Are We Postmodern Yet?

Reinhold Kramer

Are We Postmodern Yet?

And Were We Ever?

palgrave
macmillan

Reinhold Kramer
English and Creative Writing
Brandon University
Brandon, MB, Canada

ISBN 978-3-030-30568-0   ISBN 978-3-030-30569-7   (eBook)
https://doi.org/10.1007/978-3-030-30569-7

Cover illustration: SPUTNIK / Alamy Stock Photo

This Palgrave Macmillan imprint is published by the registered company Springer Nature Switzerland AG.
The registered company address is: Gewerbestrasse 11, 6330 Cham, Switzerland

To Terry Dirks, Paul Doerksen, Kelvin Dyck, Gerald Flood, Paul Henteleff, Bob Hummelt, Al Kehler, Justin Neufeld, Steve Ratzlaff, Ramon Rempel, Denny Smith, and Janis Thiessen

Acknowledgements

Over the years, my debt to David Williams—teacher, novelist, literary and media scholar, mentor, and friend—has grown to countless proportions. Many years ago, his essay "After Post-modernism" first started me thinking along this track, and now, decades later, his commentary on this manuscript has been invaluable. Terry Dirks, Paul Doerksen, Kelvin Dyck, Gerald Flood, Paul Henteleff, Bob Hummelt, Al Kehler, Justin Neufeld, Steve Ratzlaff, Ramon Rempel, Denny Smith, and Janis Thiessen, collectively known as the "Tall Foreheads," debated many of the issues that appear in these pages, sometimes in favour of, sometimes against my arguments, but always in a spirit of friendship. Much thanks to Rita Kramer and Stephanie de la Luz for providing a commentary on portions of the manuscript, and to Michelle Kramer for her work as a research assistant. Tom Mitchell and Trent Gill also provided helpful suggestions.

Contents

ABOUT THE AUTHOR

Reinhold Kramer is a professor at Brandon University in Canada. He is the author of *Scatology and Civility in the English-Canadian Novel* and *Mordecai Richler: Leaving St. Urbain*. With historian Tom Mitchell, he also wrote *Walk Towards the Gallows* and *When the State Trembled*.

CHAPTER 1

Introduction: The Contemporary Era

When his 13-year-old daughter and 10-year-old son began to grill cele-brated American novelist Michael Chabon in 2005 about his earlier use of marijuana, they hit a nerve. He had stopped toking only two years before the interrogation, three years if you subtract the single, potentially tragic incident (more on this later) that firmed up his commitment to absti-nence. About Chabon's marijuana use, his son asked, "How many times?" Chabon, just north of 40 years old, replied, "A number of times, but I don't do it anymore." A truer answer, he admits to readers, would have been "one million." Chabon didn't want his children to smoke marijuana, but he had difficulty explaining *why*: "It's just not something I'm ready to do anymore. And it's not something you guys are ready to do either. Right?"[1]

Chabon isn't alone. We cannot live without ethics—the values and practices that limit our self-interest and self-indulgence[2]—and, although the term "postmodern" has fallen out of fashion, it's still useful because it signalled a sea change in the way we approach ethics. Religious traditions gave us firm but sometimes very unsatisfactory reasons behind moral obli-gations and ethical dilemmas. Yet as tradition waned, modernity often couldn't step up to the plate with acceptable new reasons. Joseph Heath and Andrew Potter sum up the moral dilemma of contemporary pluralist societies: "we lack any common measure of 'the good,'" and must learn to live in deep disagreement, about crucial matters, such as "the value of fam-

---

[1] Chabon, *Manhood*, 29–36.
[2] Haidt, 270.

© The Author(s) 2019
R. Kramer, *Are We Postmodern Yet?*,
https://doi.org/10.1007/978-3-030-30569-7_1

istence of God, the sources of morality."[3] That's a bit overstated, — human rights *have* become a common measure, but Heath and Potter are mostly correct. In the case of marijuana, several American states and Canada have legalized it, though the US federal government still treats it as illegal.

It isn't just disparate views about how we should limit ourselves. With the rise of individual freedoms, says Gilles Lipovetsky, the *strength* of moral obligations declines.[4] Experimental evidence suggests that the greater the freedom, the weaker our sense of obligation. In "ultimatum games," one player (the proposer) is given money, say $10, to divide with a second player (the responder). The proposer offers a split and the responder can accept, or can reject the deal, in which case both players get nothing. Typically, proposers offer between $2 and $5. On a purely rational level, responders should take any offer, no matter how low. In fact, however, responders usually refuse deals under $2, and will even *pay* $1 in order to punish selfish proposers. When Joseph Henrich tried the game out in a variety of small-scale cultures, he found a few universals—mean offers ran between 26% and 58%—but also a great deal of cultural variation in what was perceived as a fair offer.[5] If no punishment is allowed (i.e. the proposer gets the share no matter what), the proposer effectively becomes a dictator. In this situation, some benevolent proposers will still irrationally offer almost half of their $10, sticking with the moral values they trust outside of the game—yet some proposers will offer nothing, attuning their moral values to their new level of power. When proposers are asked to divide the money between *two* responders, proposers tend to offer a total sum even less than what they would offer a single responder. In other words, when punishment decreases in effectiveness, self-interest grows.[6] This supports Lipovetsky's contemporary fear about moral obligation: although the responders may feel that the proposers are morally obligated to make a reasonable distribution, the more freedom we have—which in the post-modern era turns out to be a lot—the less strongly we feel obligations to others.

---

[3] Heath and Potter, 323–4, 326.

[4] Lipovetsky, 81; Bauman, *Postmodern Ethics*, 3.

[5] Henrich et al. Variation depended on the society's market integration and on whether the society contained important structures in which cooperation paid off.

[6] Hauser, 77–8, 83–5, 100–1.

The determinative word in my title—"postmodern"—lost its cachet by the end of the previous millennium, partly because some philosophers used it as a synonym for a suspect relativism, partly because it became politicized as the academic left's personal brand, and partly just because fashions change. I'm less interested in coming up with the best name for our era than in understanding the effects of its practices. Alternative names—"liquid modernity" (Zygmunt Bauman), "hypermodernity" (Lipovetsky), "digimodernism" (Alan Kirby), and "automodernity" (Robert Samuels)—imply that we have in fact accepted, and merely tweaked, the assumptions of modern rationality. There is some validity to this claim. However, if we accept the force of the naturalistic fallacy (that no matter how robust our rationality, we can never derive our ethics directly from nature) we must also recognize that we are indelibly *post*-modern. I have no inclination to argue against the newer, sexier terms, yet "postmodern" has the advantage of broad intelligibility. Bauman, Lipovetsky, Kirby, Samuels, and many other scholars, despite using new terminology, still agree that we're in a coherent *new* period that has significantly altered modernity.

The philosophers of modernity most often assumed that, once we understood the logical and social failures of religious traditions, we could rebuild our meanings by understanding the rational design in nature (as the Deists thought), or by making rational calculations about where the most happiness lay (as Utilitarians argued), or by learning to correctly interpret nature's inner voice in us (as Rousseau and the Romantics felt).[7] Modernity's line of rational calculation, especially in utilitarian form, has continued simplistically in scholars such as Sam Harris, who imagine that any moment now reason will allow us to agree on values, while the more expressivist Romantic lines of argument have found a home in what I will call postmodernity's How-I-Feel ethics, the notion that the individual's emotional responses are the best guide to interpersonal disputes, appropriate behaviour, and moral decisions.

Naming and Dating Postmodernity

To give a full account of postmodernity's historical development would require another book. Not to sidestep the matter entirely, however, I offer a brief sketch of how such a question might be approached, provided that

[7] Taylor, *Sources*, 272–4, 322, 351, 362, 373–5.

the answer remains broadly rooted in human practices, and not merely in theory, polemics, or a single discipline. Some scholars find the real beginnings of postmodernity in the Reformation, which allowed the individual, guided by the "light within," to interpret the *Bible*. The more decisive weakening of grand narratives came with the scientific revolution and the rise of "higher criticism" of the *Bible* in the eighteenth century. Only in the 1960s did the antagonism between tradition and modernity tip broadly into postmodernity when a number of factors destabilized the grand narratives of tradition and modernity both: church attendance began its slow decline; influential continental theorists such as Foucault discovered Nietzsche and cast a cold eye on rationality; European empires crumbled as postcolonial nation after nation won its independence; social groups with strong grievances against tradition—women, people of colour, and sexual minorities—began to mobilize, not on the basis of scientific rationality, but on the basis of human rights. All these tremors opened the road for an ungrounded pluralism.

The tremors were above all moral, or ethically political. The social contract is an early modern idea that took nascent form in differing ways among the English Levellers and Thomas Hobbes in the seventeenth century, and among the French and American revolutionaries in the eighteenth. The twentieth-century framers of the UN's *Universal Declaration of Human Rights*, appalled by the Holocaust, established for the first time a global agreement on the notion that the individual held a kind of sovereignty, the *Declaration* going much further than the UN Charter, which focussed on the sovereignty of nations. Expressed on a very practical level, commitment to the social contract and the new notion of sovereignty grew into a flood by the 1960s in civil rights marches, the battle for reproductive rights, anti-war demonstrations, and the Stonewall protests. For a leftist such as David Harvey, the failure of May 1968 to bring about revolution led to postmodernity,[8] and he's right insofar as group protests began to take on a very individualist cast. Strongly relativist theories also played a role, soon percolating not only into the academies, but also into popular culture, from David Bowie's attempt to avoid a singular identity to Robert Altman's multi-voiced *Nashville* (1975). But where Harvey, in his eagerness for a proletarian revolution, reports a tragedy, many would see the trickle-down effect of the 1960s protests as having created desirable social changes.

[8] Bertens, 221.

Individualism is rooted intellectually in the flowerings of Romanticism, but it reached a postmodern tipping point in the post-war period when Western wealth, together with new forms of birth control, freed many individuals from a reliance on the community and thereby from its strictures. Boomers rode their demographics, their affluence, and their libidos into a very privileged position in which their individual wishes triumphed. Where once only an aristocrat such as Lord Byron could ignore sexual conventions with impunity, millions of people could do so by the 1960s after the invention of the birth-control pill. With the weakening of the Christian grand narrative and the emphasis on women's rights, divorce also became broadly available, setting off the great increase in nonconventional households. Boomers, as they flooded the scene, could enforce their pluralist moral standards, and, subsequently, with the slowing down of the Western birth rate after 1965, individuals in subsequent generations began to count for even more.

The decline of empires and the grand narratives associated with Western imperialism likewise began in earnest after World War II, though the decline of the American empire didn't reach a critical level until the late 1960s and early 1970s, when the Vietnam War convinced at least half of young Americans that the nation was criminally fallible. Later American attempts to resume empire-building have been more tentative, at least militarily, if not culturally. Economically, the post-war Bretton Woods regime opened borders in a significant way, while still allowing nations some self-determination. Behind these more multilateral, seemingly postmodern freedoms, the US still loomed, and continued to do so in the 1990s era of globalization. For Fredric Jameson and Perry Anderson, capital in its multinational, neo-liberal phase forms the economic base for a flawed postmodernist scepticism.[9] And globalization, of course, couldn't have happened in such a thoroughgoing fashion without cyber-culture. Technologically, media such as photography and film had in the nineteenth century already given people a sense of how powerful simulations could shape human thought and behaviour, but it wasn't until the rise of electronic media and the broad availability of TV in the 1950s that people could immerse themselves for several hours of the day in visual simulations. Cyber-culture has extended that into a near-constant immersion.

Conceptually, at least, I distinguish between "postmodernism" and "postmodernity," even though the terms have often been used interchange-

---

[9] Jameson, *Postmodernism*, xviii–xxi. Perry Anderson, 55.

ably. With "postmodernism," "postmodernists," and the adjective "post-modernist," I refer to the broad, self-conscious literary and philosophical scepticism about foundations and reality. Barth and Pynchon, Foucault and Derrida represent the canonical positions. Postmodernism is strongly rela-tivist, and, in most of its incarnations, represents a limited engagement with the problems that we face after modernity. In contrast, I use "postmoder-nity," "the postmodern era," and the adjective "postmodern" to refer to post-war social developments: individualist practices, global pluralism, the decline of religious faith, powerful visual simulations, and, above all, a lack of certainty about *ethical* foundations. Postmodernity includes postmodern-ism, but refers to historical developments that cannot be reduced to a philo-sophical choice or fashion. My hope, in part, is to rescue "postmodern" from its polemical meaning, and to keep it as a description of the contem-porary era, an era that is heavily individualist, but, as I will argue, not nearly as sceptical as advertised.

Some claims arising from postmodernism—notably Foucault's asser-tion that truth is an effect of power—exaggerate far too much, even though power often does skew truth, as is increasingly evident in contro-versies about fake news. Because of this overreaching, other scholars, such as Richard Dawkins, have treated postmodernism as if it were a meaning-less fashion shopped around by charlatans who lacked scientific knowl-edge.[10] Dawkins is quite naïve about the historical aspects of postmodernity, but he has a point insofar as many postmodernists have completely ignored the 1.6 million years of human evolution, so crucial in the shaping of *every* culture, including the present West. In a more measured response to post-modernism, Charles Taylor has noted what has long been clear about postmodernists: in their push for a *valuing* of "difference," they have kept modern ethical concerns even while claiming to reject the modern order.[11]

But whatever the weaknesses of postmodernists, we are still left with the question of what to say about the contemporary *era*. Admittedly, the very word "postmodern" is illogical: in its Latin roots—"post modo"—it literally means "after the now."[12] We, travelling faster than light, expect to touch down in the future before we arrive there. One dictionary of culture

---

[10] Richard Dawkins, post to "Update: Fashionable Nonsense?" 14 June 2011, The Richard Dawkins Foundation for Science and Reason, http://richarddawkins.net/discussions/637927-update-fashionable-nonsense/comments?page=4.

[11] Taylor, *Secular*, 256.

[12] McHale, *Postmodernist*, 4.

offers the following definition: "Postmodernism: The word is meaning-less. Use it often."[13] Throwing up his hands, David Lehman says, "I am tempted ... to argue that we are not post-anything. We are, miserably or splendidly, ourselves, living now, living here."[14] Against such a studied disregard for history, I would respond that "postmodernity" is a useful name for a suite of historical changes that have given us greater and greater freedom to make all kinds of choices, ethical choices even, based on how we feel as individuals. When people begin to behave as if neither tradition and faith on one side, nor science and reason on the other, can give us full explanations of why we *ought* to behave in certain ways, it's appropriate to speak of "postmodernity." The problems to which the word "postmod-ern" gave utterance have by no means disappeared,[15] especially if we look at human *practices*. "Postmodern" has the great virtue of saying, "This is where we arrive once we've assimilated the lessons of modernity, and yet realize that it can't tell us how we *ought* to live."

Another difficulty in speaking about the "postmodern" era is that in specific disciplines "postmodern" has had various meanings. In literary usage, it usually refers to a highly self-reflexive style. In architecture, it's usually a tongue-in-cheek quotation of past styles. In sociology, it describes how institutional power determines social roles and cultural forms. In phi-losophy, it usually looks back to *The Genealogy of Morals*, where human values are revealed to be ungrounded and where, in Nietzsche's provoca-teur paraphrase of the Society of Assassins, "Nothing is true; all is permitted."[16] Unsympathetic scholars therefore argue that "postmodern" was an aesthetic term that evolved into "a wholesale relativism."[17] While this characterization is partly true, it is, again, truer of postmodernist the-orists and their followers than a good description of the *era*.

---

[13] Quoted in Lemert 6.

[14] Lehman, 14.

[15] Scholars focused on literature tend to date postmodernism from the mid-1960s until 1989 (the end of the Cold War) or sometime in the 1990s, or on 11 September 2001 (the day that the attack on the World Trade Center supposedly put irony to bed). See McHale, *Cambridge*, 3, 7; Bertens, 14; McGowan, 92; Ahmed, 140; Jameson, *Postmodernism*, xx; Kirby, "Death," Burn, *Franzen*, 8, 10–11. If we restrict ourselves to the literary *style* of post-modernism, it could perhaps, like surrealism, be periodized into a tidy 35-year era. But postmodernity, as a suite of social changes, reflected in art but not determined by it, can't be circumscribed so easily.

[16] Nietzsche, *Genealogy*, 287.

[17] Snipp-Walmsley, 405.

The best short definition of postmodernity is still Jean-François Lyotard's "incredulity toward metanarratives."[18] As my opening anecdote about Chabon implies, the weakening of grand narratives—the big stories that give meaning to our lives, that strongly influence our moral actions, and that have a significant institutional basis—goes to the heart of a contemporary ethical problem that hasn't been solved. The shaken grand narratives send waves out in many directions, allowing us to find at least some historical coherence in "postmodernity," whose common features are often said to be the collapse of metaphysics and broadly based notions of truth; the triumph of emotion; a pluralist ethics; the exaltation of individual freedom and choice; self-reflexivity; the deregulation of desire; the fear that simulacra can erase reality, especially on TV and online; the world-encircling spread of consumerism; the waning of privacy; the waning of community; the weakening of the ties of duty in relationships and in citizenship; and the weakening of national sovereignty. Jameson and Harvey interpret the era as primarily a hegemony of capitalism. Others point at the rise of subjectivity as the main feature of postmodernity.[19] Best and Kellner say that postmodernity continues modernity's disenchantments and yet they also see a break with "positivistic" science, Enlightenment optimism, and faith in reason.[20] The notion of a strong conceptual break is easier to believe in if we restrict ourselves only to postmodernist theory, but the picture is more complicated and the rupture less uniform if we examine Western social practices of the past 30 years, especially the problems of living together in an era of weakened agreement about which stories to live by. On what basis do we decide what's right and wrong? In regard to relativism, Nietzsche's inheritors are mistaken, because we *do* decide—even Nietzscheans must rely on ghostly grand narratives. But *how* do we decide?

JUST THE WEST?

In one of his favourite jokes, American novelist David Foster Wallace told of two fish swimming along when they come upon an older fish. The older fish says, "Morning boys, how's the water?" The younger fish continue on for a while. Then one of them stops, turns to the other, and says, "What

---

[18] Lyotard, xxiv, 37. Best and Kellner, *Turn*, 256.
[19] C. Smith, 101.
[20] Best and Kellner, *Adventure*, 101; Kellner, "Reappraising," 109.

the hell is water?"[21] One argument holds that postmodernity, in many of the features listed above, is now a universal condition.[22] It's not uncommon to become so incrementally acclimatized to the passing scene and engrossed in the everyday details of our lives that we can hardly conceive, for example, of a time before smartphones or a time when individual rights meant nothing without citizenship.

My focus is on the US, Canada, and, to a lesser degree, Europe. Against the notion of a universal condition, some critics claim that "postmodernity" describes only conditions in the Western capitalist nations, and that it's wrong to assume that other countries will follow suit.[23] Philip Jenkins expects that Western Christianity, for example, will be pulled back into traditional faith by what's happening in the Global South.[24] Other scholars expect that we will grow to rely on indigenous ways of knowing. I don't dismiss tradition in its various forms, but the postmodern story of the West will repeat itself in the South, though in unpredictable ways. Wherever people have significant levels of national order, financial well-being, and personal freedom—they have begun to adopt many of the West's liberalizing reforms[25] and its individualizing, consumerist expressions. Nelson Mandela's granddaughters Zaziwe Dlamini-Manaway and Swati Dlamini moved to the US, created their own reality show on COZI-TV, and began to sell a line of "Long Walk to Freedom" T-shirts, hoodies, and caps. Something like postmodernity arises, I would predict, in every society that reaches a certain standard of material prosperity, education, and structural complexity.

The Ethical Dilemma

In the West, we have arrived at a distinctly new place, and we continue to ride the energies of an individualism that exploded in the 1960s and 1970s. For the philosopher Charles Taylor, the history of the Western self looks back to Augustine's sense of interiority, Montaigne's emphasis on self-discovery, Descartes' reduction of the phenomenal world, and Locke's punctual and disengaged self. And, as Taylor convincingly argues, subjec-

---

[21] Max, 285.

[22] Vattimo, 32–3. Keith Tester in Bauman and Tester, 25.

[23] Bertens, 10.

[24] See Jenkins, *The Next Christendom.*

[25] Pinker, *Better*, 692.

tivity comes into existence precisely through what the subject strives towards, the higher-order goods that it values and that allow it to judge others.[26] If we then trace back contemporary morality, its route owes much to the Deist reduction of divine revelation and to Kant's assertion that moral responsibility starts in individual reason, before flowing through the Romantic valuing of feeling and self-expression. Taylor has little patience for "postmodernism" (which he equates with neo-Nietzschean anti-humanists such as Foucault and Lyotard), yet he speaks of a pluralist "supernova" that after World War II extended the nova of modernity, and he calls the 1960s a "hinge moment" that swung us into "expressive individualism."[27] This is a convincing account, and, since "expressive individualism" is what (according to Taylor) arises out of modernity yet paradoxically repudiates its parent reason,[28] there's good cause (despite Taylor) to fall back on the older word, "postmodernity." At the same time, contemporary practices also suggest that, even in entering the new territory, we've retained important features of our evolutionary past, our faith traditions, and the lessons of scientific modernity.[29]

The tendency, in speaking about a new era in human history, has been to lean heavily on a generalized theory or to speak only about postmodernity in very circumscribed areas—only ethics, only faith, only individualism, and so on—but it's important at least to try to pull the various strands together. While basic human psychology retains the neuro-cognitive patterns laid down during the Pleistocene, changes in the cultural environment—in technology, in patterns of social organization and regulation—are producing significant behavioural shifts. Some are adaptive; some aren't. There's something profoundly adaptive about the way that millions of people can live peaceably in our post-natural cities, though if global warming gets out of control, our reshaping of the world could destroy us. As active creators of our own niche, not just the passive subjects of evolution,[30] we stand before a myriad of possible cultural forms.

[26] Taylor, *Sources*, 36, 60.
[27] Taylor, *Secular*, 374, 716–7, 377, 473.
[28] Taylor, *Sources*, 498.
[29] Best and Kellner, for example, argue that postmodernity keeps "the best aspects of modernity—humanism, individuality, enlightened reason, democracy, rights, and solidarities—to be tempered by reverence for nature, respect for all life, sustainability, and ecological balance" (*Adventure*, 11).
[30] Laland and Brown, 181.

The more extravagant claims—for example, that postmodern people can lay aside grand narratives[31]—are not supported by the evidence of our practices, as I hope to show. In some senses, we never were postmodern—not in the 1960s, not now. Yet we are also postmodern in crucial ways. I will start in Chap. 2 by examining the logical contortions that occur when the individual becomes the arbiter of truth, and I will argue that, with respect to facts, we are not postmodern, despite strong pressures from evolutionary psychology, from continental philosophy, from political campaigns, and from certain media to reify emotion and thereby to treat knowledge as mainly an effect of power. Chapter 3 turns to Ethics, where, in contrast, the agreement to disagree and to negotiate mark us most tellingly as postmodern. A popular response to weakened grand narratives has been to base decisions on "How I feel," but neither How-I-Feel nor the proposed alternatives—tradition, reason (especially consequentialism), "Other"-based ethics, or market-based ethics—have by themselves provided a satisfactory ethic, and, in practice, people don't follow any of these exclusively. Yet we make ethical decisions every hour, and, as individual moral agents, we can't remain in the realm of "multiplicity." As Taylor insists, the self cannot operate apart from moral judgements.[32] I will argue that in practice the postmodern ethical tendency has been to start with widespread agreement on human rights, and then, unconsciously or consciously, to cobble together various approaches to create individual codes and social contracts.

Addressing the strong individualist culture that arises from multiple-sourced ethical codes, I will show in Chap. 4 that by giving a place of honour to How-I-Feel we have encouraged some vexing behavioural tendencies, but that, as societies, we can't disown postmodern individualism without losing important democratic goods. Chapter 5 turns to the technologies of cyberspace, where some of the greatest individual freedoms and the most compelling simulations have distanced us from the real. Chapter 6 examines the way that How-I-Feel and individualism play out in the public sphere. The individualist distrust of the political, the elevation of the consumer over the citizen, and the forces of globalization—all postmodern effects—have begun both to pull away the protective canopy

[31] Kellner criticizes Lyotard and Foucault for creating new grand narratives (Kellner, "Reappraising," 120). The implication seems to be that one could avoid grand narratives altogether, simply by selecting the right words!
[32] Taylor, *Sources*, 31, 36, 60.

of the nation and to weaken the dangerous powers of nationalism. Nevertheless, I will argue that the withering of the nation has been overstated.

Chapter 7 pulls together the strands of truth, ethics, and the social effects of individualism into the question of how we make larger meanings. The truth claims of religious faiths and even of secular grand narratives have undergone disenchantment, followed by a necessary accommodation of the faiths to individualism. The chapter describes the various positions that people have taken in relation to those grand narratives: trying and failing to create re-enchantment through science-based or environmentalist grand narratives; restricting themselves either to ego-based narratives or to small narratives; becoming selective adherents or pluralist adapters of traditional faiths; or turning to humanism. The most coherent positions—selective adherence, pluralist adaptation, and humanism—reveal that we are not fully postmodern, that we haven't abandoned grand narratives, and also, paradoxically, that we've been postmodern at least since the 1960s. As I will argue throughout this book, very few people have found it possible to return uncritically to grand narratives or, on the other hand, to live without them.

CHAPTER 2

Truth or Truths?

Truth as a Kind of Fiction?

In 1996, Alan Sokal, a physics professor at New York University (NYU), sent the cultural studies journal *Social Text* a paper entitled "Transgressing the Boundaries: Towards a Transformative Hermeneutics of Quantum Gravity." Quoting famous scientists and post-structural philosophers alike, Sokal appeared to argue that physical reality was merely a social construct. In some quarters, this was not a controversial claim to make. Most of those who considered themselves "postmodern" believed that our ways of speaking constituted the world. "The truth claims of science," Sokal announced, "are inherently theory-laden and self-referential; and consequently … the discourse of the scientific community … cannot assert a privileged epistemological status with respect to counter-hegemonic narratives emanating from dissident or marginalized communities."[1] To put this bluntly, he was saying that scientists have no epistemic right to challenge my claim that Echinacea cures cancer or Vine Deloria Jr.'s claim that Native Americans always inhabited the Americas and that their ancestors never crossed the Bering land bridge.[2] Sokal revealed that "the π of Euclid and the G of

---

[1] Sokal, "Transgressing," 218.

[2] The dating of the Bering land bridge theory has been questioned, since some versions of it don't harmonize well with the dates of archaeological sites such as Monte Verde, Chile, but genetic evidence makes it clear that North American native cultures descend, late in the Pleistocene, from Siberian groups. For a very brief summary, see Alan MacEachern, "The

© The Author(s) 2019
R. Kramer, *Are We Postmodern Yet?*,
https://doi.org/10.1007/978-3-030-30569-7_2

Newton, formerly thought to be constant and universal, are now perceived in their ineluctable historicity."[3] *Social Text* editor Andrew Ross found the paper convincing, asked Sokal to shorten it slightly, and published it. Soon afterwards, however, Sokal revealed in *Lingua Franca* that the paper was a hoax, a parody of the cavalier postmodernist attitude towards objective knowledge and of the popular pluralist belief that the truth of a statement was somehow relative to the individual or social group or, especially, the marginalized community making it.

The Sokal Hoax was a watershed moment in the history of the post-modernist conception of "multiple knowledges." In the humanities and social sciences, Foucault and Derrida were the oracles of the day, the scholars most cited in the 1980s and 1990s. Other scholars followed them in doubting the existence of non-discursive truth, a truth outside our ways of representing the world.[4] Baudrillard took the extreme post-structural stance, saying that we were now in the fourth and final stage of the image, the point at which the image bears no relation at all to reality. Thus, in *The Gulf War Did Not Take Place* (1991), he insisted that mediatization had made it impossible to speak of true events, only of their representation: "The war watches itself in a mirror" and asks "am I pretty enough, am I operational enough, am I spectacular enough?"[5] Although Baudrillard, like Sokal, may have been winking, Foucault and Derrida were not. For Foucault, power invariably determined which discourses were adopted as "true." Power, dispersed through a juridical, political, or social field, determined what counted as knowledge.[6]

Bering Land Bridge Theory: Not Dead Yet," ActiveHistory.ca, 6 September 2016, http://activehistory.ca/2016/09/the-bering-land-bridge-theory-not-dead-yet/. Resistance to the Beringia theory has become popular in some progressive circles. The Canadian Assembly of First Nations national chief Perry Bellegarde, while accurately detailing some of the repressive ways in which Canada treated its native population, also implied that he adhered to Deloria's archaeological revisionism. When interviewer Nancy Macdonald spoke of "the nations who have called this land home for more than 12,000 years," Bellegarde responded, "We should be adding two more zeroes on there!" Macdonald, though she clearly knew better, immediately agreed. Nancy Macdonald, "The Interview" (Perry Bellegarde), *Maclean's*, July 2017, 26. Victims of colonial oppression are allowed not only to add their formerly silenced voices to history—a crucial advance—but also, according to the notion of multiple knowledges, to rewrite history as they see fit.

[3] Sokal, "Transgressing," 222.
[4] See, for example, Best and Kellner, *Turn*, 235–6.
[5] Baudrillard, *Selected*, 236.
[6] Foucault, *Discipline*, 175.

Before the 1960s, indeed, colonial power had ruled that oral cultures were primitive, and heterosexual power had ruled that homosexuality perverted normal sexuality. The majority's norms thus threatened to erase difference, often violently. For Derrida, every discourse (except deconstruction[7]) pointed to a transcendental signified, a governing centre (God, the nation, nature, materialism) that had been invented to ground the discourse, but that could never be produced. Fiction was no longer understood as a mimetic copy of the world, and even science was suspect, riven with metaphors. In a giddy moment, eager to clear the field of "totalization" and centres, Derrida claimed that the Einsteinian constant was not a constant.[8] His and Foucault's language grew portentous, to the point of doubting whether it was still useful to speak about "humanity." Believing that the future would bear little resemblance to the past, Derrida began to talk of monsters on the horizon.[9] Foucault insisted that "the experience of madness [comes] closest to absolute knowledge"[10] and famously ended *The Order of Things* by proclaiming that "man is an invention of recent date," and would soon be erased.[11]

Contemporary deconstruction-influenced movements such as object-oriented ontology (OOO) run in the same direction. Timothy Morton's claim that there is no meta-language uncontaminated by things slides into the claim that there is no meta-language—no language that could translate between conflicting worldviews. It's uncontroversial to claim that anthropocentrism prevents us from knowing the full reality of objects, and especially of Morton's massive "hyperobjects," such as global warming. The claim is a bit like saying that we can't hear ultrasonic frequencies. But

---

[7] Derrida didn't like the term "normative," and in theory he insisted that his own writing could be deconstructed too—"What I have already written is instantly annihilated ... There is no philosophy of Jacques Derrida" (Jacques Derrida, *Points … : interviews, 1974–1994*, Elisabeth Weber, Stanford: Stanford University Press, 1995, 352, 361–2). But, obviously, as soon as deconstruction was practised, it disseminated and dogmatized a set of normative principles that stuck around for decades.

[8] Derrida, "Structure, Sing and Play," *The Structuralist Controversy*, 267. Derrida seems to mean the speed of light, though it's possible that he could instead be talking about the "cosmological constant," energy density in space (close to zero, but not zero) which Einstein hypothesized to keep the universe from collapsing into itself in his steady-state model. When the same essay reappeared in Derrida's own book, *Writing and Difference*, the discussion of the "Einsteinian constant" had been discreetly dropped. See also Bérubé, *Rhetorical*, 21, 27.

[9] Derrida, "Structure, Sign and Play," *Writing*, 293; *Grammatology*, 5.

[10] Eribon, 151.

[11] Foucault, *Order*, 387.

many of our measurements and perceptions (including many emotional ones) *are* meta-languages, since they give us true information about hyperobjects and about other humans. And, of course, Morton consistently writes as if he and OOO can provide truth, not merely a "local" and parochial *feeling* about hyperobjects. At his best, he is poetic in reshaping the deconstructive trope about the end of man—"the being of a paper cup is as profound as mine"—but here and elsewhere he leaps towards grandiose rhetoric: "the end of the world ... *might have already taken place.*" Qualifications quickly follow: the world ended in 1784 with the invention of the steam engine; the world ended again in 1945 with atomic tests; "*world* is an aesthetic concept"; "what is called human continues after the end of the (human) world." Rhetoric thus sabotages the more reasoned parts of his argument, and the ideological decision not to speak of "truth" opens the road for illogic.[12]

In ethics, I will argue, postmodernist scholars were justified in distrusting claims about truth and a centre, but post-structuralists had bigger fish to fry, and insisted that discourse constituted the world: "The *problem of language* has never been simply one problem among others," said Derrida, because it asks "the *name of man.*" To *speak* is thus a Nietzschean act of will, bringing the world under human mastery: "The sign and divinity have the same place and time of birth." While Derrida gave the linguistic sign the dignity of a founding religious Word, he simultaneously withdrew all veridical force by presuming that language was mythological and couldn't convey *things*. Not Derrida, but writing itself was supposedly the author of deconstruction. The dissemination of words meant that each time a word was used a slightly different meaning was attached to it, destabilizing language itself. Derrida, therefore, wanted to abandon the word "rationality" because writing inaugurated "the destruction, not the demolition but the de-sedimentation, the de-construction, of ... the signification of truth."[13] In the wake of such rarified qualifications, one might feel like a fool for asking what the precise distinction was between "destruction" and "demolition." Nevertheless, Jacques Bouveresse demurred, pointing out that Derrida had no theory of propositions about the world.[14] By what *deconstructive* logic would scientific descriptions of the world be exempted from the post-structural scepticism about language? By none ... though

---

[12] Morton, 2, 4–5, 7, 16–8, 23, 56, 106, 195.

[13] Derrida, *Grammatology*, 6, 83, 14, 10. Derrida's emphasis.

[14] Dosse II, 41.

after his first slip on the Einsteinian constant, Derrida was careful not to say so. He insisted that he believed science to be true, but for many scholars influenced by his thought in the humanities and social sciences, the mediated nature of linguistic representation meant that one couldn't lay hold of *any* truth in an objective way. We were "always already" postmodern (synonymous, in many quarters, with post-structural[15]), and, short of abandoning language altogether, we could never become anything else.

No objective point of view would let us compare reality and its mental representation.[16] Instead of knowledge, we had knowledges.[17] No longer, said Bauman, could philosophy separate truth from untruth, but it must attempt to translate "between separate languages, each generating and sustaining its own truths."[18] Because various cultures and disciplines speak different tongues, they must see the world in radically different ways, and we would no longer be able to call one custom better or truer than another.[19] The most eager took this notion quickly forward to the next logical step: not just every culture, but every individual must see the world in fundamentally incommensurable ways. How could *you* possibly legislate *my* perception? Already in 1940, Jorge Luis Borges had foreseen this stage.

---

[15] Briefly: although the terms have often been treated as synonymous, "post-structuralism" properly refers to the French scholars who arose in opposition to anthropologist Claude Lévi-Strauss's structuralist attempt to isolate a society's basic socio-mythic binary patterns (such as nature/culture). Post-structuralism refers also to those who subsequently agreed that binaries in general ought to be undone, and saw the world as constituted by difference. "Postmodernism," by contrast, has been a broader portmanteau term that at its loosest has been a synonym for "contemporary," or, at its tightest, has been used to describe architectural and literary self-reflexiveness. "Postmodernity" has generally referred to the period, usually beginning in the 1960s, when modernity and rationality came under strong critiques, not from tradition but from a position somewhere after modernity. In the epistemological crisis that Jean-François Lyotard called incredulity towards metanarratives, postmodernism shades into post-structuralism, but postmodernism (not post-structuralism) has been used to refer to the many cultural expressions of that incredulity: lack of ethical foundations, virtual simulations, the celebration of low culture, the focus on the individual, and many more. For my attempt to disentangle postmodernism as a philosophical stance from postmodernity as an era, see the Introduction.

[16] Frans Ruiter in Bertens 280–81.

[17] Some scholars attempted to place "non-Western and premodern knowledges" on a level with science, and only granted Darwinian natural selection "partial validity" (Best and Kellner, *Adventure*, 117, 119).

[18] Bauman, *Discontents*, 116–17. Bauman, quoted in Jacobsen et al., 45.

[19] Watson, 67.

In his fictional Tlön, "every mental state is irreducible." Far from destroy-ing the sciences, this makes the sciences uncountable,[20] presumably because not only is there a separate physics for *every person* on earth, and a separate chemistry and so on, but there must also be a separate physics (and chemistry and so on) for every *mental state* of every person on earth.

If that seems like too many knowledges, Borges wasn't far off the mark, according to some theorists. Channelling Richard Rorty, Bauman says, "The *truth* of the West, the truth of modernity found its home in the self-same work of *fiction* which it fought tooth and nail."[21] Against the homog-enizing certainties of science, this reductive understanding of fiction became the model for postmodernist knowledge and difference. Notions of performance and creative misreading convinced many literary scholars that truth was alien to literary interpretation. A historical novelist is obvi-ously free to let Hitler encounter the Hitler diaries (actually forged by Konrad Kujau in the early 1980s), but K.M. Newton goes a step further: literary commentators, too, should be free to play—to treat the Hitler diaries as true.[22] Newton must have cheered when Sony Pictures created a fictitious film reviewer in Connecticut, who gave rave reviews to Sony's *The Animal, A Knight's Tale, Hollow Man,* and *Vertical Limit* in 2001.[23] Hans Bertens explains the premise underlying Foucauldian orthodoxy: "If representations do not and cannot represent the world, then inevitably all representations are political."[24] In strong, truth-like cadences, postmod-ernists insisted that everything we say or write is a fictional claim to power, the power to create truth.

Politically, the postmodernist resistance to Truth had the salutary effect of chipping away at ethnocentrism, racism, sexism, and gender policing. "Anti-foundationalism" and "anti-essentialism"—the notion that "moral and epistemological principles derive not from divine will or so-called 'natural' law but from ordinary social practices"[25]—undercut grand narra-tives and made it more difficult to appeal to God or nature as the final authority on correct gender or sexual or moral behaviour, though such claims are still made in popular venues such as Focus on the Family's *The*

---

[20] Borges, 10.

[21] Bauman, *Discontents,* 118. Rorty, xli, xliii.

[22] Newton, 480, 483.

[23] Robert Welkos, "Sony pledges full inquiry into bogus film reviewer," *Winnipeg Free Press,* 6 June 2001.

[24] Bertens, 7.

[25] Bérubé, *Liberal,* 297.

Truth Project. Postmodernists also insisted that power, not reason-based virtues, explained why the West dominated the world; power, not psychiatric science, explained why homosexuality was treated as a pathology; power, not natural selection, explained many gender norms. Since many minority communities had their voices silenced and their rights abused, often on the basis of some foundational religious or scientific "truth," Foucault provided the tools to counter real oppression.

A major difficulty, however, remained. Despite postmodernism's liberating effects for so many people, to describe all knowledge as socially constructed was self-defeating and, above all, false.[26] One of Foucault's Group d'Information sur les Prisons pamphlets read,

These are intolerable:

courts
cops
hospitals, asylums
school, military service,
the press, television,
the State.[27]

A rather extensive list, though Foucault, like other post-structuralists, declined on principle to give normative reasons for his claims. But if Foucault couldn't acknowledge a broad standard of truth, there was no reason, except political taste, to prefer his left-wing stance to that of his right-wing opposition. Alan Sokal, for his part, agreed with *Social Text* that one must question how the government and the military *use* science, but he also insisted that scepticism must be deeply informed, and he rejected Foucault's claim that knowledge was merely an effect of power, a reflection of social forces.[28] In his parody, Sokal wanted to highlight the weaknesses of a de facto relativism. Foucault's inheritors spoke as if each culture should be free to make its own equally valid How-I-Feel truth claims, yet these same scholars treated their own positions as if they applied across cultures—women's rights and unions were supposed to be universally applicable, while anti-immigration laws and legislated minimum sen-

---

[26] For the claim about social construction, see Best and Kellner, *Adventure*, 103, 110.
[27] Eribon, 224.
[28] Sokal, "A Physicist." For the highly questionable argument that scientific epistemology was in crisis, see Best and Kellner, *Adventure*, 112–13.

tences were believed to be universally mistaken. As these cross-cultural intuitions suggest, epistemology and ontology are founded in a common human perceptual system. Despite significant differences between cultures, even morality is rooted in shared, evolution-shaped understandings of harm. In the end, even Foucault wasn't so postmodern; he mostly presumed a normative humanist stance on civil liberties, while refusing to call it humanist.

Some defensive responses that followed the Sokal Hoax argued that Sokal's joking claims were *unintentionally* true, that scientific truth was in fact relative. Severe contortions were required to simultaneously "agree" with Sokal's words and yet disparage him, especially when Andrew Ross ventured that Sokal had originally intended his essay seriously but had gotten cold feet.[29] The defenders of relativism wanted to argue, against the "hegemony" of science, that truth was "plural." At the same time, they needed to prove that their truth—the truth that there are no objective truths—was the only available truth. The arguments had to be crafted to show that only postmodernist orthodoxy could make sense of the world, that, as Mara Beller put it, the world isn't presented to us twice— once as it is and then in theoretical description—but only once, in description.[30] Of course, if that were the case, one couldn't actually argue against Sokal, since there would be no objective vantage point from which one could look down and judge between the two competing accounts. No meta-language could translate the competing languages into common terms.[31]

In a sense, this feels self-evident: how could a universal translator account for every unique quirk of every different way of speaking? But translators do exist. Firstly, modernity hadn't disappeared in the postmodern era, and even outside of the West, science was increasingly being accepted as a universal operation. Though it couldn't translate ethics, it could describe the physical world, and it did so universally, no matter the culture, language, or bias of the observer. Not only is our sensory apparatus veridical, but it is extended by new technologies that allow us to hear frequencies that our ears can't hear, and to see radiation that our eyes can't see. Secondly and more tentatively, the historical decline of violence relative to population (particularly in democracies and despite spectacular

[29] Bérubé, *Rhetorical*, 17.
[30] Beller, 6.
[31] Vattimo, 37.

events such as 9/11) suggested that communicative reason was on the rise. Whenever we argued rather than physically fought, we edged towards a universal language, however flawed and biased in practice. The Golden Rule, the categorical imperative, the social contract: all these social norms urged us to leave parochial ethics behind and to speak universally, to state our cases in ways that would extend our rights to others too.[32] With some justice, post-structural theorists countered that communicative reason's ideal, non-coerced speech situation has never been a reality, and that universalism has often been a cover for Western domination.[33] But despite these important caveats, the fact that we can argue at all is the gift of our species' common evolutionary heritage. Even when we disagree with each other—and our tribal affiliations ensure that we will—we can comprehend the basis of an opponent's argument. That even the *Social Text* defenders wanted to translate between languages suggests that, although ethical universals are far slipperier than scientific universals, even ethics leans towards communicative reason.

More astute commentators, such as Michael Bérubé, who debated Sokal in the late 1990s and eventually headed the Modern Language Association in 2012, agreed that there were objective truths in science, but that in the social sciences and humanities, all knowledge was historical. Following Rorty, Bérubé wanted to stop talking about "the Way Things Really Are."[34] He limited objective knowledge to physical facts (such as gravity and Neptune) and he also insisted that, because we can only apprehend physical facts socially, social facts are "prior" to physical facts. Therefore, "gravity" didn't mean "a universal force of nature" until Newton discovered it.[35] Like the notion that discourse constitutes the world, this "historicizing" again said very little, since it evaded the significant point that we can now talk objectively about how gravity operated not only before Newton, but also 13.8 billion years ago. More importantly, the developing science of evolutionary biology has shown that the facts of the world include facts about our species' psychology—about human social universals such as costly signalling, pro-social punishment, and, most controversially, gender dimorphism. These social facts had been shaped by evolution and by an intricate structure of hormones and chemi-

[32] Pinker, *Better*, 182.
[33] Bérubé, *Liberal*, 221–3. Grant, 29–30.
[34] Bérubé, *Liberal*, 240–41.
[35] Bérubé, *Rhetorical*, 39.

cal rewards mediated in the brain, so while gender, for example, has picked up countless socially constructed elements, gender dimorphism and the various departures from dimorphism are, nevertheless, rooted in genetic facts shaped by evolution. Past mistakes about what is natural in gender and race rightly made postcolonial theorists and many humanities scholars more wary, since by looking only at universals and by confusing Western patterns with universals, the West was responsible for much oppression. The evolutionary basis of human sociality couldn't tell us what we *ought* to do or how we *ought* to express our genders, as Bérubé, other "anti-foundationalists," and most scientists also recognized.[36] Still, scientists insisted, we can discover psychological and sociological truths about human beings.

At the same time that these academic debates were raging, postmodernist relativity filtered down into popular culture, and surfaced in such projects as "unschooling" and the movement's more respectable cousin, "emergent curriculum." Foucault might well have sympathized with these fads—in which education is tailored to the individual child by expanding on whatever the child shows interest in, as opposed to what the teacher or society considers important. How the child feels counts for more than expertise. By 2006 there were between 100,000 and 200,000 "unschooled" children in the US.[37]

In another stream of popular relativity, the Internet shifted control away from traditional news organizations and authorities in general towards the audience, making "all representations of reality vulnerable to public challenge and disbelief."[38] This sort of relativity wasn't quite the democratization envisioned by early Internet cheerleaders, for it often undermined more competent intellectual authorities. Twitter has confirmed Bauman's prophecy: "It is the number of followers that makes – that *is* – the authority."[39] Some commentators, such as Kevin Kelly, are pleased that for every fact, there is someone on the Internet who challenges it. He says, "My thinking has become more liquid ... I am less interested in Truth with a capital *T* and more interested in truths, plural."[40] A newsfeed that supplies my preferred news rather than the news supplied

[36] Bérubé, *Rhetorical*, 40–42.
[37] Twenge and Campbell, 187.
[38] Coleman, quoted in Andrejevic, 10–11.
[39] Bauman, *Liquid*, 67.
[40] Kevin Kelly, "The Waking Dream," in Brockman, 19.

by experts, even if they're not completely neutral, creates a dynamic uncongenial to Foucault's liberatory project and perhaps even to Kelly's. For, if expertise is the effect of power, and if group-specific knowledges are all valid, one can insist that Intelligent Design should have an equal hearing beside evolution in the classroom, and global warming denial beside atmospheric science. Why *can't* Rush Limbaugh, with his popular local knowledge, be a climate-change expert?[41] If discursive knowledge projects such as encyclopaedias are primarily an expression of power, then *Conservapedia*, "The Trustworthy Encyclopedia," makes sense. Born in 2006, *Conservapedia* imitates the *Wikipedia* format. For example, the article on "Barak Hussein Obama" reveals that "Obama claims to have been born in Hawaii," that his birth certificate has been questioned as possibly fake, but that "no charges have been filed."[42] The article on "gene" is one page long and cites a single reference, while lengthy articles on topics such as evolution lead off with the *Bible* and rely mostly on quotations in place of evidence. *Conservapedia* contributors can and do claim that their "subjugated knowledge" goes largely unheeded because liberals dominate universities, mainstream media, and the arts.

From a very different position, the psychoanalytic philosopher Slavoj Žižek, who calls psychoanalysis a truth experience, has argued that *rational* truths aren't available. The symbolic realm of language, humanist scholarship, and law can only be understood if we recognize that we are all impersonating authority—a "Big Other"—and that all our larger orders are ultimately deflected expressions of bodily desire. To know the pre-symbolic body of a dying animal and its imaginary expressions is to truly know ourselves. This psychoanalytic knowledge about our desires demolishes reason and radically questions the structures built via tradition and reason: religion, law, government, education. "The Master is an imposter," Žižek announces; the Big Other doesn't exist. Nobody's in charge! Yet the Master's *place* can't be abolished, and we can only speak if we impersonate the voice of the master.[43] In other words, we merely feign rational knowledge and thereby produce it. This—alongside his love of provocative statements and hoaxes[44]—is why Žižek's scholarship often

---

[41] Andrejevic, 63.

[42] Not surprisingly, *Conservapedia* articles on other presidents generally leave the president's middle name out of the article title.

[43] Žižek, *Symptom*, 98, 103. Myers, 49–50.

[44] Žižek has spoken of fabricating dreams in order to spice up his psychoanalysis with Jacques-Alain Miller. He wrote a pseudonymous review in *Problemi* (a journal he helped

feels like a game: he claims to know things, yet, according to his theory, he must be an imposter: catch me if you can. Without saying so directly, he advocates a world in which anyone can be a psychoanalyst. Does the heart surgeon's apparent surgical skill also reflect only the say-so of the Big Other?

Some postmodernists want it both ways: the world can't be described with any objectivity (our positions are rooted in our politics), and yet their description of the social world is intended to count as more than just a political stance. Charles Lemert says, "Social theorists are ... more relaxed in their science and more intense in their politics."[45] Almost in the same breath, and seemingly unaware that he's contradicting himself, Lemert explains that postmodernism must be tested against the facts of the world.[46] More conventional leftists, such as Jameson and Harvey, have understood that ethical principles must be generalized and that only a cross-cultural meta-theory could explain economic processes and the behaviour of elites.[47]

For a scholar such as Bauman, artistic simulations no longer represent something real "out there,"[48] and all disciplines must admit that their relationship to the truth is like that of an artistic production. Art, Alain Badiou explains, is the truth procedure that expresses "multiplicity in truths."[49] Indeed, in the postmodern era, many writers do foreground their ontological manipulations.[50] In Charlie Kaufman's captivating *Synecdoche, New York* (2008), it becomes increasingly difficult to disentangle the life of theatre director Caden Cotard from the ongoing play he is directing

---

edit) attacking his own book; he reported a fictional "roundtable" discussion on feminism, depicting himself as a boorish chair, and he claimed to have published an article on Rossellini without seeing his films. He calls himself a conservative who only plays at subversion. See Robert Boynton, "Enjoy Your Žižek," *Lingua Franca* 8:7 (October 1998), available online at https://www.robertboynton.com/articleDisplay.php?article_id=43.

[45] Lemert, 25.

[46] Lemert, 26; Lemert's italics.

[47] See Jameson, *Postmodernism*, 337–8, 346, 409, 417–8; "Postmodernism and Consumer," 1971; Harvey, *Condition*.

[48] Bauman, *Discontents*, 106.

[49] Badiou, 66.

[50] This is true even in the 2000s, after the postmodern literary movement has, according to some accounts, ended. Many scholars simply dropped the term "postmodernism." Others, such as Brian McHale, placed the end of postmodern literature sometime around 9/11, but then explained that one of the most important things about "post-postmodernism" was "the new phase's continuity with postmodernism" (McHale, *Cambridge*, 1, 3, 177).

and from Kaufman's film of that play. Truth is most obviously simulated in the entire-life reality show *The Truman Show* (1998) and likely so in Jonathan Lethem's *Chronic City* (2009), where the chaldron that the characters seek may or may not be real. Like *Chronic City*, both of Marisha Pessl's novels leave the reader with multiple uncertainties. At the end of *Night Film* (2013), the journalist Scott McGrath wants to know whether the reclusive filmmaker Stanislas Cordova is a Satanist and child molester or just a run-of-the-mill horror director, but Pessl doesn't supply an answer. *Special Topics in Calamity Physics* (2006) ends rather uniquely with a final exam. Formally, the novel—a whodunit—exploits the wish for truth. And many of the novel's answers correspond to carefully placed clues, but on the "Final Exam," some questions about Blue's father Gareth's disappearance are left hanging, and the "Essay Question" turns self-reflexively back upon questions of how American authors approach "the generalized bewilderment of living." Pessl makes Gareth a spokesperson for postmodernism, as he complains that Americans would "rather be shot in the arm with their own semiautomatic rifle" than confront the indeterminacy of life.[51] Gareth also happens to be the most untrustworthy character in the novel.

I will later argue, contra Bauman and Badiou, that for many important fiction writers, literature *does* attempt to describe something real "out there." Nonetheless, British novelist Tom McCarthy, influenced by post-structural theory, suggests that truth and even self are illusory. Repeated insectoid and technological metaphors in *C* (2010) make the point that human life is a sophisticated version of other carbon-based lifeforms (the *C* of the title) and that *we* are what our technology produces. It's not a human voice but language that speaks: "The [wireless] clicks were somehow speaking on their own and didn't need the detectors, keys or finger-twitching men who cling to them like afterthoughts."[52] Likewise, Montese Crandall, the novelist supposedly responsible for Rick Moody's *The Four Fingers of Death* (2010), says, "It's the words that have the ideas. I just assemble."[53] In *C*, Sophie "looks like a tethered radio mast" and Serge turns into "a giant, tentacular wireless set."[54] But as such metaphors accumulate, the book comes to seem more like a disquisition than a novel.

[51] Pessl, *Special*, 513, 411.
[52] Tom McCarthy, 365, 82–3.
[53] Moody, 37.
[54] Tom McCarthy, 91, 376.

In *C*, one cannot finally get outside of oneself, an unsatisfactory conclusion since we live in a world of so many others whose signals we are constantly trying to decode accurately, and since McCarthy expects the earth, dung, black bile, or ink growing inside Serge to *aptly* describe psychological and worldly conditions. To say that the *language* speaks is to completely ignore what John Searle calls the "word-to-world" fit that occurs whenever we make assertions, even in novels.[55] Literature's fit can never be exact, since neither Serge nor the most realistic characters exist outside language, yet literature has no sense apart from its fit to the world.

Emotion as the New Truth?

What takes the place of truth in contemporary understandings of the world? With modern rationality corroding trust in traditional faiths, and postmodernity corroding trust in rationality, many people turned to the old standby—emotion. This has happened across the political spectrum, from conservatives to liberals to leftists. In the next chapter, we'll see emotion's appearance in How-I-Feel morality, but here I'll examine emotion primarily as a truth-substitute. In a variety of contexts, emotion has come to be treated as an all-purpose decision-maker, truer than reason. The reliance on emotion, of course, is far older than the human species, since the emotions are mechanisms for promoting adaptive behaviour.[56] We've evolved to rely on and sometimes overrate our emotional intuitions. If problems are phrased in purely logical forms ("If P then Q"), we have a much harder time solving them than, say, if they are presented in a form that engages our cheater-detection module ("If drinking then must be over age 21").[57] Our emotions, shaped by evolution through millennia, can sometimes grasp the truth intuitively. Playing with a rigged deck of cards, we become aware of aversive emotions long before our reason can explain why.[58] Yet when confronted with abstract problems or problems in which the solution goes against our adapted emotional biases, we are stumped.[59] And some "common-sense" moral emotions that evolution

---

[55] Fotion, *John Searle*, 40, 48.
[56] Boyd, *Origin*, 205.
[57] Laland and Brown, 166–9.
[58] Greene, 141–2. See chap. 3 for this study by Antonio Damasio.
[59] Laland and Brown, 166–9.

has selected for, such as bias towards our own groups, lead us to immoral results—such as juries' biases against racialized defendants.[60]

New in the postmodern era is the perception that emotion belongs not to regressive, unthinking tradition, but rather to a progressive politics. Throughout the 1960s, emotion was hailed as a smart bomb that could explode the minions of Western rationality: the military-industrial complex, Cold War philosophies, and bourgeois existence. If the Enlightenment and modernity gave us total social control exemplified in Nazi concentration camps and Soviet gulags (a highly questionable thesis favoured by Bauman and Adorno), then postmodernism was what could resist reason's imperialism. Whereas emotion since time immemorial had been associated politically with tribalism and nationalism, in the postmodern era emotion was mobilized in two main ways *against* one's own nation: first, the growing sense of individualism made it horrifying that I should be sacrificed for my nation's advantage; and, second, rational scepticism about a divine warrant for my nation freed me (in postmodernity's extension of modernity's reasoning) to empathize personally and politically with foreigners slaughtered for my nation's advantage, particularly in the Algerian War (1954–1962) and the Vietnam War (1964–1975).

This anti-tribalism has a long history in the major world religions, in the Humanitarian revolution of the eighteenth century, and in the Rights Revolutions of the twentieth century,[61] but the immediate outcome of the 1960s anti-war protests was ambiguous. The heavily politicized May 1968 protests in Paris failed to transform France into a leftist utopia, while, in the US, successful protests in favour of civil rights and against the Vietnam War helped to cement a feeling that an emotional, victim-centred approach was the most moral one. The latter attitude heralded many advances in human rights. At the same time, if I hold that my emotion is truer than any general truth, then why should any larger institution have a say over my life? As young protesters throughout the West slowly learned to cherish social perks and material goods, and *became* the despised bourgeoisie, they, nevertheless, held onto the first lesson, that emotion was a dependable expression of human motivation, morality, and truth.

By the 1990s and 2000s, emotion's public reach went far beyond war protests, and could be measured in how the news increasingly covered celebrities and appealed to audience emotion. Jameson thought he saw a

[60] Greene, 212.
[61] See Pinker, *Better*.

waning of affect in selected high-culture literary works, yet news outlets revelled in politicians' personal lives, popularity, shifting alliances, misdeeds, and eventually tweets, rather than discussing policy. Faced with a shortage of political misdeeds, reporters ask candidates, "What's playing on your iPod?" During the 2008 American presidential campaign, the top Internet searches in relation to John McCain were about his wife, then his family, and then his daughter, and in 2016, those interested in Hillary Clinton wanted more information on her crying before the New Hampshire primary.[62] These interests aren't strictly postmodern: as social creatures, we've always wanted social information, yet gossip overwhelms policy issues. Bauman puts the matter succinctly: "No one ... proposed the impeachment of Bill Clinton for abolishing welfare as a 'federal issue.'"[63]

It's not just media, but politicians too, who recognize the primacy of emotion. Conventional political wisdom now dictates, "Forget about policies and rational arguments in politics – you need to make people *feel* for your side."[64] Websites such as Britain's pro-Jeremy Corbyn *The Canary*, on which writers are partially paid by the click, and political blogs that attract big audiences are generally the most partisan, with greater emphasis on emotion and a punchy style.[65] Yet even spiked with rage, politics isn't emotional enough to entertain most Internet surfers, who would rather read "PISTOL PACKIN' PLAYMATE! Former Playboy model gets gun permit from NYPD."[66] According to Hitwise, a company that formerly measured Internet surfing, politics accounted for less than a quarter of 1% of all Internet visits, behind fashion, insurance, lotteries, and gambling.[67]

Personal emotion crowds out truth on TV. Despite widespread scorn for the reality of Reality TV, people were still surprised when it became evident that a scene in *Kourtney & Kim Take New York* was falsely presented as having been filmed before the break-up of Kim Kardashian's marriage to Kris Humphries. In the scene, Kardashian and her mother appear to discuss the state of Kardashian's marriage, but viewers, tipped off by the stars' clothes, realized that the scene must have been manufac-

[62] Tancer, 41.
[63] Bauman, *Liquid*, 71.
[64] Heath, "Reason."
[65] Ball, 114. Maich and George, 191.
[66] This was one of the headlines for the *New York Daily News* on 11 April 2016, http://www.nydailynews.com/.
[67] Tancer, 41.

tured post-break-up. Rehearsed scenes, staged confrontations, and planned controversies have become the staples of Reality TV, since unscripted reality simply isn't emotional enough.[68] One anonymous *Bachelor* producer told NPR that the show sometimes did "frankenbite" editing, "where you take somebody saying, 'of course I'd like to say that I love him' and cutting the bite together to say 'of course I love him.' ... [It's] misleading to the viewer and unfair to the cast member, but they sign up for this."[69] It has been argued that young viewers seek the unvarnished truth in these shows, that instead of "the airbrushed perfection of *Friends*" they want "actual arguments between genuine young people being authentically solipsistic,"[70] but, since most viewers are aware of the manipulative nature of the genre, that can't be true. It's more likely that they want the emotional buzz that comes from a voyeuristic window into other people's love and rejection, success, and delicious humiliation. In 2016, Americans chose as their president a Reality TV star, who based his entire political appeal on emotion.

Emotion is the defining feature of Facebook, blogs, and TV's political punditry. As Jean Twenge puts it, "Opinion is a lot cheaper to obtain than actual news."[71] Advertisers have long sought emotional responses to their products, but the technological mapping of emotion is relatively new. An entire industry—neuro-marketing—has arisen in an attempt to dispense with reasoned pitches and to access our brains' soft emotional underbellies directly. Campbell Soup, for example, took two years to design its label in 2008, measuring consumers' "heart rate, respiration, skin conductance, facial expressions, and pupil dilation." Social media, "the world's biggest focus group," are stocked with emotionally inflected messages about products and popular culture, so we should be able to measure not just people's survey answers, but what they "truly" think (i.e. feel). "Sentiment analysis" can supposedly tell companies what the Internet as a whole is thinking (i.e. feeling).[72] Marketers analyse consumers' "word-clouds"—the frequency, not the meaning, of the words—and even argue that having access to big data is "better than having a hypothesis."[73]

[68] Weinman, 63.
[69] Pozner, 26.
[70] Alice Marshall quoted in D. Shields, 110.
[71] Twenge and Campbell, 64.
[72] Andrejevic, 125, 96, 82, 15, 42, 45–6.
[73] Andrejevic, 54. Morozov, *Save*, 265–6.

The emotional data apparently speak for themselves, bypassing representation and even comprehension.[74] It's ironic that Google, Intel, Daimler Chrysler, and Microsoft[75] use neuro-marketing in an attempt to get at a real "truth" beyond representation—modernity's goal—and then use that "truth" to create fantasy representations of the company, a postmodern evasion of the truth. Chrysler has nothing to do with Detroit rapper Eminem or black gospel choirs, but if neuro-marketing "Builds Brand Through Emotion," then a company that also happens to be located in Detroit can be presumed to be as gritty as a rapper and still full of God's grace.[76] More troublingly, George W. Bush spoke about making his policy decisions based not on research, but on "feel." Laura Bush said of her husband, "He has good instincts, and he goes with them. He doesn't need to evaluate and re-evaluate a decision. He doesn't try to *overthink*. He likes action."[77] When Joe Biden queried Bush about the next steps of occupation if the US were to defeat Saddam Hussein in Iraq, asking, "How can you be so sure when you know you don't know the facts?" Bush put a hand on Biden's shoulder, and responded, "My instincts."[78] Heath notes the irony that while the American Republicans and Canadian Conservatives have crafted many of their social policies to appeal primarily to voters' intuitions rather than reason, the parties nevertheless ensure that experts in polling and statistics run election campaigns.[79] The pessimistic interpretation of all these symptoms is offered by Jonathan Haidt: often we can't convince anybody unless we appeal to their intuitions, and even *reason* is designed not for truth, but for justification, especially justification of the self and the tribe.[80] In other words, we are all savvy politicians, truth doesn't matter, and postmodernity has merely made this explicit.

Kathryn Lofton calls the ascendancy of emotion "Oprahfication." In the place of hard news or talk about social structures, Oprah solicited sto-

---

[74] Andrejevic, 4–5.

[75] Andrejevic, 100.

[76] "Chrysler Eminem Super Bowl Commercial - Imported From Detroit," YouTube, published 5 February 2011, accessed 18 April 2016, https://www.youtube.com/watch?v=SKL254Y_jtc. Nielsen, "Solutions: Consumer Neuroscience, Benefits," accessed 18 April 2016, http://www.nielsen.com/us/en/solutions/capabilities/consumer-neuroscience.html.

[77] Andrejevic, 16.

[78] Suskind.

[79] Heath, *Enlightenment*, 257.

[80] Haidt, 48, 74.

ries, which got converted into slogans about victory over hardship.[81] Even though Oprah, early in her career, was hired to do the evening news in Baltimore, she was too uninformed and had trouble writing news copy, so she was transferred to the morning talk show. Her show really took off on 5 December 1985 when she revealed that she had been molested as a child by male relatives: "She had broken the silence for millions of women, and in that moment Oprah Winfrey became Oprah – Everywoman battling and overcoming victimhood."[82] This history forces us to pause and remind ourselves that, although emotion often ignores reasoned truths, for us to therefore sideline emotion would be to ignore, among other things, the voices of women, of victims, and of stories generally. Anne Kreamer suggests that notions about what constitutes "professional" behaviour have historically come from men, which has meant that women, if they wanted to be taken seriously, had to suppress their femininity—"their nurturing impulses" and "aspects of their intrinsic emotional biology," such as crying. To succeed, women were forced "to simulate maleness," a process that valued modernity and denied their neurobiology—for example, their higher levels of prolactin. Yet tears aren't automatically a sign of weakness, but may announce that a significant issue isn't being dealt with,[83] and that the concept of "professionalism" is behaviourally too narrow.

The issue is much too complex to address here, but it could be argued that the growth of women's political and social power after the 1960s has contributed to the cultural inroads made by emotion and has significant implications for the forms that rationality now takes. On some important questions, such as animal rights, men and women are divided: 62% of men favour the use of animals in research, while only 42% of women do so. Should we bow to our best reasoners, the scientists, 95% of whom favour the use of animals in research?[84] Or should emotion be an important factor in our decision? In hypothetical scenarios, heightened activity in the amygdala and other emotion-processing regions of the brain is associated with our reluctance to save five people by pushing one individual onto a track to stop a trolley. Only with emotional input from the limbic system can the prefrontal cortex avoid purely utilitarian calculations and instead make

---

[81] Lofton, 216–7.
[82] Packer, 59–60.
[83] Anne Kreamer, "Tears don't tell the truth," *Winnipeg Free Press* 17 August 2011, A10.
[84] Pew, "Scientific," 41.

better, "all things considered" decisions.[85] Steven Pinker has argued con-vincingly that an important factor in the decline of violence in the West has been the rising influence of women and their interests.[86] One reason for valuing the arts, which from a certain angle might seem like a massive waste of resources, is that the arts integrate the neocortex's rational infor-mation with the limbic system's emotional knowledge. Distrustful of intellectualization, David Foster Wallace tried to push his writing students towards the emotional potential in their work. When they relied too much on intellect, he'd order, "Write about a kid whose bunny died."[87] If, as Haidt argues, we generally seek out rational arguments that confirm what we have already concluded,[88] then reason will never be a cure-all. We could say, therefore, that the postmodern movement towards emotion in news-papers or TV news broadcasts doesn't signify only cultural failure but important gains as well.

Despite these important caveats, we must protest when an appeal to emotion impoverishes or biases rational arguments. Evolution has ensured that quick emotional calculations are necessarily biased towards our tribe, our kin, and ourselves. Linda's funny defence of her cat Bobby's right to kill as many birds as it pleases in Jonathan Franzen's novel *Freedom* only slightly exaggerates the arguments we make every day on behalf of ourselves, our family, our team, our nation, or our religion. Walter complains, "Why does [Bobby's] mild preference for being out-doors trump the right of songbirds to raise their families?" Linda confi-dently replies, "Because Bobby is part of our family. My children love him, and we want the best for him. If we had a pet bird, we'd want the best for it, too. But we don't have a bird, we have a cat."[89] There is a certain dogged logic here, but it's grounded entirely in familial emo-tion—a bit of emotion for her cat and a lot of emotion for her children. The argument is no more reasoned than were Donald Trump's popular emotional appeals against Muslims and Mexicans during the 2016 American election campaign.

With our sense of truth often manipulated via emotion, it's not surpris-ing to see a corresponding decline in trust of news outlets. High on the list

[85] Greene, 122, 126.
[86] Pinker, *Better*, 684–5.
[87] Max, 188.
[88] Haidt, 76.
[89] Franzen, *Freedom*, 543.

of distrust ought to be Fox News, correct? In fact, a 2010 survey showed Fox News to be the US's most trusted news organization at the same time that Fox was encouraging racist scepticism about whether President Obama had been born in the US. Infotainment rules. The more emotionally engaging the news is, the bigger and more trusting the audience.[90] This was the thrust of Stephen Colbert's famous "Truthiness" parody: "I don't trust books. They're all fact, no heart. And that's exactly what's pulling our country apart today." For Colbert it's not only politicians but also media pundits who bring back the heart by killing the head: "What about Iraq? Sure, if you *think* about it maybe there are a few missing pieces to the rationale for war, but doesn't taking Saddam out *feel* like the right thing? Right here … right here in the gut? Cause that's where the truth comes from, ladies and gentlemen, the gut … Anyone can read the news to you. I promise to feel the news *at* you."[91] Even when it was confirmed beyond all doubt that Obama was an American citizen, born in Hawaii, that his healthcare initiative didn't include "death panels," and that no connection existed between Saddam Hussein and Al-Qaeda, such emotional claims continued to find many adherents.[92]

Donald Trump certainly benefited from this new climate in which emotion reigned and there was presumed to be no neutral truth. In George Saunders's description of the Trump campaign, "The speeches themselves are nearly all empty assertion. Assertion and bragging. Assertion, bragging, and defensiveness. He is always boasting about the size of this crowd or that crowd, refuting some slight from someone who has treated him 'very unfairly,' underscoring his sincerity via adjectival pile-on (he's 'going to appoint beautiful, incredible, unbelievable Supreme Court Justices') … He is not trying to persuade, detail, or prove: he is trying to thrill, agitate, be liked, be loved, here and now. He is trying to make energy." Reporting from Trump rallies, Saunders felt saddened by both the Trump supporters and anti-Trump protesters who shouted insults at one another. In part, Saunders blames the Internet's "custom informational universe" that splintered TV and emasculated the local newspaper. The older media do have biases (linguistic analysis suggests that newspapers on average do

---

[90] Andrejevic, 3, 47–8.

[91] Stephen Colbert, The Colbert Report, October 17, 2005, http://www.gametrailers.com/user-movie/truthiness-the-colbert-report/33403.

[92] Andrejevic, 60.

slant somewhat to the left because their readers slant in that direction[93]) but at least people had a shared public space.[94]

The ascendancy of emotion isn't just a problem with right-wing agendas. The left's new focus on "microaggressions"—small, seemingly inoffensive comments or subtly critical body language—has created new and esoteric crimes defined mainly by emotion. The comments "You speak English very well," "Where are you from?" and "America is the land of opportunity" are deemed to be aggressions that unconsciously exclude the recipients from mainstream culture or perpetuate the "myth" that merit brings success.[95] There is validity in the notion that small aggressions can have a cumulative effect, and that minorities are more commonly on the receiving end of small aggressions. However, there are inherent flaws when one bases offences entirely on the emotions of the receiver. The first flaw is the idea that one can be guilty of an unconscious crime, an idea that runs directly counter to the *mens rea* aspect of criminal law: in order to be guilty, one must *intend* a harmful or illegal action. Some microaggressions, such as "Not wanting to sit by someone because of his/her color," truly are small aggressions, because they express racist feelings. Other supposed microaggressions, such as "Female doctor mistaken for a nurse," are incoherent, because they require the "aggressors" to know precisely what they don't know—otherwise they wouldn't have made the mistake. Best to assume that everyone is a doctor: nurses, healthcare aides, cleaners, visitors, cafeteria workers. In order to counter the *mens rea* defence, those condemning microaggression give lists of statements that are impermissible, so that no one can plead ignorance. But this leads directly to a second flaw. The fact that the most innocuous statement can be made aggressively should alert us that it's important to separate the propositional content of the statement from the emotional tenor added by body language. It's possible that "America is the land of opportunity" can mean, as Derald Wing Sue claims, "People of color are lazy and/or incompetent,"[96] but it's absurd to claim that it commonly means that. No one can specify all the contexts of its meaning from a neutral context, to a context in which the speaker is *justly* criticizing the merits of a minority receiver, to a context in

---

[93] Stephens-Davidowitz, 95–7.

[94] G. Saunders, "Who." Andrejevic, 130.

[95] Derald Wing Sue. See also Twenge, *iGen*, 256–8; and Kathy Wyer, "Microaggressions: What You Need to Know," *Ampersand*, UCLA Education and Information Studies, 2 June 2015, https://ampersand.gseis.ucla.edu/microaggressions-what-you-need-to-know/.

[96] All the cited microaggressions in this paragraph are from Derald Wing Sue.

which the speaker is *unjustly* criticizing the merits of the receiver for *non-racist* reasons, to a context in which the speaker is being racist. The suggested solution is to ban the statement entirely. If we agree that such statements can be banned because of the emotion or identity of the receiver rather than because of an objective incitement to hatred, then in effect we deny that the statement has any propositional content, with the corollary that *any* statement upsetting the feelings of the receiver is potentially culpable. Those troubled by "microaggressions" seem to want to criticize rudeness or lack of decorum in relation to race, ethnicity, gender, and sexuality, but consider "rudeness" or "lack of decorum" as too loose for something that they'd rather pursue with the rigour of hate speech laws.

Often emotion crowds out journalism and democracy, as the Internet becomes the primary source of news and as social media and search engines create filter bubbles that cater to our established prejudices. In late 2016, a fake news story about prominent Democrats running a child-sex-trafficking ring out of Washington's Comet Ping Pong restaurant led a North Carolina man to fire an assault rifle several times in the restaurant.[97] After a 2009 Fort Hood shooting that was eventually found to be workplace violence, News app entrepreneur Jason Calcanis, upon hearing the shooter's name, Nidal Malik Hassan, immediately characterized the killings as terrorism. Defending himself against criticism that he should have waited until he knew the details, Calcanis said, "We shouldn't wait for facts … Facts are, of course valuable, but speculation gets me further and builds better webs in my mind."[98] By late 2016, 805,000 people followed the website LibertyWritersNews.com, started by Paris Wade and Ben Goldman. "CAN'T TRUST OBAMA – Look At Sick Thing He Just Did To STAB Trump In The Back" and similar incendiary headlines allowed the two unemployed restaurant workers to rake in huge profits, especially during the ad-rich US presidential election. Referring to another headline—"THE TRUTH IS OUT! The Media Doesn't Want You To See What Hillary Did After Losing"—Wade says, "Nothing in the article is anti-media, but I've used this headline a thousand times … You have to trick people into reading the news." He admits that "in a perfect world," he would like to write a complex, nuanced, and balanced article, but "no

[97] Associated Press, "Fake news led to D.C. restaurant shooting: police," *Winnipeg Free Press*, 6 December 2016, A8.
[98] Jason Calcanis, "Trust Nothing, Debate Everything," in Brockman, 238.

one would click on it." Since emotion leads, Wade and Goldman never have to leave their apartments or interview anyone to create their stories.[99]

Through reporter Leila Helou in *Purity* (2015), Jonathan Franzen ably stages the threats to rational journalism in the postmodern era that also come from our fondness for spectacle. Leila's rants against Andreas Wolf, the Assange-like character who runs the fictional Sunlight Project, are described as follows: "You didn't need Washington journalists when you could read the tweets of congressmen, didn't need news photographers when everyone carried a phone with a camera, didn't need to pay professionals when you could crowdsource, didn't need investigative reporting when giants like Assange and Wolf and Snowden walked the earth." It's not just Trump who wants to bypass the traditional media gatekeepers. There is clearly something spectacular and insufficiently rational about a leak—leakers value truth, but they don't always value expertise.[100] Leila, whom Franzen makes one of the most reliable characters in the novel, calls leakers such as Edward Snowden and Chelsea Manning just "glorified sources." The real danger comes from unfiltered outlets such as WikiLeaks and the Sunlight Project. She says, "Filtering isn't phoniness—it's civilization."[101]

The limits of emotion as a guide to truth can be seen in other arenas too. To take one example, body language experts claim that they can bypass speech and get directly at the truth by observing the body's emotional signals. Choice Compass, a new decision-making app, is supposed to measure heart-rate-variability (HRV) so that if you're having difficulty making a choice, your "body's natural wisdom" will make the choice for you. Deborah Rozman, president and co-CEO says, "If you're angry, anxious or depressed, your HRV is disordered and jagged, like an earthquake," but if you're thankful and loving, the HRV is "beautiful and smooth like a sine wave." That makes you more empathetic and able to make better choices.[102] Like Napoleon Dynamite,[103] the company website advises, "Listen to your heart." "As you concentrate on each of two dif-

[99] Terrence McCoy, "All the News that's Fit to Fabricate," *Washington* Post, rpt *Winnipeg Free Press*, 26 November 2016, D4–5.

[100] Franzen, *Purity*, 240–1. Franzen isn't referring to any actual Sunlight Project. The Citizens for the Republic's "Sunlight Project" appears to be a borrowing and repurposing of Franzen's fictional group.

[101] Franzen, *Purity*, 524.

[102] Rosemary Counter, "The heart knows, and the phone tells you," *Maclean's*, 30 March 2015, 57.

[103] *Napoleon Dynamite*, 1:18:40.

ferent choices for one minute (example: ask for a raise vs. switch jobs), Choice Compass detects your heartbeat patterns to help you learn what the right decision should be; i.e. what choice reflects the calm and joyful feelings that will benefit you."[104] No doubt, the body often reveals more than our words do—we can more easily shape our language to deceive than we can our skin conductivity—but there's no sure way to get from an increase in skin conductivity or a change in heartbeat to the *meaning* of the change. Users want to access a true realm beyond reason, but *reasoned* cognition, which includes emotion, still gives us the best route to truth.

A central problem is that emotion generates the illusion of truth. Even a moderately engaging story can convince us to believe untruths—for example, that mental illnesses are contagious.[105] In one experiment, Jeffrey Strange gave readers a historical account of the Panama Canal, then a fictional story based *only* on the historical account. Afterwards, not surprisingly, readers sometimes misremembered bits of the fiction as history. More troubling, however, was the readers' propensity to treat the fiction as historical even when they remembered that the "information" was *fictional*. One reader explained, "If it was in the second text and not in the first, it wouldn't have any real basis, *unless it made sense to me*."[106] Such findings don't recommend a postmodernist or emotional approach to multiple knowledges. Fiction's counterfactual speculations are of immense value, but it's also crucial to distinguish history from myth, and truth from fiction, even in literature. There is no special, completely separate truth procedure for the arts. Against Derrida's attempts to deconstruct the difference between literary and non-literary speech acts (through his notion of the supplement), I will argue later that even our *literary* analysis (never mind our view of the world and our relationships with others) will be juvenile if we pretend that literary and non-literary speech acts have similar truth-values.

Truth, Act II

Are we postmodern yet? In Jodi Dean's opinion, emotional intensity nowadays trumps content, but Mark Andrejevic argues convincingly that "the reality-based community persists in various guises."[107] We are postmodern

---

[104] Mossbridge Institute, "Listen to Your Heart," (Main page for Choice Compass), http://www.choicecompass.com/, accessed 6 April 2016.

[105] Foy and Gerrig.

[106] Strange, 271–3. My emphasis.

[107] Andrejevic, 139.

to the extent that we no longer trust reason as the sole arbiter of truth. But we do trust reason, and this was always so, even at the height of post-modernism. All claims, from the physical forces inside the sun to the behaviour of crowds to the validity of tears in a certain situation, are subject, in different ways, to verification. When we now argue against former consensus "truths" in the West (that women weren't as fully rational as men, that dark-skinned races were intellectually inferior, that gender non-conformity was a sin or a mental illness), we don't argue that the new truth is merely an effect of new powers held by women, racialized people, or gender minorities. Rather, we argue that the old "knowledge" was not *true*, that it wasn't *knowledge*, but rather belief based on an emotional prejudice. It makes little sense to say that these social questions were only questions of value, with disinterested reason playing no role.

What evidence is there that even in the postmodern era truth is still accessible? Firstly, evolution has always selected for accurate depictions of the environment, and human perceptual systems are "accurate enough to bet one's life upon."[108] Studies confirm how adept we are at tracking the eye movements, and thus the attention, of others. Not surprisingly, there is also an emotional reward system associated with true propositions.[109] Knowing precise truths about the world and other beings is usually adaptive, and is mediated by the medial prefrontal cortex. During a hunt, it's adaptive to have learned about animal behaviour, while during a social situation it's adaptive to know (even if unconsciously) that people who blush are more likely to tell the truth. At the same time, of course, evolution doesn't place a premium on the truth, and false beliefs can be selected for, as long as they promote adaptive behaviour.[110]

Sam Harris goes much further than evolutionary psychologists do, rashly claiming that reward systems for truth mean that the brain doesn't separate truth and value, and that "values reduce to a certain type of fact."[111] Against such unsupportable claims, one can easily point to disjunctions between reward systems and value. Drug addiction, successful violence, and rape are all rewarded with dopamine. Successful aggression is usually rewarded in the brain, yet when aggression is directed *against* us, we have no difficulty calling it immoral. Deception—untruth—is also

[108] Anderson and Anderson, 352.
[109] Harris, *Moral*, 121.
[110] D. Wilson, *Darwin's* 41. Boyd, *Origin*, 205.
[111] Harris, *Moral*, 121–2.

clearly adaptive in many situations and has been selected for. Here's the complexity: believers get dopamine rewards when thinking about heaven, and their belief in implausible heavenly crowns can convince them both to slaughter the "heathen" and to act altruistically, especially towards fellow believers. Harris is thus wrong on both counts: the brain's reward system doesn't always favour positive values, and it doesn't favour only facts. Nevertheless, despite Harris's overreaching, moral truth has been selected for as well. Blushing, an involuntary signal, ought to be selected *against*, we think, since it can cause the blusher trouble by exposing a lie. However, blushing also signals the blusher's adherence to the social code—they are embarrassed by the lie—so people tend to treat the blusher more sympathetically than they treat the brazen. Blushing is a costly signal of truth.

Secondly, the reality-based community persists in language too. Noam Chomsky's universal grammar revealed how mistaken the Sapir-Whorf Hypothesis of linguistic relativity was. Subsequently, linguists have been able to show the stable, cross-cultural structure of the language instinct. Pinker cites the case of Simon, a deaf boy: despite only seeing his parents use defective American Sign Language (ASL), Simon, nevertheless, invented proper ASL verb inflections on his own. Severe intellectual deprivation in youth (such as occurs when children are exposed to *no* language at all) can prevent language development, but Simon's case—"creolization by a single living child"—is one of many pieces of evidence that language (contrary to the "multiple knowledges" dogma) is not relative to culture in depicting the world: it accurately represents time and a host of other features of the world.[112]

Truth is also accessible in that we have multiple methods of gauging the trustworthiness of language. Responding to critics who disparage the return to the personal voice in postmodernism, Charles Lemert counters that non-postmodernist writing (including Kant's *Critique of Practical Reason*) is also highly personal, just not in obvious ways.[113] While postmodernism greatly deepened the humanities and social sciences by showing that the personal is political, Lemert's claim ridiculously simplifies the process of rational argument. Kant's arguments, no matter what their personal source, are more *objective* than the tweets of Donald Trump. If

---

[112] Pinker, *Language*, 69–73, 46–8, 52–3, 27. Culture can limit what we know, but language is determined by thought, not thought by language. See Pinker, *The Stuff of Thought*, New York: Penguin, 2007, 124–51.

[113] Lemert, 87.

power determined knowledge, then the best we could hope for would be balance, always quoting both sides of any issue. Savvy PR experts quickly jumped on the balance bandwagon, with the result that global warming deniers for a long time received equal press to scientists who warned against rising temperatures. Yet, as Mark Andrejevic astutely observes, "the fact-checking cottage industry" arose in response to 1980s and 1990s journalism which, despairing of objectivity, planted its flag on the problematic concept of he-said/she-said balance. Objectivity resurfaced as a separate division.[114] *FactCheck.org*, *PolitiFact.com*, 150 fact-checking organizations around the world, and the embryonic development of software such as Squash (which in a 30-second delay assesses the claims in political speeches[115]) all show an affinity with Habermas's communicative reason against Foucauldian scepticism.

The Doublespeak Award for grossly deceptive language[116] … what could such an award mean other than that language is capable of transmitting truths about human social interactions? Kellyanne Conway won the award in 2017 for defending Sean Spicer's falsehoods about the Trump Inauguration attendance by calling the falsehoods "alternative facts." President George W. Bush won in 2008 when, instead of setting a deadline for the US Army's withdrawal from Iraq, he spoke of an "aspirational goal." Had he set a deadline, or had he refused to set a deadline, or had he named factors that might induce the US to postpone a deadline, he would have failed to win the award: his words would either have been truthful or could have had their truthfulness objectively measured in the light of subsequent events. Instead, "as textbook Doublespeak, 'aspirational goal' is both a tautology and a paradox. Aspirations and goals are the same thing; and yet when the terms are combined, the effect is to undermine them both, producing a phrase that means, in effect, 'a goal to which one does not aspire all that much.'"[117] It's easy to forget that, as Michael Tomasello has shown, language itself is a product of joint attention, a cooperative, conventionalized, reason-giving enterprise whose evolution required

---

[114] Andrejevic, 138.

[115] Jonathan Rauch, "Autocorrect: How advances in real-time fact-checking might improve our politics," *The Atlantic*, June 2019, 11–14.

[116] National Council of Teachers of English, "The Doublespeak Award," accessed 16 March 2016, http://www.ncte.org/volunteer/groups/publiclangcom/doublespeakaward.

[117] National Council of Teachers of English, "Past Recipients of the NCTE Doublespeak Award," accessed 17 March 2016, http://www.ncte.org/library/NCTEFiles/Involved/Volunteer/Appointed%20Groups/Past_Recipients_Doublespeak_Award.pdf.

humans to take a second-personal point of view. This doesn't necessarily mean objectivity and truth, since language is oriented to *group* values, yet doublespeak only works because it is set against the baseline expectation that speakers are committed to giving reasons and favouring joint goals, not just the *speaker's* goals.[118]

Similarly, George Saunders's satire in the diminished future of "Pastoralia" (2000) isn't funny unless we assume a more truthful way of speaking that doesn't only convey the goals of a single corporation. He satirizes corporate communications in an inter-departmental memo: "Truth is that thing which makes what we want to happen happen. Truth is that thing which, when told, makes those on our team look good, and inspires them to greater efforts." The same memo denies the rumour that firings will soon take place (they will).[119] Saunders and other contemporary writers influenced by postmodernism are unlikely to return to literalist or parochial notions of truth, but these writers do insist that language, in the right hands, is never purely political. Nicoline Timmer, summarizing one of the features of what she calls the "post-postmodern" novel, turns to Wittgenstein's notion that a relationship between people is a precondition of language.[120] Earned trust defines the evolving relationship between novelist and reader, politician and voter, journalist and citizen, fact-checking organization and audience.

With the rise of photoshopping, Voco, and Deepfakes, facts are under even more pressure from several directions. Donald Trump's political success, despite his stunningly low scores on fact-checking websites—much lower than any other politician—shows how often group loyalties and confirmation bias outweigh facts. This is exacerbated by filter bubbles and by the growing tendency of the young not to follow the news. A 2014 poll found that nearly two-thirds of 18- to 29-year-olds and over half of 30- to 50-years-olds got their political news mainly from Facebook. CNN posts news on Snapchat, because that's where the people are,[121] and many reliable news organizations post "sponsored links" that look like news links and that take viewers to dubious celebrity news and deceptive advertisements—the news organizations sabotage themselves for advertising reve-

---

[118] Tomasello, 51–2, 71–2, 111–12.
[119] G. Saunders, *Pastoralia*, 62–3.
[120] Timmer, 360.
[121] Cecilia Kang, "News in a Snap," *Winnipeg Free Press*, 7 March 2015, D9. She cites a 2014 Pew Research poll.

nue.[122] Still, despite targeted news, it has never been easier to check out the truth of a claim, and we don't spend two minutes on the Internet without making finer and finer distinctions about the affiliations and niches of various websites. What level of language is the writer employing? Do they have any obvious biases? Do they use a wide range of references? And so on. The main difficulties are not a lack of facts or an inability to distinguish them, but our emotional and social ties to particular groups. My lack of knowledge about health insurance may make it easier for a website to fool me by catering to my group prejudices. Nevertheless, my continued relationship with various websites allows me slowly to orient myself as to the level of objectivity in the places I visit. According to John Searle, we join an infinite number of language games—from a testimony in court, to a weather report, to a neighbourhood conversation—and every type of speech activity has its own conventions. The games aren't chaotic, just complex, though still rules-based, and we're constantly on the lookout for cues to help us estimate levels of truth,[123] as long as we *want* the truth.

Thirdly, there is a common misconception that truth isn't accessible in fiction. Giacomo Rizzolatti's discovery of mirror neurons in the 1990s revealed that language, fiction, and film are *real* in fundamental and mimetic ways: I say the word "grasp" and *your* neurons fire, the same ones that fire when you actually grasp something. More recently, film theorist Torben Grodal has shown how movies stimulate specific bodily reactions. In this aspect, cinema builds upon the ways in which stories and language consist of cues to perceptions, emotions, and actions.[124] As well, fiction involves complex calculations of whether the fictional events would be plausible in the world as we know it. Even fantasy isn't exempt: although the characters in the *Harry Potter* books cast spells, teen readers also ask whether the books reflect convincing teen emotions and character psychologies. Hypothetical thinking, such as occurs in all forms of fiction, allows us to apprehend the world, other people, and other cultures in their complexity. Grodal gives a more accurate assessment than either Bauman or Derrida: fiction isn't an "unreal" activity, since our ability to imagine alternate worlds is tied to our understanding of prototypical behaviours in

[122] See Ball, 200–5, 212.
[123] Fotion, "Speech," 40–1.
[124] Grodal, *Embodied*, 162–4.

the real world.[125] No *general* statement (i.e. that fiction carries truth, or that fiction has little disputational use, or that fiction is the destabilizing supplement of serious speech acts) can identify the truth-value of individual works of fiction. Postmodernism has taught us that each individual speech act and each fiction may bear a different relationship to reality.[126] Only careful analysis reveals the nature of that relationship.

Pinker argues that it's no coincidence that torture, slavery, and capital punishment all declined during the rise of literacy and of the novel, a hypothetical form that allows readers to enter the emotional truth of other people's lives and to empathize with them.[127] By inventing counterfactual narratives, we open up a variety of new possibilities from which we select better cultural adaptations.[128] Children with imaginary friends actually perform *better* in distinguishing between the real and the imaginary,[129] because art develops a flexible mind through play. Rats deprived of play tend to become abnormal, veering between behaviour that is too passive or too aggressive. A new line of research suggests that, although psychopaths seem to have no common background, 90% apparently had reduced play in childhood.[130] In a democratic society, the best fiction (including the forms practised on TV and the Internet) is neither a deception that diverts us from reality nor the ironic hallmark of a post-objective world, but a flexible, exploratory form that allows us to grasp truth and human difference in ever more complex ways.

Certainly, as we've seen in the Panama Canal history/story, fiction can no doubt sway us emotionally to believe untruths, and for Twenge this includes the cynicism that accompanies the satirical news on *The Daily Show* or in *The Onion*.[131] In Canada, a CBC radio show *This Is That* provides documentary reports about issues such as dog parks in Québec where dogs are required to understand owners' commands in both of Canada's official languages (English and French), and about children's soccer leagues that, to prevent over-competitiveness, have done away with scoring and don't use balls. To build self-esteem, children are free to

[125] Grodal, *Moving*, 26.
[126] Grodal says it well: "Fiction as a category does not have a fixed reality-status" (*Moving*, 34).
[127] Pinker, *Better*, 477–8, 169–76. See also Hunt.
[128] Storey, 105.
[129] Boyd, *Origin*, 183.
[130] Boyd, *Origin*, 192–3, 86–7, 179–80.
[131] Twenge, *Me*, 147.

imagine themselves having scored as many goals as they like. Were you fooled by these reports? I'd wager no, though these stories fooled less sophisticated news-aggregating organizations such as the *Washington Times* and the *Drudge Report* into reporting the satire as fact.[132] Is this a sign that too much fiction inoculates us against truth? No. News-aggregating sites are vulnerable because, unlike real news organizations, they don't send reporters out to investigate the truth of a story. The fact that educated people rarely confuse satire and fake news, despite the documentary-style reporting, tells us that we have robust social knowledge and a finely honed ability to understand counterfactual cues. *This Is That* listeners make larger, less literal political and social inferences: about the overreaching of Canadian bilingualism and about the anxieties of helicopter parents who fear that a bit of soccer competition will traumatize their children, and even about the ways in which the documentary form can be manipulated.

Earlier I showed literary writers such as Kaufman, Lethem, and Tom McCarthy arriving at multiple incompatible truths, but many other great fiction writers of the late twentieth and early twenty-first centuries—Jonathan Franzen, Richard Powers, David Foster Wallace, Salman Rushdie, Mo Yan, Margaret Atwood, Alice Munro, David Mitchell, Peter Carey, to name a few—have leaned towards communicative reason, seeking to assess historical forces and human aspirations accurately, even when they created future worlds (Atwood) or used magic realism (Rushdie). Wallace's early work, for example, was indebted to the postmodernism of Barth and Pynchon,[133] but later he dismissed his own major work of the period, *The Broom of the System* (1987), as having been written by "a very smart fourteen-year-old."[134] By the 1990s, *Infinite Jest* gave sympathetic treatment to the AA counsellor Don Gately, with critical treatment to Hal Incandenza, who descends into drug-fuelled depression, and to James Incandenza, whose funny, "anti-confluential" films become increasingly detached from the world. Clearly, Wallace sought a role for traditional

---

[132] John Bowman, "CBC Radio show strikes again with ball-less soccer satire," 6 September 2013,   https://web.archive.org/web/20131003140042/;   http://www.cbc.ca/news-blogs/yourcommunity/2013/09/cbc-radio-show-strikes-again-with-ball-less-soccer-satire.html. "Youth soccer league: No balls, scoring to halt negative effects of competition," *Washington Times*, 5 September 2013, http://www.washingtontimes.com/news/2013/sep/5/just-pretend-ontario-youth-soccer-league-eliminate/.

[133] McHale, *Cambridge*, 136–7.

[134] Max, 48. See also Lipsky, 35.

virtues and a way around his predecessors' insistence that truth was evasive. When the character Geoffrey Day arrives at Ennet House, he sabotages the former prostitute Charlotte Treat and her hope for sobriety with
his satiric commentary on Alcoholics Anonymous clichés: "I came here to
learn to live by clichés ... One day at a time. Easy does it. First things first.
Courage is fear that has said its prayers ... I live my life by the dictates of
macramé samplers ordered from the back-page ad of an old *Reader's
Digest* or *Saturday Evening Post*." Gately, who has a lot more sobriety
under his belt than Geoffrey Day does, comments, "It's the newcomers
with some education that are the worst ... They identify their whole selves
with the head."[135] Here, common sense comes out better and truer than
postmodernist intellectualizing. Alongside *Infinite Jest*'s wonderfully
hyperbolic invention of a future lies an emotionally intense and *realistic*
description of depression and drug dependency.

In the next chapter, we'll see that we really are on the horns of a postmodern dilemma, not in relation to truth, but in the field of ethics, where
postmodernity has given currency to a pluralist world of multiplying differences and beliefs. Nevertheless, with evolutionary adaptations that
favour truth, language's ability to convey truth, and literature's mimetic
qualities, the reality-based community persists in the postmodern era.
Pinker explains that crucial for the decline of violence were the rise of science and the slow growth of reason, "a species-wide self-consciousness,
encouraged by literacy, mobility, and technology ... Increasingly we see
our affairs from two vantage points: from inside our skulls ... and from a
scientist's-eye view."[136] Douglas Kellner, harbouring a postmodernist suspicion of rationality, argues that since maps and theories are distortions of
reality, a "postmodern cartography" would recognize maps and theories
as "rhetorical and political devices."[137] To which, one must reply that rhetoric and politics are only a small part of any valid theory's function, because
valid theories also convey veridical information about the world and about
people. We couldn't have built massive cities, complex medical facilities,
educational institutions that question truth, and intricate systems of governance without stepping outside of our own biases and learning, accurately, what other humans are and want. These developments strongly
challenge the postmodernist belief in separate truths for separate people

[135] Wallace, *Infinite*, 270–2.
[136] Pinker, *Better*, 569–70.
[137] Kellner, "Reappraising," 111–14.

and cultures. In relation to truth and multiple knowledges, we are less postmodern than has been claimed. Despite significant cultural differences, we continue to access species-wide psychological truths, without which it would be almost impossible to create a dialogue across cultures, across religions, or, as we'll see, across ethical positions. Echoing Max Planck, scientists have been able to safely continue speaking of data as "mysterious messengers from the real world."

CHAPTER 3

Ethics: "How I Feel at the Time"

MORAL DILEMMAS

Despite the many weaknesses of the postmodernist dethronement of reason and truth, one salutary effect has been a passionate defence of pluralism. Rational truths can't solve the postmodern ethical dilemma—our lack of a common measure of the good. At the same time, the notion of a thoroughgoing post-rationalist approach to ethics is seriously flawed, leading to a How-I-Feel ethics, an ethics circumscribed by the individual's own interests, but also an ethics, as we will see, that even its defenders fail to practise with any consistency. Set above our pluralism, we do have at least one widely agreed-upon rule—the human rights obligation, "Do No Harm." The good that we call "security of person" historically deployed modernist reason against religious traditions, yet in the postmodern era this good has found broad assent, from religious people to postmodernist relativists. Modernity, trying by means of the 1648 Treaty of Westphalia to escape the wars of religion, upheld the right of every sovereign nation to determine its own internal affairs, including moral ones, but postmodernity, responding to the trauma of the Holocaust with the UN's 1948 *Universal Declaration of Human Rights*, has increasingly pulled away from the nation as the force that determines right within its borders. With the UN caught between modernity's injunction not to interfere with a nation's sovereignty, and postmodernity's belief that the human individual is the supreme good, UN peacekeepers in Rwanda were ordered to sit on their weapons as a genocide took place.

© The Author(s) 2019
R. Kramer, *Are We Postmodern Yet?*,
https://doi.org/10.1007/978-3-030-30569-7_3

Looking back at Rwanda 1994, hindsight makes it remarkably easy to declare what sort of interference should have occurred to protect human rights; and in re-enactments such as *Hotel Rwanda* (2004), certain sequences loom large: Rwandan orphans and nuns arrive at the hotel believing that they will get passage out of the horror, but brief, hand-held shots jump-cut through a melee as French military personnel separate the French nationals from Rwandans, then a pan slowly crosses the troubled, relieved white faces safe inside a bus, and finally the camera cuts to a static shot of the stranded black children. In such moments, it doesn't matter that critics seriously challenged the self-serving motives behind hotelier Paul Rusesabagina's selective autobiographical narrative,[1] because the separation of white from black, and even of citizen from non-citizen is now experienced as highly offensive, an affront to *human* rights, which place infinite value on human individuals, not on their group identities.

Ethical requirements in the context of a genocide seem clear, if difficult, to us in the postmodern era, but when we turn to everyday life, ethics cloud up, especially when human rights and harm can't be invoked. Although several factors made Michael Chabon uneasy about his marijuana habit mentioned at the outset of this book, it was the near graduation of his habit into the category of harm that made him quit smoking. Alone for an evening, he got high, not expecting to have to drive. But he was surprised by a call to pick up one of his children from an abortive sleepover. He drove, stoned, aware that he was courting tragedy. With the potential for harm so clear, the ethical pressure afterwards to abstain from drugs felt irresistible to him. But what if his children vowed in their teenage years always to call Operation Red Nose or some other designated driver service instead of driving high? Would he still urge them to stay away from marijuana? For those who no longer assent automatically to tradition's firm answers, ethical choices wherein human rights are not at stake have become increasingly blurry. Cases of self-harm (physician-assisted death, drug use), cases in which no individual is harmed (cheating on tests, desecration of holy symbols, genetic engineering), cases in which two sets of interests collide (child welfare) are the kinds of issues that

---

[1] See Okaka Opio Dokotum, "Re-membering the Tutsi Genocide in *Hotel Rwanda* (2004)," *African Conflict & Peacebuilding Review* 2:3 (Fall 2013): 129–50. Linda Melvern, "Hotel Rwanda – without the Hollywood Ending," *Guardian*, 17 November 2011, https://www.theguardian.com/commentisfree/2011/nov/17/hotel-rwanda-hollywood-ending.

dumbfound contemporary ethics. Even when the morally right decision is clear, individual human harm and the attendant emotions are much easier to feel than is harm to an institution or to a cultural practice. A study of several colleges found between 67% and 80% of students admitting that they had cheated. Cheating among American high school students increased from 34% in 1969, to 61% in 1992, to 74% of in 2002.[2] Set beside the great advantage that cheating gives me—how I feel—it becomes difficult for me to put much weight on the harm done to the integrity of grades, to merit-based hiring that relies on grades, or to my own moral integrity.

Similar competing moral interests appear in arguments about reproductive rights. In Canadian writer Theresa Shea's moving novel *The Unfinished Child* (2013), Margaret, who gives birth to a Down syndrome child in 1947, is crosscut with Marie, who in the 2000s must decide whether to abort an unwanted Down syndrome foetus. Shea avoids the political rhetoric of Pro-Life/Pro-Choice debates, concentrating on the human face of the ethical dilemma that colours a host of smaller problems: What will people think? How will my other children react? Can I live with myself after giving my child away? Margaret's 1947 decision is rooted both in tradition (abortion isn't a legal option even had she been forewarned about Down syndrome) and in modern authority (the doctor recommends institutionalization). Margaret doesn't question the doctor, even though his advice goes against her gut instincts. Marie's ethical dilemma in the 2000s, however, is postmodern. In Canada, as in most Western democracies, moral decisions, including about abortion, lie squarely with the individual. Neither traditional religious authorities nor modern medical authorities can choose on Marie's behalf. Shea notes that the abortion of Down syndrome children has gone up to about 90%, though a 2012 systematic review of termination studies puts the figure between 67% and 85%.[3] The numbers shouldn't surprise: decisions such as Marie's are often made without a divine warrant and in a context where harm is difficult to weigh.

---

[2] Twenge, *Me*, 27; Twenge and Campbell, 206. James, 16. Men were more likely to justify their cheating than women were.

[3] Shea, 237–8. Jaime L. Natoli, Deborah L. Ackerman, Suzanne McDermott and Janice G. Edwards, "Prenatal diagnosis of Down syndrome: a systematic review of termination rates (1995–2011)," *Prenatal Diagnosis* 32: 2 (February 2012): 142–153, Wiley Online Library, http://onlinelibrary.wiley.com/doi/10.1002/pd.2910/full.

In 2008, sociologist Reginald Bibby asked Canadian 15- to 19-year-old Millennials, "Generally speaking, on what do you base your moral views?" Almost half (43%) replied, "How I feel at the time"—a moral guideline that goes, in its momentariness, beyond even Rousseau's "what I feel to be right is right, what I feel to be wrong is wrong." Far fewer Millennials (the generation born between 1980 and 1995) said that they based their views on their parents' views (16%) or on religion (10%).[4] Might they be cobbling together ethics from a variety of sources? Bibby did offer precisely this alternative, and only 7% chose it. Most likely, these Millennials understood that parental influence and tradition wouldn't restrain them from actions that they *felt* were permissible. Perhaps they were confused about their views and unaware of their moral debt to parents, to surrounding social norms, and to traditional religion? This "confusion" interpretation is supported by a 2015 Angus Reid poll of Canadians generally, not just Millennials, in which half agreed that "what's right or wrong is a matter of personal opinion," and yet three-quarters also agreed that "the Ten Commandments still apply today."[5] This means that at least a quarter of Canadians hold the irreconcilable positions that morality is fundamentally a matter of personal opinion and that it fundamentally isn't. Bibby's percentage—43%—may even underestimate the How-I-Feel category by almost 20%. Those Millennials who claimed that they based their moral views on "nothing" (12%) or on "personal decisions" (7%) may also effectively belong to the How-I-Feel group. A How-I-Feel ethics is not quite ethical egoism, but it does insist that ethical demands external to the individual can't be determinative. Maybe the Ten Commandments are merely Pascal's insurance wager.

We might defend Millennials by explaining that the rise of the modern subject has allowed us to value ordinary life against spiritual asceticism and to value bills of rights against hierarchical oppression,[6] yet self-indulgence looms when individuals, not the community, decide the shallowness or depth of their moral obligations. One American Millennial says, "What's right for me may be wrong for somebody else or what's wrong for me may be okay for somebody else." A minority of young Americans criticized this as "self-indulgent rationalizing of wrong choices and behaviors," but one young man explained, "Unless you do something really horrible, you

[4] Bibby, 8, 213.
[5] Angus Reid, 10, 21–2.
[6] Taylor, *Sources*, 211–47, 188–93.

know, kill someone, it doesn't really matter, right or wrong."[7] Right-for-me, wrong-for-you: this makes it difficult for Boomer parents to enforce moral rules in their children. Parents and even supposed experts can't articulate why promiscuity or getting drunk might be morally wrong. Kate Ruby-Sachs, a Toronto social worker, explains that parents must set boundaries for their children. For example, "If you're using mood-altering substances, using the car is off the table."[8] That should clear up a lot of moral agonizing. Only by steering the problem directly towards harm can Ruby-Sachs arrive at a moral distinction, simplistic as it is. However, complex questions about finer moral distinctions—about alcohol use or commitment or appropriate behaviour during relationship conflicts—can rarely be reduced to simple "harm." Without some agreements about various kinds of moral responsibility, I may easily be tempted to defect from my public commitments and from my private responsibilities.

Even the intellectually sophisticated stumble when they try to base a moral calculus on How-I-Feel. Talented American novelist William Vollmann tries to anchor his wide-ranging survey of human violence *Rising Up and Rising Down* (2003–4) in a How-I-Feel ethic: "I declare that I am sovereign over myself because I want to be." The first right, *ex nihilo*, is self-defence. He very quickly gets to a human rights ethic, saying that if he feels so strongly about his own autonomy, then he can't trample on the choices of others, unless they cause "unjustified suffering."[9] But he soon returns to individual choice. Although Hobbes fears that it would be poison for "every private man" to be "Judge of Good and Evil actions,"[10] Vollmann rather likes the idea and says that to surrender individual sovereignty in order to bring peace and order is a "doctrine … appealing to tyrants." He leans towards a libertarian ethic: few deeds are categorically evil, individual sovereignty demands that we allow others mostly to do what they want,[11] and, except for "direct incitement to violence," free speech should be absolute, including all forms of pornography, hate speech, and blasphemy.[12] When he tries to arrive at a moral calculus, the determinedly individualist character of his premises clashes directly with his conclusions. Local norms, the Golden Rule, and the necessity to some-

[7] C. Smith, 48–9, 52, 203.

[8] Rebecca Eckler, "Hey mom, I'm so high right now!" *Maclean's*, 22 February 2016, 79.

[9] Vollmann, *Rising*, 85, 93.

[10] Hobbes, Ch. 29, 365.

[11] Vollmann, *Rising*, 94.

[12] Vollmann, *Rising*, 467.

times break social norms in order to choose the right all figure in his instructions on how to form a moral code. On the other hand, he thinks that universal norms often fail—the same principle applied in a different situation can result in a completely different outcome[13]—and so his first instruction is highly subjective: "Follow your own inner logic and feeling in order to postulate laws of conduct which seems to you good."[14] This postmodern, nearly How-I-Feel, approach gives us no help on which social norms to follow. Once Vollmann gets more detailed in his moral calculus, he allows for violence not only in self-defence, but also in defence of individual rights, defence of honour (under some conditions), and defence of class (under some conditions).[15] How did he leap from the self to honour and class? Unfortunately, *his* calculus, too, would delight tyrants. Vollmann's is not a naïve recourse to How-I-Feel and he recognizes that his moral calculus often includes mutually exclusive items,[16] but he doesn't know what to do about that.

In *Europe Central* (2005), Vollmann's profound redaction of World War II into a tour-de-force novel, composer Dmitri Shostakovich asks his student Galina Ustvolskaya, "Can music attack evil or not?" She responds, "Certainly not. All it can do is scream."[17] Of course, films and novels, including Vollmann's, do a lot more than scream. Richard Joyce argues that morality bonds individuals "in a shared justificatory structure."[18] Novels and films explain our actual moral stances and make ethics seem natural.[19] While art can't replace the functions of religious faith, politics, and moral choice, it depicts moral problems and negotiations, at times imagines solutions, and occasionally outlines some ways in which the social order *depends* on moral choices. Most crucially, literature, including its postmodernist varieties, undermines libertarianism and How-I-Feel by broadcasting social control, sometimes through poetic justice (punishing evildoers), but usually more subtly by implying which of the characters' deeds are shameful or praiseworthy, and by identifying which social structures the sympathetic characters accept and which they rebel against.

---

[13] Vollmann, *Rising*, 34.
[14] Vollmann, *Rising*, 448.
[15] Vollmann, *Rising*, 461–71.
[16] Vollmann, *Rising*, 414.
[17] Vollmann, *Europe*, 645.
[18] Joyce 117.
[19] Boyd, *Origin*, 170, 196. Sugiyama, 188–9.

Europe Central certainly does this through the agonizing of the characters Shostakovich and Kurt Gerstein. Without the punishment of cheaters, neither social cooperation nor a stable society is possible. Beyond the first-order moral temptation to cheat comes a second-order temptation: to let everyone else bear the cost of punishing cheaters. This is why literature and film, even beyond their aesthetic value, are so important in assessing contemporary practices. William Flesch goes so far as to say that altruistic punishment (our willingness to punish a cheater, even if it costs us) is a central motive for stories.[20] In stories, even minor anti-social deeds like cutting in a queue are *noticed* and despised, making altruistic punishments *public* and enlisting the audience's feelings.[21]

A black comedy such as Morris Panych's *Benevolence* shows how unworkable, even murderous, a How-I-Feel ethic rooted only in the desires of the individual would be. The play's moral problems cry out for a generalized moral structure, even though this was not necessarily Panych's intent. The panhandler Terence Lomy kills the dog that Oswald Eicherson detests, his girlfriend Audrey's dog. Lomy then asks Eicherson, "How did you honestly feel?" Lomy means that if the feeling is "honest," it has a kind of moral force, that we are entitled to be happy, and that he is merely acting as Eicherson's "agent" in killing the dog. Eicherson replies that happiness is a mirage—clearly an evasive response— and his main argument against Lomy's canicide is that it's *illegal* to kill animals. He ignores the humane reasons behind the law. Because Eicherson is such a limp rag, one is tempted to side with Lomy, who wears his beliefs confidently and who goes for the jugular: "The law is a line in the middle of the road. OK? A *line*: in the middle of the fucking road. You *are* the road." Halfway through the play, we discover that Eicherson detests Audrey and might be pleased if she, too, were killed, so even if we fell for Lomy's pitch earlier, we can no longer do so. Eventually, Lomy announces, "I see you setting a match to the whole world," a rather apocalyptic conclusion to a project that began as the freeing of Eicherson's individual feelings. The playwright Panych won't offer a norm, but Lomy's position is clearly untenable. Even without murder or apocalypse, he is evasive when it comes to questions of self-harm. Preaching about the inevitability of desire, Lomy never answers

---

[20] Flesch 4, 10. Readers anticipate vindication of the innocent and punishment of the guilty (Flesch, 163–4).
[21] Flesch 78–81, 90–1.

the question that Eicherson stumbles towards, "What if my desires are bad for me?"[22]

As I begin to address postmodern responses to such questions, it's important to remember that contemporary moral dumbfounding is just part of the story. Violence and crime are down between 1990 and 2017, so laments about a loss of ethical standards only tell part of the postmodern story. Clearly, there are currents arising both out of postmodern How-I-Feel ethics and out of Enlightenment standards of justice that have led to ethical gains. I will examine several weak (yet popular) responses to the postmodern dilemma: moral relativism, traditionalism, and market-based ethics. I will also consider the attempt to put ethics on a scientific footing, an attempt that fails to solve ethical dilemmas, but that can limit the excesses of both traditionalism and moral relativism, before we turn to postmodernity's most characteristic response—contract ethics.

Scepticism About Ethical Foundations

One characteristic postmodernist approach takes a sceptical position. Law theorist Costas Douzinas recognizes, but decries, the fact that "human rights" language has become the dominant way of speaking about harm. If both the owner of Harrods and former king of Greece have "glossed their claims in the language of human rights," if nations regularly use that language to discredit adversaries,[23] and if people speak of the right to party or to watch reruns of *Star Trek*,[24] the language must be flawed. In order to "defend human beings" Douzinas attacks "humanism," which he calls "a banal combination of classical and Christian metaphysics."[25] The ghosts of Nietzsche and Foucault hover nearby: human rights have no foundation—we constructed them socially, so we ought to be more, not less, sceptical about ethics. This claim accounts for the postmodern dilemma we face in struggling to decide which rights should take precedence, but errs badly in suggesting that human rights haven't really

[22] Panych, 37, 40, 57, 92, 87–8.
[23] Douzinas, 50, 55. For human rights as a "hegemonic ideology," see Freeman, 204.
[24] Douzinas in Goulimari, "Introduction," 6.
[25] Douzinas, 52. Douzinas applies Lacanian psychoanalysis to the human rights subject, who supposedly desires a missing object to fill her lack, "the unattainable 'right to be loved'" (Douzinas, 66). Applying Occam's Razor to this overly complex psychic process, I would say that people simply don't want to be harmed.

advanced historically, and that tyranny has merely been rerouted into disciplinary norms.[26]

Why must we attack humanism? Because, claims Douzinas, the twentieth century has seen more human rights violations than previous epochs.[27] This is incorrect. Steven Pinker has shown that violence has historically declined at *logarithmic* rates as a percentage of population, especially in the movement from non-state to state societies (belying, among other misconceptions, the popular image of peaceful hunter-gatherer societies). Pinker's numbers hold despite genocides in Nazi Germany, Stalin's USSR, Mao's China, Rwanda, and elsewhere. In the US, lynchings, hate crimes against African-Americans, corporal punishment, spousal abuse, and child abuse have all fallen greatly. All American children in the last half of the eighteenth century were beaten with sticks or other implements.[28] In 2014, Minnesota Vikings star running back Adrian Peterson was taken to court and suspended from his $86 million contract for beating his four-year-old son with the same kind of switch used freely on Peterson as a boy. More broadly, torture and capital punishment in Europe and the US declined precipitously leading into the twentieth century. The number of countries worldwide that discriminate against ethnic minorities and homosexuals has steadily declined since the 1950s. Even the rights of non-human animals have seen increasing protection.[29] Douzinas invokes raw numbers of human rights abuses, but with a world population that rose from under 2 billion in 1900 to over 7.7 billion by 2019, his argument would be like chastising Canada for having nearly twice as many homicides (512) as Detroit (316) in 2013. The relevant statistic, most scholars would agree, is murders per 100,000 of population, a statistic in which Canada at one-and-a-half murders comes off somewhat better than Detroit at 45 murders.[30] The twentieth century comes off better than all other previous

---

[26] One of the most devastating critiques of Foucault's thought belongs to Habermas: Foucault can give no account of the *normative* functions of his own discourse (James Miller, 458).

[27] Douzinas, 51.

[28] Pinker, *Better*, 384, 386,411–12, 429, 436, 438, 440.

[29] Pinker, *Better*, 149–52, 390, 45, 454–71; Pinker, *Enlightenment*, 223.

[30] Statistics Canada, "Homicide offences, number and rate, by province and territory," 2014-12-01, http://www.statcan.gc.ca/tables-tableaux/sum-som/l01/cst01/legal12b-eng.htm.

FBI Uniform Crime Reports, Crime in the United States, 2013, Table 8, Michigan, http://www.fbi.gov/about-us/cjis/ucr/crime-in-the-u.s/2013/crime-in-the-US-2013/tables/table-8/table-8-state-cuts/table_8_offenses_known_to_law_enforcement_michigan_by_city_2013.xls.

centuries in terms of violence, and the period after 1945 comes off best of all. Douzinas is on firmer ground when he criticizes the US for its hostility towards the International Criminal Court, and notes that human rights are still strongly delimited by citizenship.[31]

But American evasiveness does not mean that, as Douzinas claims, "universal humanity does not exist empirically and cannot act as a transcendental principle philosophically."[32] On the contrary, it is precisely in an empirical sense that universal humanity exists—the concept of "species" is uncontroversial. And while rights include beliefs, rights are not mysterious transcendental principles but "claims or entitlements" that arise out of moral and sometimes legal agreement.[33] If nations have used their sovereignty as a shield for rights abuses, and thus undermined universality, it's also true that they have felt increasing international moral pressure to limit abuses. Affirmed by so many countries, the UN's *Universal Declaration of Human Rights* was the first set of moral declarations that could make "a plausible claim to universality."[34] The moral pressure to host and resettle refugees, as inadequate as the response often is, testifies that "universal humanity" and "rights" have become increasingly salient. In his complaints about national sovereignty, Douzinas arrives at mutually exclusive claims: on the one hand, human rights don't exist; on the other, we shouldn't deprive Third World people of rights just because they aren't citizens. Clearly, he smuggles a conception of universal human rights in through the back door. When all is said and done, Douzinas doesn't finally decry human rights language. Instead, like the former king of Greece, though less self-servingly, Douzinas necessarily relies on it.

Popular expressions of postmodernist scepticism about ethical foundations, unlike the high-cultural expression by Douzinas, tend to treat desire as sufficient for ethics, and are even more prone than Douzinas to slip unwittingly into the certainties that they claim to be battling. Pastafarianism, with its feigned worship of the Flying Spaghetti Monster, wittily parodies religious belief and mocks the certainties of religious "foundations." Of course, humour takes priority over ethical deliberation, as in the graphs showing the historical correlation between the declining numbers of pirates and the increase in global warming. Yet Pastafarians, despite soften-

[31] Douzinas, 53–4.
[32] Douzinas, 56.
[33] Freeman, 11.
[34] Freeman, 42.

ing the Ten Commandments into "the 8 I Really Would Rather You Didn'ts," clearly want to offer alternative ethical commandments, not just How-I-Feel options. "Our Noodly Lord" commands, "I'd Really Rather You Didn't Use My Existence As A Means To Oppress, Subjugate, Punish, Eviscerate, And/Or, You Know, Be Mean To Others. I Don't Require Sacrifices, And Purity Is For Drinking Water, Not People." The ban on purity and absolute belief means that one must abandon the commandments to worship God alone, to avoid idols, and to treat God's name as holy. On the other hand, some Rather-You-Didn'ts repeat the Mosaic Code, updated to reflect a more contractarian age: "I'd Really Rather You Didn't Indulge In Conduct That Offends Yourself, Or Your Willing, Consenting Partner Of Legal Age AND Mental Maturity. As For Anyone Who Might Object, I Think The Expression Is Go F∗∗∗ Yourself, Unless They Find That Offensive." The commandment forbids harm more broadly than Mosaic Commandments 6 through 10. At the same time, the ethical foundation is both disavowed ("I'd *rather* you didn't," instead of "Thou shalt not") and yet voiced very aggressively—"Go F∗∗∗ Yourself."

The focus on consent has merit (consent *is* often a good way of limiting harm), but it is self-contradictory in its hedonist, libertarian tendencies. All ethical approaches, Pastafarianism not excepted, build on previous traditions in making moral claims. The difference between the Flying Spaghetti Monster (FSM) and Yahweh is that the FSM is more tolerant, permitting leather and lubricants between consenting adults, promising "a Stripper Factory AND a Beer Volcano,"[35] and refusing to specify actions that are wrong in all circumstances. For Gilles Lipovetsky and Sebastien Charles, "Postmodern hedonism has two faces: it is de-structuring and irresponsible for a certain number of individuals, prudent and responsible for the majority." In other words, narcissism can potentially be mature and responsible, a limited hedonism, not just pure libertarianism.[36] But on what basis, beyond direct harm, would hedonism limit individual desires to produce a working social consensus between competing groups? On what basis would we resist the pleasurable self-harm of drug use? According to Robert Putnam, Boomer libertarian attitudes in comparison with their parents—greater emphasis on autonomy; less respect for authority, religion, and patriotism; less moralism about drug use; greater tolerance—

[35] Henderson, 78–9. Church of the Flying Spaghetti Monster, "Flying Spaghetti Monsterism" brochure, http://www.venganza.org/images/spreadword/sk_brochure.pdf.
[36] Charles in Lipovetsky, 8, 11.

have had positive effects on a number of issues, "but as a syndrome [Boomer] attitudes have had a high social cost."[37] Depression has increased with every generation since the 1940s. Suicide, too, especially among adolescents and young adults, tripled or quadrupled between 1950 and the mid-1990s, dipped a bit, then rose again after 2008.[38] This doesn't necessarily invalidate Boomer attitudes, but it does ask how we might better respond to the postmodern ethical dilemma than we have done so far.

Like the Pastafarians, Quentin Tarantino revels in a playful ethics. His *Django Unchained* (2012) pays lip service to the modern consensus about "Do No Harm": slavery is violent and harmful, so it must be stopped at any cost. Both the black revenger Django and the courteous white Dr. Shultz free slaves, so we must applaud them no matter the bloodbath. As with any Tarantino film, harm avoidance becomes more and more of a pretext as the body count rises and the violence becomes increasingly entertaining. Not coincidentally, in *Django* Tarantino invented a movie that allows characters to say the word "nigger" a thousand times, supposedly without giving offence. Since Tarantino takes the correct position (slavery is bad), it's easy for commentators to find a moral purpose in the film. Documentary filmmaker Michael Moore tweeted that "Django Unchained is one of the best film satires ever. A rare American movie on slavery and the origins of our sick racist history."[39] For A.O. Scott, the *New York Times* film critic, "regenerative violence" is important when it is employed against the historical grain to make white audiences uncomfortable. *Django* is "crazily entertaining, brazenly irresponsible and also ethically serious in a way that is entirely consistent with its playfulness."[40] Tarantino's own comments on film violence have been less preachy and more postmodernist. Of *Pulp Fiction* (1994), he said, "I have no more problem with violence in movies than I do with dance or subtitles or slapstick … It's an aesthetic thing. People will attach a moral thing to it, but that's bullshit." Young people raised on videos are more likely, he thinks, to see violence as he sees it—*formally*, not morally. In fact, he goes so far as to insist that his films nearly obey the old Hays Code, in which violence

---

[37] Putnam, 258–9.

[38] Putnam, 261; CDC 2013 survey; Twenge, *iGen*, 88.

[39] Michael Moore, MichaelMoore.com, 1 January 2013, https://twitter.com/mmflint/status/286023749197774848, retrieved 28 April 2015.

[40] A. O. Scott, "The Black, The White and the Angry," *The New York Times*, 24 December 2012, http://www.nytimes.com/2012/12/25/movies/quentin-tarantinos-django-unchained-stars-jamie-foxx.html?pagewanted=all&_r=1, retrieved 28 April 2015.

is permissible as long as the bad guy dies.[41] What, one wonders, would Will Hays have made of the early scene in *Pulp Fiction* in which the hitman Jules blasts three bullets into Brett's friend, then turns to Brett and says, "Oh, I'm sorry. Did that break your concentration?"[42]

For all of Tarantino's self-consciousness about the history of cinema, and despite his self-directed ironies (he casts himself as a slaver in *Django*), he is curiously unreflective about what aesthetic violence might mean culturally. In the films, funny talk about moral problems punctuates violence: morality is only superficially at issue. Before they kill Brett and his friends, Vincent and Jules in *Pulp Fiction* argue about whether their boss Marsellus was morally correct to have thrown Antwan Rockamora off a fourth-floor balcony for having given Marsellus's wife Mia a foot massage. Vincent absolves Marsellus of moral blame: "Is it as bad as eatin' her pussy out – no, but you're in the same fuckin' ballpark." Jules disagrees: "Touchin' his lady's feet, and stickin' your tongue in her holiest of holies, ain't the same ballpark, ain't the same league, ain't even the same fuckin' sport." Of Marsellus's outsized revenge, he concludes, "That shit ain't right, man."[43] Later on, when Vincent has a chance to commit adultery with Mia, he tries to talk himself out of it. He phrases it in terms of virtue theory—as a question of his loyalty to Marsellus—but, of course, that fourth-floor balcony looms large. That's called expediency, not morality.

In *Pulp Fiction*, moral reflections are meant to be funny. In 2018, it was tied for #5 among the Internet Movie Database's highest-rated movies of all time[44]: alongside aesthetics, does it also strike a congenial *moral* chord in postmodern audiences? While shooting up with heroin, Vincent complains that someone keyed his Malibu: "You don't fuck another man's vehicle … It's just against the rules." His companion, Lance, agrees: "No trial, no jury, straight to execution." In another scene, Vincent responds to The Wolf's orders with "A 'please' would be nice."[45] Tarantino milks laughs out of the hitman's expectations of civility, and despite Tarantino's professed lack of serious moral reflection, one can't help notice that Vincent's outrage belongs to How-I-Feel ethics—he feels harmed when someone attacks his property. Vincent wants to generalize a few moral

[41] Tarantino, *Interviews*, 74, 95–6.
[42] Tarantino, *Pulp*, 29–30.
[43] *Pulp Fiction*, 22.
[44] As of 7 May 2015.
[45] *Pulp Fiction*, 42–3, 156.

maxims, but it would be difficult to do so in a Kantian sense, since any larger moral scheme might just possibly invite a moral scrutiny of his job as a hitman. Irony and wit don't free Tarantino from the albatross hanging on all gangster films: if we feel sympathy for Vincent, then surely we must feel sympathy for his victims; and if we feel sympathy for his victims, how can we possibly feel sympathy for Vincent? We can't praise *Django Unchained*'s "regenerative violence" and "playfulness" in the same breath, no matter how righteous the cause. Spike Lee tweets, "American Slavery Was Not A Sergio Leone Spaghetti Western. It Was A Holocaust."[46] Tarantino complicates the issues slightly by having Vincent killed (poetic justice served, the Hays Office mollified) and letting Jules resign from his hitman job. But this is a moral bait-and-switch: Jules isn't significantly more moral than Vincent. It's troubling that what makes Vincent and Jules more sympathetic than their victims is that Vincent and Jules are more hip.

On the other hand, can I really ask for Miltonian moral reflection from a filmmaker who insists, "All my stuff is the funny part"?[47] The repeated ironies and visual beauty, even in violence, all pull away from ethical reflection. With any kind of art, we do value a thing for aesthetic reasons, not just for immediate social, political, or ethical use-value, and we allow speculative play outside of our conventional moral categories. Other postmodern filmmakers such as the Coen brothers give a more considered role to moral reflection, especially in *Fargo* (1996) and *A Serious Man* (2009). If *some* of our stories display a moral weightlessness, we can perhaps be cautiously optimistic about a social contract that has room for this form of ideological dissent, but if our most *popular* expressions—#5—display moral weightlessness, we may have reason to worry.

TRADITIONALIST ETHICS

At the opposite extreme from postmodernist scepticism about ethical foundations, traditionalists call for a return to earlier ethical foundations, a divine command deontology. They warn of potential abuses when How-I-Feel becomes the ethical litmus test, and rightly point out that even postmodernists who distrust "foundations" assume fundamental

[46] Spike Lee, Spike Lee Twitter, 22 December 2012, https://twitter.com/SpikeLee/status/282611091777941504, retrieved 28 April 2015.
[47] Tarantino, *Interviews*, 91.

civilities, ground rules for their social interactions. David Bentley Hart, bitingly, says, "The truth of no truths requires the plurality that it be civil."[48] We need strong motivations to set aside our own desires in order to allow another's needs to take priority, and in the past religious faith helped us to do this. Coming from a variety of disciplines, traditionalists such as Hart, Christian Smith, Alasdair MacIntyre, and Brad Gregory often provide apt critiques of postmodern ethics. But they are far less convincing when they try to solve the postmodern dilemma by straight-forwardly returning to earlier ethics, usually religious.

According to Smith, young adult Millennials express the default North American ethical approach: moral relativism. All answers to questions about norms begin with "everybody's different, but for me."[49] Alasdair MacIntyre and Brad Gregory go farther than Smith, diagnosing "emotivism" as the root of the postmodern ethical quandary, and advocating a return to late-medieval ethics, "rooted in God's self-revelation." According to Gregory, our inability to agree on common goods means that the highest political good is now "the maximization of individual choice, and the greatest social virtue is toleration of others' choices and actions." Gregory drags into the interrogation room a surprising accused: the Protestant Reformation. The Reformation, by turning the individual into his or her own moral authority, opened the path to How-I-Feel secularism: "Truth is whatever is true to you, values are whatever you value ... In short: whatever."[50]

One may agree on the shortcomings of "whatever" without wishing away the Protestant Reformation, or in other ways renouncing the contemporary world. As we will see in the chapter on faith, most Westerners are no longer persuaded by the argument that only belief in God can foster morality.[51] What does Gregory make of the medieval propensity for torture and violence, or of the drop from a thirteenth- and fourteenth-century homicide rate in England of 10–100 per 100,000 to 1 per 100,000 in twentieth-century London,[52] where "personal preference" supposedly damns morality? He has an answer: medieval Christians behaved badly because, although churchmen and rulers had the true rev-

---

[48] Hart, 420.
[49] C. Smith, 48.
[50] Gregory, 182, 190, 184, 77.
[51] Pew, "World Publics," 33–4. Angus Reid, 21.
[52] Pinker, *Better*, 60.

elation, in exercising power they somehow never quite arrived at the exact formula for "consistently combining *caritas* with coercion."[53] But Gregory's excuse reveals a major weakness in the traditionalist position: a dogged historical selectivity that in Gregory's case recommends Thomist principles but glosses over medieval ecclesiastical and political *practice*. In fact, it's no puzzle at all why the medieval church countenanced unchristian practices. Inquisitors didn't suddenly repent their lack of love; rather, the reshaping of the public sphere in a secular and democratic direction reined them in. As limits were placed on its power, the church miraculously improved its ethical performance.

In other words, despite Gregory's claim, we don't live in "the current kingdom of Whatever."[54] In the US, the 1990s and 2000s saw a decline in abortion, "divorce, welfare dependency, teenage pregnancy, dropping out of school, sexually transmitted disease, and teenage auto and gun accidents" since the 1970s and 1980s. Despite a popular culture awash in "punk, metal, goth, grunge, gangsta, and hip-hop," pornography, and increasingly violent movies and video games, violence *declined* in the US and Canada, though not to the levels of the 1950s.[55] Between 1991 and 2013, fewer American high school students carried weapons, and fights were cut in half, though there hasn't been much change in rape numbers.[56] A variety of factors have been identified in the crime drop—better security, the ability of cellphones to easily record and report crimes, even the *simulated* violence on the Internet and in video games, so much more enchanting than real crimes.[57] Fewer students had their first serious drink before age 13 and fewer were involved in binge drinking.[58] Smoking, alcohol use, and hard drug use mostly declined in Canada and the US between the 1980s and the 2000s though some drugs, especially marijuana and

---

[53] Gregory, 196.

[54] Gregory, 378.

[55] Pinker, *Better*, 127–8, 427–8. Statistics Canada figures, reported in McKnight, 38–41. Some of these social problems declined from the 1970s to the 1990s, but rates were still higher than in the early 1960s.

[56] CDC 2013 survey.

[57] McKnight, 38–41.

[58] Pinker, *Better*, 128. Centers for Disease Control and Prevention (CDC), 2013 survey. According to Pinker, the statistics on drug use and overdoses point to decreases in use by younger generational cohorts, while Baby Boomers still account for the majority of the drug problem as they age. Pinker, *Enlightenment*, 184.

opioids, saw greatly increased use,[59] and the uptick in crime in 2017 has been attributed mainly to meth addictions. All told, the teens of the 2000s grew up valuing freedom and equality, diversity, individual rights, civility, female empowerment, and social compassion.[60] These values are compatible with certain vices—selfishness, drug dependency—but strongly censure other vices that tradition didn't find so troubling, such as racism, sexism, and homophobia.

The historical violence/religion correlation argues strongly against the belief that a "return to faith" would in itself solve the postmodern ethical dilemma. Social violence is sometimes caused by too much, not too little morality, according to Pinker.[61] For example, when homosexual acts are moralized, homosexuals become targets for violence. It's also interesting that children, people of lower classes, and those with less education tend to moralize more than adults, wealthy people, and those with more education.[62] Still, it's far too simplistic to point at violence in earlier eras (as do Dawkins and Christopher Hitchens, for example) and then finger religion as the culprit.[63] If the West were to lose its prosperity, Gregory warns, we'd quickly jettison the pluralism we're so proud of.[64] Indeed, our affluence and social structures protect us from the far more difficult ethical choices that medieval people had to make.

The place of tradition in any moral order, including postmodernity, is complex. Jonathan Haidt, coming from an evolutionary direction, argues that religious faith solves the problem of cooperation without kinship, and that we shouldn't underestimate the ethical value of altruistic punishment. His evidence is historical, sociological, and psychological. Historical: in the nineteenth century 39% of religious communes lasted more than

[59] In Canada, 16% of young people smoked marijuana or hashish in 1984, 18% in 1992, 37% in 2000, and 32% in 2008. Other illegal drugs were used at a rate of 11% in 1984, 8% in 1992, 14% in 2000, and 12% in 2008. Smoking dropped from 30% in 1984 to 23% in 2008, while the consumption of alcohol dropped slightly from 76% in 1984 to 71% in 2008 (Bibby, 75–6). For American high school students, marijuana use increased (though down from a high in 1999), while smoking and the use of most hard drugs declined between 1991 and 2013. Pinker, *Better*, 128. Centers for Disease Control and Prevention (CDC), 2013 survey.

[60] Bibby, 211.

[61] Pinker, *Better*, 84.

[62] Haidt 22.

[63] Pinker's much broader analysis in *The Better Angels of Our Nature* points at the complex interrelation of a number of historical factors: the state's increasing monopoly on violence, the growth of commerce, feminization, cosmopolitanism, and the escalator of reason.

[64] Gregory, 189.

...us, but only 6% of secular communes did. Costly sacrifices demanded of members *increased* the likelihood of religious communes surviving, but not of secular communes. Sociological: the *least* religious 20% of the population give 1.5% of their incomes to charity, while the *most* religious 20% of the population give 7%, mostly to religious organizations. More surprisingly, religious people also give as much or more to *secular* charities as secular people do.[65] Volunteering runs along a similar divide: religious people do more volunteering, though mostly for religious organizations. Social and civic engagement is higher among those who are involved with religious groups, and civic engagement predicts volunteering.[66] Churches create a generalized reciprocity, and those who trust their fellow citizens "volunteer more often, contribute more to charity, participate more often in politics and community organizations, serve more readily on juries, give blood more frequently, comply more fully with their tax obligations, are *more* tolerant of minority views, and display many other forms of civic virtue."[67] Those disengaged from faith, on the other hand, tend not only to be more suspicious of others, but are also themselves more likely to lie, cheat, and steal.[68] Psychological: in "public goods" games (such as those mentioned in the Introduction), contributions to the public pot decline whenever players have no opportunity to punish free riders. However, when players can *punish* selfish players ("altruistic" punishment), cooperation skyrockets. Without faith traditions' positive reinforcements and negative consequences, we tend to become free riders.

The evidence of community cooperation partly confirms Gregory's intuition that expressions of Christian love (and cognate virtues in other faiths) do confer social and ethical benefits. Still, against Gregory's idealization of faith, the evidence also suggests that faith has a parochial quality. In some studies, although religious people expressed a lot of altruism, their actions under experimental conditions weren't so different from those of secular people. We don't blindly empathize, Haidt observes; we empathize in the socially productive ways that our evolutionary psychology nudges us towards: with "nice" not "selfish" people, and with people from our own group.[69] Of American contributions to charity, half go to

[65] Haidt, 257, 265, 267.
[66] Putnam 66–7, 117.
[67] Putnam, 136–7.
[68] Putnam, 137.
[69] Haidt, 236, 266.

the donor's church, contributions that sceptics like to call "selfish" since the donor gets personal returns on the gifts.[70] The sceptics' critique has some validity, but it demands a saintliness not demanded of secular people, and then feigns disappointment when the idealized saintliness fails to appear. People of faith will recognize that even reciprocal altruism within faith groups is not easy—it still requires one to set aside selfish instincts, at least for the time being, and the returns are not guaranteed. In addition, when pure altruism briefly arises, it usually comes from those with practice in reciprocal altruism.

Given these complexities—the violent past of religious faiths, the importance of faith in relation to volunteering and charity—one cannot make unqualified generalizations about the moral value of tradition. However, as to the belief that revelation provides an absolute foundation for contemporary morality, the evidence goes against tradition. Gregory rightly criticizes "Woody Allen's emotivist maxim … 'The heart wants what it wants,'" because such a solipsistic statement pretends that one can't reason about desire, and that desires don't need to be justified. Gregory, however, commits the either/or fallacy, arguing that only revelation can save us from this subjective morality.[71] Yet, according to the fossil record, as long as 100,000 years ago, paralysed humans and humans unable to chew survived into adulthood: someone *without* Christian revelation must have cared for them with "Christian" love.[72] To invoke "revelation" is, oftentimes, to excuse oneself from having to give a rational explanation for why the claimed "foundation" really is a foundation. Gregory is hard on those who make assertions in place of arguments, and he mocks Thomas Jefferson's appeal to the "self-evident" truth that men are "endowed by their creator with certain inalienable rights." What audacity, scoffs Gregory, since we've neither been able to define "rights" and "dignity," "nor indeed has a person ever been observed."[73] But religious language is even *more* susceptible to Gregory's critique: any metaphysical claim begins with a bald assertion, how much more so when the assertion is about God's existence and God's intentions rather than about human rights. Not only are Gregory's assertions just as ungrounded as modern or postmodern assertions, but, in view of the Inquisition, it's clear

[70] Hauser calls such donations selfish, 288.
[71] Gregory, 231, 182.
[72] de Waal, *Bonobo*, 56.
[73] Gregory, 213, 381.

that a "foundation" alone won't secure morality. Faiths have used revelation to cut through the Gordian knot of moral questions for better ("love your neighbour") and for worse (the prejudice against same-sex relationships) just as Jefferson did with "inalienable rights." Why is a religious prejudice against same-sex marriage more "grounded" than, for example, How-I-Feel in favour?

Gregory claims that no convincing secular foundation for ethics arose in the wake of Aquinas's virtue ethics.[74] Both modernity and postmodernity fail, because reason offers us no guidelines for moral choice, and because individual subjectivity—How-I-Feel—can't decide moral questions. Yet Gregory's appeal to virtue ethics overreaches in several ways. Firstly, virtue ethics don't solve the postmodern dilemma. We acknowledge the importance of the virtues and of the wise teachers who pass them on to us. Yet, instead of blindly obeying the teacher or God, we give *reasons* why the virtue or action is good. As soon as we do this, the moral reasons, not the wise teacher's or God's say-so, make the actions right or wrong.[75] The reasons and the virtues thus exist not at any "foundational" level, but at the level of moral argument. What *foundational* principle will tell a social worker at what moment compassion for a child should override compassion for parents to remove the child from its home? Only moral reasoning, not virtues alone, can tell us how to act.

In a study of the virtue of charity, Ara Norenzayan left $10 in coins on the table, instructing his subjects to take what they wanted and leave the rest for the next person. He primed the experimental group with religion by having them correct the grammar in sentences that included words such as "God," "prophet," and "divine." Unprimed people left an average of $1.84, but primed subjects left $4.22, almost half the money. The subjects' religiosity didn't matter—those who claimed to have no religion performed the same way as the others. Norenzayan's conclusion was that "watched people are nicer people," and Gregory would have agreed.[76] However, in another study, Norenzayan primed his subjects with the words "civic," "jury," and "court." These terms had an effect slightly more pronounced than the religious terms. People who had been primed left on average $4.44 on the table,[77] suggesting that religious traditions

[74] Gregory, 219.
[75] Shafer-Landau, 270.
[76] Norenzayan, quoted in De Waal, *Bonobo*, 219.
[77] De Waal, *Bonobo*, 220.

don't have a monopoly on our community-mindedness and our sense of right and wrong. But partially supportive of Gregory's critique are the gaps that Bibby discovered between young women and young men. More women than men valued several of the virtues: trust, 90%–76%; honesty, 87%–74%; concern for others, 73%–56%; politeness, 70%–57%; and forgiveness, 66%–53%.[78] Such figures, likely rooted in evolutionary adaptations, should shake our postmodern complacency and make us take traditionalist critiques seriously. Nevertheless, because contemporary people—women evidently more so than men—do believe in ethical virtues, it's deceptive of Gregory to say that we live in "the Kingdom of Whatever."

Some virtues are bequeathed to us by tradition (ethical responsibility for one's neighbour), some come from modernity's social contracts (justice free from religious prejudice), and some from postmodern pluralism (equality for those who express alternate forms of sex and gender). Near the end of this chapter, we will examine one method of cobbling together moral consensus, John Rawls's contractarianism, but for Gregory, any sort of contractual cobbling is anathema. The 1992 US Supreme Court majority decision in *Planned Parenthood v. Casey* reads, "At the heart of liberty is the right to define one's own concept of existence, of meaning, of the universe, and of the mystery of human life." In other words, says Gregory disparagingly, "answers to the Life Questions can be literally anything human beings can invent and affirm." Gregory mocks the Rawlsian notion of a liberal consensus, implying that without any agreed-upon philosophical means of adjudicating disagreements, rights have no foundation. "Secular humanism lacked," Gregory says, "any shared criteria for deciding among the rival truth claims."[79]

Though Gregory is right that shared criteria are a serious problem, he, like many others, blurs the distinction between foundations and adjudication. For all of his critique of modernity, Gregory several times invokes "human flourishing"[80] to arbitrate between competing notions of "the good." If we discover universal aspects of human moral behaviour (rooted in our evolutionary psychology) and if we find increasing agreement across many societies about certain goods (life, security of person, freedom of conscience and religion, freedom from arbitrary arrest), then even if we balk at the word "foundations," we aren't so very far from significant

---

[78] Bibby, 10.
[79] Gregory, 77, 188, 357.
[80] Gregory, 245, 254, 308.

agreement on some principles. Why ignore political means of adjudicating disagreements—democratic votes, constitutional rights, the courts—when political means, not metaphysical agreement, have always been the way disputes have been adjudicated, no less in the early Christian church councils than in postmodernity? It's possible to have courts that are widely seen as legitimate, but to ask for an "agreed-upon *philosophical* means of adjudicating disagreements" is to demand exactly the consensus that doesn't exist. Will we *all* be required to submit to late-medieval beliefs in order to come to an agreement?

SCIENCE-BASED (MODERNIST) ETHICS

If traditionalism can't save us from the postmodern ethical dilemma, can the science and reason of modernity? The venerable E.O. Wilson says yes: contemporary moral reasoning may be a mess, but once we set ethics on a properly researched biological foundation, we'll make cause-and-effect predictions about behaviour and "it should be possible to adapt the ancient moral sentiments more wisely ... to modern life."[81] Steven Pinker, likewise, assumes that reason, without any prodding from tradition, can direct us to provide to others what we expect for ourselves.[82] Neuroscientist Sam Harris even assumes that science can provide an objective consequentialist morality. Since conscious creatures feel pain, they can easily and "objectively" distinguish between good (a well-fed, laughing mother and child) and evil (a mother and child tortured by famine). As long as he sticks to extreme contrasts, the objective approach works. But nobody's arguing that famine is good. The moment Harris sends his "objective morality" to sort out a real controversy—should Muslim women wear veils or not?[83]— he fails. It's possible, he suggests, to find a better balance between the extremes of Islam covering up women and the West insisting that women constantly display their bodies for male pleasure. What he can't do is to say what the balance is—the ethical position that would both protect individual freedom and prevent gender-based discrimination. His attempt to say why women shouldn't cover up confirms the postmodern suspicion that science, on its own, can't make moral determinations. Asked, at a TedTalk, what he would say to Islamic women who insisted that they

---

[81] E.O. Wilson, *Consilience*, 278.
[82] Pinker, *Enlightenment*, 11.
[83] Sam Harris, *Moral*, 65.

wanted to wear a veil, Harris replied that their freedom to dress as they chose was important, but their cultural context exerted so much control that we couldn't trust their decisions. In other words, *our* moral knowledge about patriarchy should trump the *women's* freedom to choose. Driven to such a highly questionable position, Harris flails about. In the future, he says, science will make the choice easier: we will be able to *measure* love in the brain, we'll measure fathers' love for daughters in a strict Islamic society, compare it to the fathers' love in a democracy, and, presto, make an objective moral decision![84]

Perhaps it's unfair to show Harris answering off the cuff. But in his systematic argument for science-based values, *The Moral Landscape* (2010), he fares no better. His argument is that the suffering caused by various moral answers can be measured or will be measurable in the future. Moral answers that cause less suffering must be preferred. But, again, how does one measure the degree of suffering in moral dilemmas and how far should we go to end suffering? How many Syrian refugees should my country accept? Harris cannot answer Patricia Churchland's objection to measurement: "No one has the slightest idea how to compare the mild headache of five million against the broken legs of two, or the needs of one's own two children against the needs of a hundred unrelated brain-damaged children in Serbia."[85] Should I prefer duty and an unhappy marriage or should I choose freedom, divorce, and unhappy children? Brain science, no matter how advanced, cannot answer such questions because they involve competing moral claims, not juvenile questions about whether famine is good or bad. The brain itself is of little help, since moral decisions aren't localized in one spot: cortical executive functions play a significant role assessing input coming through emotional centres such as the hippocampus and amygdala.

At his most convincing, Harris turns to something that is highly subjective: "human flourishing."[86] He would like to leave right and wrong, good and evil, behind and speak merely about how to maximize well-being.[87] This is, of course, impossible. In order to decide *what* maximizes well-being and *what* destroys it, we are forced to smuggle in good and evil. A

[84] Sam Harris, "Science." Even the usually more circumspect Joshua Greene holds out hope that brain imaging will give us a real way of measuring happiness (Greene, 166).
[85] Churchland, quoted in Sam Harris, *Moral*, 68.
[86] Sam Harris, "Science."
[87] Sam Harris, *Moral*, 64.

novel such as Canadian Trevor Cole's *Practical Jean* (2010) puts a point on the difficulty. Jean goes on a mercy-killing spree, ending the lives of friends who are no longer living in conditions of maximal well-being. Like Harris with veils, she does on *their* behalf what they are (she thinks) too craven or conflicted to do for themselves. The novel lacks alternatives to Jean, either formally (the action is focalized through her consciousness) or ideologically (there is no systematic reply to her veterinarian's approach to human ethics), yet we inevitably apprehend the novel as satire. This response suggests that the rational calculus that Jean applies to the evil of her friends' suffering must wilt before the good of self-determination. Here How-I-Feel, rather than any objective standard, does define flourishing. To a degree, we all rely on some form of consequentialism—Harris is right about that—but consequences don't remove good and evil from the discussion, and we're reluctant to trade our necessarily subjective approach for someone else's supposedly objective reasoning about our well-being.

Other scientists, such as Richard Dawkins, arrive at self-contradictory positions because they are quite certain how we *ought* to behave, yet they insist that ethics are primarily a matter of programming. Can science tell us how we ought to behave? No, Dawkins seems to say, we just do what our selfish genes have programmed us to do in order to ensure their own replication. We are generous to our families (kin altruism), to people who can repay the favour (reciprocal altruism), and to others when our charity advertises our social dominance (costly signalling). These self-serving mechanisms become important forms of social "glue." Lingering at the level of species, Dawkins attributes individual ethical decisions to the genetic substrate: "Our Good Samaritan urges are misfirings, analogous to the misfiring of a reed warbler's parental instincts when it works itself to the bone for young cuckoo." Evolution has selected in favour of a rule of thumb that tells us to care for children, so when humans adopt children our programming is similarly misfiring.[88] This gloomy lack of choice sounds like the cartoon in which a woman at a cocktail party asks Dilbert (the hapless engineer with the muffintop hair), "Tell me a little about yourself and be totally honest." He replies, over several panels, "I don't believe in free will, soul-mates, or following my passion ... I only associate with other people because I have biological and economical needs. I think all human actions are driven by selfishness." The woman, a bit taken aback, continues gamely on, "Um ... Okay. Do you have any questions for me?"

[88] Dawkins, 247, 250, 252.

Dilbert responds, "Am I still being totally honest or should I act curious?"[89] Dawkins—recognizing that in a book designed to show why religion is bad for people, cynicism might not win the day[90]—calls the misfirings "blessed, precious mistakes.[91] Yet, even in this more cheerful formulation, the genetic substrate does almost everything, while individual choice, culture, and faith contribute very little.

If ethics are simply a matter of firings and misfirings, then logically we can't be responsible for our actions, can we? Yes, we can, Dawkins insists. He lists ten new commandments that he borrowed from an atheist website. Some commandments echo the Golden Rule of Hinduism, Buddhism, Confucianism, Hillel the Elder, and Jesus: "Do not do to others what you would not want them to do to you." Some arise more directly from a contemporary human rights idiom ("In all things, strive to cause no harm"), from science, and from democracy (we ought to value facts, reason, learning, questioning, free speech, and tolerance). Dawkins quotes H.L. Mencken, who said, "People say we need religion when what they really mean is we need police."[92] Fair enough, enforcement structures play a crucial role in ethics, but will the police enforce the Golden Rule? Dawkins also adds some new commandments, exhorting us, for example, to allow sexual liberty. This freedom has become important in Western democracies, but when we see the claim expressed at a popular level—an Oregon high school student says, "I don't think it's wrong to have sex when you're 14 or so. Your body is ready, so why isn't it right?"[93]—we can see how easy it is to sidestep *moral* considerations and to claim that *nature* alone tells us what we ought to do.

Though his insistence on the absolute dominance of biology would seem to dismiss the entire discipline of sociology, Dawkins also commands, "Value the future on a timescale longer than your own," and "Do not discriminate or oppress on the basis of sex, race or (as far as possible) species."[94] The broadening out of rights is morally significant, so I won't ask Dawkins what kind of blessed misfiring would make our *genes* so sensitive to animal rights; or whether it would be ethical to clone a Neanderthal,

---

[89] *Winnipeg Free Press*, 23 May 2015.

[90] Indeed, Putnam has shown that political cynics, for example, volunteer less than other people do (Putnam, 132).

[91] Dawkins, 253.

[92] Dawkins, 298–300, 261.

[93] Twenge, *Me*, 162.

[94] Dawkins, 300.

as George Church, a Harvard geneticist proposes; or whether a Neanderthal, once cloned, would have "human" rights.[95] What's more of a problem is the escape hatch "as far as possible." This is not a slip of the pen, but goes to the heart of the postmodern ethical problem: we want a rule to help limit our selfish disregard for other species, yet there's little in nature to tell us *why* we ought to obey such a rule, and still less to tell us what the *content* of the rule should be, so we pretend to make a rule but really only offer a soft suggestion. The original Ten Commandments were quite specific, but Dawkins's secular commandments are general enough to make little direct claim on us.

One can find an even hazier list of Ten Commandments in A.C. Grayling's *The Good Book*, where we're commanded to "Love well," "Respect nature," "Do your utmost"—a level of generality that would have allowed even Hitler to bat .900, striking out only on "Harm no others."[96] There are also better, more specific lists, such as the "10 Humanist Commandments," which defend life and property, ban wars, mandate assistance for those in need, and demand conservation.[97] Dawkins, less absolute about what to enforce and what to ban, quotes, "Do not overlook evil or shrink from administering justice, but always be ready to forgive wrongdoing freely admitted and honestly regretted." But why *should* we (not just why *do* we) behave in empathetic ways? And what, specifically, is evil? To answer such questions, we are forced to return to tradition for commandments that we should obey (thou shalt not kill), and to humanist rejections of or updates on tradition (stop killing homosexuals; prohibit discrimination based on sexual orientation).

More careful philosophers such as Richard Joyce and Joshua Greene argue that we can't derive ethics from an understanding of our evolutionary past. Greene gives examples of values that run counter to our evolutionary and genetic heritage (birth control, charity for strangers),[98] while Joyce shows why evolutionary justifications for morality don't work. One weakness found in evolution-based ethics is the tendency to privilege the

---

[95] See Nicholas Wade, "*Scientists in Germany Draft Neanderthal Genome,*" *New York Times*, 12 Feb 2009, https://www.nytimes.com/2009/02/13/science/13neanderthal. html, and Zach Zorich, "Should We Clone Neanderthals?" *Archaeology* 63:2, March/April 2010, https://archive.archaeology.org/1003/etc/neanderthals.html.

[96] Grayling, 8:11–12.

[97] Dr. Rodrigue Tremblay, "TEN COMMANDMENTS FOR A GLOBAL HUMANISM," 2007, http://www.thecodeforglobalethics.com/pb/wp_ff9e877a/wp_ff9e877a.html.

[98] Greene, 25.

Environment of Evolutionary Adaptedness, the notion that what was adaptive in the Pleistocene is a guide for contemporary human "goods." Secondly, evolutionary ethicists make the unlicensed leap from a description of how we act, to a prescription about how we *ought* to act. Joyce counters, "If it is 'an unavoidable condition produced by evolution' that humans are constructed to act so as to benefit the community (i.e., be moral), then the conclusion we might have expected is that each *will* act so as to benefit the community (i.e., be moral). What business does this 'ought' have in making a sudden appearance?"[99] Thirdly, evolutionary ethicists display a pronounced tendency towards instrumentality: a particular moral act (helping your neighbour) is good because it works (creating a socially cohesive group). But proving *instrumental* value is not the same as proving *moral* value, and, indeed, if you are a kinsman of Genghis Khan, then your group's social cohesion and your own neighbourliness to fellow warriors may well be immoral.

Any evolutionary "ought" would be highly problematic. The social consensus in most cultures insists that evolutionary adaptive strategies such as rape are morally abhorrent. Although evolved mechanisms such as mirror neurons and Theory of Mind have assisted in the development of empathy, humans have also been selected for hunter and warrior traits, allowing us to block empathy and to use our knowledge of other minds as a strategic military advantage.[100] The evolutionary connection between dominance and mating opportunities[101] explains the massive over-representation of young men in violent crime. When the narrator (Edward Norton) in the *Fight Club* (1999) ends his first fight, he feels that he has arrived at something more viscerally and elementally true than any do-gooding. His impulse to defy the feminization and moralization of the contemporary world appears in a funny exchange with his guru, Tyler Durden:

> Narrator: I'd fight Gandhi.
> Tyler: Good answer!
> Narrator: How 'bout you?
> Tyler: Lincoln.[102]

---

[99] Joyce, 159.
[100] Grodal, *Embodied*, 191.
[101] Pinker, *Better*, 90.
[102] *Fight Club*, Dir. David Fincher, Twentieth Century Fox, 1999, 46:55.

In 2018, *Fight Club* ranked up near *Pulp Fiction*, tied for #9 on the IMDb list of the highest-rated movies of all time. Can evolutionary history or scientific reason insist that a young man ought to prefer reasoned negotiation and a peaceful old age rather than violence, glory, and the attendant mating opportunities? No. Only a moral community can do that. But communities are split about the morality of violence.

Features of our evolutionary psychology, such as our instinctual preference for kin and in-groups over strangers, can issue in many good deeds, as well as in many that we judge as immoral—from nepotism to suicide bombing to genocide. Far from disappearing in the postmodern context, this adaptation in favour of parochial altruism has managed to express itself in surprising ways. A University of Zürich study by Hein et al., for example, showed that soccer fans were prepared to sacrificially receive electric shocks intended for another fan of the same team. Yet when soccer fans watched supporters of a *rival* team get a shock, not only were the fans far less likely to take the rival supporters' shocks, but the shocks activated the dopamine *reward* pathways in the fans' brains.[103] If the suffering of rival groups gives us pleasure, it must have been adaptive at some point. Yet if we now find it morally abhorrent to torture people even if they cheer for the Golden State Warriors against the Toronto Raptors, then instincts are an insufficient basis for keeping the peace across groups, never mind for maintaining democracy and some level of equality.

It gets worse for an evolution-based morality. When I become angry with my spouse, not only my feelings, mediated by my limbic system, register outrage, but even my prefrontal cortex rushes into the fray,[104] justifying my outrage with reasons that, on calmer reflection, are highly biased in my favour. A famous experiment by Isen and Levin showed that finding as little as a dime will make a person more likely to help a passer-by who has dropped a sheaf of papers.[105] Disgust reinforces moral norms, but this "natural" reaction can be easily hijacked: in another experiment, subjects were given post-hypnotic suggestions that a certain word—"often" or "take"—was disgusting. Later, when subjects were given short vignettes about moral violations, they judged the characters more harshly if the

---

[103] Hein et al. Activation occurred in the nucleus accumbens.
[104] See Roberts, 68.
[105] Joyce 227.

words "often" or "take" were used. The experimenters expected that a neutral vignette about a discussion facilitator, Dan, who "often" picked appealing topics, would show that in some cases disgust *can't* be manipulated; but, surprisingly, 30% of subjects found Dan to be morally reprehensible. When asked to justify their condemnation, these subjects unwittingly revealed how fallible instinct is, saying, "Dan is a popularity-seeking snob," and "I don't know, it just seems like he's up to something."[106] Instinct isn't quite synonymous with postmodern How-I-Feel morality (which may also express inarticulate or shorthand aspects of tradition and reason), but the hijacking of instinct reminds us how insufficient How-I-Feel is as an ethical principle. Joyce is left in the postmodern dilemma. He places morality within the category of "useful fictions": things that may be important and helpful, but aren't epistemically justified.[107]

Ethical Universals

In terms of my larger argument, such evidence seems to confirm that postmodern scepticism about ethical foundations is justified, and that scientific appeals to human adaptation leave us no closer to addressing the postmodern ethical dilemma than a simple return to tradition did. Scrupulous scientists admit that reason can tell us what *is*, but not how we *ought* to behave.[108] But that's not quite the end of the story. Firstly, moral intuitions do often lead to moral goods—emotions can't be dismissed, even if they can be hijacked. Secondly, intuitions point at moral universals. This corrects the postmodernist claim that there are no common measures of the good, and yet also corrects the traditionalists' claim that only their specific faith can bring moral goods. Even if universals do not solve moral dilemmas such as abortion, and even when universals have the *potential* to lead to deeply immoral behaviour (nepotism, rape), shared moral instincts make moral negotiation possible. Thirdly, reasoning about morality undercuts flawed arguments that have been used to elevate social conventions to the level of moral universals. Science by itself can't tell us what we ought to do, but it can clear up misconceptions and flawed arguments that have used morality to support various kinds of oppression.

Firstly, despite Dan and his reprehensible use of the word "often," intuitions and emotions do often lead us to actions we wouldn't hesitate to call

---

[106] Haidt, 53–4.
[107] Joyce, 159–63.
[108] Shafer-Landau, 77, 88. de Waal, *Good-natured*, 38; *Bonobo*, 163. Greene, 184, 186.

morally good. When the syndicated Québec TV show *Just for Laughs* filmed a prank in which a baby trailer pulled by a "mom" cyclist "accidentally" detached, sending trailer and the (assumed) baby rolling into a pond, most victims of the prank immediately, without pausing to analyse the situation, chased the trailer and pulled it out of the water. We laugh, yet we approve of the moral action, even if it looked instinctive.[109] In another prank, a smoking "mother" sits beside a baby carriage in a park. The inside of the carriage is shielded from view, but a soundtrack plays of a baby crying. Finally, the annoyed mother appears to offer the "baby" her cigarette. Exhaled smoke rises from the carriage, along with sounds of a baby coughing. In this case, onlookers do nothing—we live in a pluralistic age! But if looks could kill….[110] In each case, the situation was new, but the moral response was instinctive. Alongside our instinct to care for a baby that isn't ours, it would be easy to come up with thousands of other situations showing that we value the instinctual moral attention to care and harm.

In humans, evolution selected for emotions such as pride and shame that push us to coordinate our actions with the goals of our group. So it's not surprising that even in the postmodern era, the most powerful predictor of whether we will conserve energy isn't the wish to save the environment or even money, but the pressure to do what everyone else is doing.[111] In some situations, a rational, more utilitarian approach to ethics can be advantageous, but often it's not. Neuroscientist Antonio Damasio allowed his experimental subjects to either win or lose money by picking cards from decks. Two of the decks on average gave good results, while the other two on average gave bad results, despite the occasional large payout. Subjects with normal brain connectivity soon began to show increasing sweat on their skin when picking from the bad decks, long before they could consciously explain which decks were bad. Subjects with ventromedial prefrontal damage to their brains showed no changes in skin conductance, and continued to pick from the bad decks, hoping for a large payout. Emotions influence heartbeat, breathing, body temperature, and muscle tone, producing hunches that the prefrontal cortex incorporates into its

[109] JustForLaughs TV, "Baby Stroller Falls in Water Prank," uploaded 22 May 2011, https://www.youtube.com/watch?v=MNOvlymO_sw, accessed 6 May 2015.
[110] JustForLaughs TV, "Smoking Baby Prank," uploaded 24 February 2011, https://www.youtube.com/watch?v=yvUgUKguDsc, accessed 6 May 2015.
[111] See McGonigal, 195–7, 202.

calculations.[112] Because of the limits of emotion and intuition, it's presumptuous to say, as Bauman does, "I am moral *before* I think,"[113] but it would be equally presumptuous to dismiss the hunches of seemingly irrational moral intuitions. Postmodern How-I-Feel ethics can be self-serving, but can also lead to some good moral decisions outside of tradition's commandments and modernity's reason.

Moral intuitions lead us into the second point less congenial to postmodern moral pluralism: there are universal moral values. Characteristically, postmodernists claim that morality has no foundation. Richard Rorty says, "When the secret police come, when the torturers violate the innocent," we can't say to them, "There is something within you that you are betraying. Though you embody the practices of a totalitarian society which will endure forever, there is something beyond those practices which condemns you." The pragmatist's certainty that we can't appeal to God or some internal moral arbiter is, Rorty admits, "hard to live with," but "there is nothing deep down inside us except what we have put there ourselves," and Michael Bérubé adds, "Rhetorical strategies of persuasion, and nothing else, are the bases for human moral codes."[114] Speaking of his son, a person with Down syndrome, Bérubé denies that rights for the disabled are somehow written on our hearts. "Rather, Jamie's rights were invented, and implemented slowly and with great difficulty. The recognition of his human dignity … was invented." A truly democratic community is a community in which everybody recognizes that "human solidarity," not a transcending knowledge, leads to human rights.[115]

But how can persuasion have any effect, and whence comes this sudden solidarity? Working across cultures, Haidt, in his Moral Foundations Theory, isolates six types of moral values that appear universally in every culture, though they vary in expression and strength: care/harm, fairness/cheating, authority/subversion, loyalty/betrayal, sanctity/degradation, liberty/oppression. For each pairing, Haidt explains the evolutionary challenges that the value addressed, the original and current triggers, the characteristic emotions, and the relevant virtues. Haidt's work is descriptive, not normative.[116] There's no necessary connection between the fre-

---

[112] Greene 141–2.

[113] Bauman, *Postmodern Ethics*, 61.

[114] Rorty, xlii. Bérubé, *Rhetorical*, 45, 51; and *Liberal*, 241–2.

[115] Bérubé, *Liberal*, 249, 256–7.

[116] Haidt, 125, 271. Haidt calls himself a utilitarian. This is strange, considering that consequentialism tends to distrust instinct and emotion in favour of a rational calculus. Haidt

quency of a behaviour (its statistical "normality") and its moral value (its *normative* force).[117] Yet even other primates such as chimpanzees, brutal in some respects, recognize variants of our fairness/cheating dichotomy. As social creatures, from a very early age we learn to perceive the thoughts of others and to empathize, especially with close kin. It would be quite incredible if this group solidarity were merely the fruit of convincing rhetoric, rather than an evolutionary adaptation. Indeed, social questions of morality and politics precede individual existential questions. Female chimps will sometimes "drag reluctant males toward each other to make up after a fight, while removing weapons from their hands," and "high-ranking males regularly act as impartial arbiters to settle disputes in the community."[118] What varies historically and between cultures are the exceptions to the rules—for example, the conditions under which a child may be abandoned,[119] or how precisely to treat a person with a disability. Haidt can't tell us how an individual culture ought to define inappropriate aggression or cheating, but he can tell us that we have a basis for comparison, a foundation that allows us to understand and sometimes to argue against another culture's socially accepted position on aggression. It is only upon adaptive foundations that we "invent" rights, and among the most important inventors were those who appealed to transcendence—Jesus, the Buddha, Mohammed—to find new meanings in our groupishness.

Thirdly, looking back to Kant, who called on us to use our own reason in ethical deliberation, a scientific approach exposes issues in which tradition has mistaken culture-bound conventions for universals. Reason couldn't tell us that racism or homophobia were wrong, but it exposed flawed conceptions of race underwriting racial segregation, and corrected mistaken claims that LGBTQ orientations are "not natural." In this way, science, alongside political activism, countered both traditional ethics and How-I-Feel ethics by pushing issues such as same-sex marriage onto the footing of argument rather than just revelation or personal feelings. Not only the natural sciences but also the social sciences and humanities, including literature and film, engage in this form of "reasoning," for

---

seems to recognize this, and at moments he caricatures both the utilitarian and the Kantian positions. Haidt, 272, 126.

[117] de Waal, *Good-natured*, 38.

[118] de Waal, *Bonobo*, 20.

[119] Hauser, 44.

example, in *Brokeback Mountain* (2005), *Milk* (2008), and *Dallas Buyer's Club* (2013). These films owe much to the history of Romantic expressivism that Charles Taylor identified, in that they access moral norms via feeling,[120] but they also require a reasoned disengagement. Examining heterosexual norms from the outside, effectively objectifying them, these films place us in an expressive identification with the homosexual characters. If we return to the soccer fan study, Hein et al. showed that when the participating men knew only the fans of the same team, empathy for the rival team was low. But meeting the members of the rival team and getting more information about them tended to increase empathy. Greene distinguishes between our "automatic" moral settings and a "manual mode" that appears when we start reasoning carefully about moral problems.[121] We begin with an innate moral grammar that is almost effortlessly acquired, and with rapid, nearly unconscious judgements based on that grammar's evolutionary sources. Conscious, principled reasoning and the broader generalizations that arise out of it appear later and make heavy cognitive demands.[122]

Reasoning doesn't *cause* good behaviour—typically, we use reason to justify our actions, not to arrive at truth[123]—yet our manual mode allows us to distinguish between convention and morality. Asked whether it would be okay to work on Sunday if God said so, 100% of Amish and Mennonite children in one study said "yes." Asked whether it would be okay to steal if God said so, over 80% said "no." In a different study, children agreed that it would be fine for boys to wear dresses to school if the teacher permitted it, but not to punch another student on the teacher's say-so.[124] Children distinguishing between convention and morality are clearly engaging in an internal moral argument with tradition. The major world religions used principled reasoning to broaden automatic morality beyond the tribe; a scientific approach broadens it beyond faith communities. In separating convention from morality, the children are also generalizing their moral intuitions into a reasoned universal rule and, we could say, spontaneously inventing modernity and maybe even postmodern pluralism. If we tried to define postmodernity only according to

120 Charles Taylor, *Sources*, 284.
121 Greene, 133.
122 Greene, 137–43.
123 Haidt, 89, 74.
124 Joyce 130, 136.

the Nietzschean/Foucauldian notion that power determines ethical stances, then we have never really been postmodern, because, despite power's important role in constructing and applying moral systems, power can't explain the fact that we have moral instincts, the existence of moral universals, or our ability to partly distinguish between conventions and morality. At the same time, we are postmodern because, despite the helpful role that reason plays, it can't, without help from faith or humanism, say what is morally right.

POSTMODERN "OTHER"-BASED ETHICS

Although tradition and science by themselves fail to provide secure foundations for morality in the contemporary era, their bequeathal of moral communities and reasoned argument, respectively, allow us to evaluate Bauman's signature postmodern argument that there can be no ethical *system*. For Bauman, postmodern ethical dumbfounding is a good thing, since no system (a concept that Bauman equates with scientific modernity) can tell us how to treat our neighbour. Ethics are completely individual and can only be expressed in the face-to-face encounter, the law being a very poor expression of ethics. Whereas Foucault derided both reason and moral rules for "their monotonous nights,"[125] and helped open the gates for same-sex desire, Bauman, less sure that the new freedoms were enough, but similarly mistrustful of reason and moral regulation after his experience of Polish totalitarian politics, followed Levinas, looking not to the system but to the individual—the Face—for morality. Something like Bauman's argument stands behind many contemporary deontological appeals to human rights, tolerance, and pluralism. He rightly wants to avoid How-I-Feel ethics, but his resistance to moral and legal *systems* leaves a massive gap with respect to the reasoned, generalizing side of ethics, ignores actual ethical practice, and resists the community's crucial role in morality even today. In this way, he is symptomatic of the gaps in postmodern ethics.

According to Levinas, e*very* Other, not only a kinsperson or fellow citizen, makes an infinite moral demand on me. As Bauman explains, "I *am* my brother's keeper," whether or not my brother takes the same stance towards me—"I am denied the comfort of the already-existing norms."[126]

---

[125] Foucault, *Madness*, 64.
[126] Bauman, *Postmodern Ethics*, 49; *Discontents*, 51.

This responsibility arises in the West out of Judaism and Jesus, flows into Kant's demand that the Other be treated as an end not a means, and into the humanist commandment, "Proclaim the natural dignity and inherent worth of all human beings."[127] Postmodernity, Bauman senses, can undermine ethics when we apprehend other people more as aesthetic objects, or simulations, rather than as moral partners.[128] Bauman departs from tradition and from modern systematizing when he insists that neither repentance nor continual correct action will absolve me morally. The judge may be satisfied if I obey community standards, but that doesn't justify *me*, as I stand before the Other's face: "No universal standards, then. No looking over one's shoulders to take a glimpse of what other people 'like me' do."[129]

Self-sacrificial obligation appears in novels such as Neil Gaiman's *The Ocean at the End of the Lane* (2013), the sacrifice bolstered by a dim sense that some barely apprehended transcendence might approve. A film such as Guillermo del Toro's *Pan's Labyrinth* (2006), however, like Bauman, treats infinite obligation more baldly alongside a postmodern scepticism about foundations and transcendence. Although tempted by a faun to trade her baby half-brother's life for her own, the adolescent hero Ofelia will spill her own blood rather than her brother's. In contrast, the Spanish fascist Captain Vidal, who is Ofelia's stepfather and the baby's father, tortures Republican prisoners. A humanist ethic arises out of the human rights value of not harming others, and the ethic is mythologized when Ofelia is invited to rule the underworld with her dead parents. For much of the film, del Toro stays in conventional moral territory, in that the characters line up neatly as good (those who try to minimize harm) or evil (those who violate human rights). However, by showing Ofelia speaking to thin air instead of to the mythological creatures who supposedly tested her and rewarded her moral choices, del Toro hints that she may be hallucinating her apotheosis. In other words, as in Rorty's and Bauman's moral scene, there may be no independent warrant, no foundation for Ofelia's actions.

It's true that without an initial respect for the Other as an end, any larger moral system seems bound to fail. Bauman easily shows how sacrifices for the "greater good"—kin, nation, church, or political party—often

---

[127] Dr. Rodrigue Tremblay, "TEN COMMANDMENTS FOR A GLOBAL HUMANISM," 2007, http://www.thecodeforglobalethics.com/pb/wp_ff9e877a/wp_ff9e877a.html.

[128] Bauman, *Postmodern Ethics*, 180. Bauman, quoted in Jacobsen et al., 178.

[129] Bauman, *Postmodern Ethics*, 54, 53.

use people as means to immoral ends.[130] Morality, he argues, does not belong to a code; neither education, nor faith, nor political leanings are correlated with the heroic resistance against evil.[131] He may be right about instances of individual heroism, but statistics disprove a general disjunction between the system and morality. The best *general* predictor of altruistic behaviour turns out to be education.[132] Educated people didn't necessarily defy the Nazis or resist colonialism, but in any open society, the educated are crucial in the formation of altruistic groups. There may be a number of reasons for this: they may have greater self-control, a greater sense of social interdependency, or more social capital.

Because systems of ethical behaviour encourage thoughtlessness (orientation to the rule, not to the Other), Bauman prematurely insists that there can be no such thing as, for example, a Christian morality.[133] He quotes resistance fighter and rescuer of Holocaust victims Wladyslaw Bartoszewski: "Only those who died bringing help can say that they have done enough."[134] While we admire Bartoszewski's heroic rescues and the humility of his statement, only rarely does an ultimate sacrifice help future victims. If we value the saving of lives rather than spectacular sacrifices, then we ought to recognize not just Oscar Schindler, but also the less glamorous toilers who saved millions of lives without endangering their own: Norman Borlaug, whose painstaking development of better wheat, corn, and rice prevented an estimated 305 million people from starving; Abel Wolman and Linn Enslow, whose water chlorination strategy saved 189 million lives by 2018; many others who helped eradicate or control various diseases; and even the anonymous bureaucrats who developed safety standards for our highways, workplaces, and homes.[135] At the same time as praising Bartoszewski's actions, Bauman also avoids mentioning Bartoszewski's Christian motivations. This is not to say that a Christian

---

[130] Bauman, *Postmodern Ethics*, 55–6.

[131] Madeleine Bunting, "Passion and pessimism: Zygmunt Bauman." *Guardian*, 5 April 2003, http://www.guardian.co.uk/books/2003/apr/05/society/print.

[132] Putnam, 118–19.

[133] Bauman, *Postmodern Ethics*, 78–9.

[134] Bartoszewski, quoted in Bauman, *Postmodern Ethics*, 80.

[135] The numbers are totals as of 3 July 2018, taken from the website for *Scientists Greater than Einstein*, ScienceHeroes.com, http://www.scienceheroes.com/index.php?option=com_content&view=article&id=258&Itemid=27#Lifesavers%20in%20Book. See also Pinker, *Enlightenment*, 62–7, 75–6, 176–90; and Amy R. Pearce, "About the Numbers," Science Heroes, http://www.scienceheroes.com/index.php?option=com_content&view=article&id=44&Itemid=57.

system determined Bartoszewski's deed, but that he and many others, Christians and non-Christians, came to their actions via particular systems. In fact, studies of people who rescued Jews during the Holocaust suggest that many of these rescuers weren't motivated by infinite obligation or other forms of independent moral thinking, but were conforming to humane authority figures and to the humane communities to which they belonged.[136] In the end, Bauman's postmodern ethics is at once very well behaved—ready to sacrifice all to the Other—and curiously without force, unable to say why this should be done.

Bauman's critique of modernist ethical systems harmonizes well with his fears of Eastern Bloc totalitarianism, though less well with his youthful role as a political cleanser. Although he has denied the charges, evidence has been published in Poland that between 1945 and 1953, when he was in his 20s, Bauman helped suppress Polish dissidents. Later, because of his father's Zionism and his own growing political dissent, he himself was purged.[137] His collaboration took place under the aegis of a systematic moral goal—to create a society shorn of the evils of class difference. I have no desire to criticize Bauman, who was in a very difficult position, nor will I argue that his personal failings disqualify his arguments. Yet ironies abound in his unwillingness to acknowledge the communal aspects of morality. It's common to repent our youthful ideological fervour and to wish that we had acted more morally instead of protecting our own skins, but for the young Bauman, who worked in the army's secret service to keep public order, it was the *community's* regulations, not his own moral intuitions, that proved decisive. John Carroll suggests that the principal Other whom Bauman in his later writing most commonly envisions is his wife, Janina.[138] However, without downplaying the moral party of two, one can't help but point out that since the older professor Bauman no longer performed a difficult public role, his moral dilemmas became simpler, more individualized. He could afford to forget the community and its sometimes cruel demands. In Bauman, there is always a wish for a

[136] Freeman, 108.

[137] Thomas Urban. Aida Edemariam. For the evidence against Bauman, see the web portal, *WPolityce.pl*, "Kim naprawdę jest Zygmunt Bauman?" ["Who Really Is Zygmunt Bauman"], 25 June 2013, http://wpolityce.pl/polityka/160560-kim-naprawde-jest-zygmunt-bauman-przeczytaj-tajny-dokument-bezpieki-i-tlumaczenia-socjologa-dla-brytyjskiej-prasy. Bauman's interpretation of the Holocaust as a failure of "modernity" cannot be wholly independent of his experience of Communist "modernity."

[138] John Carroll, 147.

human solidarity that would give force to positive political interventions, yet his distrust for larger groupings and his cleavage of morality from public justice cut off the route to solidarity.[139]

Bauman's ethic is too demanding—completely self-sacrificial—and also too weak, lacking the community's enforcement mechanisms for gross violators and lacking subtle community pressure to engage in small sacrifices. In lieu of *infinite* obligation, might we at least see *great* obligation practically expressed in our circles? Not so much: in the postmodern era, with the decline of community, we see a decline even in small obligations. In charitable giving and volunteering, most of us fall nowhere near discharging meagre, never mind infinite, obligations. Yet by suggesting and obeying various tax regulations, we have built hospitals. I glimpse over my shoulder to make sure that my neighbour is paying a fair share too, and I'll offer a meagre 10% of my income for charity. My contributions won't rescue the victim of genocide, though they may help to keep society civil and to heal the sick. More ominously, however, even our *small* obligations are shrinking. Putnam's landmark study, *Bowling Alone* (2000), measured the many ways in which Americans have become more individualistic in practice—eager to spend more time with TV and the Internet, but increasingly less willing to join social and political organizations, to give to charity, or even to invite others over for supper.[140] Contra Bauman, some trends point to the ethical importance of religious and non-religious *communities*, not individuals. Both religious and non-religious group joiners donate ten times more time and money than non-joiners do.[141] It would be quite remarkable if our face-to-face personal sacrifices—visiting the elderly in nursing homes, say, or helping a friend shingle a house, or sharing food with a homeless person—were greater than our charitable giving, which requires so little of us.

Another ethical practice, volunteering, has shown a more positive trend, with increases among people over 60, and, to a lesser degree among people under 30. Partly, the increase among the young may be occurring because some high schools and colleges have wisely begun to require volunteering as part of the curriculum and because volunteering looks good

---

[139] Bauman, *Discontents*, 208; Jacobsen et al., 240.

[140] Putnam proves that percentage-wise, the economy has little effect on these changes. Putnam, 123. Twenge, *iGen*, 174–5.

[141] Putnam, 120.

on entry-level job applications.[142] Unfortunately, *regular* volunteering (once a month or once a week) has changed little. The main increase was to those who volunteered "sometime in the last year."[143] Because volunteering (slightly up) and community projects (greatly down) are headed in opposite directions, volunteering increasingly depends on weak "single-stranded obligations."[144] In this regard, community and faith are invaluable. Volunteering was higher among those who embraced religion (45%), lower among those who rejected it (27%), or who were ambivalent (31%).[145] Regular worshippers are far more likely than non-religious people to join groups, even secular groups, though non-religious people who *have* joined groups tend to be more involved than religious people are.[146] If motives are rooted in the popular individualist trope "I want to make a difference" rather than in community ties, then volunteering will be difficult to sustain.[147]

Asking young adult Americans in the late 2000s to comment on these practices, Christian Smith discovered that most of his respondents didn't volunteer, or give to charity, or feel a general obligation to help others. It's great to help, they said, but even in the event of a natural disaster, there was no *obligation*. Someday, when they were much better off, they might consider it. They mostly saw charity as the responsibility of very rich people, such as Bill Gates,[148] unaware, no doubt, that the wealthy give a lower percentage of their income than do the poor to charity.[149] (Possibly the Giving Pledge, initiated by Gates and Warren Buffett, could change this, if donations aren't funnelled mainly into foundations that further the political will of the donors.) Among high school seniors, only 33% gave to charity, down from 46% in the 1970s, even though, by some estimates, young people in the 2000s *spent* five times as much (adjusted for inflation) as their parents had spent when they were young.[150] Not surprisingly, Smith's young adults spoke in individualistic ways, with little sense of depending "on a larger social infrastructure or shared institutional

---

[142] Twenge and Campbell, 252–4.
[143] Twenge, *Me*, 241; Twenge and Campbell, 252–4.
[144] Putnam, 128–9.
[145] Angus Reid, 35.
[146] Putnam, 119, 67.
[147] Twenge and Campbell, 252–4.
[148] C. Smith, 68, 71.
[149] Putnam, 119.
[150] Twenge and Campbell, 251, 83.

goods"—the system. Nearly as troubling, the few who *did* feel an obligation couldn't explain why, and agreed that people didn't have a moral
responsibility to help others.[151] These practical ethics are clearly based on
How-I-Feel, a far cry from infinite obligation: the postmodern prioritizing
of the individual limits ethics.

If we lack *systematic* and communal measures of the good, then what
prevents me (as a free rider) from low-balling you by insisting that my
obligation depends only on How-I-Feel? Theodore Melfi's film *St. Vincent*
(2014) exemplifies the limitation. Vincent uses prostitutes, abuses alcohol,
doesn't work, lives in squalor, and is obscenely rude to others (often in
very funny ways). He is a free rider ... except that he saved a number of
men decades ago in Vietnam, he does his dementia-suffering wife's laun-
dry, and (at $11 per hour) semi-befriends his neighbour's son. For this,
Vincent is acclaimed as a modern-day saint. He represents the kind of anti-
communal and low-ball ethical offer that a relativist ethics sometimes
calls adequate.

The broad standard of virtues and vices matter little: ethical achievement is measured in relation to a salient individual (How-the-boy-feels)
and this turns out to be good enough for Vincent's sainthood. This sort
of How-I-Feel can produce a positive moral outcome, when we're faced
with a single sympathetic victim, less so when we're faced with many.
Solicitation for money to help one child in need of medical treatment
tends to succeed; solicitation to get money for eight such children tends
to be less successful. Even numbers as small as *two* diminish our charity.[152]
In the postmodern media context, charities have learned that the image of
a single photogenic face can bring in donations. This fact of evolutionary
psychology is good news for the one whose face is shown. To use the language of Levinas and Bauman, the Face—whether mediated via filmic
close-up or via photographic portrait[153]—can bring us into empathetic
communion with another, into an I/Thou relationship that is basic to our
humanity. But this humane spectacle is not such good news for the many
anonymous sufferers, whom we won't help unless something more systematic than our evolved sympathies is operative.

The lack of behavioural standards and of enforcement are another way
in which Bauman expresses a general postmodern underestimation of

---

[151] C. Smith, 71, 68, 175.

[152] Greene, 263–4.

[153] On the significance and rise of the close-up, see David Williams, *Imagined*, 168–9.

the community's ethical role. Law and legitimacy, not merely person-to-person ethics, are vital for any ethics that wants to move beyond family and village into impersonal cooperation, without which municipal, national, and global systems cannot function. For Douzinas, the codification of ethical principles into law transfers ethical decisions to legislators—"false prophets and fake tribes"[154]—allowing us to evade everything except our legal duty, narrowly defined. Certainly, duty is not enough. Legally, a non-citizen has no claim on us, so for refugees to survive, we must recognize their human, not legal, claim. However, the postmodern anti-systemic bias forgets that it's through positive law that refugee rights have expanded, and without legal recognition of refugees, our good ethical intentions offer little. The notion of an ethics/law split creates a false dichotomy. Why have most EU countries accepted so many Syrian refugees while the US accepted so few? Because EU countries were legally obligated. Why do some countries such as Portugal, Spain, Italy, and Greece have such high rates of income tax cheating (19.7%–25.2%), while other countries such as the US, Switzerland, Austria, Japan, New Zealand have much lower rates of cheating (7.8%–9.9%)? Because of systemic reasons: enforcement, history, belief in the *system's* legitimacy. Malcolm Gladwell argues that people in countries with low cheating rates see their legal system as legitimate, with low corruption and fewer insider deals for the wealthy.[155] In practice, moral behaviour—contribution to community goods in this instance—rises as the belief in the legitimacy of the law rises. Enforcement is not a false veneer added to ethics, but is just as important in a postmodern world as ever. In practice, chaos and harm operate far more freely, even in ordered societies, the moment that enforcement is suspended or perceived as suspended—witness Montreal's "night of terror" (7 October 1969) during a police strike, and the many riots after sporting events, such as the 2011 Vancouver Stanley Cup riots. Franz de Waal recognizes an internalized "one-on-one" morality among even non-human primates, but he is more realistic than Bauman about sources and outcomes. Empathy and the threat of physical consequences, says de Waal, form the two great

---

[154] Douzinas, 66.
[155] Gladwell, 291–3. Crime rates rise when people question the legitimacy of their government, as in the US during the 1960s and in post-Soviet Russia (Pinker, *Enlightenment*, 173–4).

supports for one-on-one morality, and the outcome is a modus vivendi, a social code.[156]

"No universal standards," says Bauman, a moral approach that is, in practice, consistent with the contemporary affirmation of the individual over the community. He goes on to say that since "moral responsibility is the first reality of the self," it has no foundation or cause.[157] A lofty postmodern claim, but false in a very basic way. It ignores the millions of years of evolved primate sociality, mediated by the increasing size of our frontal lobes, a change attributable to increased social calculations and by hormones (such as oxytocin) that act as social lubricants. Among chimpanzees, high-ranking males will police the fights of subordinates. As well, although males in the wild can rape females by taking them to out-of-the-way locations, in captivity females will sometimes band together to chase off a male whose sexual advances are too insistent. Not surprisingly, #MeToo depends on rudimentary cultural affordances and on social pressure to limit violence. "A social hierarchy is a giant system of inhibitions, which is no doubt what paved the way for human morality … Impulse control is key."[158] Indeed, we can speak of Adam Smith's "impartial spectator" when we recognize the individual voices of #MeToo as a form of technologically mediated, communal surveillance. In other words, among all primates, including humans, the moral party is rarely just a party of two.[159] Even Bauman—who seemingly distrusts the objectifying gaze[160] and yet as a writer calls the individual to account—functions as Smith's third party and as a collective inhibitor.

Despite valid postmodern fears about the oppressiveness of community and duty, it is the community that pulls us partway out of the potentially self-serving How-I-Feel. Even if we can't decide what is fundamental, there are many rules that cut across cultures, for example, "Help people who can't help themselves and return favors to those who have given them in the past. The first represents a norm of social responsibility, the second a norm of reciprocity." [161] It might surprise us that narcissists, too, respond to the socializing pull of community. In one experiment, actors insulted participants, who were then allowed to retaliate by blasting their insulters

[156] de Waal, *Bonobo*, 160.
[157] Bauman, *Postmodern Ethics*, 13.
[158] de Waal, *Bonobo*, 172–3, 150.
[159] de Waal, *Bonobo*, 170–1, 175–6.
[160] Bauman, *Postmodern Ethics*, 111.
[161] Hauser, 289.

with a painful noise. As predicted, narcissists showed the most aggression, but if they were told of something they had in common with the insulter, narcissists were no more aggressive than non-narcissists. Connectedness weakens egotism.[162] Of course, we can't naïvely trust the community—it loves and perpetuates itself. Yet when it criticizes us for our individual failings, it is often correct.[163] In a coffee room, where people paid on the honour system, researchers put up pictures of eyes, then pictures of a flowerpot to see if payment patterns changed. They did; people were more likely to pay when other eyes, even painted eyes, were present. Bruce Hood explains, "When we are made self-conscious, we become more accountable,"[164] and he ought to have added that in practice we become self-conscious precisely when the *community* looks at us.

Even in the postmodern era, then, the larger community is still crucial, morally, for its *ability* to limit harm, yet, since the early 1970s, faith in the institutions of government, education, and news media has declined.[165] So who will have the necessary power to make social changes? In what social arena will the change be made?[166] De Waal, taking his news from Hobbes, sees two political alternatives: "unmitigated competition" or "a social order partly shaped and upheld by aggression."[167] Both minor (don't litter) and major (don't rape) aspects of ethical behaviour can be influenced simply by people's feeling that there are rules and that the rules will be enforced. This is a function of the community as an agent. Evidence of vandalism in a neighbourhood actually suggests that no one is in charge and that we can get away with crimes. A Dutch study showed that when people were in the presence of graffiti or saw unreturned shopping carts, they were more likely to litter. When they saw a €5 note sticking out of a graffiti-covered mailbox, a quarter of passers-by stole it; only half as many did so when the mailbox was clean. Attention to appearances signals that

---

[162] Twenge and Campbell, 286.

[163] Vetlesen argues that while Bauman fears the state's threat to individual morality, he doesn't fully consider the ways that the state *safeguards* against the individual's *immorality*—Bauman prefers Foucault to Durkheim (Vetlesen, 258). If it's true that we'd always rather fight the previous war than the one we're in, it may be that Bauman (like many others) is still fighting previous war against totalitarianism, admittedly an important struggle.

[164] Hood, 187.

[165] Twenge, *iGen*, 279.

[166] Vetlesen, 256.

[167] de Waal, *Good Natured*, 183.

residents care about their environment and will uphold social rules.[168] In practice, the rules help us to be moral, and it is the community that both authorizes and enforces the rules.

Bauman's notion that there are no general rules, only actions that fit individual situations, is a popular notion, defended by many of Christian Smith's interview subjects. On the contrary, however, Western society's moral calculus has grown into a fine mesh of rules in a thousand areas, from healthcare ethics to consumer-protection laws to property bylaws. We hardly think of morality when we think of city bylaws, but the careful specification of our duties in relation to one another reduces conflict. Bylaws tell me how close to my neighbour's property and how high I may build my garage. Here, my infringement on his right to property is either restricted or penalized to the point that it's not worth my while to make a moral choice that brings conflict, perhaps violence. The rules specify my obligations, sometimes to the smallest tittle, and they effectively call on me to treat my neighbour as a face rather than as a potential antagonist in an unregulated Wild West.

Since no ethical rule works well in every case (if it did, we'd never go to court), Bauman too hastily concludes that each ethical response must be unique. This is palpably untrue. If moral codes couldn't be generalized, then we could never criticize anyone who refuses to accept the moral code—around bullying, for example—and we'd be left with subjectivism.[169] Human rights, where our moral agreement is widest, are premised upon universal principles, and therefore don't fit with relativism.[170] Most features of the Geneva Conventions and the UN's *Universal Declaration of Human Rights* (especially those features related to harm) receive increasingly broad global assent. A World Bank survey of 60,000 poor people worldwide in the early 2000s showed great support for the *Universal Declaration*.[171] Even the more limited 1990 *Cairo Declaration of Human Rights in Islam* copies much of the UN document while still trying to maintain a literalist interpretation of the *Qur'an*. Instead of moving to a state in which rules can't be generalized, we've taken some laws—such as the prohibition against sodomy—off the books, but more often we've multiplied laws, as when, for example, sexual orientation became a

---

[168] Pinker, *Better*, 124.
[169] Shafer-Landau, 301.
[170] Freeman, 125.
[171] Freeman, 120.

prohibited category of discrimination throughout the law, and as the responsibility to accommodate transgender people became a requirement.

The push to turn moral values into generalized rules is ironically attested among criminals in the Coen brothers' movie *Fargo* and in Denis Johnson's novel *Nobody Move* (2009). *Fargo*'s car salesperson, Jerry Lundegaard, lures two customers to the dealership by agreeing to sell a car for $19,500, but once they arrive, he insists that they will need to pay extra for Tru-coat sealant. They grudgingly pay; advantage Jerry. A short time later, having arranged the kidnapping of his own wife in order to solve his money woes, Jerry finds the kidnappers reneging on the deal and refusing to share the ransom. Jerry protests, "We had a deal here! A deal's a deal!"[172] Jerry appeals to the universal value of fairness, though he had previously exempted himself from any categorical imperative. As Heath and Potter lucidly put it, "This is why petty crime has a tendency to become organized crime. Everyone can benefit from having some rules, even those who are doing their utmost to break the rules."[173] In *Nobody Move*, the low-life Jimmy shoots the enforcer Gambol, who was about to beat Jimmy up for a gambling debt. But then Jimmy also calls 911. After Jimmy hits Gambol's boss Juarez, drawing blood, Juarez says, "I love getting pistol-whipped. It means I'm dealing with a *puto*. He can't pull the trigger."[174] Of course, this is precisely what differentiates Jimmy ethically from the more ruthless Juarez: Jimmy recognizes a generalizable Kantian ethic outside of himself. His survival seems to demand that he kill, but, because he doesn't want to be killed, he finds it difficult to justify killing others. De Waal argues that it is precisely the movement towards universal standards that differentiates human morality from that of other primates— universal standards, along with a system to monitor and punish offenders.[175]

For Bauman and many others, morality is non-rational—no legal code or calculus will solve our ethical dilemmas[176]—and he is right to the extent that individual choice will always remain at the heart of morality, that codes cannot specify everything, and that codes can become evil. However, since our non-rational moral intuitions evolved over millennia to favour kin, people in our group, and people like us, only "the universalizing

[172] *Fargo*, 62.
[173] Heath and Potter, 77.
[174] Johnson, 181–2.
[175] de Waal, *Bonobo*, 17–18.
[176] Bauman, *Postmodern Ethics*, 11, 13. *Discontents*, 48.

boost of reason" can bring us to policies and social norms that effectively reduce violence.[177] Generalizing Enlightenment arguments about torture, emancipation, and universal human rights played a crucial role in the historical decline of violence. Because of their groupish intuitions, white colonialists found it possible to rationalize policies and atrocities against indigenous cultures, policies and atrocities that the colonists would have understood as highly immoral if applied to themselves. More recently, the African National Congress justified atrocities (such as the rubber-tyre "necklace" burnings of suspected collaborators) because the fight against Apartheid was a "just war," and South African president Thabo Mbeki refused to criticize Zimbabwe's tyrant Robert Mugabe because Mugabe was African. Against such group-identity approaches, Chair of the Truth and Reconciliation Commission, Archbishop Desmond Tutu, turned to universalizing reason: "Human rights are human rights and they are of universal validity or they are nothing."[178]

Market-Based Ethics

If Bauman's individualized morality cannot fully describe how we ought to act, or even how we do act, perhaps a more worldly approach would solve the postmodern ethical dilemma. If our self-interest or desire runs up against someone else's, one contemporary solution is market pricing. The argument, favoured by Heath and Potter, runs thus: since no fixed metric can determine whether your wish to fix your bike tire is more or less important than my desire to replace the washer in my faucet, the only way to solve the problem of where resources should be allocated is to ask how important the tire is to you, and the washer to me. In short, how much would you be willing to give up for the tire? In a pluralist world, where there is no objective method of determining what is valuable and what isn't, pricing plays the intermediary role, revealing how valuable each thing is to each person. Where postmodern other-based ethics and "acting locally" can't address large problems such as global warming that require communal negotiation and cooperation, pricing could solve the problem. Global incentives to limit emissions and disincentives against atmospheric pollution (a carbon tax or other price that factors in environmental costs) could address our environmental dilemma.[179]

[177] Pinker, *Better*, 691.
[178] Meredith, 657, 673–4.
[179] Heath and Potter, 326–7, 332.

In support of Heath and Potter, one could point at the role of commerce in the historical decline of violence and increase of free expression.[180] The zero-sum game of war (always highly moralized) has increasingly been overshadowed in the West by the win-win character of economic exchange (which often sets morality aside). Pinker, using Alan Fiske's categories, argues that a broad historical shift in economic models from "Communal Sharing" to "Authority Ranking" to "Equality Matching" to "Market Pricing" helped reduce violence by "retracting the moral sense from its traditional spheres of community, authority, and purity." Whatever qualms we might have about the market's libertarian ethics (encouraging prostitution, drug use, and gambling), market pricing organizes society in an increasingly "Rational-Legal" way, crowding out moralizing violence.[181]

As well, arguments can be made in favour of pricing in formerly moral areas: home care for seniors, for example. To put a price on work that children formerly owed to parents eases the children's load. Seniors might feel abandoned if their care becomes a paid job, but they might also feel freer, less indebted, and no longer obligated to put up with inadequate care. From Bauman's point of view, such pricing is an abdication of moral responsibility, since it is merely transactional. And in a business relationship, I only fulfil my obligation if my partner *deserves* it. I escape moral obligations at a time when—in a world of deregulated markets with people and companies fleeing their obligations—we need *greater* moral intervention, not less.[182] Nevertheless, Lipovetsky insists that ties of affection and empathy can still be maintained alongside market values, and that the real danger occurs when weakening community ties throw people onto their own resources, making them more fragile and emotionally unstable.[183] Here the market can help.

Unfortunately for Heath and Potter's case, even in the postmodern era business transactions and contracts need moral rectitude to get started. From where will this unpriced rectitude come? More importantly, some things inherently resist pricing—how much should a polluted lake cost? How much for a foetus? Market pricing works very well for bike tires, faucets, and the value of your time in comparison to mine; not so much

---

[180] Freeman, 99–100. Pinker, *Better*, 682–4.
[181] Pinker, *Better*, 628, 636–7.
[182] Bauman, *Postmodern Ethics*, 57–9. Jacobsen et al., 241.
[183] Lipovetsky, 84–5.

for collective action problems such as global warming. A carbon tax is an excellent tool, but, in practice, human ethical intervention, not the invisible hand of the market, will legislate a carbon tax. The market, apparently, has other ideas. In 2018, when the Canadian government brought in carbon pricing, it kept the price low enough that emissions will be reduced only slightly. If I want a washer for my faucet, I can quickly determine how valuable a functioning faucet is to me. In a collective action problem, it's very difficult to get agreement. Which actions are necessary to slow down global warming? Or, harder yet, how should we rate the value of lower future temperatures against immediate economic prosperity? Given the "licensing effect," it's too simple to say that "people and corporations pollute whenever they lack an incentive not to."[184] Economists have shown that if we pay for bad behaviour—paying to plant trees as penance for our high electricity use—we tend to use *more* electricity, whereas if we pay extra to use *green* energy sources, the licensing effect disappears. In the first case, we've bought a licence to be wasteful. In the second, we're paying a price for our moral commitments.[185]

Collective action problems are political problems—they are solved (or not) by means of moral arguments in the public sphere. When pricing oil, we should account for "negative externalities" such as the global warming wrought by carbon. However, before we price the negative externalities, we must jointly make a *moral* decision about how important a clean environment is. We must agree on a "good" that cuts across pluralistic lines. The moral decision *precedes* the pricing. Therefore pricing, as significant as it is, puts us no further ahead in the postmodern dilemma of deciding morally between two alternatives. That's the nice part. In practice, things get much more vicious. In the past, when pricing became the arbiter, multinational companies raced to the bottom, as jurisdictions desperate for economic growth offered better prices—lower and lower emission standards in order to retain the offending industry. Such practices are at the heart of Jameson's warnings about postmodernity as the multinational stage of capitalism. While instituting a carbon price, Canada's Liberals also championed the Trans Mountain Pipeline against a lot of opposition to bring highly polluting tar sands oil more cost-effectively to market, since

---

[184] Heath and Potter, 313. Even those who defend the moral value of markets recognize that markets rely on virtues derived from other institutions such as the family or the church. See Wight, 130.

[185] McGonigal, 103–4.

oil is important to the Canadian economy. Just as vicious (Heath and Potter acknowledge this) is the way that pricing can magnify economic inequities into serious injustices. Price measures how important something is to you. The company Myriad patented breast cancer genes, and in 2015 charged $4000 to perform the detection tests.[186] How much would you be "willing" to pay as a Congolese with an average annual income of $450? In a similar vein, how badly do you need a kidney? In 2004, if you were a poor Brazilian, you could *sell* one of yours for $6000. You couldn't afford to buy one—at a retail value of $60,000—but a middle-class North American could.[187]

Novelists such as David Mitchell and Margaret Atwood have, in their near-future scenarios, satirized the notion that market pricing could successfully address ethical problems. In *The Bone Clocks* (2014), the participants at the 2015 Hay Festival pass by a smoking tent, "sponsored by Win²Win: Europe's premier facilitator of ethically sourced organs for medical transplant."[188] In *The Year of the Flood* (2009), Ren, as sexual performer at the Scales and Tails nightclub, praises her boss, Mordis: "He never took freebies from us. He had ethics … Also he didn't like waste; we were a valuable asset, he'd say."[189] The market doesn't eliminate the values of love and human rights, yet they are irrelevant to pricing. For the child prostitute Oryx, in *Oryx and Crake* (2003), money value is no substitute for love, but love is undependable, and having a market value is preferable to having no value: your owners will feed you and ensure that you are "not damaged too much."[190] Oryx is a survivor, but Atwood, with that casual "too much," clearly wants to horrify us with how little price cares about moral right. Market pricing will play an increasingly valuable role in a wide swath of human endeavour, but it can't solve our ethical dilemmas.

Contractarian Ethics

Despite problems with tradition, scientific modernity, postmodern individualism, and the market as arbiters of ethics, postmodernity has found

---

[186] Stiglitz, 206. Elizabeth Lopatto, "Genetic testing for breast cancer gets more affordable," *The Verge*, 21 April 2015, https://www.theverge.com/2015/4/21/8458553/color-breast-cancer-gene-testing-brca-myriad.

[187] The prices and nationalities appeared in the *Winnipeg Free Press*, 23 May 2004.

[188] Mitchell, *Bone*, 299.

[189] Atwood, *Year*, 7.

[190] Atwood, *Oryx*, 126.

ethical consensus on two fronts: in terms of ethical content, consensus has largely galvanized around human rights; in terms of process, around contractarianism, the notion that for moral demands to have force, they must be mutually agreed upon. Fundamental agreement on individual human rights caught on globally (not just in the West) with great speed, highlighted by the adoption of the *Universal Declaration of Human Rights* by the UN General Assembly in 1948,[191] with over 80% of members voting in favour and none voting against. Practice, of course, lags far behind declarations. If I make human flourishing my goal, warns Taylor, there is no transcendent voice to tell me that I should work towards universal human welfare rather than just towards my individual material benefit.[192] It's true that there may be no single foundation for human rights, but, as Freeman argues, "This is not a serious blow to the concept … because the very idea of philosophical foundations is itself problematic. We can find strong reasons for supporting human rights, based on respect for human dignity (Donnelly), the bases of moral action (Gewirth), the demands of human sympathy (Rorty), or the conditions of human flourishing (Nussbaum)."[193] These conceptions go further than simply right action and rest on an attitude towards other people,[194] something like love. The framers of the *Universal Declaration of Human Rights* sought agreement on the actual rights (the norms) rather than on foundations, and therefore reached agreement. In Jacques Maritain's account of this "thin" justification, the framers, though ideologically opposed, agreed about the rights "*on condition that no one asks us why.*"[195] Even those who criticize the conceptual gap in human rights rely heavily on human rights norms. According to the model developed by Christopher Fariss, human security rights (freedom from killings, torture, and political imprisonment) have been steadily increasing worldwide between 1949 and 2014, despite the very uneven performances of

---

[191] Freeman, 4–5, 37. Charles Taylor sees human rights—"the notion of rights as prior to and untouchable by political structures"—as the clearest expression of a modern moral order "underlying the political, which the political has to respect" (Taylor, *Modern*, 173).

[192] Taylor, *Secular*, 572.

[193] Freeman, 65, 87.

[194] Hunt, 27.

[195] Freeman, 41. Pinker, *Enlightenment*, 418–9. Hunt, 20. Jean Cohen, too, thinks that the search for the *foundations* of human rights is not a priority, and that we shouldn't rest human rights on any *particular* conception of the good (Cohen, 181, 188).

many countries, including the US.[196] In democracies, both sides of almost every difficult ethical issue tend to be articulated in terms of human rights. We argue over which rights take precedence (should our right to life and liberty override a terrorist's right to be free from torture?), but almost no one argues that the rights themselves should be abolished. Postmodern individualism coheres well with human rights: if I want freedom, I need security of person and I need guarantees that I won't be treated as a symbol for my group or as expendable in a particular ideology. How I feel actually matters.

The content of rights segues into the process advocated by contractarians. As explained by John Rawls, contractarians try to imagine themselves behind a veil of ignorance—as if they didn't know which place in society they would be born into—before negotiating the rules that would limit self-interest and give structure to that society.[197] The point in negotiating morality is, again, not to push for agreement on fundamental philosophical principles (a potentially Big Brother-like process), but, more practically, to find rights and rules that disparate groups can agree should be honoured. For example, we can have widespread agreement that no one shall be subjected to torture despite disagreeing whether this freedom flows from God or from the inherent value of the human being. Vollmann says, "Carry out your program, please, not your ideology. People have improved conditions in sweatshops, temporarily and in finite localities, but no one has ever 'reorganized the means of production' with happy results, because it is difficult to know when to declare victory."[198] One of the hopeful aspects of postmodern ethics is that we are less and less comfortable with an ideology or a faith as the *only* warrant for individual actions. Instead, we require programmes that are acceptable to a variety of ideologies and traditions. Human rights and contractarianism fit with the belief that political and religious ideology should no longer override other concerns. According to Pinker, if we think that our ideological opponents are evil, we will allow "any number of eggs to be broken to make the utopian omelet."[199] If human rights are the standard, however, breaking eggs

---

[196] Christopher Farris and Keith Schnakenberg, "Human Rights Protection," in Roser, Human Rights I.1, https://ourworldindata.org/human-rights. As well, capital punishment has declined steeply, so that now only one-fifth of the world's countries still execute people. Pinker, *Enlightenment*, 209.

[197] Rawls, 118–23.

[198] Vollmann, *Rising*, 130.

[199] Pinker, *Better*, 556.

becomes more difficult. This is not to claim that contractarianism is some-how post-ideological. It's a liberal programme, but even if we see in it a blindness to class or other ideological considerations, what contractarianism demands—and what the *Universal Declaration* demands—is that any ethical proposals retreat from large philosophical or religious claims into practical effects.

In addition to freedom from physical harm and other negative rights, the UN has an increasing list of positive rights, some of which (the right to favourable conditions of work and to protection against unemployment) are still widely seen as privileges, not rights. Out of a sense that racialized groups, the poor, and other disenfranchised minorities did not have equal access to resources and practical freedoms—that the liberal social contract wasn't serving everybody—grew the "capabilities" approach to justice. Nobel laureate Amartya Sen and Martha Nussbaum emphasized human flourishing, including senses, imagination, thought, emotions, affiliation, and play,[200] sometimes over, sometimes alongside the basic rights that a social contract is supposed to ensure. Sen notes that one can have freedoms that are useless if economic deprivation blocks the opportunities that are available to more privileged citizens. Like contractarianism, the capabilities approach takes postmodern pluralism as a starting point (i.e. people will have conflicting notions of the good), but Sen criticizes Rawls by proposing a parable in which three children argue over a flute. Who should get the flute? The best player, the neediest, or the one who made it? The parable envisions three differential lines of argument, with no possibility of arriving at an impartial agreement via Rawls's original "veil of ignorance." But contractarians, of course, never denied the priority of human flourishing, and Sen cannot solve the postmodern ethical dilemma either, since he is able to speak only of a "partial ordering" of priorities,[201] which, in terms of process, offers no advance on Rawls. What Sen accomplishes with much greater success is to argue that a moral social contract must address *needs* no less than freedoms.

Despite widespread agreement on basic human rights, they are conceptually limited in that they don't reach far beyond egregious harms. How do we address morally complex issues? How do we decide whether free expression means (as was the case in 2015) that anti-Muslim crusader Pamela Geller should be free to hold a contest for the best anti-Mohammed

---

[200] Nussbaum, 314, 306.
[201] Sen, 226–9, 13–15, 399–400.

cartoon? Mostly, people argued How-I-Feel, based on their group loyal-ties, but the more consistent traditionalists argued vehemently that to allow anti-Muslim blasphemy was to allow hate speech that undermined everyone's religious freedom. Libertarians insisted that freedom of speech must override everything, unless violence were directly advocated against a specific group. Consequentialists might say that the dangers of violent reprisal are too high to allow such a contest, but rule consequentialists and virtue ethicists might point out that rules allowing free speech encourage a greater degree of human flourishing than do rules prohibiting blas-phemy. Ultimately, the Texas contest did proceed, on the principle of free speech, but many defenders of free speech criticized those who used free speech mainly to offend others.

When we examine such attempts to reach public consensus in the post-modern era, it's evident that contractarianism has become the default pro-cess. However artificial and abstract Rawls's imagined "veil of ignorance" might be, many features of actual governmental decisions, legal judge-ments, human rights codes, and constitutions proceed from pluralist assumptions. No matter how I feel, I can't convincingly argue that 'because America is a Christian country, we should allow anti-Muslim cartoons.' Although my moral grounding may be in a particular faith, I must justify the moral decision on a pluralist basis, as something that will benefit Muslims, Christians, and atheists. Even in personal morality, we can see ways in which the veil of ignorance is gaining importance. It has become rare for Christian relief organizations to direct their efforts only at the welfare of other Christians. A social contract forces me to move beyond How-I-Feel and to consider the world from the perspective of others, but not so much that I sacrifice myself. Without setting individual morality or tradition aside, contractarianism insists that we treat these obligations pre-cisely *not* as infinite, but as matter for social negotiation, in which emotional responses are set within a rational set of procedures (a fair trial, for exam-ple, or the duties of a parent towards a child). Morris Panych, whom we saw earlier satirizing the freeing of individual desire in *Benevolence*, shows how socially unsustainable it would be to disregard the veil of ignorance. The aggressive panhandler Lomy expects cash from Eicherson, but admits that had their situations been reversed, he'd have kicked Eicherson's face in.[202] For Lomy, his position matters: depending on his level of power, he will act very differently. Yet, if I look disenchantedly (through Nietzsche

---

[202] Panych, 30.

and Foucault) at a social order that subordinates me, I can't give a *moral* reason (apart from my desire) why the social order should change; nor can Lomy. All he can say is that he wants greater power. Lomy will not in imagination temporarily relinquish his subjectivity, so he can't approach anything like a social consensus.

Contractarianism reveals a troubling concord with the postmodern dilemma, since under the initial veil of ignorance contractarians cannot, by definition, know where a moral consensus might lie. The contract is thus ideologically liberal in a broad sense, allowing many liberties for each individual so long as those liberties don't harm others or restrict their liberties.[203] Moral stances that become public policy are required to be compatible with many positions. In other words, contractarianism provides a negotiating process without actually *solving* the postmodern ethical dilemma. Of course, as individuals, contractarians do take particular moral stances and may adhere to a particular code. The content of the contract may come, variously, from the evolved parent-child bond, from a faith tradition, from humanism, even from highly subjective individual claims. Yet the content of each position is measured by how well it can meet the challenges set by *other* approaches. Because negotiations happen repeatedly, contractarianism has a pluralist face, but it doesn't remain only in a pluralist situation (where the postmodern dilemma weighs so heavily), since each ongoing negotiation results in a provisional social consensus that allows certain freedoms and enforces certain moral limits.

Against contractarianism, Greene argues that human happiness, broadly construed, should overrule human rights and the contracts that flow from them. Greene defends utilitarianism/consequentialism—"a deep pragmatism about making principled decisions"—as a workable meta-morality. If an abortion, for example, will bring more happiness and less suffering to the people involved, then abortion is justified. Greene's scientific-modernist argument is important, in that the Western movement away from tribalism partly depends on putting more and more of a premium on individual happiness. Human rights alone can't be a basis for morality because we don't have a way of deciding which rights should take precedence, says Greene, and the idea that rights should always trump consequences is troubling because it makes all counter-evidence irrelevant. According to Greene, the right to life, the right to choose, the right to self-defence, have all been used to rationalize our gut feelings into seem-

[203] Rawls, 53.

ingly objective human rights "principles." "Rights and duties are *absolute*," we say, "except when they're not."[204]

Yet, contra Greene, rights have also defended us against utilitarian-minded leaders who would sacrifice people for a desirable outcome. As well, Greene's notions of happiness and of pragmatism as the essence of morality owe much to the traditionalist's Golden Rule,[205] which he mentions, and to the human rights ideals of equality, which he doesn't. Like all Utilitarians, Greene stumbles when he wants to measure happiness. How and when, for example, should we begin to account for the foetus's happiness in abortion? On the question of waterboarding that dogged the presidency of George W. Bush, how should we measure the definite agony of a few torture victims against the agony of many civilian victims of a terrorist attack that might or might not happen? Greene is forced to go outside of rational happiness calculations in order to arrive at one of his crucial first principles—that everyone's happiness must be considered equal—precisely what the Rawlsian state of ignorance and the Golden Rule seek to approximate. In effect, he makes happiness broad enough to include all the virtues and values (including rights) that he thinks are important, thus losing the sense that reasoned consequences or "deep pragmatism" can always be decisive, and arriving, once again, at the dilemma of postmodern ethical pluralism.

In the postmodern era's contractarianism, we have become more reluctant to prejudge that some objective standard can tell us what might make another person happy. We look back to tradition and to deontic claims for some of our moral choices, affirming some (the prohibition on false witness), and rejecting others (the prohibition of homosexuality), but, most commonly, we negotiate modifications: we don't proscribe usury—economic growth requires the charging of interest—yet we legislate against the predatory interest rates that the market, left to its own resources, approves. We thus try to make happiness calculations, but not by assessing what would make the *most* people happy. Rather, we consider what sorts of rules we'd prefer, if we didn't know whether we'd be creditor or debtor.

If contractarian notions are important in contemporary society, we would expect to see them reflected in literature and film. Looking at contemporary Anglophone literature, John Su argues that it shies *away* from providing normative ethical codes and towards a Levinasian attentiveness

<hr/>

[204] Greene, 16, 147, 184, 176, 302–3.
[205] Greene, 173, 163.

to the individual's needs.[206] Since fiction focuses on individuals, we shouldn't be surprised that the individual's needs play a starring role, but literature doesn't actually shy away from normative codes. On the contrary, we can see in much fiction the signs of contractarian negotiations leading to normative codes. Moral questions in *The Year of the Flood*, for example, gravitate towards a social contract, even though in Atwood's post-apocalyptic world there are no longer legal authorities. As Toby hovers between pacifism, self-defence, and aggression, we see the social argument staged via the individual. Toby's internal negotiation forms a basis for the future *public* contract. When the sexually abusive Painballers are captured, Toby will not execute them. There's no immediate vengeance—the decision on what to do with them is postponed. Instead, she gives them soup, appalling their victim Amanda and failing to elicit gratitude from the Painballers.[207] But that's not important to Toby. With the disappearance of state authority after the Waterless Flood, it's no surprise that the Painballers gravitated towards a Hobbesian state of nature. Atwood, however, doesn't go down the well-trodden right-wing path of revenge fantasy, which regresses into a kinship-based or religious normative code. Instead, she imagines a proto-court system and the beginnings of a new social contract. This doesn't mean that the Painballers will escape punishment—execution is still likely—but the community will negotiate its way to a temporary order, weighing various rights and consequences. Late in the final novel of the trilogy, *Maddaddam* (2013), Toby finds herself advocating *for* the Painballers, not because they are innocent, but because some of her colleagues refuse to consider the Painballers as people, and because she wants to establish whether they ought to be treated as criminals or as prisoners of war. Eventually, they receive the death penalty, based on votes by humans and pigoons (pigs with human neocortical tissue).[208]

We can see an incipient contractarianism in literature when writers examine larger social patterns. The contract or normative code is often imagined not as a social consensus, but as a protagonist pulling together a traditional culture and Western democratic attitudes into a personal hybrid. In David Mitchell's *Cloud Atlas* (2004), Sonmi, agitating for rights for fabricants (human worker clones), speaks in the terms of Western human rights. Zach'ry, a traditionalist living hundreds of years later, treats

---

[206] Su, 12, 175.
[207] Atwood, *Year*, 430.
[208] Atwood, *Maddaddam*, 263, 367, 369, 378.

her as a deity, yet what he worships is in large part her human rights ethic. He recognizes value in the Prescients' non-faith-based culture (they belong to modernity), and he learns not to despise their "mansome" women, such as Meronym.[209] In *A Thousand Splendid Suns* (2007), hybridity appears when author Khaled Hosseini tries to be partially faithful to the Islamic tradition, using the *Qur'an* as a general basis for ethics, while also moving towards Enlightenment and postmodern understandings of women's equality. In *White Teeth*, Zadie Smith shows little sympathy for Millat's radical Islamic stance, but she does allow the protagonist Irie to find a rapprochement with her Jehovah's Witness grandmother Hortense. Despite Hortense's anachronistic faith, her position must be taken into account. We can find similar attempts at social rapprochement in the works of David Foster Wallace, Richard Powers, Gary Shteyngart, Jonathan Franzen, and Michael Chabon, and we can find many works that lament the tragic destruction of political contracts, no matter how faulty, as Mitchell's *The Bone Clocks* does in the final section, where an unjust, but semi-stable international system degenerates into petty kleptocracies. Whatever the inequities of the international social contract, it is *morally* far superior to the disorder that follows.

Given the rise of human rights, the post-Westphalian direction of international society, and the continuing importance of social contracts in postmodern morality, we can in some cases predict (barring a disaster that overwhelms civil society) the direction that postmodern moral contracts will go. Christian Welzel, using World Values Surveys, has attempted to measure liberal values, what he calls "emancipative values," over the last century by collapsing gender equality, personal choice (divorce, homosexuality, abortion), political voice (freedom of speech), and childrearing philosophy (emphasis on independence over obedience) into a single number. According to Welzel's statistics, *every region* of the world has gotten more liberal over time, and this is not only a factor of generational change or of a generation's youthful liberalism, because *every* recent generation has gotten more liberal as it has gotten older.[210]

Despite present moral confoundings in issues such as child welfare, one reason that we are justified in believing that postmodern ethics haven't

[209] Mitchell, *Cloud*, 248.

[210] Christian Welzel, cited in Pinker, *Enlightenment*, 224–8. This social liberalism, however, doesn't necessarily imply a belief in liberal democracy, as can be seen by youth support for anti-system parties of the left and the right. Mounk, 120–3.

gone off the rails into the Kingdom of Whatever is the historical decline in violence. Violence has declined logarithmically throughout history, and features of the social contract, such as the state's monopoly on violence, have been a major factor. From the 1960s in the early postmodern era to the 1990s, rates of violence did rise in North America and Europe, most drastically in the US, though never anywhere near to medieval rates or rates in pre-state societies,[211] before declining *everywhere*, including the US, after 1990.[212] The factors are many and complex, but for our purposes, the complex rise and fall of violence makes it impossible simply to blame the factors favoured by the left (imperialism, racism, gun culture, and capitalism's inequalities) or the factors favoured by the right (immigrants, bad parenting, relativism, a weakening of social control). Pinker points at a measurable drop of trust in social institutions[213] and a culture-wide process of informalization beginning in the 1960s, with adolescence valued over adulthood, and rebellion valued over conformity. "Decivilizing,"[214] he calls it, but that's too strong. When people don't feel that they're part of a contract, they act less ethically and violence increases. The positive developments in the 1960s—the civil rights movement, women's liberation, anti-war protests—were all born out of a sense of a faulty or failed social contract. Once the movements attained some success, members of the affected groups could begin to feel that they did have some say in the social contract and that their needs were being addressed. Targeting crimes such as "rape, battering, hate crimes, gay-bashing, and child abuse" gave a progressive valence to law and order.[215] A belief that the social contract was becoming more inclusive helped lead to the declining violence of the 1990s and 2000s.[216] Contractarianism hasn't solved the difficult moral issues that confront us, and because of power differen-

---

[211] In the 1960s, the homicide rate in the US more than doubled, "from a low of 4.0 [per 100,000] in 1957 to a high of 10.2 in 1980. The upsurge included every other category of major crime as well, including rape, assault, robbery, theft, and lasted (with ups and downs) for three decades" (Pinker, *Better*, 107). Nevertheless, the worst homicide rate in that 30-year period—"10.2 per 100,000 in 1980—was a quarter of the rate for Western Europe in 1450, a tenth of the rate of the traditional Inuit, and a fiftieth of the average rate in non-state societies" (Pinker, *Better*, 116).

[212] Pinker, *Better*, 117–18.

[213] Pinker, *Better*, 109–10; Twenge, *iGen*, 279.

[214] Pinker, *Better*, 106.

[215] Pinker, *Better*, 125.

[216] Putnam notes that the percentage of guards, police, and lawyers grew a great deal since 1970, and this no doubt had an effect too (Putnam, 144–5).

tials, contracts can be highly unjust, but contracts help to create a background for ethical behaviour and a basis upon which ethics can be negotiated.

Are we postmodern in our ethics yet? Yes, increasingly so. The postmodern rise of How-I-Feel ethics is a direct result of tradition's and modernity's failure to, by themselves, deliver us from evil. In a social species, How-I-Feel, of course, is utterly unworkable as a moral arbiter, and we'll see some of the costs of individualism in the next chapter. By definition, others, too, must make judgements based on how *they* feel, judgements that might directly counter my feelings, my wishes, and my autonomy. So we fall back into a pluralism of virtue and consequences, tradition, and reason. But the way of deciding the proportions of these in our moral decisions is increasingly through a variety of social contracts. Though rooted in the older notion of covenant, contractarianism is a modern invention, arriving with the scientific revolution and underwriting revolutions against the "God-appointed" authority of kings. Paradoxically, contractarianism is also postmodern in disallowing a final appeal to reason or utility as much as to God or virtue, though any of these may be important to us as individual contractors. In terms of factual truth and in terms of our universal ability to reason about ethics, we aren't postmodern, but in our unavoidable reliance upon negotiation and contracts rather than on absolute ethical truths, we are postmodern. This extends the postmodern dilemma, as we'll see, to everything from one-on-one relationships to the national polity.

CHAPTER 4

Individualism: "I Believe in Me"

"I wasn't cut out to be a worker," says Z in *AntZ*. "I'm supposed to do everything for the colony. What about my needs? What about me?"[1] Ever since Dr. Spock in 1946 advised parents to put newborns to sleep in a separate room,[2] to treat children as individuals, and to gear their expectations to the children's needs, succeeding generations have increasingly been taught that how they feel—not just as members of a group but also as separate individuals—is important. "I've always been a country of one," says Nick Shay in Don DeLillo's *Underworld* (1997).[3] When advertisers for the US Army realized that appeals to individuality and self-actualization worked, they came up with the slogan "Be All That You Can Be." It lasted throughout the 1980s and 1990s, a rather ironic slogan for a strictly hierarchical group premised on subordinating the individual to the team. From 2001 to 2006, the slogan became—was it possible?—even more individualistic: "An Army of One." Although the army hadn't suddenly decided to make obedience optional or to send out strike forces of one, recruiters understood that Millennials liked to *think* of themselves as armies of one. But the bait-and-switch foundered. Cutting the cognitive dissonance between the ads and the realities of army discipline, advertisers fell back to more traditional methods through the "Army Strong" slogan. The individualist refrain still rang—"I am a warrior," "I am an expert and a professional, "I am a guardian

---

[1] Eric Darnell and Tim Johnson. *Antz*. DreamWorks Pictures, 1998.
[2] Klinenberg, 51.
[3] DeLillo, *Underworld*, 275, 796.

© The Author(s) 2019
R. Kramer, *Are We Postmodern Yet?*,
https://doi.org/10.1007/978-3-030-30569-7_4

of freedom and the American way of life," I, I ..."[4]—but recruits were shown that they could only attain their powers through a powerful group. With individualist appeals, the army embraced the ethos of Oprah, on whose show guests explained how to uncage your "inner stripper," "not for your guy—it's about celebrating you!"[5] It would be a sin to choose plastic surgery in order to conform to someone else's ideal of beauty, but it's a cardinal postmodern virtue to let plastic surgery direct you towards "your more authentic self."[6]

The Costs of Postmodern Individualism

Many roads led us to this spot, from Augustine's inward turn, to the Deist notion that God's goodness consists mainly in his benevolence to *us*, to a host of historical factors, among them the Protestant emphasis on spontaneous prayer, congregational discipline, self-scrutiny, and companionate marriage, all tied to a radical shift in Cartesian epistemology on the thinking self. In the wake of these religious and philosophical developments followed new eighteenth-century childrearing practices, an artistic emphasis on originality, the rise of privacy, markets and contracts, voluntary associations, and the valuing of sentiment.[7] Postmodernity extends modernity's developments by imagining the free individual as paramount, even though the structural importance of community has *increased*, not diminished. Because of our socialization, we don't recognize how very many unspoken cultural constraints we still follow,[8] some nearly unconsciously—how to wait in lines, when to smile to defuse conflict, and what bodily distance from others is appropriate. However, although we have strict new rules on many things, from race to gender to disability, and although we have a myriad of new laws on health and safety, we mainly notice the expanding individual freedoms of speech and of sexual expression. We indeed have greater individual freedom from direct police and government intrusion into our private lives, even as greater portions of our lives come under

[4] THE US Army Media Center channel, "THE NEW US ARMY STRONG COMMERCIAL," YouTube, posted 4 April 2009, https://www.youtube.com/watch?v=cq-ZVIZJaI8; Army of One Commercial "Fight Back" - Deuce Four Infantry, posted 4 August 2012, YouTube, https://www.youtube.com/watch?v=H5ySBWOCNnA; *Wikipedia*, "Slogans of the United States Army," https://en.wikipedia.org/wiki/Slogans_of_the_United_States_Army.
[5] Lofton, 103.
[6] Lofton, 125.
[7] C. Taylor, *Sources*, 143, 267, 206.
[8] Heath and Potter, 48–9.

public surveillance. In the West, most of the surveillance that affects us is business-oriented (digital tracking cookies) and self-inflicted (Facebook), not initiated by authoritarian governments or police. *Slate*'s Farhad Manjoo speaks for many people when he admits that he likes the idea of software adjusting itself to fit his tastes.[9]

In a 1970 song, "God," John Lennon bore witness to the decline of grand narratives and collective beliefs in early postmodernity:

> I don't believe in Jesus
> I don't believe in Kennedy
> I don't believe in Buddha

Throughout the song, Lennon cuts adrift a whole series of grand narratives, those collective stories of faith, humanity, science, politics, economics, race, nation, or gender that told us why we should or shouldn't do certain things. More heretically (for the time), he mocked his own celebrity status, saying that he didn't even believe in Beatles. What do you believe in, then, John?

> I just believe in me
> Yoko and me ...[10]

Lennon's congregation of one (or at most one couple) encompassed the so-called "end of metaphysics" and expressed somatic effort (the individual organism doing what's best for its survival and pleasure). Not a faith with enough reach, however, to account for the simple fact that humans live in groups. What Lennon gained in honesty, he lost in terms of commitments, mediation between competing interests, and the tools for maintaining social order.

Eighteen years deeper into the postmodern era, U2 offered, in "God, Part 2," a more self-critical update on individualism:

> Don't believe in excess
> Success is to give
> Don't believe in riches
> But you should see where I live
> I ... I believe in love[11]

---

[9] Morozov, *Save*, 234.

[10] John Lennon, "God," *John Lennon/Plastic Ono Band*, Apple, 1970.

[11] U2, "God, Part 2," *Rattle and Hum*, Island, 1988.

If the song's ethics are traditional—moderation, charity, and love—Bono, nevertheless, implies that simply agreeing with an ethical position doesn't abolish Lipovetsky's "cult of the self,"[12] as the speaker's wild thoughts, Uzi, and cocaine clearly sabotage his beliefs. "You should see where I live": the cult of the individual self appears in the size and organization of our homes, with a bedroom, private TV, and laptop for every person; in free-form dancing and the decline of the scripted dances of the past; in couples writing their own wedding ceremonies. Our communications devices are increasingly individual, and Nokia made big profits by allowing young people to make their ringtones unique at a couple of dollars a pop.[13] By the time of "Mockingbird" (2004), Eminem could promise his daughter that Daddy shared in her prayers, and yet, a few seconds later, without sensing too much discordance, could add to the words of the nursery rhyme that "if that mockingbird don't sing ... Ima break that birdy's neck." [14] And if the diamond ring didn't shine, the jeweller, too, would be in danger of grievous bodily harm. Eminem is joking, but the joke depends on an aggressively high valuation of the self.

The cult of the self also appears in the drive for unique baby names. The same trend that gave us celebrity children such as Blue Ivy Carter (the daughter of Beyoncé and Jay-Z) has made putty of everyday names, turning, in the service of individuality, Jason into to Jayson, Jaysen, Jaycen, Jacen, Jaisen, Jaison, Jasen, Jasin, Jasun, Jace, Jase, and Jayce. Every year in the 1990s and 2000s, hundreds of children, especially girls, were given the name "Unique." It's hard to tell if this somewhat self-defeating trend is tapering off a bit: in the 2010s, there are fewer children being named "Unique,"[15] though *londonmumsmagazine.com* has offered 30 unique ways of spelling it, all the way from Youneek to U'Neeque.[16]

Across North America, the cult of the self invaded educational books such as *I Believe in Me: A Book of Affirmations, 1-2-3 Special Like Me!*, and

---

[12] Lipovetsky, 40.

[13] Maich and George, 82.

[14] Traditional nursery rhyme, with half a line added by Eminem, "Mockingbird," *ENCORE*, Aftermath Entertainment, Shady Records, Interscope Records, 2004.

[15] In 2013, only about 150 babies were named "Unique," down from a high of over 300 in 2009. "Unique," The Name Meaning, 2015, http://www.thenamemeaning.com/unique/.

[16] Michael Schilling, "30 Unique ways to spell the name Unique," 26 March 2014, http://londonmumsmagazine.com/2014/30-unique-ways-spell-name-unique. See Twenge and Campbell, 181–2.

Celebrate Yourself: Six Steps to Building Your Self-Esteem.[17] The schooling of my own daughters included a unit called "I'm a Thumb-Body" (Reader, I encourage you to recite this motto, stretching out your fist, thumb up.) Kenneth Wilson's *Tools for Energized Teaching* (2006) contains many good teaching tips, but it also recommends the following technique for buttering up children in the classroom: "Any person may ask for a standing ovation. The group then gives that person stupendous cheers and applause, and the person demonstrates proud acceptance of the acknowledgement."[18] No achievement, no kind deed necessary. The National Association for Self-Esteem advises, "On the back of a business card or small index card, write out a statement such as 'I like and accept myself just the way I am,' 'I am the master of my destiny,' 'I am somebody, I love myself, I believe in myself.' Carry the card with you. Repeat the statement several times during the day, especially at night before going to bed and after getting up in the morning."[19] An organization such as Artists for Humanity, which is much more broadly focused and which has successfully mentored Boston inner-city youth, nevertheless, runs down the same path. The 95-page resource guide says nothing about learning from earlier artists or traditions, or even about aesthetics.[20] Rather, art is a synonym for the self. The young artists declare, "I could express myself through art and not be judged by it." "AFH is a place where I can be me." "I was able to find myself, and know who I am."[21]

Belief in the self apparently eliminates all obstacles. The rabbit Judy Hopps in *Zootopia* (2016) knows that she can become a police officer in a city of predators if she believes in herself. A largish University of Kansas professor, well aware of her physical limitations, heard her students repeat this mantra, and challenged them: "You're saying that I could be a ballerina?" "Sure," a student responded, "if you really wanted to." Similarly, 24-year-old Rosa's career plans needn't be tempered by reality. She won't follow her mother (an optician) or her father (who travels the world doing ship maintenance): "I knew I wanted to be somewhere that I could grow as a person, but I don't see them growing as individuals."[22]

---

[17] Maich and George, 32–3.

[18] Kenneth Wilson, *Tools for Energized Teaching: Revitalize Instruction with Ease.* Greenwood: Westport, CT, 2006, 76. Wilson also includes the thumb-body advice.

[19] NASE.

[20] Bauerlein, 173.

[21] Artists for Humanity, Impact, "Success Stories: What Do You Love About Artists For Humanity" (video), http://afhboston.org/impact.html, accessed 6 June 2016.

[22] Twenge, *Me*, 78, 80.

Contrast the I-Believe-in-Me approach to the seemingly opposite approach in the traditionalist comments of Rachael Harder, named "Young Alumnus of the Year" by Briercrest College, an evangelical college in Saskatchewan. Harder worked for a market research firm and was in the process of studying why some youth raised in Christian homes chose to leave their faith. She gave a couple of reasons: "One is a misunderstanding of identity. The second is a misunderstanding of right authority ... We have lots of young adults running around engaging in false identity. They're wanting to build a life for themselves rather than inheriting the identity that Christ has already given them."[23]

This alternative approach, bowing to an identity given by tradition, firmly denies that we're postmodern. But traditional, group-oriented identities don't evade the postmodern problem. And it's not just that traditional roles put a straightjacket on those who don't fit for reasons of gender, sexual orientation, temperament, or heterodox beliefs, but that Harder's own context doesn't evade postmodern individualism. Her speech was recorded because, as "Young Alumnus of the Year," she was part of Briercrest's effort (all colleges and universities do this) to attract students by making a momentary "star" out of an individual who has excelled after graduation. Even as she speaks for tradition and communal identity, the young alumna steps into the celebrity spotlight as an expressive individual. Christian identity, she suggests, is truer, more organic than other identities—one need only affirm it to enter it. Yet she also belongs to a market research firm working on behalf of retailers and churches to identify likely customers, to discern their tastes, and then to tailor the advertising and the product to the customer. The process actually exalts the simulated over the organic, and treats the individual as a consumer. It's not that Harder is completely mistaken—those devoted to various faith communities do generally have better life outcomes[24]—but it's naïve to think that we can simply refuse postmodern individualism. The increasing valorization of the individual is proportional to the decline of faith in grand narratives and in the belief that tradition or modernity can solve our ethical problems. But this valorization carries a number of liabilities: self-indulgence, incivility, lack of empathy, a decline in community, and an increase of social distancing.

---

[23] Julie Cole.
[24] C. Smith, 261–75. A fuller discussion of this appears in the faith chapter.

Self-Indulgence

The first liability in postmodern individualism is this tendency to self-indulgence, a privilege formerly restricted to nobility and to the rich. Early Christians gospels emphasized individuals of negligible social importance; Augustine and eventually Protestant Reformers such as the Quakers validated the individual's "inner light"; Dickens showed even orphans rising to high status; and now Oprah preaches that anybody can have it all. Say yes to the dress. At the top of the wage scale, financial executives in the 2000s became the watchword for self-indulgence. They demanded sky-rocketing levels of compensation, the logical reward, they explained, of their companies turning record profits. When profits turned into losses during the Recession of 2007–8, many executives—holding fast the basics of self-esteem—still felt entitled to the same compensation. Yet the 99% have little reason to vaunt their moral superiority over the 1%. Between 1950 and 2000, the size of the typical American home rose from 983 sq. ft. to 2200,[25] not always because people could afford it. Before the Recession of 2007–8, many homebuyers leapt at "Pick a Pay" mortgages, choosing their own special How-I-Feel payment plan, often set *below* the accumulating interest.[26] Some lenders even offered a down payment rate of –2%.[27] They got houses that they felt good about, but, in this negative amortization, their debt increased every time they made a payment. A recession waited in the wings. As recently as the mid-1980s, Americans saved an average of 10% of their earnings, but by the mid-2000s, they had, on average, stopped saving completely,[28] even though 60%, when polled, said that they regretted buying the things that had run them into debt. In Paul Beatty's *The Sellout* (2015), the protagonist, known only by his last name "Me," isn't overly enchanted with his father's racial retooling that produces "Plantation Barbie." In fact, Me has no problems with the original Ken and Barbie, "Because the white people got better accessories." His individualism comes under critique from his friend Hominy who updates "You can't see the forest for the trees" by admonishing Me with "You ain't seeing the plantation for the niggers." Eventually, Me does seem to see an oppressive plantation, as his court case "*Me v. the United States of America*" suggests.[29]

[25] Klinenberg, 49.
[26] Packer, 193.
[27] Twenge and Campbell, 129.
[28] Pozner, 144.
[29] Beatty, 35, 80, 21.

:ators have contributed to the cult of the self by blaming bad
ur, crime, and poor academic performance on low self-esteem.
Like Oprah, they hoped to start a virtuous cycle: plant self-esteem, creating better behaviour and higher achievement, bringing more self-esteem,
leading to even better behaviour and achievement. As hoped, self-esteem
rose.[30] But it didn't improve academic performance or work performance.
Low self-esteem is a risk factor for suicide, depression, teen pregnancy, and
being bullied, but it doesn't lessen cheating, crime, violence, juvenile
delinquency, welfare dependency, or drug and alcohol abuse.[31] Although
US students in the 2000s missed more classes, felt greater boredom in
class, and did less homework, twice as many got an A average than in the
1960s and 1970s.[32] Far more beneficial than self-*esteem* is self-*control*,
which limits self-indulgence without necessarily destroying individualism.

Faith can counter many kinds of self-indulgence, but some of the most
popular pastors and artists have chosen to surf the self-esteem wave. Joel
Osteen, pastor of Houston's Lakewood Church, the largest church in the
US, explains how to set aside self-indulgence—by praising others, apolo-
gizing, building better relationships—yet he also preaches self-esteem: "If
you don't love yourself, you're not going to be able to love others"; "God
didn't create you to be average"; and "To win is to honor God."[33] Many
of the songs sung in evangelical churches orbit around the self. Talented
singer Chris Tomlin's "Whom Shall I Fear (The God of Angel Armies)"
moves from the common (if hard-to-swallow) trope of God as a good
buddy towards a self-centred reinterpretation of Isaiah 54:

> The God of angel armies
> Is always by my side …
> And nothing formed against me shall stand.

Whereas in the gospel of *Matthew* Jesus refuses to call down angel hosts in
Gethsemane, nowadays the angels are primed for war on my behalf.

[30] The average college student in the mid-1990s had higher self-esteem than 86% (for
men) and 71% (for women) of those in 1968. Self-esteem in children declined during the
1970s, a finding that Twenge blames on divorce, the economy, crime increases, and promiscuity. After 1980, the self-esteem of Generation X and Millennials rose, and by the mid-
1990s, children's self-esteem rose to pre-1970 levels even though divorce rates remained
high and "the kid-friendly stability of the 1950s and early 1960s" didn't return (Twenge,
Me, 52–3).
[31] Maich and George, 37.
[32] Twenge and Campbell, 84; Maich and George, 31, 37; Twenge, *iGen*, 31.
[33] Twenge and Campbell, 248.

Civility

Another predictable result of postmodern self-indulgence generally, and of self-esteem particularly, has been a decline in the need for social approval. Some of Twenge's interview subjects are charmingly naïve in this regard. Maria, 20, says, "It doesn't matter what other people think … What really matters is how I perceive myself. The real person I need to please is myself."[34] Although we angle for Facebook "Likes," the approval is requested for images of social status, not for behaviour. Researchers found that college students in 2001 gave more individualistic survey responses compared to students in 1958, whose responses skewed towards answers that were seen as socially desirable. The upside may be less herd pressure on outsiders; the downside is that we care less about other people, and lean towards How-I-Feel moral choices. Twenge argues that the need for social approval bottomed out in the late 1970s and early 1980s, but her own studies show declines even in later years.[35] In the 2010s, to blurt the phrase "Fuck her right in the pussy" became a trending, supposedly funny, way to disrupt media interviews on the street. Toronto CityNews reporter Shauna Hunt said, "It happens daily, sometimes numerous times a day, depending on the scenario." Even sober men and ten-year-olds yell it.[36] If the *individual* is the measure, then there is no real way to speak of decorum as a social good.

The advent of social media has only accelerated this trend. People who post web comments often take great pleasure in anti-social self-expression, and the Internet can make manners seem superfluous, since the social costs accompanying face-to-face rudeness often don't apply on the Internet.[37] One can see this in the online argument about the conclusion of the spy film *Kingsman: The Secret Service* (2014), where the Swedish princess promises that if the hero Eggsy frees her from her prison cell and saves the world, she'll let him penetrate her anally. Some fans complained, civilly, that the ending was crude and sexist. Those who liked the scene, however, usually took a less well-mannered line:

[34] Twenge, *Me*, 37.
[35] Twenge, *Me*, 42.
[36] Shauna Hunt (interview), "Come on, again? *Again?*" *Maclean's*, 1 June 2015, 38. "Fired Hydro One employee apologizes to Shauna Hunt," News 1130, 15 May 2015, http://www.news1130.com/2015/05/15/fired-hydro-one-employee-apologizes-to-shauna-hunt/.
[37] Hood, 269, 187.

Peter: "People knows whats best for themselves and they don't need puritanical
shits like yourself telling them what to do" [sic].

If how I *feel* determines my moral stance, then my manners, no matter how rude, will be, by definition, an honest expression of my feelings. In Marisha Pessl's *Special Topics in Calamity Physics* (2006), a high school teacher, Hannah, whose attitudes were formed in the counter-cultural 1960s, is deeply suspicious of conformity. What are manners but a kind of conformity? On a camping trip, she encourages the protagonist Blue and her classmates to shout out anything, from *"Fuck you!"* to *"Be–be true to yourself!"* and she only reprimands one boy, who, unaware of the shamefulness of his words, had shouted, *"Behave yourself!"*

Decline of Empathy

With self-indulgence rising, and with our feelings determining our manners, it's not a shock that empathy seems to be declining in the postmodern era. Examining the period between 1979 and 2009, Sara Konrath et al. found a decline in empathy among American college students, with the greatest decline coming after 2000. She found no decline in the ability to *identify* with fictional characters. What declined was "Perspective Taking" (the ability to imagine another's point of view) and "Empathic Concern" (the feelings of sympathy for another's misfortunes).[38] But isn't identifying with fictional characters the same thing as imagining another's point of view? Sometimes. Literature is, indeed, an empathy technology,[39] as long as the focus isn't just on our own response. A longitudinal study that revisited children after 26 years found several factors correlating with higher empathy: fathers took part in child-care, mothers allowed dependent behaviour, mothers controlled their own aggression as children, and mothers were happy in their roles.[40] On the negative side, we can predict that too much postmodern self-indulgence by parents—increased screen time, more emphasis on individual freedom, a sense that How-I-Feel should determine my response to others—will decrease empathy. Alan Kirby argues that despite the "feminine" empathy and emotivism valued

[38] Konrath et al., 185, 187.
[39] Pinker, *Better*, 478.
[40] Konrath et al., 189.

by our culture, such "digimodern" devices as iPods and cellphones isolate us in private worlds that, in their extreme forms, approach "masculine" autism.[41]

Lack of Larger Commitments Beyond the Self

Some important historical trends do run counter to the decline in empathy: the growing importance of human and animal rights, the increase in volunteering, and the decline in crime. However, an upshot of I-Believe-in-Me is the decline of commitments beyond the self. As Putnam has shown, altruistic *attitudes* play a much smaller role in getting people to volunteer or donate than does *involvement* in social networks. "Simply being *asked* to give is a powerful stimulus to volunteering and philanthropy." The most common reason why people join a group or activity is that someone asks them to.[42] The less people are committed to groups, the less likely it is that they will be asked. The irony is that in the long run only larger commitments can sustain *individual* rights.

In this way, we are indeed postmodern. Because of our individualism, whether counter-cultural or simply hedonistic, we have great difficulty with certain "collective action problems" such as global warming.[43] Many of the profound group goods arising out of the turmoil of the 1960s—gay rights, racial equality, equality for women, for example—mesh well with individualism. I commit to a group, take part in protests, and make sacrifices very willingly when the rights gained by the group are my gains too. Stopping global warming must be approached at a similar institutional level; but, unlike asserting new rights, stopping global warming will *limit*, not expand, my freedoms and pleasures. Ulrich Beck describes us as "easy-coming, easy-going, easy-partying and easy-parting neo-tribes" on the lookout for "ever new, ever more intensive sensations."[44] We may display the correct political attitude, but balk at the tedious but important work of political organizing.[45]

---

[41] Kirby, *Digimodernism*, 232.
[42] Putnam, 121–2.
[43] Heath and Potter, 75.
[44] Bech, 372.
[45] Heath and Potter, 62.

Visiting the *Canadian Idol* tryouts, Hal Niedzviecki repeatedly heard the same story from contestants: I'm special; I'm going to become a star; soon I'll be liberated from everyday life.[46] Yet Canadians also saw a huge jump in anti-depressant prescriptions, marking the gap between the high expectations and the low rate of fulfilment.[47] After spending most of *Hello: I'm Special* cataloguing the delusions, the vanities, the solipsism of focusing on the self, Niedzviecki arrives at a strangely selfish conclusion: "We must learn to take an active role in our own sublimated desires. We can no longer afford to settle for anything less than what we have been promised," which turns out to have been individual *power*.[48] Hard upon mocking a North American culture in which nobody identifies with the "system," and everybody is apparently a nonconformist, Niedzviecki discovers that the solution is a more effective individualist rebellion.

Social Distancing

With decreased social commitments, by the mid-2000s Americans were four times more likely to call themselves lonely than in 1957.[49] Nevertheless, since 2005, the most common type of American household (28%) has consisted of one person living alone.[50] By the 2008 census, 31 million Americans were living alone,[51] and the number has been rising. The percentage is higher in Canada, and rises to an astonishing 39–47% in Germany and the Scandinavian countries, with Britain the first country to appoint a Minister of Loneliness. In one sense, living alone is "a collective achievement"—people in developed nations have attained this freedom, while people in poor nations aspire to it. Indeed, the global rate is growing, led by China and India.[52] However, according to Putnam's extensive evidence, close friendships have declined, and entertaining friends at home declined by almost 50% between the 1970s and late 1990s.[53] Perhaps, like Lars

---

[46] Niedzviecki, *Special*, 62–5.

[47] Prescriptions jumped 95% between 1988 and 2002. Niedzviecki, *Special*, 99.

[48] Niedzviecki, *Special*, 234.

[49] Twenge, *Me*, 110.

[50] Klinenberg, 5. In the US between 1970 and the mid-2000s, single-person households of 15- to 24-year-olds doubled, while those of 25- to 34-year-olds tripled (Twenge, *Me*, 114).

[51] Pew, Decline, 109.

[52] Klinenberg, n.p., 10, 212. DePaulo, 221–2.

[53] Putnam, 98.

Lindstrom in *Lars and the Real Girl* (2007), we prefer robotic companions and sex dolls. There is already a robotic nurse prototype, called Flo, and the French company Robosoft has made a robotic companion called Kompaï.[54]

Claude Fischer disputes Putnam's thesis about the decline of togetherness, arguing that electronic ties enhance connectedness generally,[55] and (more plausibly) that social media specifically enhance the ties of people who are already close. Susan Pinker counters that to physically touch fewer people and to make less eye contact deprives us of the pleasurable oxytocin release that binds us in our personal commitments and that has done so among primates for 60 million years.[56] Often, living alone is not an attainment but a fate. For some, like Paul alone in New York's Chinatown, the great challenge is to fill all the empty hours. Helen, middle-aged in Greenwich Village, laments, "Ten thousand mornings I wake up and just go through the day, and the aloneness is like a cubic force in me ... It's dark."[57]

As cable TV and the Internet make entertainment options more individualized,[58] we isolate ourselves even further. Don DeLillo already understood this in *Underworld*, where Nick's wife wants to watch TV alone because "another's presence screws up ... the integrated company of the box."[59] In Douglas Coupland's *Generation A* the fictional drug Solon is, arguably, a symbol for the media environment. One character says, "You stop caring about the tribe." Another explains, "You live in a constant present. It makes life more intense. You're not needy. You don't stress about things. You can take people or leave them."[60] Putnam has argued that factors such as the huge increase in screen time have contributed significantly to the growing unhappiness of people under 55 since the 1940s and 1950s. Among the Amish, who spend much less time alone with television and other media, depression is much lower, even though the rates of other mental illnesses are comparable to those of the general population.[61] One need not advocate an Amish lifestyle to argue that too much time alone, even if we're accessing social networks, is bad for the individual.

[54] Klinenberg, 192, 195.
[55] Fischer, 95–6.
[56] Susan Pinker, *Village*, 37, 65.
[57] Klinenberg, 178, 99.
[58] Putnam, 216.
[59] DeLillo, *Underworld*, 116.
[60] Coupland, *Generation*, 146, 135.
[61] Putnam, 263–5.

Pleasure

Yet I-Believe-in-Me also results in more pleasure accruing to the individual. Increases in pornography, obesity rates, [62] consumer spending,[63] and even school grades all suggest that we postmoderns are increasingly kowtowing to our desires. The year 2005 was a watershed year: for the first time since the Depression of the 1930s, Americans outspent their paycheques.[64] Predatory banks couldn't have jump-started the Recession of 2007–8 without the individual's sense of entitlement to pleasure. After borrowing $110,000 to build a house in a subdivision near Tampa Bay, Ron and Jennifer Formosa refinanced, then took out an equity loan for a new roof, refinanced again to pay off their cars, a new patio, and a new boat. They spent the rest on cruises and trips to Disney World with their children.[65] They were far from alone. By 2007 average credit card debts tripled those in 1990, rising to over $9000 per account, with debts particularly high for those aged 25–35.[66] Unearned pleasure is also a driving force behind school grades. In 1968, 18% of American college freshmen reported an "A" average in high school. Between 1968 and 2004, their time spent studying and therefore their SAT scores decreased, yet by the end of that period, almost half were reporting A's.[67] In one way, the decreasing cost of A's makes perfect sense. If the student is a consumer, teachers are obliged to make the customer happy.

Many films, including, for example, *American Beauty* (1999), *Runaway Bride* (1999), and Anthony Minghella's 1996 screen adaptation of *The English Patient*, celebrate the notion that our primary allegiance ought to be to our self-actualization and pleasure. *What Just Happened* (2008) briefly satirizes this self-actualization when divorced movie producer Ben (Robert DeNiro) complains to movie writer Scott Solomon (Stanley Tucci):

---

[62] McGonigal, 185. Ferguson, *Colossus* 295. Twenge and Campbell, 174. According to the Center for Disease Control, those in the 95th percentile of weight rose from 10.6% to 13.7%, while those in the 85th percentile rose from 14.1% to 16.6% (CDC 2013 survey).

[63] Ferguson, *Colossus* 268.

[64] Twenge and Campbell, 124; Roberts, 64.

[65] Packer, 193–4.

[66] Twenge and Campbell, 124; Roberts, 64; Barber, 137; CreditCards.com press release, "Taking Charge: America's Relationship with Credit Cards," 6 June 2007, http://www.creditcards.com/press-releases/Taking-Charge-Americas-Relationship-with-Credit-Cards-June-06.pdf.

[67] Twenge, *Me*, 62–3.

Ben: You're seeing my ex-wife.
Scott: What does that matter?
Ben: You're married.
Scott: What does that matter? I'm not happy.

We do occasionally see works such as Ian McEwan's *On Chesil Beach* (2007), where the newly married Edward's valuing of his desires against Florence's near-asexuality ends in tragedy, as he drives her away. An aching sense of loss appears as he slowly recognizes that love would have offered more than pleasure. Even when extra-curricular desires are punished, as in *Sideways* (2004) and *Mulholland Drive* (2001), or satirized, morality still sits like a wallflower beside gorgeous desire. The husband of the beautiful Mrs. Riorden in Peter Unwin's story "Halloween" is "a premature drunk who would rather watch naked women squirm around in a vat of Jell-O instead of reading *The Berenstein Bears* to his children."[68] In the wake of such ambivalence, schooled in self-actualization and pluralism, younger generations have become more accepting of even violent forms of pornography. Interviewing teenagers, MIT psychologist Sherry Turkle found them able to articulate sensible rules about avoiding AIDS and pregnancy, yet on the inter-relational and philosophical side, they had difficulty explaining what sort of sexual conduct is appropriate.[69]

CASE STUDY: THE NOVELS OF DAVID FOSTER WALLACE

One story of the desiring postmodern individual is that of talented and troubled American novelist David Foster Wallace, who examined individual freedom and the pursuit of pleasure in brutal and human detail in his epoch-expressing, 1079-page novel *Infinite Jest* (1997). At times, he attributed the novel's themes to his generation. He sensed a sadness in people under 45: "It has to do with pleasure and achievement and entertainment. And a kind of emptiness at the heart of what they thought was going on." At other times, Wallace grew more personal. Speaking about the origin of *Infinite Jest* after an extended dry period in the early 1990s, during which he wrote very little apart from his essay on TV, he said, "I decided that maybe being really sad, and really sort of directionless, wasn't just that I was fucked up … Maybe it was *interesting* in a way … I just had

---

[68] Unwin, *Life*, 28.
[69] Turkle, 308.

so many friends, who went through terrible times exactly when I did."
Wallace, the critic of America's entertainment addiction, read a lot as a
child, but also watched "*hellacious* amounts of television," calling it his
primary addiction. Individual freedom was a factor in his directionlessness
and addictions. His parents were "really '60s parents," who not only
didn't push their children into particular roles or jobs, but also consciously
avoided giving overt direction.[70] This seems like a considerate thing to do,
and Wallace thanks them for it. Yet, if a society "idolizes self-fulfillment"[71]
without setting that fulfilment inside a larger meaningful story, one result,
according to Bauman, is that greater pressure falls on the self to supply all
the meaning.[72] Marijuana helped with some of Wallace's anxieties, but he
became addicted and more distanced from other people. After he received
his MFA from Arizona and taught at Amherst in the late 1980s, Wallace
was quite lonely, watching TV 6–8 hours a day, drinking, doing drugs.[73]
Things grew more difficult after his younger sister got married, because
he, too, wanted to marry and have children.[74]

It's tempting to treat Wallace's 2008 suicide as an exemplum of the
failings of postmodern culture. We can't do that: his psychological difficulties began when he was a child, long before he encountered the problems of desire, the pursuit of happiness, and the addictions that *Infinite
Jest* examines. By the time Wallace was in his 20s, he had already been
under suicide watch in Boston and had been treated with electroconvul-
sive shocks.[75] Although he blamed himself, calling his life in 1996 "pretty
selfish" and impulsive,[76] Wallace's self-diagnosis doesn't sufficiently take
mental illness into account. But neither can we declare postmodernity
innocent in his death. Since so many readers declared that *Infinite Jest*
expressed their experience, the novel's reception, coupled with the its
unarguable artistic and cultural depth, prevents us from shrugging off
Wallace's critique of the individualized pursuit of pleasure or his descrip-

---

[70] Lipsky, 274, 237, 51, 144, 52. Wallace's emphasis.

[71] Lipovetsky, 37.

[72] Bauman, *Discontents*, 183.

[73] Max, 104.

[74] Lipsky, 251. Max, 197.

[75] Lipsky 57, 147; Tim Adams, "Karen Green: 'David Foster Wallace's suicide turned him
into a celebrity writer dude,'" *Observer*, 10 April 2011. http://www.guardian.co.uk/
books/2011/apr/10/karen-green-david-foster-wallace-interview.

[76] Lipsky, 293.

tion of "a real feeling of deprivation" when his generation wasn't experiencing pleasure.[77]

Infinite Jest tries to imagine ways out of the impasse of postmodern individualist desire. In the 1990s, Wallace (in his 30s) realized that his promiscuity and his attempt to always make different women fall in love with him by pretending to care made him a lot like "the people selling Tide."[78] The selfishness Wallace despised in himself appears metaphorically and in concentrated form in Orin Incandenza—whose girlfriend-of-the-week is often called "the subject"—as well as in his brother Hal, who is slowly imploding because of his psychological problems, compounded by a marijuana addiction. Hal calls marijuana "Bob Hope," while sobriety, when Hal "Abandoned All Hope," is nothing short of Dante's hell.[79] Addictions abound in the novel: Joelle van Dyne to crack, the father James Incandenza to Wild Turkey whiskey, the Saudi Minister of Home Entertainment to Toblerone, and his medical attaché to an entertainment cartridge so pleasurable that he *never* stops watching. Ken Erdedy switches entertainment cartridges every few seconds: "The moment he recognized what exactly was on one cartridge he had a strong anxious feeling that there was something more entertaining on another cartridge."[80] He is Buridan's Ass at the dawn of the Internet, though Tinder and other swiping apps are still a decade and a half away.

Hal tries to find a Narcotics Anonymous meeting, but instead stumbles upon a group-counselling session in which the clients learn therapeutic techniques sanctified by postmodern individualism. Clients give rein to their non-drugged "Inner Infant." Rather than signs of recovery, we see tantrums and crawling,[81] which meshes well with the novel's larger consumer culture: in the Year of the Depends Adult Undergarment, not only have naming rights to Anno Domini been sold to commercial interests—the novel calls this "subsidized time"—but, in a great coup of product placement, the Statue of Liberty wears a diaper. In interviews, Wallace turned to high school as a metaphor for the postmodern era: "the party gets louder and louder, and you run out of drugs … and you gradually start wishing your parents would come back and restore some fucking order in your house."[82]

---

[77] Wiley, 11, 13.
[78] Max, 234.
[79] Wallace, *Infinite*, 796.
[80] Wallace, *Infinite*, 26.
[81] Wallace, *Infinite*, 800–1, 806–8.
[82] McCaffery interview in Daverman 2.

Given his critique of the pleasure-seeking individual, one might expect
Wallace to unequivocally affirm tradition and self-sacrifice. Not necessarily
so, and for postmodern reasons. Marathe, a Québécois character who
insists that pleasure can't form the basis for a morality,[83] argues against the
American government agent Steeply, who defends the pursuit of happiness. Steeply seems to lose. Yet the fact that Marathe is member of the
Wheelchair Assassins somewhat taints his victory. Similar ironies surround
Gerhardt Schtitt, the too-German head coach at the Enfield Tennis
Academy, who wants his junior athletes "to sacrifice the hot narrow imperatives of the Self ... to the larger imperatives of the team (OK, the State)
and a set of delimiting rules (OK, the Law)." For the postmodern writer,
a team or state *can't* carry transcendent meaning. "What's the difference,"
the third brother, Mario Incandenza, silently and astutely asks in response
to Schtitt, "between tennis and suicide?" We also know that Schtitt, who
supposedly wants to demote the self, had to resign his previous position
"because of an unfortunate incident involving a riding crop."[84] The closest
that Wallace gets in the novel to a way out of the impasse created by How-
I-Feel and I-Believe-in-Me is in the co-protagonist Don Gately's self-
limiting commitment to Alcoholics Anonymous. Hal's difficulties are
heightened by a lack of larger commitments, while Gately's recovery seems
predicated on his commitment to AA, its grand narrative of a vague faith
in God, impulse control, healing, and Gately's tough-love parental concern for the well-being of the Ennett House inmates.

Wallace's final novel, *The Pale King*, incomplete at his suicide, turns to
the problem of how to limit adolescent pleasure in favour of an admittedly
more boring adult life. Wallace challenged himself "To be, in a word,
unboreable," and two characters—Chris Fogle and Shane Drinion—point
the way. Fogle seeks a way out of his "wasteoid" life of TV and drugs,
eventually disciplining himself into a career as an accountant, and despite
Fogle's verbose and off-putting manner, he seems to have come to some
form of enlightenment. Fellow-accountant Drinion is even more blessed
(or perhaps weird). He says, "Almost anything you pay close, direct attention to becomes interesting." In an age and among a species tormented by
emotional manipulation, Drinion's even-keeled telling of the simple truth
in a conversation full of potential emotional landmines bespeaks his sanity.

[83] Wallace, *Infinite*, 428.
[84] Wallace, *Infinite*, 82–4, 79.

He intends neither to *make* people uncomfortable nor to *stop* them from being uncomfortable. When he is engrossed in a matter, Drinion levitates slightly, and one night he is seen in the IRS office "floating upside down over his desk." In his notes to the novel, Wallace was more direct: "Drinion is *happy*. Ability to pay attention."[85] Wallace corresponded with Stephen Lacy, who called the tax code postmodern because it was "relativistic and constructed of words." But Wallace treats the code as a necessary structure, something closely tied to "ethics and civics and consent of the governed."[86] The very boredom of the code recommends it, signalling that to review a tax return is to engage in an adult task, to forgo entertainment, and instead to discipline oneself to the necessary.

A failure, William Deresiewicz justly calls *The Pale King*. Although he admits that Wallace may have been the best mind of their (late-Boomer) generation, Deresiewicz isn't ready to agree that the "thorny path of solitary asceticism" is the road to adulthood. To see adulthood as boring is still to look through adolescent eyes, and the part of the story that Wallace could never finish, Deresiewicz says, was "the one where we all grow up."[87] Wallace's biographer, D.T. Max, on the other hand, considers the novel *too* grown up: "It had to show people a way to insulate themselves from the toxic fanaticism of American life. It had to be emotionally engaged and morally sound, and to dramatize boredom without being too entertaining. And it had to sidestep the point that the kind of personality that conferred grace was the opposite of Wallace's own … He saw that he could not write it because he could not himself tune out the noise of modern life."[88] Although Deresiewicz won't concede that "the congregation of AA"[89] in *Infinite Jest* provides the sort of answer that *The Pale King* lacks, I would argue that Wallace, through Gately, did imagine a mature, intriguing adulthood. But it's fair to say that instead of resting in adult consolations, *Infinite Jest* accepts the plague of self-conscious individualism. Wallace tried to write his way out of the burden of postmodern individualism. In Gately, he did. In Hal, he purposely didn't. In *The Pale King*, he tried to and failed.

[85] Wallace, *Pale*, 437–8, 456, 485, 546.
[86] Max, 292.
[87] Deresiewicz.
[88] Max, 292.
[89] Deresiewicz.

The Goods and Limits of Postmodern Individualism

Are we postmodern yet? It would seem so, because it wasn't just Wallace but Boomers and succeeding generations who embarked on a more individualized quest for pleasure. Still, there are reasons to defend postmodern individualism, despite its pitfalls, against the alternative of a strongly duty-bound existence. Firstly, postmodern individual freedoms—continuing Augustine's, the Reformation's, and Romanticism's turn towards the interior—have limited the oppression of the state and other powerful social institutions. Secondly, some have argued that gratification of desire is inherently a good thing. Thirdly, despite the increase of self-indulgence and pleasure in some areas of our lives, in other areas self-control and agency have increased.

Freedom: Completing the Work of Modernity

Postmodern individualism extends the work of modernist demythologizing by weakening our obligations to kin, tribe, and faith community, and by supporting the postcolonial resistance to the oppression of empires. Constitutions and other social contracts, invented in early modernity, slowly elevated the rights of the individual. Because big-tent groups such as the nation (in the eighteenth century) and class (in the nineteenth century) crossed sectarian boundaries, they were often allied with modernity, but the big-tent community can easily regress into a new form of tribe. Signal examples are Nazi Germany and Pol Pot's Cambodia, but every strong identification—including Americanism—runs the same risk, and the concept of citizenship presumes a supra-tribal tribe: citizens are in; others are out. Postmodern expansions of individual human rights resisted the larger tribalism of nation, race, and faith, yet, paradoxically, because of its mistrust of rationalism and because of imperialist abuses, postmodernity often celebrated weaker postcolonial manifestations of tribalism via "local knowledges."

Must the community and its local knowledge be emasculated? Yes. If we agree that human rights apply to citizen and non-citizen alike, then we're postmodern enough to recognize that, to a degree, the nation, tribe, and race must be emasculated in favour of the individual, even if the cost is sometimes a lack of larger commitments. Evolution *hasn't* wired us for specific categories such as race, since experiments have shown that, for example, team membership overrides race membership. But we *are* wired to treat fellow group members better than outsiders, a groupishness that can take many forms, convincing us to overvalue our race, nation, church, political party, team, and even (as experiments have shown) blue-eyed children over brown-eyed.[90] However, the relative decline of war, not just in the West but especially there, could not have happened without many legislated limits on group oppressions that were once considered legitimate expressions of community. The American state, after the protests of the 1960s, eventually exited the Vietnam War, unable to ignore "casualty dread," as individualist Americans became less and less willing to sacrifice themselves, their sons, and their daughters for dubious national goals.[91] In other Western nations, casualty dread was even more pronounced. When the US called for an invasion of Iraq in 2003, only Britain and Spain showed up, with Spain exiting as soon as was polite. Canada, Germany, and France all declined the American invitation. Even support for the War in Afghanistan, which began with a broad coalition and had UN approval, quickly dwindled. Casualty dread doesn't necessarily prohibit bombing raids and drone attacks, but it does make us sensitive to civilian casualties, sometimes even on the enemy side.

Another important good of postmodern individualism is the individual's increased control over his or her body. Although Lynn Hunt neglects the crucial role of the English Levellers in the seventeenth century, she has shown how the notion of "human rights" was developed in the eighteenth century through the civilizing process, which pressured people to keep their bodily excretions to themselves; through silent appreciation of music and theatre, which interiorized emotional response; through portraiture, which gave dignity to individuals of lesser social importance; through novels, which focussed on individuality, creating empathy outside of communal lines; and through arguments against torture, arguments that treated the individual body, not the community, as sacred.[92] In the postmodern era, courts in Canada have been particularly likely to rule against parliament when it conflicts with individual rights, for example, in the right of heroin addicts to use a safe injection site at a Vancouver clinic,[93] in Lou-Gehrig's-disease-sufferer Gloria Taylor's request for physician-assisted

[90] Greene, 52–4; Hood, 193–4.

[91] Pinker, *Better*, 264.

[92] See Hunt, Chapters 1 and 2. On the Levellers, see David Williams, *Milton's*, especially 3–8.

[93] Sniderman, 18.

death, and in the striking down of a number of prostitution laws because they led to a secrecy that threatened the prostitutes' security of person.

Placing a premium on individual freedoms correlates with a decline in domestic violence against women; countries where community interests override individual rights still have higher rates of violence than do "individualistic" countries.[94] Children, based on their rights as autonomous individuals and even against the wishes of some parents, have been sent to school, removed from abusive homes, given vaccinations, given blood transfusions, protected from female circumcision, and protected from most forms of corporal punishment.[95] These are all progressive features of I-Believe-in-Me.

BlyssPluss

Such insistence upon basic individual freedom from community oppression is no longer controversial even among traditionalists, but a second claim, that the freeing of individual desire is necessary and good,[96] has proved more controversial. Already in 1961, Levinas had insisted that egoism isn't some shadow overlaying true being, but that, despite our group commitments, "egoism is life ... the very pulsation of the I." It's what withstands totalization (and, we could add, totalitarianism). According to Levinas, "subjectivity originates in the independence and sovereignty of enjoyment."[97] If this is the case, individualism and desire can deliver not only the goods, but also "The Good." "The age of emptiness has dawned, but 'without tragedy or apocalypse,'" announces Lipovetsky, referring to the moment at which we take the institutional brakes off self-fulfilment and let people chase their own desires, no matter how frivolous: "Hypermodern individuals are both better informed and more de-structured ... more adult and more unstable, less ideological and more in thrall to changing fashions, more open and more easy to influence, more critical and more superficial, more skeptical and less profound."[98] Would you rather hear a fireside Anansi tale or watch a superhero movie? In popular Christian churches, Jesus's parables now

---

[94] Pinker, *Better*, 414.
[95] Pinker, *Better*, 437.
[96] Best and Kellner, *Turn*, 6.
[97] Levinas, 57, 175, 113–14.
[98] Charles in Lipovetsky, 8–10, 12.

compete with movie clips and concert-style music. We may lament the advent of Wolverine as the new messiah, but we want our desires "on constant display."[99]

Despite critiques offered by Jameson, Bourdieu, Bauman, and other leftist critics, the evidence suggests that we *like* the superficial interplay of new fashions, new products, and new experiences much more than the dull work of safeguarding freedoms or reining in the corporate domination of government. Because the primitive dopamine reward system arose precisely to get us to discount the future and act on our pleasures (prioritizing food acquisition and reproductive success), it's too simple to speak of our desires being "hijacked" by advertisers. In the uproar about New York mayor Michael Bloomberg's 2013 attempt to ban super-size high-calorie soft drinks in certain venues, many voices cried against the "nanny state" and in favour of individual consumer freedom. Nevertheless, Bloomberg's defence of "choice architecture" and "soft paternalism" has a strong moral basis not only in reducing social costs, but also in the welfare of *individuals*,[100] as laws enforcing motorcycle helmets and high taxes on smoking have shown. Negative amortization loans, payday loans, and Americans' $650 billion in high-interest credit card debt all reveal the lack of self-control, the individual's eagerness to discount the future in favour of pleasure now. In response, the "nanny" state acts as a prefrontal cortex against our dopamine reward systems, limiting interest rates and offering food vouchers instead of money to low-income people as "a rational self-binding strategy."[101]

Although emancipated desire and non-conformity have value in the quest for individual freedom, they are fabulously ill-equipped to solve the problem of living in groups. Some of the trade-offs posited by the prefrontal cortex—heaven, for example, or a socialist utopia—are falling by the wayside, so some of the associated self-control is failing too. Contra Lipovetsky, theologian David Bentley Hart sees a darker calculus, in which postmodernist thinkers deny metaphysical categories, discover that desire motivates all human action, and then treat the desiring self as if it were a transcendent metaphysical category.[102] Hart has a point. As with our larger

---

[99] McGonigal, 122.

[100] Sunstein, 4, 52.

[101] Heath, *Economics*, 260–76.

[102] Says Hart, postmodern thinkers call this self "event rather than substance" but that by no means lessens its transcendent power (Hart, 111).

commitments, our ability to place limits on ourselves—to delay gratification, to empathize, and to commit to larger social goals—is necessary not only to sustain communities, but to sustain *individual* freedom.

Against Hart's warning, however, we would expect humans, given our evolutionary history, to become adept at making sophisticated trade-offs between the pleasure/reward centres in our brains and the prefrontal cortex's longer-term calculations. And indeed, alongside the evidence of increasing desire and gratification are trends that pull in a less worrisome direction. Between 1991 and 2015, fighting, drinking, drinking and driving, car accidents, traffic tickets, and smoking have decreased among American high school students, while marijuana use was up (though lower than in the 1970s).[103] Crime is down, and more students graduate from high school.[104] The rate of those who had intercourse before age 13 was almost cut in half from over 10%, while the percentage of high school students engaging in sexual intercourse dropped somewhat from 54% in 1991 to under 47% in 2013, possibly due to the Internet's greater attraction. Condom use rose from under half in 1991 to 63% in 2003, then dropped slightly by 2013.[105] Such results and feelings aren't an expression of self-denial, since those with one sexual partner were happier than those with no partners or those with multiple partners.[106] On a variety of fronts, we can still speak with Norbert Elias of a civilizing process and with Charles Taylor of a modern "buffered self," as we exert greater control over our impulses, while still satisfying our desires.[107]

* * *

Broadly aware of both the costs and goods of individualism, Turkish Nobel laureate Orhan Pamuk introduces his novel *My Name Is Red* (1998) by quoting a fifteenth-century Persian historian, who said that "the greatest sin of the Devil was to say 'I.'" The miniaturists of 1590s Istanbul, in this postmodern novel, are both inspired and appalled by the advent of Frankish (i.e. Renaissance) portraiture, in which "even a poor foolish tai-

[103] CDC. Twenge, *iGen*, 144–50.
[104] Twenge, *Me*, 109.
[105] CDC. The percentage of those who had intercourse with four or more persons during their lives declined slightly from 18.7% to 15%, as did the percentage of the sexually active, from 37.5% to 34%.
[106] Wheelan, 183.
[107] Taylor, *Secular*, 33, 38, 84.

lor" may be convinced "that he's not an ordinary simpleton, but an extraordinary man." Nowadays, the Renaissance's nascent I-Believe-in-Me flowers as blogs and as comment sections of Internet pages. In Pamuk's genealogy of modernity, even Allah does not escape blame, as Satan reminds Him, "Was it not You who instilled man with pride by making the angels bow before him? Now they regard themselves as Your angels were made to regard them; men are worshipping themselves, placing themselves at the center of the world … This narcissism will end in their forgetting you entirely. And I'm the one who will be blamed."[108]

The cunning narrator of *My Name Is Red* understands that his killing of two people cannot be separated from his self-affirming portrait. He says, "I suspect that I did away with them so I could make this picture. But now the isolation I feel terrifies me."[109] Similarly, Bauman notices how the individual, not the larger group, has in our era become responsible for human failure and success, for joy and suffering—thus privatizing moral action and letting governments off the hook.[110] Twenge, looking at the increase of anti-depressant use and the apparent increase in anxiety, comes to a similar conclusion, arguing that our unparalleled freedoms put a great deal of pressure on the individual.[111] The larger picture is ambiguous. In 2006, more than three-quarters of young American adults rated their lives as excellent or good, and claimed to be happy. Those who feel that their individual decisions (not outside forces) determine their fates cope better with stress, feel less depressed or anxious, and perform better in school. Yet, paradoxically, depression and loneliness have increased over the same period that the sense of agency increased.[112]

Growing individualism is one of the salient features of the contemporary era, and is a trend that seems unlikely to abate anytime soon. The ability to take full charge of one's body and to act on one's desires is deeply implicated in our sense that we cannot return to ethical absolutes. In this way, we are profoundly postmodern. Our ethical and political negotiations will limit or contain our individualism, but our ability to sustain a community in the teeth of I-Believe-in-Me is not certain, and it will also depend on how we assimilate the new cyber-technologies, a question to which we now turn.

[108] Pamuk, xiv, 189, 319.
[109] Pamuk, 436.
[110] Bauman paraphrased in Jacobsen et al., 86–7.
[111] Twenge, *Me*, 106–9.
[112] Pew, "How Young," 5; Putnam, 261, 263; Twenge, *Me*, 157, 213; *iGen*, 110, 87–8.

CHAPTER 5

Adventures in Cyber-Culture

Internet Gains

In the mid-1990s, John Perry Barlow's *Declaration of the Independence of Cyberspace* predicted a robust and unproblematic individualism—new freedoms but without any postmodern ethical dilemma—as humans migrated onto a new plane: "Governments of the Industrial World, you weary giants of flesh and steel, I come from Cyberspace, the new home of Mind. On behalf of the future, I ask you of the past to leave us alone.... You have no sovereignty where we gather.... Our identities have no bodies, so, unlike you, we cannot obtain order by physical coercion. We believe that from ethics, enlightened self-interest, and the commonweal, our governance will emerge.... The only law that all our constituent cultures would generally recognize is the Golden Rule."[1] Five years earlier, Stuart Moulthrop had voiced similar hopes. Cyber-writing and hyperreality would knock down the notion of language as property, undermine referential utterances, particularly those that authority called absolute and definitive, and yet renew literacy. If he didn't share Barlow's grandiose sense that our identities would be uncoupled from our bodies, Moulthrop hoped that at least our language would be made of light and wouldn't need to refer back to the material world. He worried that a CIA-controlled technocracy could arise, yet believed that it would effectively be countered by "Populitism," because now anyone could change the rules of the game

---

[1] Quoted in Heath and Potter, 302.

© The Author(s) 2019
R. Kramer, *Are We Postmodern Yet?*,
https://doi.org/10.1007/978-3-030-30569-7_5

by publishing on the web. We would arrive at a postmodern carnival of simulation in which no grand narrative would hold sway over the free individual.[2] Barlow and Moulthrop could not have fully predicted the expressivist ways in which every individual has become a self-published author, yet Facebook, Snapchat, and Twitter are indeed on the road to surpass Borges's infinite Library of Babel. To the question, "Are we postmodern yet?" Barlow and Moulthrop in the 1990s answered with a resounding "Yes, and it's about time!"

More realistic evangelists for the Internet still enumerate its astounding gains: the enchanting visuality, the creative possibilities (unlike TV, it lets us speak), the boundless variety of voices and faces we meet, "the wonders... for those who were else condemned to be odd outsiders,"[3] not to mention global connectivity, crowd intelligence, and information, information, information. Once upon a time, TV anaesthetized us, but now, insists Clay Shirkey, we are beginning to use our "cognitive surplus" on unpaid collaborative projects.[4] *Wikipedia*, with 2.5 million English articles in 2008 already, "more than all the world's paper encyclopedias combined," grew to 5.9 million articles by mid-2019 (48 million if we include all of its 250 languages).[5] Although *Wikipedia* isn't infallible, a sampling of science articles by the journal *Nature* has pegged the *Wikipedia* error rate as comparable to that of the *Encyclopaedia Britannica*—very impressive for an encyclopaedia 70 times *Britannica*'s size at the time.[6] Jaron Lanier complains that *Wikipedia* makes porn stars as important as Nobel Prize winners,[7] but that's part of the pluralist marvel: the old encyclopaedias neglected popular culture, and if the pendulum has now swung too far in the opposite direction, it's still a delight to find Vampire Weekend as easily as Martin Van Buren.

In 2003, before *Wikipedia* had become a significant cultural force, Atwood mocked the Internet's eagerness to give us a quick rundown on *Madame Bovary* or the Theory of Relativity.[8] By 2010, Atwood was defending Twitter—"Let's just say it's communication, and communication is something human beings like to do," while the Library of Congress

---

[2] Moulthrop, 74–5, 85, 77–9, 84.
[3] Bech, 374.
[4] Young, 82–3.
[5] Gleick, 379; Lanier, 174; "Wikipedia: About," *Wikipedia*, as of 3 July 2019.
[6] Hood, 268; Pinker, *Enlightenment*, 260.
[7] Lanier, 142.
[8] Atwood, *Oryx*, 78.

decided to preserve every tweet.[9] That young people are online so much has even been cited as a reason why violence and crime have declined,[10] for real violence can't match the glamour or the dopamine rush of *World of Warcraft*. Claims that the number of people googling the word "flu" could be an early warning signal for regional flu trends have been confirmed by medical researchers.[11] It's a bit deceptive to speak of visual *literacy* (since literacy as such has declined), yet we are being visually educated. The Flynn Effect—the rise of IQ scores in the twentieth century—appears in abstract reasoning, analogies, and visual matrices. The gains in abstract reasoning and analogies can be attributed to the dissemination of scientific ideas into many areas of education, but for the gains in visual matrices we can thank our rich visual culture, including TV and the Internet.[12] Characters in Zsuzsi Gartner's story "Once, We Were Swedes" plan to go off-grid for their electricity but worry about losing access to Netflix.[13] Who can blame them?

Looking back, we can admit that Barlow and Moulthrop were right insofar as we've found a home in this alternative, heavily simulated new space. According to a venture capital firm, one-fifth of American adults and more than one-third of 18-to-29-year-olds say that they are online almost constantly, and, on average, Americans spend about 7½ hours daily looking at a screen. If that seems high, it's less than the screen time of Chinese, Brazilians, and Vietnamese. At the top of the scale, Indonesians and Filipinos sit in front of a screen for 9 hours a day.[14] With increased freedom for, and hiving off, of the individual, the Internet's powerful simulations are making us more postmodern in a very *practical* sense, and postmodernity is partly the result of technological change in the advent of TV and then the Internet.

[9] Gleick, 420.

[10] McKnight, 42.

[11] Hopkins Researchers Find "Google Flu Trends" A Powerful Early Warning System for Emergency Departments, News Release, Johns Hopkins Medicine, 9 January 2012, http:// www.hopkinsmedicine.org/news/media/releases/_hopkins_researchers_find_google_flu_ trends_a_powerful_early_warning_system_for_emergency_departments).

[12] Pinker, *Better*, 650–7.

[13] Gartner, *Better*, 36.

[14] Canadians watched their screens for 6¼ hours per day. Meeker, 2014, slide 96. Meeker, 2018, slide 11. See also Ansari and Klinenberg, 29–30. Another study, by Ball State University's Center for Media Design in 2009, found an even higher amount of screen time—8.5 hours per day—in the US. Carr, 87. See also Pew and Perrin, "One-fifth," and Twenge, *iGen*, 51.

But has the Internet, like a flight simulator or a good novel, made us more adept at navigating the real world or less adept? As Benedict Anderson argues, the novel and newspaper gave us the nation *here* and *now*, the sense that we are all deeply implicated in a local group that belongs not to eternity, but to other local groups living day upon day in secular time.[15] And immersion in the digital simulation makes the *now* even more immediate than the novel or newspaper, if at the price of losing much of the *here*. Back in 2000, Putnam showed statistically that "Nothing – not low education, not full-time work, not long commutes in urban agglomerates, not poverty or financial distress – is more broadly associated with civic disengagement and social disconnection than is dependence on television for entertainment."[16] Barlow's and Moulthrop's hopes that, by entering cyberspace, humans would arrive at a state of pure "carnival," slough off evil, and transcend governance look impossibly utopian now. "Populitism" turned out to be not much more than populism. Only if carnival is an endless party can we say that we have arrived: the music of almost any artist is available online for free; games are freely available; pornography is everywhere; all sorts of personal connections, legal and illegal, can be made online; anybody can post a response to the latest novel, movie, or news story; Hilary Clinton, Bernie Sanders, and Donald Trump can even be forced (via Songify) to sing and dance their speeches.[17] Yet, if carnival (in the Bakhtinian sense) means an effective and egalitarian humbling of the powerful, we have not arrived. Alongside its wonderful gains, the Internet is making us more postmodern in three potentially debilitating ways. With massive increases of on-screen time, both our memory and our literacy are declining. This tends, secondly, to undermine reading as well as reasoning, and, thirdly, to weaken our connections to each other. Two claims in favour of Internet-driven change—that we've become more adept at multi-tasking and that the Internet makes us more democratic—fail to hold up. With all the changes, we're moving more resolutely into a world of simulation. Even forward-thinking science-fiction writer Stanislaw Lem has lamented the effects of the Internet: "We

[15] Benedict Anderson, 24–6. See also David Williams, *Imagined*, 21–4.
[16] Putnam, 231.
[17] The Gregory brothers, "Bernie VS Hillary- Battle of the Bands," 7 March 2016, https://www.youtube.com/watch?v=GFbQZU1iPSU&list=PL08FD35E184A24E7F, accessed 22 April 2016.

are like a man who jumped off the roof of a fifty-story building and reached the thirtieth floor. Someone looking out of the windows asks: 'How are you doing?' and the falling man replies: 'Everything is fine, so far.'"[18]

INTERNET LOSSES

A Decline of Memory and Literacy

As our computer simulations get better, we lose interest in older simulations: by 2008, time devoted to reading print materials had fallen to less than 2.5 hours per week, an 11% drop over the previous four years. Online time hasn't been carved out of TV-watching time, but has been piled on top of it.[19] Already in 2007, a Nevada college student could say, "My dad is still into the whole book thing. He has not realized that the Internet kind of took the place of that."[20] Patricia Wallace, senior IT director at Johns Hopkins University Center for Talented Youth, cheers such sentiments; she explains that because cell phones are so portable, high school students, while waiting for the bus or a friend, can use "micro time slots" to complete a quick lesson.[21] Possibly the pre-teens I saw in the movie theatre pulling out their cell phones during a slow-moving part of *Harry Potter and the Deathly Hallows, Part 2* were completing a quick biodiversity assignment. Possibly; but so far, cell phones are primarily used to visit social networking sites.[22] Nevertheless, those pre-teens have soulmates among the elite. Kevin Kelly often finds the trailer better than the movie and he intones that, "the depth, complexity, and demands of [online massive] games can equal... any great book."[23] A bit more playfully, Adrian Chen asks, "Do you remember 'books'? A book is basically thousands of tweets printed out and stapled together between pieces of cardboard.... These days, the majority of books are read by people who don't know how to use the Internet."[24] With the rise of cinema and subsequently TV, the

[18] Peyman Esmaeili.
[19] Carr, 86–7.
[20] Bauerlein, 41.
[21] Lunau, "Touch," 60.
[22] Hood, 258–9.
[23] Kevin Kelly, "The Waking Dream," in Brockman, 21, 23.
[24] Adrian Chen, "What Would You Buy for People Who Read Books? A Gift Guide," Gawker.com, 19 November 2012, http://gawker.com/5961827/what-would-you-buy-for-people-who-read-books-a-gift-guide.

image—"its immediacy, its presentism, its total immersion in the moment"—appeals to us in a visceral way that cancels out the past, as David Williams argues.[25] Back in 1965, TV soundbites clocked in at a sleep-inducing 42 seconds. Who can stay on a single track that long? By 1995, even before our twitchy Internet trigger-fingers got into the game, we had shaved the soundbites down to 8 seconds.[26] Images appeal to the brain's automatic response system, honed by evolution to give heuristic, not reasoned responses. Our attachment to smartphones and computer screens extends "the primacy... of the image over the word," and allows for serial immersions and repeated escapes from immersion. If the cinematic image immerses us in a past world by effacing the past in the present rush of the image,[27] the digital world caters rather to our second-by-second shifts in attention, and involves a more troubling de-structuring of time. What is gained in critical distance from cinematic simulations is paid for by a temporal nomadism that is at home neither in the past nor in the present.

Less enchanted than Kevin Kelly and Patricia Wallace by the digital revolution, Nicholas Carr has detailed how the Internet is geared to short-term memory, in contrast to the "deep reading" associated with books, which is more reliable for long-term recall. Socrates, who complained in *Phaedrus* about a threat to memory from the new technology of writing,[28] turns out to have been right: conversations with friends still provide better memory recall than do reading books or watching TV.[29] But books are linguistically far richer than either conversations or TV.[30] The Internet effectively decreases memory, since in web-browsing we divert mental resources away from comprehension and deep thinking, applying a larger share to navigation. Links, so useful, also increase the reader's cognitive load. Eye-tracking of Web users shows that we read in the pattern of the letter F, concentrating on the tops of pages and beginnings of lines, usually leaving a page within 19–27 seconds on average. This brevity of devotion holds true not only for high school students, but for academic researchers as well.[31] According to Microsoft, the average attention to a

---

[25] David Williams, "Film," 168–9.
[26] Homer-Dixon, 321, 454n13.
[27] David Williams, "Film," 184, 179; *Media*, 8, 110.
[28] Plato, *Phaedrus, Collected Dialogues*, trans. R. Hackforth, Princeton: Princeton University Press, 1961, 275a.
[29] Small, 117.
[30] Bauerlein, 128.
[31] Carr, 122–5, 126–9, 134–6.

webpage fell from 12 seconds in 2000 to 8 seconds in 2013.[32] As these statistics suggest, people scan rather than read webpages, alighting on words and sentences non-sequentially, as if they were viewing *images*, not linear text.[33] In the Pleistocene, distraction was usually adaptive, so neural pathways favourable to the Web are easier to develop than are the cortical pathways for deep reading. Neuroplasticity, the brain's ability to partially restructure itself at a cellular level, is an important evolutionary adaptation to changing environments,[34] and a mere 5 days on the Internet seems to be enough to begin rerouting neural circuitry for Internet efficiency.[35] But comprehension suffers.

Jameson's claim in the early 1990s that postmodernity effaces history was too sweeping in regards to art and literature, but has proven to be prophetic at the micro level of everyday behaviour, with disturbing cultural and political implications. In 1999, Putnam was still hopeful about the effects of the Internet on reading, since 42% of Internet users said that the Internet cut into their TV time, while only 16–19% were reading fewer magazines and newspapers.[36] Sixteen years later, however, the more time that youths spent on the Internet and on gaming, the *more* TV they watched.[37] Although high school math scores remained steady between 1999 and 2008, reading and writing scores went down, literary reading showing the biggest decline.[38] The American *Survey of Public Participation in the Arts* found that, despite Harry Potter, reading rates had dropped significantly between 1982 and 2002, with the biggest drop among 18–24-year-olds.[39] In 2006, only 39% of 18- to 29-year-olds said that they enjoyed reading a lot, compared to 53% of adults generally.[40] Indeed, if your webpages continue to look like book pages, you can forget about having people read them, a Nielsen report has found. Website managers

---

[32] Alter, 28.

[33] Bauerlein, 143.

[34] Carr, 63–4, 24–5, 31, 122–5.

[35] Small, 16.

[36] Putnam, 179.

[37] Bauerlein, 80.

[38] Carr, 145–6. Bauerlein, 89, 108. Bauerlein cites the 1992 and 2005 NAEP reading tests of grade twelves and the 2005 Kaiser Report *Generation M*. See also NAEP (2013) and Twenge, *iGen*, 64.

[39] Bauerlein, 44–6.

[40] Bauerlein, 59. See also Twenge, *iGen*, 60–4. She quotes one 12-year-old "A" student, who says, "I just can't sit still and be superquiet."

have grasped this: keep your home page at a grade six reading level; subsequent pages may be bumped up into the grade eight stratosphere.[41]

Both cognitive and metacognitive factors seem to be implicated in the lower reading comprehension. Grade 10 students had lower reading comprehension when they read articles or stories digitally rather than on paper. The primary difference is spatial, given the fixity of print on paper. When we remember, we partly remember where the words were placed—in a particular book, near the beginning or end, high or low on a page—but in the spatial flow of the Internet, such placing aids vanish.[42] Kindle, too, turns books into "something very like a Web site," and readers have testified how difficult it is to stay with *Nicholas Nickleby* rather than to jump "down the Internet rabbit hole."[43]

An Israeli study found that when engineering students (all of them digital natives) were given longer texts to read in a limited time, performance didn't vary much between screen and print. In a second situation, however, with time constraints removed, screen performance proved worse than print. Yet, ironically, the students *believed* that their screen comprehension was better. The study's authors speculate that the differences are metacognitive. In other words, the differences aren't just in performance, but in how we approach the screen.[44] We *expect* to jump around when we're on-screen, a prophecy that fulfils itself in the erratic management of study-time.

Psychologist Alison Gopnik hopes that her grandchildren will not have "the fragmented, distracted, alienated digital experience" that she does. Instead, as digital natives, they will have cortical areas newly developed in relation to the new technology, not "hijacked by print."[45] Gopnik is wrong: the higher children's screen time is, the lower their academic achievement. Interest in school has been declining for a while, but it plunged significantly for 12th-graders in 2012, when iGen, the first digi-

[41] Bauerlein, 148, 151.

[42] Mangen, Walgermo, and Brønnick. See also Alan Kirby's comments on the "antisequentiality" and "ultraconsecutiveness" of Internet surfing. He argues that "in the absence of a logical overarching shape" the brain has difficulty reconstructing surfing sessions and therefore can't easily remember individual items (Kirby, *Digimodernism*, 64).

[43] Carr, 103.

[44] Ackerman and Goldsmith.

[45] Alison Gopnik, "Incomprehensible Visitors from the Technological Future," in Brockman, 274, 271.

tal natives (born beginning in 1995) reached that grade.[46] For toddlers the effect is multiplied, so that greater exposure to TV correlates, later in life, with lower future classroom engagement, lower math scores, greater consumption of junk food, higher weight, less physical activity, greater behavioural and social problems, and more victimization by classmates.[47] When he sees his young girlfriend Eunice struggling to read Milan Kundera, Lenny, a character in Gary Shteyngart's *Super Sad True Love Story* (2010), says, "People just aren't meant to read anymore. We're in a post-literate age."[48] Millennials and iGen make far more use of postmodern technologies than do previous generations, and with each generation, fewer people get their news from newspapers and radio, while more get it from the Internet.[49] Eunice, evidently a Millennial, is wedded to her device.[50] Shteyngart, a Generation Xer who, in contrast, had to hire an intern to get himself onto Facebook and iPhone, likewise succumbed quickly to the pleasures and costs of instant gratification.[51] But there is good news: the children of Steve Jobs, of former *Wired* editor Chris Anderson, and of many other cyber-heavyweights are being spared some of the deleterious effects, since their parents strictly limited their screen time.[52]

The weakening ability to concentrate on written words is a broad phenomenon. In only 20 years, *Time* cover stories dropped from 4500 words to 2800.[53] This change in prose length and attention span has accelerated with Twitter, so that between 2005 and 2014, the average message length on OkCupid dropped from almost 400 to 100 *characters*. Now young singles are finding even 100 too long: the highest response rates are reserved for messages between 40–60 characters.[54] With the arrival of

---

[46] Twenge, *iGen*, 169–71.

[47] These results come from Linda Pagani's study of 1314 Canadian children, cited in Susan Pinker, *Village*, 167.

[48] Shteyngart, *Super*, 277.

[49] Pew, "Millennials," 35. TV news is in decline too, but more slowly.

[50] Coupland, the author of the prophetic *Generation X* (1991), is actually a baby boomer, born in 1961.

[51] Gary Shteyngart, Interview with the *Guardian*, 14 Apr 2011, https://www.youtube.com/watch?v=Y737fdfJE2o; also http://www.youtube.com/user/kevinpkavanagh#p/u/40/Y737fdfJE2o, 4:47, 5:45.

[52] Alter, 1–2.

[53] Homer-Dixon, 321, 454n13. *Scientific American* and *New York Times* showed similar declines.

[54] Rudder, 65–6.

Donald Trump, Twitter became a preferred arena of political debate, so that instead of reasoned arguments about policy, the briefest and sharpest barb wins. Newspapers and online commentators then dutifully write stories about the most outrageous and insulting tweets. According to one study, 59% of those sharing links on Twitter have never even clicked on those links themselves.[55] Although some teachers and some small-scale studies without control groups have reported that Twitter encourages active learning, a broad study of 1465 students at 70 randomized Italian high schools found that use of Twitter and micro-blogging in literature classrooms *reduced* student test scores by 25–40%. Barbetta et al. cite the "short-cut effect": brief Twitter interventions convince students that they've adequately understood a complex literary work, and may even convince teachers to reduce their effort.[56] Twitter, I would argue, is an expression of postmodern How-I-Feel: in how many words I feel like reading, in what attitudes (not reasons) I feel like expressing, and in which of yesterday's pronouncements I and Trump feel like conveniently forgetting.

Writers and publishers are worried. Graphic novels accept the brevity of our linguistic devotion and bow to the visual. Even the best books make concessions. In Jennifer Egan's *A Visit from the Goon Squad* (2010), one (very moving) chapter consists entirely of PowerPoint slides. Marisha Pessl's *Night Film* (2013) gives disturbing glimpses of the dark web, where fans of horror director Stanislas Cordova find room for their darker urges. She prophesies the extinction of "the slow printed word" and satirizes the iEverything phenomenon: "With the iPiano, anyone can be an iMozart. *Then, you could compose your own iRequiem for your own iFuneral attended by millions of your iFriends who iLoved you.*"[57] Yet, amid the satire, Pessl's book itself also boasts many faux-webpages and invites readers to download apps to find "easter eggs" inside the book. Alongside Lenny's literary references in *Super Sad True Love Story*, Shteyngart places the semi-literate and brand-heavy (and already-dated) emails of the young. To market the book, he did a faux YouTube documentary, which "revealed" that the celebrated Shteyngart could only read at about

[55] Gabielkov Maksym, Arthi Ramachandran, Augustin Chaintreau, and Arnaud Legout. "Social Clicks: What and Who Gets Read on Twitter?" *HAL Archives*, ACM SIGMETRICS/IFIP Performance, June 2016, https://hal.inria.fr/hal-01281190/document.

[56] Barbetta et al.

[57] Pessl, *Night Film*, 50, 292, 194.

a Grade 2 level. For his subsequent autobiography, *Little Failure*, Shteyngart did a 4-minute YouTube skit in which Random House forces the book's derogatory title on him, and he discovers that his "husband," James Franco, will pre-empt *Little Failure* with the tell-all memoir: *50 Shades of Gary: An Erotic Journey*. In one sense, such concessions to populist cyber-culture do what writers have always done—turn the world into fiction—but publishers clearly fear that in the new regime of postmodern visual culture, word-heavy books will sink if they neglect YouTube buzz.

Studies of the research habits of British students and staff members indicate "a general tendency to shallow, horizontal, 'clicking' behavior in digital libraries." Massive Open Online Courses (MOOCs) enrol hundreds of thousands, but about 90% drop out,[58] and people tend to either read offline or not at all.[59] Carr cites a number of educated people—including editor and Publish2 founder Scott Karp, Rhodes Scholar Joe O'Shea, and others—who have stopped reading books altogether and have begun to graze on the Internet, where they feel that they can gather more informational snippets.[60] C. Gordon Bell, the Microsoft engineer who has been trying to document his whole life in the MyLifeBits project, can't abide books anymore. Experiences that can't be "stuffed into a hard drive" annoy him: "I get [books], I look at them, I occasionally read them. But then I give them away, because they're not in my memory. To me they're almost gone."[61] Still, our postmodern individualism ensures that, although we read less, we write more: one in five American adults publishes a blog.[62] We see almost a parody of the postmodern valuation of "my truth" and "How-I-Feel" above the complexities of inherited wisdom. Venn, in Tom Rachman's *The Rise and Fall of Great Powers* (2014), complains, "Everybody's putting out press releases on what they ate for breakfast."[63] In that novel, the decline of the bookstore (now a showroom for online buying) and the seeming availability of all human knowledge on smartphones is symbolically associated with Venn's and Tooly's unmooring in the world.

[58] Bethune, "End," 42.
[59] Williams and Rowlands, 19.
[60] Carr, 7–8, 138.
[61] Morozov, *Save*, 270; Turkle, 300.
[62] Hood, 258–9.
[63] Rachman, 339.

A Decline of Reason

As the printing press did in the fifteenth century, and the cinematic image did during World War I,[64] the digital image partially frees us from older authorities. However, the reading habits developed by TV and cyber-culture diminish rational engagement, confirming what some philoso-phers have argued: that the brain reasons much more with sentences than with images. We are most likely to understand something when we can explain it in speech.[65] Although such terms as "distributed cognition" and "collective intelligence" are trotted out to designate the ability to collabo-rate digitally and to use digital tools such as search engines, children who spend excessive amounts of time in front of a screen show a greater likeli-hood of irritability and a diminished ability to pay attention.[66] Critics praised and gave awards to *SpongeBob SquarePants*, a TV show for young children, and even Barack Obama declared it a family favourite,[67] but researchers, testing its effect on four-year-olds, found that its frenetic pac-ing (a scene change every eleven seconds on average) had negative effects on planning and self-control. Four-year-olds who watched the slower-paced educational show *Caillou* (scene changes every thirty-four seconds) did better on the tests. The control group, which drew pictures instead of watching TV, did best of all.[68]

Teachers in the U.S and Australia are now using Kate Pullinger's online novel *Inanimate Alice*—with its multimedia effects and audio track—in Grade 7 classrooms. Pullinger explains that as technology changes, the way we tell stories must change as well, and some teachers report success in engaging reluctant readers. The novel fits nicely alongside comic books under the shibboleth of "multiple literacies" and promises "audience participation,"[69] but the language and content are impoverished. Worse, it's difficult to concentrate on the words with the audio-visual images con-stantly flashing by. The cure is no more than the disease repackaged. Phil Davis, a Cornell doctoral student, blogs, "I should be reading a lot – only

---

[64] David Williams, "Film," 184. See also David Williams, "Representations of Time: Film and Great War Writing." *Options for Teaching Representations of the First World War.* Debra Rae Cohen and Douglas Higbee, eds. New York: MLA, 2017, 242–8.

[65] Heath, *Enlightenment*, 52–4, 143.

[66] Small, 27.

[67] Joyce Eng, "What's on Obama's Must-See TV List?" *TV Guide* 8 April 2009, http://www.tvguide.com/news/obamas-favorite-tv-1004874/.

[68] Susan Pinker, *Village*, 172.

[69] Browne, 87.

I don't. I skim. I scroll. I have very little patience for long, drawn-out, nuanced arguments, even though I accuse others of painting the world too simply." Nevertheless, Davis is convinced that he's on the right track, because the Internet provides more external influences on his thinking: "I hate reading the humanities literature, where there are no abstracts, and the thesis could be hidden somewhere in the long, unstructured paragraphs…. The Internet may have made me a less patient reader, but I think that in many ways, it has made me smarter."[70]

Like Davis, three-quarters of people would rather read news briefs than full articles, yet when 6300 American students were tested on their Information and Communications Technology (ICT) literacy, they gave no evidence of "smarter" reading. Half failed to judge the objectivity of particular Web sites, and more than half couldn't formulate a proper research statement. When preparing PowerPoint slides, 8% created completely irrelevant presentations, and 80% combined relevant and irrelevant points.[71] Clearly, just because one uses information technology, doesn't mean that one knows how to use it intelligently. The obvious point that we rely on others for our cognitive information ("distributed cognition") is used to justify our lack of individual knowledge. Alan Kirby fears the flux of *Wikipedia*—the never-finished nature of each entry.[72] Flux, however, isn't a major cause for worry: it *invites* rational engagement, as editors argue about what should and shouldn't appear, and as articles are improved. Instead, the salient point is that reasoning (for the most part) is "explicit linguistically structured thought,"[73] acquired only through deep reading and study, not by cycling quickly through a series of webpages.

Increasingly, we only want to hear about the present. Sampling a set number of books from every year since 1800, Google Books found that the percentage of mentions of the present or previous year have gone up astronomically.[74] Although some commentators, such as former *Wired* editor Chris Anderson, bet that YouTube's "big-*n* statistical game" would bring more thought-provoking material than network TV, others have pointed out that the most-watched user-generated material is juvenilia—

---

[70] Carr, 7–8. Davis.

[71] Bauerlein, 144, 114. A Nielsen alert on the "Usability of Websites for Teenagers" showed that despite their wired lifestyles, teens were less able than adults to complete ordinary tasks on the web (Bauerlein, 146).

[72] Kirby, *Digimodernism*, 117.

[73] Heath, *Enlightenment*, 143.

[74] Rudder, 64.

"News of the Weird," funniest home videos, and Fails.[75] Kangaroo with five legs! Brevity and spectacle, the inherent limitations of broadcast journalism, are ratcheted up to a further level on the Internet, and the algorithms that raise a link to the top of a Google search favour novelty over trustworthiness.[76] Despite the IQ increases in visual matrices, some areas of IQ have shown little gain: verbal abilities (reading, writing, vocabulary), arithmetic, and learned cultural knowledge (civics, history, science, foreign affairs).[77]

Video games are among the culprits that diminish rational engagement. Adolescents who played video games for more than an hour a day showed more symptoms of Attention Deficit Hyperactive Disorder (ADHD) and inattention. Although there are many causes for ADHD and serious questions about the looseness of ADHD diagnostic criteria in DSM-IV (*Diagnostic and Statistical Manual of Mental Disorders*) and DSM-5, it has been argued that the huge increase in diagnoses points to the technological rerouting of neural circuitry in children. Even simple addition activates neurons from various brain regions, mostly the frontal lobes, but video gaming is *inversely* connected with frontal lobe use. The brain initially works hard, but relies on the motor and visual cortices further back in the brain. Then, after a few months of practice, video game scores go up, while brain activity goes down.[78] It's not worrying that some of our activities engage our frontal lobes and other activities don't, but it would be worrying to produce a culture that reasons less and functions more on autopilot.

Illusory Gains in Multi-tasking

A popular argument has it that postmodern technologies compensate for their attack on our memories and rational engagement by allowing us to multi-task, but the evidence suggests otherwise.[79] Ellen, in her early 30s, surreptitiously does her email while Skyping with her grandmother, and admits, "I'm not really paying attention to our conversation." Sixteen-year-old Audrey would prefer that her mother look up from the cell phone

[75] Lanier, 98, 122, 182.
[76] Morozov, *Save*, 150, 152.
[77] Pinker, *Better*, 650–7. Bauerlein 93–4.
[78] Small, 66, 68, 36–8.
[79] Ophir, Nass, and Wagner's 2009 study of 3400 girls is reported in Susan Pinker, *Village*, 174.

when she picks Audrey up at school. But Audrey can't complain too loudly, because she does the same, texting when she's with her friends.[80] Data obtained from the Moment app found that users spent an average of 3 hours on their cell phones daily.[81] It's not unusual to see people at conferences attending to their cell phones rather than to the speaker; and even in church, people reverently gaze at their phones. For the digital natives of iGen, cell phone use is acceptable anywhere, including their own future weddings.[82] Older people, too, have learned to pull out their phones during funeral services, and one woman, in her 60s, confessed, "I couldn't stand to sit that long without getting on my phone." No longer must the free postmodern individual participate fully in the group's ritual confrontation with death. "Even a simple [!] cell phone brings us," as Turkle says, "into the world of continual partial attention," so that we only give other people and important tasks small chunks of ourselves. A 16-year-old sophomore, Julia, sensing an incoming text when she is in class, begins to feel "antsy" and heads to the bathroom in order to open the crucial text. Usually, it's just someone saying hello. But fear of missing out (FOMO) on what's happening elsewhere lets the cyber-mediated now alienate us even from the immediate present. The upside is that one never has to *feel* alone; the downside is that we're often handcuffed to the trivial, and even in groups we *are* still alone.[83]

Tech guru Don Tapscott shies away from the term "multi-tasking": "What we're actually watching," he says, "is adaptive reflexes – faster switching and more active working memories."[84] Of course, he's still describing (and surreptitiously praising) multi-tasking as adaptive. But he wisely skirts around the word, since multi-tasking doesn't live up to its inflated name. People who stay on "a single sustained task" get better results than "fast switchers" do.[85] Psychologist Larry Rosen observed 263 secondary and post-secondary students for 15-minute blocks as they studied in their homes. On average, they stayed on task for only 5 minutes at a time. Facebook and text messages beckoned. To a lesser extent, video games, TV, the Internet, music, food, and drink also encouraged them to

---

[80] Turkle, 13–14, 164, 189–90.

[81] This doesn't include listening to music or making phone calls. Alter, 14–16.

[82] Caitlin Gibson, "Getting Inside Kids' Heads." *Washington Post*, rpt *Winnipeg Free Press*, 4 June 2016, D4.

[83] Turkle, 295, 161, 245, 243.

[84] Kingston, "Get Ready," 44.

[85] Small, 34, 68.

switch away from work. Even when their phones weren't vibrating, they felt the irresistible urge to check their messages. Those who could stay on task longer tended to be better students. The worst students switched back and forth among several tasks, but even students who checked Facebook only once during the 15 minutes had lower grade-point averages. Imposed discipline didn't help matters, for if they were forbidden to check their phones, they became very anxious, a debility for anyone trying to study.[86] Like the students who believe that their screen comprehension is better than print comprehension, multi-taskers *feel* more productive, because the brain sends a little dopamine reward at each task switch, seeming to confirm the truth of their self-deception.[87] Sticking to one task is boring, as polls confirm.[88] Our *intuitive* judgements do involve multi-tasking, but *rational* thought involves a selection between competing stimuli.[89] The bad news is that chronic multi-tasking may delay frontal cortex development, making children less able to delay gratification, plan, or reason abstractly.[90] It may even be that ethical choices based on "how I feel at the time" are not so much conscious decisions as an effect of this mediated inability to delay gratification.

A Decline of Human Connections

Particularly troubling in the loss of attention and reason is cyber-culture's role of increasing distance between human beings, our waning attention to the Other. A positive side of mediated relationships is that, just as the book and the newspaper helped create the nation-state, allowing people to live in imagined communion with fellow-citizens whom they would never see, cyber-culture creates a necessary form of mediation in the contemporary world, allowing us to imagine ourselves, though at a distance, as part of a global community. Eric Klinenberg reads the entrails positively, citing a 2009 study in which the Internet mitigated depression among older people, and a Pew poll in which heavy Internet users had larger, more diverse social networks, visited public places more, and volunteered more often. Since young adults are living solo more than they ever have histori-

[86] Rosen, Carrier, and Cheever.
[87] Turkle, 163.
[88] Williams and Rowlands, 16.
[89] Heath, *Enlightenment*, 72–3.
[90] Small, 32.

cally, Klinenberg interprets the rise of network society and social media as young people knitting together new connections to replace the lost old ones.[91]

Like Klinenberg, young Gabe in Richard Powers's novel *Generosity* anticipates a critique of the online game Futopia: "Mom No!" he cries, "It's completely social."[92] Translation: it's a multiplayer game. As Adam Alter notes, part of the addictive quality of life online (for example Instagram or *World of Warcraft*) is indeed the *social* connection.[93] Yet Gabe's attention is degraded, his language clipped and inconsequential when he plays. It's true that some features of the Internet—such as collaborative-input memorials for people who have died—can bring people together,[94] but neither having a diverse social network nor being in a public place tells us much about the quality of these social connections.[95] For one experimental group, merely the *presence* of a cell phone (sitting idly nearby) during a conversation made the conversational partner less able to connect, less able to empathize, and less trusting of the other person. Why wouldn't a pad of paper (as the control group had) do the same thing? Because the cell phone promises a freer, richer, more exciting world beyond the limits of the present face-to-face conversation.[96]

The postmodern speed, ease, and simulated attractiveness of our technology may make us frustrated and bored when things don't go as planned in real life.[97] Watch families in fast-food restaurants, and see if your observations match what Jenny Radesky and her colleagues found. Although they saw some joint use of cell phones that made both parent and child happy, usually the children either accepted the parent's cyber-immersion or pestered the parent until the parent grew angry.[98] A study found that one-year-olds instinctively follow their parents' eye movements, so that

[91] Klinenberg, 64, 111, 196, 231.

[92] Powers, *Generosity*, 125.

[93] Alter, 9.

[94] Quan-Haase, 181–182.

[95] Pew confirms that cell phone users have larger social networks than non-users. But cell phone users have less contact with their neighbours and show less integration into their local communities (Susan Pinker, *Village*, 15).

[96] Alter, 15–16.

[97] Konrath et al., 188.

[98] Radesky, Jenny S. et al. "Patterns of Mobile Device Use by Caregivers and Children During Meals in Fast Food Restaurants," *Pediatrics* 133:4 (1 April 2014): 843–9; online 10 March 2014, http://pediatrics.aappublications.org/content/133/4/e843.full?sid=bd4d9e74-dfa8-4894-b2e4-4ea47d1650b6.

---

parents who constantly check their phones teach their children distracted behaviour.[99] It's not unusual to see groups of people seated together, but isolated, each gazing at his or her cell phone. I watched a family of six in a restaurant: the youngest boy (about 2 years old) horsed around with his brother (about 7), while father and mother and the eldest daughter (about 16 years old) remained firmly glued to their cell phones. Only the eldest daughter acknowledged the existence of another person, sharing something on her phone with her sister (about 13). The meal came and briefly the family interacted, but after the last bite, the parents returned immediately and exclusively to their phones. Similarly, Aziz Ansari describes going out for brunch with a number of people, hearing a Nelly song, and then diving into his phone for Nelly's Wikipedia page, "as one must do anytime Nelly-related questions plague one's mind."[100]

Although most of us want less "village-level" contact, says Susan Pinker, "we have been making trade-offs we haven't understood."[101] She cites a study on the hormonal effects of various kinds of contact. After trying to solve math and word problems in front of an audience, pre-teen girls received from their mothers a visit, or a phone contact, or a text message, or nothing. Both the mothers' presence and their voices caused an increase in the girls' oxytocin (the pleasurable bonding hormone) and a decrease of cortisol (the stress hormone), but girls who received texts felt no increase of oxytocin, while their cortisol levels remained as high as those of girls who received nothing. In other words, the medium, not just the message, is crucial—some form of direct human presence, whether in body or voice.[102]

The positive effects of Internet use that Klinenberg saw among the elderly may be the result of the isolation many seniors feel in our society. And the large social networks that he noted among heavy Internet users may appear because the young, who are the earliest adopters of technology, are also at the stage of life when sociability is highest, as they search for mates and try to establish themselves in the world. For some teens, social media are an extension of personal contact, and therefore not a problem, but for the socially poor, the more time they spend on the

---

[99] Cited in Alter, 39–40.
[100] Ansari and Klinenberg, 30.
[101] Susan Pinker, quoted in Brian Bethune, "How face-to-face contact makes us happier," *Maclean's*, 1 September 2014, 43.
[102] Susan Pinker, *Village*, 178–9.

Internet, the lonelier they feel.[103] To arrive at a fuller picture of social distancing, it's necessary to measure contemporary young people against young people of previous generations, not (as Klinenberg did) young people against their contemporary elders.

Sophisticated simulation technologies facilitate a turning away from crucial aspects of the real, particularly from the bodies and conversation of other people. Turkle warns, "When we Tweet or write to hundreds or thousands of Facebook friends as a group, we treat individuals as a unit." On a smaller scale, a 21-year-old college student says, "I don't use my phone for calls anymore. I don't have the time to just go on and on. I like texting, Twitter, looking at someone's Facebook wall. I learn what I need to know." Because of that distancing, we are becoming less adept at understanding how other humans feel. Forty-three-year-old Adam gets the feeling that he is *humane* when, during the computer game *Civilization*, he switches his country from "despotism" to "monarchy"! Given that his job is slipping away because he spends up to 15 hours at a time immersed in the game-world, it's a stretch to think that much humanity is involved. He used to play one game—*Quake*—with groups of people, but does so more rarely now. The bots he plays against simulate real-player chat well enough.[104] Similarly, the most disturbing part of Spike Jonze's postmodern fable, *Her*, isn't that Theodore falls in love with his Operating System, "Samantha," but that in some shots *most* of the people in the film are speaking to their digital devices. Everybody, it seems, has hooked up with a compliant OS (possibly, as the movie hints, the same OS). At the end of the film, Theodore and Amy sit on a rooftop, mourning the loss of their OS. They are bereft. Although Peter Unwin's narrator Jack Vesoovian, in the novel *Searching for Petronius Arbiter* (2017), is a fool and a caricature of masculine self-importance, he knows enough to resist full digital immersion. The novel predicts Edible Drone Technology—ready-to-eat "fibre optic fried chicken" sold by the Leggit corporation, and, more destabilizing in a Baudrillardian sense, holographic simulations of everyone who ever lived. Jack thinks that his ex-wife Elaine's back is a non-reproducible reality, but, evidently, Leggit has digitized Elaine too.[105] The temptation, already prophesied in William Gibson's prophetic novel *Neuromancer* (1984), is to prefer the digitally simulated lover over the real one.

---

[103] Susan Pinker, *Village*, 193–4.
[104] Turkle, 168, 15, 222, 219–223.
[105] Unwin, *Searching*, 29, 222.

Contemporary virtuality via Second Life, Facebook, robotic companions, and even cell phones has widened the fault lines between people. Pete, a 46-year-old father, accesses his buff and handsome Second Life avatar, "Rolo," while caring for his two young children. Older simulation technologies such as movies and novels rely on fantasies of youth, beauty, and wealth too, but Pete develops his fantasies more thoroughly than he could have in the past. In Second Life, he courted and "married" a female avatar, "Jade," "a pixie with short, spiky blond hair." Mornings, Pete logs onto Second Life as "Rolo," "talks" to Jade, and then, using special animations, has sex with her. He doesn't want to meet the real woman behind Jade—that would destroy the illusion. Although he can't communicate his anxieties to his real wife, Allison, talking is easier with "Jade": "Second Life gives me a better relationship than I have in real life. This is where I feel most myself. Jade accepts who I am. My relationship with Jade makes it possible for me to stay in my marriage, with my family." The turnover in these "better" relationships is high. Time, relationships, and emotions speed up, and the ability to make and break connections at will is a major part of the attraction. "The self" becomes "reassuringly protean," as Turkle puts it, while other humans come to seem like enhancements, extensions of the self.[106]

Online relationships are also flatter, with many of the areas of conflict edited out. When "Dave Barmy" met "Laura Skye" on Second Life, he was a tall, dark, and handsome nightclub owner who lived in a chalet and flew a Cobra helicopter, while she was a club DJ who liked to wear tight-fitting Western clothes. The people behind the avatars—David Pollard and Amy Taylor—decided to meet in real life, and eventually got married. Predictably, real life wasn't as compelling as the simulation: Pollard and Taylor were both on social assistance, and neither was nearly as slim as advertised. Taylor soon caught Pollard's avatar (not Pollard himself) cheating with another attractive Second Life avatar, and Taylor filed for divorce.[107] Clearly, social simulations can bring people together, but real life can also come to seem grey. Although non-mediated relationships, too, involve idealization and fantasy-projection, reality's corrections seem particularly harsh when applied to the simulated world.

[106] Turkle, 159, 217, 160, 285, 154.
[107] Hood, 280–3, Steven Morris, "Second Life affair leads to real life divorce." *Guardian*, 13 November 2008, http://www.theguardian.com/technology/2008/nov/13/second-life-divorce.

Facebook: Gains and Losses in Community

Facebook profiles are avatars too, displaying idealized selves, and social media play a major role in screen time's conquest of our bodies, as we simulate images of ourselves and consume the images of others. By 2018, 88% of Millennials took part in social media, as did three-quarters of Generation Xers, and almost two-third of Boomers.[108] Amina, a Stanford biology student, found it difficult to stay off Facebook at home and even in class. "Because there was always something more to do on Facebook—reading updates about her friends, looking at photo albums, following links—the temptation was endless."[109] By 2017, Facebook users spent an average of 2¼ hours daily on the site.[110] Screen time is just part of the story. Also problematic is the image-crafting process. J.D., 24, always reserves two spots in his Top 8 for his most attractive female friends, and here, too, research confirms that the more attractive their friends, the more attractive Facebook page owners are considered to be.[111] "Friends are things you collect and display," as Steve Maich and Lianne George put it.[112] For Hannah, a 16-year-old, Facebook has become "an all-consuming effort to keep up appearances," while another girl admits that she gets anxious if people haven't posted to her wall for a week: "it looks like you're a nerd.... People are going to judge you." The proper technique, reveals a youth in his late teens, is to write on other people's walls every day. They'll write on your wall and you'll look popular. Even those who want to be honest on Facebook can't avoid crafting an image.[113] We've evolved as social animals who respond to emotion whether we want to or not, and Facebook's overwhelming success—boasting 1.56 billion daily active users by March 2019[114]—comes from the fact that it can indeed foster already-existing relationships, though it rarely creates new friendships.[115] People feel less alone, and as a 36-year-old nurse testifies, Facebook makes it feel as if people are present. Of course, those not on

---

[108] Pew, "Who uses social media," "Social Media." This represents a significant increase since 2010, especially for Boomers (Pew, "Millennials," 25).
[109] Quoted in McGonigal, 166.
[110] Meeker, 2018, slide 187.
[111] Twenge and Campbell, 112.
[112] Maich and George, 53.
[113] Turkle, 250–1, 273.
[114] Facebook Newsroom, "Company Info," https://newsroom.fb.com/company-info/, accessed 3 July 2019.
[115] Quan-Haase, 177.

Facebook feel left out. Kara, a 50-year-old in Portland, Maine, feels like she's the only person not plugged in. She complains, "No one is where they are. They're talking to someone miles away."[116]

Mark Zuckerberg makes a bold claim for his mediated polity, insisting that misunderstandings and wars would cease if everyone were on Facebook.[117] Studies of 12th-graders did find that 10+ hours on social media per week was correlated with increased support for gender equality and racial intermixing. On the other hand, these high social media hours also correlated with increased materialism and sense of entitlement.[118] Two-thirds of college students in a 2009 national American poll agreed that their generation was more narcissistic and attention-seeking than previous generations, and the majority (57%) blamed social networking sites,[119] not a particularly good sign for the polity. In one study, experimental group members edited their MySpace accounts and wrote about the process, while control-group members used Google maps to plot their route to campus and wrote about that. Both groups then took a narcissism inventory test. MySpacers were twice as likely to show greater narcissistic tendencies, scoring especially high on such items as "I always know what I'm doing" and "I am a born leader."[120] Such findings cohere with the shift towards ethical decisions based on How-I-Feel. At the extreme end of narcissism, a 16-year-old gang-affiliated girl in Winnipeg was dubbed the "Laughing Girl" when, after being caught in a speeding stolen SUV that killed a 55-year-old taxi driver in May 2008, she bragged about the crash on social media. She posted pictures, and, under the wrecked cab, wrote, "Holy, can't get enouugh of me…. (Expletive) deaaadly."[121] Police have begun to use social media to catch criminals, and to quote their unapologetic online banter alongside their apologies in court. Usually, of course, self-regard expresses itself in more quotidian ways: Kirby wryly

[116] Turkle, 204, 277.
[117] Morozov, *Save*, 292.
[118] Twenge, *iGen*, 176.
[119] Twenge and Campbell, 34.
[120] Twenge and Campbell, 114.
[121] Mike McIntyre. "Boasts, then busts." *Winnipeg Free Press*, 6 May 2013. Mike McIntyre, James Turner and Bruce Owen. "Perspective: Chill. Thrill. Kill: A night in the life of Winnipeg's car-stealing subculture." *Winnipeg Free Press*, 29 March 2009, http://www.winnipegfreepress.com/local/chill-thrill-kill-42072227.html.

observes that, "As time goes by, your input into Facebook comes to feel like the electronic nourishment of your friendships."[122]

Ironically, while Facebook primes self-regard, it also makes us feel that the fun is happening elsewhere, that the lives of others are more filled with friends and adventure. This is a significant downside of postmodern simulation: the carefully polished images of our friends make us feel dissatisfied with our own lives, and, by increasing simulation in our friendships, we decrease joy. To examine Facebook's effect on well-being, Ethan Kross and Philippe Verduyn text-messaged 82 people 5 times per day for two weeks. Not only did high use of Facebook at any given time predict people feeling worse the next time they were text-messaged, but, even in the short two-week period, people who used Facebook more showed a drop in *life* satisfaction levels, no matter the size of their Facebook network or its supportiveness. Even gender, loneliness, self-esteem, or depression didn't affect the results.[123] The decline in satisfaction was strongest among people with *moderate* or *high* levels of face-to-face social contact. People who had little face-to-face contact weren't affected as much, presumably because their satisfaction levels and expectations were lower to begin with.[124]

Twenge floats the possibility that our love affair with the smartphone is implicated in both the decline of homicides and the rise of suicides.[125] This connection is too precise, given that the decline in homicide is a long-term trend, and given that suicide rate rose between the 1950s and 1990s, fluctuating without a clear pattern thereafter.[126] However, the evidence does support her more measured claim that screen time is contributing to unhappiness and depression in teenage Americans, even as worldwide happiness levels are generally increasing, especially in poorer countries as wealth increases.[127] It's well established that high TV-use and lack of sleep have significant connections to depression, so it should come as no sur-

[122] Kirby, *Digimodernism*, 122.

[123] Kross and Verduyn.

[124] The effect is based in "people's perceptions of social isolation" rather than in any objective measure (Kross and Verduyn).

[125] Twenge, *iGen*, 4, 87.

[126] Putnam, 261, 263; Twenge, *Me*, 157, 213; *iGen* 110, 87–8. Canadian statistics can be seen at Statistics Canada, "Description for Chart 6: Age-specific mortality with suicide and accident rates, per 100,000, ages 15 to 19, Canada, 1974 to 2009," http://www.statcan.gc.ca/pub/82-624-x/2012001/article/desc/11696-06-desc-eng.htm, and "Description for Chart 8: Divorce and suicide rates, per 100,000, Canada, 1950 to 2008," http://www.statcan.gc.ca/pub/82-624-x/2012001/article/desc/11696-08-desc-eng.htm.

[127] Pinker, *Enlightenment*, 268–71, 325.

prise that our new screens, also linked to lack of sleep, should contribute to depression.[128] Most young people ensure that their phones are within arm's reach as they try to sleep, and thirteen-year-old Athena admits, "I think we like our phones more than we like actual people." Among high school students, time spent with friends began to drop significantly around 2000. Unhappiness, loneliness, and depression correlate to the amount of time spent on texting, the Internet, and social media, especially among teen girls (the highest consumers of social media), so that young people's gains in happiness since 1980 were wiped out after 2011, just as smartphone use became ubiquitous. This correlation makes sense when we hear Olivia, 18, say, "a lot of my friends are addicted to their phones – they seem like they do not want to talk to me." In contrast, happiness increased with participation in sports, in-person social interactions, and religious services.[129]

If Facebook unhappiness occurred merely from a comparison of our social status to that of others, then face-to-face social encounters should dissatisfy us too, since status comparisons infect every social encounter. On the contrary, Kross and Verduyn found that face-to-face social interactions led people to feel better over time.[130] It seems that in most face-to-face social interactions, social ranking is mitigated by the Other's bodily proximity, by the social pleasure of each other's company, and therefore by the feeling that perhaps life is happening here, not elsewhere. As Turkle points out, if we nourish face-to-face friendships, those friends, unlike our cyber-friends, might actually come by when we're

---

[128] Susan Pinker, *Village*, 172; Putnam, 234–5; Twenge, *iGen*, 3, 292, 114–15. The best correlation with happiness appears when people engage in one hour or less of screen time per day. No screen time and two hours per day are about equal in their correlation to happiness, and then unhappiness rises with every additional hour of screen time (Twenge, *iGen*, 85). Steven Pinker, using a much wider historical lens, notes that suicide rates are presently much lower than in the early 1900s and during the Depression, so that while suicide rates are presently fluctuating, they are falling over the long term (Pinker, *Enlightenment*, 278–80), but that doesn't eliminate social media and smartphones from consideration as possible causes for the recent increases. As well, Pinker is skeptical about the rise of depression, arguing that *Diagnostic and Statistical Manual* (*DSM*) criteria for mental illnesses have been getting more and more sensitive to smaller and smaller symptoms (Pinker, *Enlightenment*, 280–3). His argument may have merit in terms of diagnosis of clinical depression, but it has little to say about people's reports of unhappiness and loneliness.

[129] Twenge, *iGen*, 2, 49, 70–2, 78–82, 95–9, 102–3, 112, 54, 293.

[130] Kross and Verduyn.

sick.[131] *Super Sad True Love Story* satirizes cyber-mediated social ranking. The novel's cell phones, called äppäräti, feature "RateMe Plus" and "Form a Community" (FAC) apps so that anyone at any time can call for nearby people to rate each other in various categories. Relaxing in a bar, the protagonist Lenny eyes an attractive woman before he discovers that she has ranked him 630 out of 800 for Sustainability (net worth), but only 450 for Personality, and an abysmal 120 for Hotness. Out of the seven males, he ranks 7th. Social ranking wasn't invented by Facebook or by RateMe Plus, but the constant presence of social media on our phones, combined with our literal and psychological distance from others, is allowing our simulated images to dominate the human encounter in the postmodern era. Some celebrities have taken the next step in simulation and distancing, by hiring writers to compose "their" tweets,[132] while marketers have taught people how to monetize their friendships via "Likes."[133]

As Facebook use soars and its "Likes" remind us that we have an ever-wider circle of "friends" geographically, surveys suggest that we have *fewer* real friends. Not surprisingly, Passenger (Mike Rosenberg) sings in "Life's for the Living" that everyone has new iPhones but nobody has anyone to call, and, in "I Hate," that people befriend each other on the Internet, but can think of nothing to say to each other in real life.[134] In-person relationships that have an online component generally grow stronger, but relationships that move from in-person to online usually disappear in about 18 months.[135] Facebook, argues Susan Pinker, has siphoned off many of our social interactions. By 2004, Americans on average had fewer friends than in 1985,[136] and a quarter of all people said that they had no one with whom they could discuss important matters, more than double the number in 1985. The drop included both family and non-family, but the greatest loss was in non-family connections.[137] Our immersion in postmodern simulation is increasing the distance between people.

[131] Turkle, 153.
[132] Hood, 267.
[133] "Generation Like," PBS, *Frontline*, http://www.pbs.org/wgbh/frontline/film/generation-like/. Rudder calls "Likes" a new microcurrency (225).
[134] Passenger (Mike Rosenberg), "Life's for the Living," "I Hate." *All the Little Lights*, Black Crow Records, 2012.
[135] Bethune, "End," 42.
[136] Susan Pinker, *Village*, 9–10. Turkle, 280.
[137] McPherson et al., in Turkle, 280, 341–2, n2. Susan Pinker, *Village*, 9, 11.

Empathy Losses

Any technology—a drug, a cell phone, even a book—that significantly limits our face-to-face interactions with others will also limit communal action and, perhaps, even empathy. When computer-based groups are assigned a problem, they come up with more alternatives than face-to-face groups, but they also find consensus harder to reach and trust that much harder to establish. The distance created by computer-mediated communication seems to license cheating and the breaking of promises, because it does without "eye contact... nods, a faint furrowing of the brow, body language, seating arrangements, even hesitation measured in milliseconds." Unlike cyber-mediation, face-to-face communication invites interruption, correction, and feedback.[138]

Print technology is more individualistic and isolating than oral communication, yet people who had read a non-fiction story on paper were drawn in more and had more empathy for the characters than did people who read the story on iPad.[139] Some forms of print, such as the novel, have been particularly vital in the creation of community. Newspapers and novels fostered the sense that the people in a nation belonged together, that they shared common interests even though they would never meet.[140] Cognitive theorist Lisa Zunshine goes further, arguing that theory of mind (whereby, already at age 4 or so, we begin to understand people's minds and to predict their behaviour) is not only important in social functioning, but is also one of the goods of fiction, as readers sort through complex suppositions that characters make about each other, and as readers infer the mind of the author. Understanding minds is not sufficient for empathy, but without such understanding empathy is impossible. Steven Pinker, building on the work of Martha Nussbaum, argues that literature is an empathy technology. These empathic features, along with the spread of literacy generally, made major contributions to the Humanitarian Revolution of the eighteenth century and to the more recent Rights Revolution, by showing us what it was like to be a slave, a woman, even an

---

[138] Putnam, 175–6.

[139] Mangen and Kuiken. Gatehouse, 47. The empathy difference wasn't evident when the participants read a fiction story, but there may have been a number of reasons for this, including the unusualness of the format (stapled booklet rather than book) and the way that the instructions may have led the participants to consider that the story's reality was primarily what they should consider. Most importantly, Suzanne Keen has shown that empathy arises less out of mere reading than out of subsequent *discussions* of the text (Keen, 146, 166).

[140] See Benedict Anderson.

animal. Print and education figure prominently in the relative decline of violence over recorded history, so it's a worrying trend that men, in particular, are reading less.[141] Suzanne Keen qualifies Pinker's argument, saying that empathy forms more easily in literature because it doesn't require us to actually *do* anything altruistic in the real world.[142] She's partly right—it's easier to empathize with a fictional character than to take on a costly obligation—but fiction does turn distant categories of people into human faces, and reveals their inner lives. Unaided, our empathy tends to stay within the bounds selected by evolution, running towards kin, groupmates, and people like ourselves,[143] but fiction can get around our evolutionary defences. After hearing the story of James, who killed his neighbour, people became more empathic towards him but only slightly more empathic towards murderers as a group. Two weeks later, however, a "sleeper" effect kicked in, and the same people showed greater empathy for prisoners generally.[144]

It remains to be seen what effect cyber-communications will have. According to Pinker, any communications technology aids the Rights Revolution.[145] The truth is somewhat more complex, both for print and for Internet technologies. When Canadian Amanda Todd was 14, a Dutch man convinced her to reveal her breasts on webcam, and subsequently used the images to blackmail her. Cyber-culture didn't invent bullying, but it vastly extends bullies' reach in the postmodern era.[146] Ghyslain Raza, also at age 14, filmed himself pretending to use a golf ball retriever as a light sabre. Other students got hold of this video, digitized it, and posted it on the Internet. The video received millions of hits, and Raza started receiving messages from people mocking him and recommending suicide. Since no laws were broken, police could do nothing.[147] Other victims of cyber-bullying did commit suicide. A Rutgers roommate used a webcam to film Tyler Clementi having sex with a man, and Clementi subsequently jumped off New York's George Washington Bridge to his

[141] Pinker, *Better*, 169–76, 292, 477–8. Keen, 109. Film can be an empathy technology too, though the effect can be weakened in popular film (as in popular literature) when spectacle is emphasized.
[142] Keen, *Empathy and the Novel*, vii, 4.
[143] Pinker, *Better*, 691. Keen, 15.
[144] Batson et al. 1997 study, cited in Pinker, *Better*, 588.
[145] Pinker, *Better*, 292.
[146] James, 12–13.
[147] Jonathan Trudel. "Return of the 'Star Wars Kid.'" *Maclean's*, 27 May 2013, 28–9.

death.[148] Amanda Todd changed schools, but her tormenters pursued her online, poisoned her new school environment, and she, too, committed suicide.

The sympathetic response to the YouTube video that Todd posted online before her death suggests that cyber-mediation can convey inner lives—Levinas's "face" of the Other—and increase empathy. So, also, with the cyber-mediated movements Black Lives Matter and #MeToo. Nevertheless, some features of our personal cyber-technologies are also reducing empathy: the short attention span and the need to always be entertained. The decline of empathy discussed in the chapter on individualism was strongest after 2000, convincing researcher Sara Konrath that the increase in time spent online might be a contributing cause.[149] Nearly a third of tweens and over half of teens and young adults suggested that disrespectful speech didn't matter as much if it occurred on the Internet, and a third of young respondents would not be upset about a hate group targeting a teacher.[150] More pervasive is a subtler change to human engagement that Nick Bolton lays bare: "We tweet the birth of a child or announce an engagement. And we are completely unaware of the viewers we talk with. I suspect we don't even care. (I know I don't.).... The Internet gives each of us a bullhorn."[151]

The decline of empathy piggybacks on declines in organizational involvement such as in meetings, family dinners, and friendly visits. When Putnam published *Bowling Alone* in 2000, community participation was already in significant decline,[152] but cyber-communication has hastened that decline. Every hour spent on a computer cuts face-to-face interactions by half an hour and sabotages our face-to-face interactions with awkwardness.[153] At the focus group meetings held by Klinenberg and Ansari, the parents, grouped at one side of the room, started to talk to each other, while at the other side the younger people all silently consulted their phones.[154] Over-exposure to cell phones and screens seems to have the

[148] James, 1.
[149] Konrath et al., 185, 187–8.
[150] James, 82, 90–1.
[151] Nick Bolton, "A Real-Time Perpetual Time Capsule," in Brockman, 388.
[152] Putnam, 128.
[153] Small, 2.
[154] Ansari and Klinenberg, 41.

same effect as excessive testosterone—decreasing eye contact and empa-thy[155]—in effect making the brain more "male."

Texting
Instead of face-to-face communication, younger people prefer texting, a communicative form that simplifies complex feelings. As one 18-year-old boy says, there's a difference between "someone laughing and someone *writing* that they're laughing."[156] The brevity of texting destroys print's advantage of rational complexity, but it's precisely the affective limitations that are attractive. Young people fear that a telephone call reveals too much. It doesn't allow them to *compose* themselves—they don't have time to veil their emotional reactions. Although some have argued that texting is so popular because it's cheap, Sherry Turkle's research subjects dis-agreed, a 16-year-old boy saying that telephones expose too much, when he'd rather craft a deliberate performance in such a way as to make it seem spontaneous. Meredith, a high school junior, is glad that news of a friend's death came by text, rather than by phone: "I didn't have to be upset in front of someone else." Whenever people feel somewhat anxious, out pop the phones.[157] One of Jennifer Egan's characters in *A Visit from the Goon Squad* sees texting as the best way to manage a moral disagreement: "It's pure – no philosophy, no metaphors, no judgments."[158] If such actions seem decorous, they also shut other people out of our emotional lives, and although people want online honesty for themselves, they won't give it to others, because it's easier not to.[159]

Audrey, 16, goes further, linking texting to How-I-Feel ethics: "The phone, it's awkward. I don't see the point. Too much just a recap and sharing feelings. With a text… I can answer on my own time. I can respond. I can ignore it. So it really works with my mood. I'm not bound to any-thing, no commitment…. Later I'm going to need to talk to people on the phone. *But not now*."[160] This rationale suggests that, as strong as the fear of self-exposure is, so, too, is the unwillingness to give up one's time. Audrey broke up with a boyfriend online, a shortcut that makes her feel

---

[155] Small, 92.
[156] Turkle, 268. Speaker's emphasis.
[157] Turkle, 200, 205–6.
[158] Egan, *Visit*, 321.
[159] Ansari and Klinenberg, 66.
[160] Turkle, 190. Speaker's emphasis.

ashamed,[161] but was more efficient. Individualism is coming to mean the rationalization of all relationships, Taylorism writ small. The culture of spectacle may also hasten the flight from the telephone. Hugh, 25, understands that he'd better not bore his friends. If he telephones, asking them to set aside their multi-tasking and attend only to him, he'd better produce something worth hearing: "They're disappointed if I'm, like, not talking about being depressed, about contemplating a divorce, about being fired.... You ask for private cell time, you better come up with the goods." Clearly chiming with the self-indulgence of postmodern individualism, Dan, a law professor in his mid-50s, admits that the reason he would rather not phone people is because *he* doesn't want to be interrupted, while Mandy, a high school sophomore, explains, "You wouldn't want to call because then you would have to get into a conversation." As for conversations, "you only want to have them when you want to have them." And when does she want to have them? "Almost never," she admits. "It is almost always too prying, it takes too long, and it is impossible to say 'goodbye.'"[162] People want to express themselves, yet balk at granting others the same privilege.

Some cell phone "pathologies" that Turkle warns of—too many young people tied to the apron strings because they text their parents—aren't pathological at all, unless one subscribes to an American ideology of Emersonian self-reliance. And some effects she foresees—if we treat others as objects, we will see ourselves as objects—seem highly unlikely. But Turkle's assessment of the distancing effects of cyber-mediation is in most other ways quite accurate. Attention, while desperately longed for, is increasingly difficult for ordinary people to command. A common complaint is that people only have time for their friends when they're online.[163] When the multi-tasker speaks, he expects a listening ear, but as soon as his companion begins to speak, the cell phone suddenly becomes irresistible. Why not attend to his companion *and* the phone at the same time! Such self-indulgent forms of individualism will prove unsustainable.

A high school senior tells how his father, a doctor, used to sit and read books, and wouldn't mind being interrupted. But after the father acquired a BlackBerry, that was no longer the case. The teens that Turkle interviewed often admitted that they were relieved when parents forced them

[161] Turkle, 197.
[162] Turkle, 204, 200.
[163] Turkle, 178, 168, 172.

to lay aside their phones to talk face-to-face. But if parents won't put down their own phones, why should teens do so?[164] Despite all this, people in general, and Millennials to a slightly higher degree, do *not* agree that the new technologies make people more isolated.[165] There is an argument to be made that increased distance between human beings is in some ways a good thing. Over-crowding produces conflict, while some of the more desirable effects of postmodern individualism—freedom, self-determination, self-expression—are much easier when one isn't dominated by one's community. For the most part, however, the distance created by cyber-mediation is troubling, and generational changes mean that we haven't seen its full impact yet.

More Democratic?

When we turn from individual connections to political connections, popularizers often speak as if the Internet's free market of ideas and its postmodern pluralism make it an agent of democracy, much like print in the Early Modern era. Print allowed the Reformation to explode publicly in imaginings of social equality, binding together communities such as the English Levellers, whose line extended through Milton, down to the American constitution.[166] Like print, the Internet gives us privacy against the intrusions of the village and the authoritarianism of the grand narratives that threaten to bind us. Extending John Perry Barlow's utopianism, Don Tapscott and Anthony Williams claim that, "digital natives" are "skeptical of authority as they sift through information at the speed of light." They bring "a new ethic of openness, participation, and interactivity to workplaces, communities, and markets."[167]

Evgeny Morozov counters that a 2010 study shows 18 to 24-year-olds to have the poorest grasp of Internet privacy policy labels, particularly of the way Internet companies trade their clients' private information.[168] Circumspection can be taught; more intransigent is the power of spectacle and image to undermine democratic reason. Former Google CEO Eric

---

[164] Turkle, 267–8.

[165] Only 35% of Millennials agreed that the new technologies increase isolation, compared to 36% of Generation Xers, 42% of Boomers, and 44% of the Silent Generation (Pew, "Millennials," 26).

[166] David Williams, *Milton's*, 6–7.

[167] Tapscott and Williams, quoted in Morozov, *Save*, 46.

[168] Morozov, *Save*, 46.

Schmidt predicted that since people wouldn't want to see long mono-
logues on the screen, it would take speed, humour, and excitement to
reach people, and, indeed, in the 2008 US election, Sarah Palin's beauty
pageant footage and the Obama Girl rose to the top of political discourse.[169] In 2013, Morozov warned of a gap between the elite who used
the superb new digital tools for research, and the "cyber lumpen proletariat" who could be sucked into gossip, social media, and xenophobic
sites. Just wait, he predicted, until the cyber lumpen proletariat heads to
the polls.[170] Morozov's prophecy was fulfilled not three years later in
Donald Trump, whose tweets included photos comparing Melania to Ted
Cruz's wife—tweets that were juvenile and outrageous and partisan and
entertaining enough to get him elected.

In the Internet's free-for-all, we've been mostly taught to think of
openness and accessibility as great virtues, and they are. In developing
countries, cell phones have been a boon to entrepreneurs such as small
farmers and fishers, locating the best market for their wares. Each cell
phone adds an estimated $3000 to a country's GDP.[171] With cell phones
recording everything, including the deaths of Eric Garner and Walter
Scott that gave fuel to the Black Lives Matter protests, police have had to
rein in brutality.[172] Social media played a huge role in organizing movements such as the Arab Spring, Occupy Wall Street, #MeToo, and Black
Lives Matter. As to the long-term effects of these movements, the jury is
still out. Wael Ghonim, the Google executive who spoke on behalf of
Egyptian protesters, expressed the cyber-democracy fantasy: "In
Revolution 2.0, no one is a leader – everyone is a leader." But, as Morozov
points out, without a leader, the young liberals eventually defaulted to the
Muslim Brotherhood in the subsequent election, and then to the Army in
a coup.[173] As Tom Rachman's character Venn observes, "Don't imagine
that digital code topples generals. It's analog human beings. Not tweets
and viral videos."[174]

Some features of cyber-culture have undermined democracy, either by
making the Internet more hierarchical, or, in the opposite direction, by

---

[169] Maich and George, 153.

[170] Evgeny Morozov, "What Do We Think About? Who Gets to Do the Thinking?" in
Brockman, 230.

[171] Pinker, *Enlightenment*, 95.

[172] Ronson, 14.

[173] Morozov, *Save*, 127–8.

[174] Rachman, 340.

making it so individualistic that the communal base for democracy is lost. During Occupy Wall Street, much venom was directed at the wealthiest 1%, but hardly anyone complains that in the Twitterverse, the 1% control three-quarters of the followers, and the 0.1% control just over half.[175] New digital hierarchies appear in the gap between most of us who can't afford to access big data and the corporations who can.[176] It may be reasonable to let employers monitor, through RescueTime, how employees are spending their work hours, whether on Facebook or on work spread-sheets, and for centralized healthcare systems to read GPS-enabled asthma inhalers so as to tag areas with poor air quality.[177] But the cyber-elite may track us in ways that bring more pain than gain. The data science company Kaggle, which crowd-sources algorithms, offered a $3 million Heritage Health Prize for whoever could predict people's hospitalization based on their medical histories. Theoretically, such predictions could improve health through early intervention, but Morozov is correct to warn that insurance providers could use the data to deny coverage to customers for whom the insurers predict hospitalization.[178] He worries that automated facial recognition will undermine privacy, and that eye-tracking software will tell marketers how many seconds our eyes lingered on their ads.[179] We see the ad, but it sees us too, first via our GPS, then via our clicks, and eventually by actually watching us. Here postmodernity merely repeats earlier hierarchies.

In some cyber-culture advances, such as data-driven policing, which nudge people away from opportunities for crime, Morozov's warnings seem misplaced. He decries "choice architecture" because it gives the illusion of agency. Better to have people drive an energy-efficient car for the right reasons than to save money on gas. But such an idealized misunderstanding of morality is very naïve. What are pedestrian crosswalks or laws against libel if not strong nudges? These nudges have made us *more*, not less sensitive to pedestrians and to truth. As long as they remain under democratic control, big data accretions such as accident- or crime-maps, can have very positive effects.

[175] Rudder, 214.
[176] Andrejevic, 34.
[177] Young, 20, 122.
[178] Andrejevic, 38.
[179] Morozov, *Save*, 223, 282.

Yet Morozov is right that without controls big data can be oppressive. Facial recognition and government surveillance, already used to ticket jay-walkers in China and to simplify airline check-in, has now allowed Chinese police to pinpoint and arrest a 31-year-old fugitive among 60,000 people at a Jacky Cheung concert. According to the government, the plan is to "allow the trustworthy to roam everywhere under heaven while making it hard for the discredited to take a single step." But China has also used big data to target ethnic minorities in Xinjiang province.[180]

On a more mundane level, Target, like every major retailer, collects and buys huge amounts of data about individual shoppers: your purchases, your demographic information, the websites you visit. One customer complained to a manager that his daughter, still in high school, was receiving coupons for baby clothes and cribs from Target. When the manager called a few days later to apologize a second time, the father's tone had changed. The baby was due in August. A Marketing Analytics algorithm had spit out a verdict of "pregnant" by associating the consumer's age and gender with the purchase of items such as dietary supplements, unscented soaps, hand sanitizers, and washcloths. The advertising technique, ironically enough, is called "behavioural targeting." With big data, corporations can predict major life changes, times when we are susceptible to forming new buying habits. But in order to keep their big data intrusions from spooking people, marketers have grown more subtle. Noticing your musical taste, great; noticing that you're pregnant, not so great. With pregnant women, marketers now throw in an ad for a lawn mower beside the diapers to fool customers into thinking that they haven't been spied on.[181]

The pregnancy algorithm is just a more sophisticated and intrusive version of "people who bought *The Loss of Happiness in Market Economies* also bought *The Paradox of Choice.*" Companies such as Taboola and Outbrain monetize webpage content by suggesting "things you may like." The content monetizer pays *Newsweek*, advertisers pay the monetizer, and you have the privilege of linking from *Newsweek* to "16 Women You'd Never Want to Meet in Real Life" and "The Full Beauty Photo Project:

---

[180] Rene Chun, "Machines that Scan Your Face," *The Atlantic*, April 2018, 14–15. Amy B. Wang, "Chinese Use of Big Data Recalls Big Brother," *Washington Post*, rpt *Winnipeg Free Press*, 21 April 2018, F2.

[181] Charles Duhigg, "How Companies Learn Your Secrets." *New York Times Magazine*, 16 February 2012. http://www.nytimes.com/2012/02/19/magazine/shopping-habits.html?_r=0. See also Andrejevic, 25.

Big Women Bare All." Every month, Taboola makes 150 billion content suggestions. Blame yourself, not the monetizer, says CEO Neil Moody, because "The stuff that gets clicks is salacious material…. Kim Kardashian's cleavage shouldn't be promoted in an article about the Ukraine crisis, but it's there because readers are clicking on it."[182] Cyber-culture isn't postmodern in the sense of creating a pluralist democracy, for wealthy corporations control the supposedly free individual; yet cyber-culture *is* postmodern ideologically, for we seem to agree (marketer and customer alike) that desire rules all. Nevertheless, Moody is being disingenuous, since corporate advertisers are also paying a lot to overwhelm "things you may like" with things the monetizer wants you to like. After I click on talented Canadian singer Veda Hille's song "Lucklucky," the YouTube algorithm recognizes that I like Veda Hille, and it provides more of her songs in positions #2 through #6. But in the #1 position, the default song that plays if I do nothing, the algorithm manages to forget Hille and her 2000–18,000 views per song, providing instead a bland song by Edward Sharpe & The Magnetic Zeros that some corporation has paid YouTube to foist upon me and upon 37,112,506 other viewers.[183]

Much wisdom has been attributed to "crowd intelligence," which is usually just another name for the algorithms of big data. Bill Tancer points out that if only we could have properly interpreted Internet searches during the summer of 2007, we could have predicted the Recession of 2007–8. Many people were searching "homes for sale," but few homes were being sold, a sign, had we only divined it, that worried homeowners were investigating, via prices in their area, how much their own homes had dropped in value.[184] What he fails to mention is that long before the crowd came up with its brilliant prophecy, many economists had given frequent warnings about the housing bubble. The appeal of crowd intelligence is that it promises answers to complex questions without "thinking" about them.[185] No in-depth analysis necessary: the postmodern surface tells us all we need to know. "Thinking without thought," Mark Andrejevic calls this process of getting answers merely by aggregating data. Certainly, numbers are crucial in any kind of sociological analysis, and something is gained by moving from anecdotal judgements to "socially distributed" judgements

[182] Hertz.
[183] The example is from YouTube, 3 August 2016.
[184] Tancer, 169.
[185] Stephens-Davidowitz, 71.

on Metacritic (movie reviews), Edmunds.com (used car ratings), or Google Scholar (academic citations).[186] But here postmodern pluralism is deceptive, trading scientific and constitutional forms of deliberation for populism: popularity determines what is *good*.

In 2012, Alistair Croll warned, "Big data is our generation's civil rights issue, and we don't [yet] know it."[187] Cyber-culture's more direct threats to democracy and the polity exploded onto the scene when Mark Zuckerberg was hauled before a joint congressional committee in 2018 to explain why Facebook sold users' private information to the data mining company Cambridge Analytica, allowing Russian agents and bots to influence the 2016 American presidential election. With 50,000 Russian bots (many posing as Americans) tweeting fake news or retweeting Donald Trump's comments in the 10 weeks before the election, the evidence suggests that a foreign power elected the American president. Among the two million retweets by these simulated Americans, Trump was favoured in a 10-1 margin over Hilary Clinton; WikiLeaks, the organization that hacked Clinton's email account, was retweeted 200,000 times.[188] Politics is a particularly fertile ground for fake online news, or Soviet-style disinformation: in a study of 126,000 news stories, Vosoughi, Roy, and Aral found that false stories—calculated to appeal emotionally—were 70% more likely to be retweeted than true stories, that false stories tended to go far deeper into the Internet (cascading into 19 generations of retweets, while true stories rarely went beyond 10 generations deep); and that false stories peaked during important political events, including the 2016 election campaign.[189] Equally troubling in a democracy is the use of Facebook information to target voters. Teams of Trump staffers and outside ad buyers competed against each other, trying to convert Facebook users into campaign donors. The teams tested images and provocative remarks on Facebook users, then repeatedly introduced slight variations and retested the ads. The campaign averaged 40,000 to 60,000 ad variations *per day*,

---

[186] Geoffrey Miller, "My Judgement Enhancer," in Brockman, 288–9.

[187] Andrejevic, 104, 131, 43, 163.

[188] Emily Shugerman, "Russian bots retweeted Donald Trump 10 times more than Hillary Clinton in the last weeks of the campaign," *The Independent*, 28 January 2018, http://www.independent.co.uk/news/world/americas/us-politics/trump-russia-twitter-bots-automated-accounts-congress-russia-investigation-latest-a8182626.html.

[189] Vosoughi, Roy, and Aral. The authors found that humans retweeted false stories as often as bots did.

each tailored to Facebook users' Likes, an ultra-high-speed evolutionary process designed to produce the most effective viral combination.[190]

Yet if political and big data interventions undermine democracy and freedoms in corrosive ways, the Internet's decentralized individualism is no less culpable, undermining democracy from the opposite end. Firstly, anonymity and personal distance of the Internet welcomes trolls onto the public stage. These hybrid children of freedom demand the right to free, nasty-as-they-wanna-be expression, and yet (by name-calling, not by argument) demand that others adhere strictly to the troll's ostensible social code. Which online posts will unleash outrage and the vigilantism of online shaming depends very much on who's doing the scolding. Justine Sacco, heading to Africa, tweeted, "Hope I don't get AIDS. Just Kidding. I'm White!" The tweet, intended to be ironic, wasn't taken that way. Sam Biddle, working for Gawker, immediately posted it, and by the time her plane landed a number of hours later her tweet had gone viral, she had lost her job, and many of her friends had abandoned her. BuzzFeed, on its front page, posted her picture with LOL across it, and pictures of her family were posted online so that they could be shamed too. Men threatened her nephews with rape.

Outrage is easy online: the medium distances us from what we apprehend as a despicable attitude, not a person, so we can express righteous indignation, How-I-Feel, without restraint. We also know that in whatever social circles we move, to be first to share news is to gain followers and retweets. As a result, as one web designer put it, "Every outrage [becomes] the exact same size, whether it [is] a US president declaring war on a foreign nation, or an actor not wearing the proper shade of a designated color to an awards ceremony."[191] Nothing of the outrage against Sacco, Christian Rudder reminds us, helped fight AIDS, and he calls Sacco's case a stoning, since no single individual was the executioner, adding, "it shows we fight hardest against those who can least fight back." A year later, when Sacco asked to see Biddle, he was fearful to encounter the person whose life he had ruined on a whim. Although she had recovered from the trolling, she wanted him to be able to see her as "a person, and not a meme."[192]

---

[190] Matea Gold and Elizabeth Dwoskin, "Fuelled by Facebook," *Washington Post*, rpt *Winnipeg Free Press*, 14 October 2017, D4.

[191] Alexis Madrigal, "The Case Against Retweets," *The Atlantic*, April 2018, 17.

[192] Sam Biddle, "Justine Sacco Is Good at Her Job, and How I Came To Peace With Her," Gawker.com, 12 December 2014, http://gawker.com/justine-sacco-is-good-at-her-job-

At the same time, decentralized viral populism can, of course, bring democratic gains: the #MeToo movement, despite valid concerns in some cases about libel and due process, has brought about far greater equality in situations where individuals' subordinate roles had made them vulnerable to sexual harassment and assault. More commonly, however, populist feeding frenzies ignore reasoned arguments, constitutional protections, minority rights, and laws against hate speech. In 2009, in order to attack financial donors to the Proposition 8 campaign against the legalization of same-sex marriage in California, activists went beyond legitimate measures such as boycotts and protests, setting up Eightmaps.com to harass donors by revealing their personal information and linking it to Google maps. No matter that we might disagree with Proposition 8 (eventually ruled unconstitutional), the individual freedom to harass donors at their homes rather than arguing against the proposition is a troubling new cyber-form of vigilantism. Similar websites can be opened to cyber-bully people on *any* issue.[193]

A second way in which the Internet's individualism can undermine democratic rights is by freeing us from governmental and legal oversight. Internet sexual freedom has been important for LGBTQ people, but PayPal founder Peter Thiel, who joined the libertarian Seasteading Institute in hopes of escaping governmental rules, and who agitated for minimal controls on freedom of speech,[194] also experienced harm in a Wild West of individualized Internet freedom when Gawker outed him as gay. It's precisely the *rules*, some written by governments and some unwritten, that ensure our individual freedom. And more broadly corrosive than the breaching of individual privacy has been the use of cryptocurrencies, such as bitcoin, to free the individual from government oversight of transactions. With a decentralized currency that can be traded freely across borders, organized crime immediately jumped at the opportunity to hide transactions involving drugs, child pornography, guns, and other illegal merchandise. By 2017, it was estimated that a quarter of all bitcoin users and half of all bitcoin holdings were involved in illegal activities. The ability of bitcoin to escape regulation is a significant contributor to its mone-

and-how-i-came-to-pea-1653022326. Jon Ronson, "The Interview," (with Brian Bethune), *Maclean's*, 30 March 2015, 14–15. Rudder, 141–3, 145, 149,

[193] Morozov, *Save*, 64.
[194] Packer, 126, 390. Morozov, *Save*, 129–30.

tary value,[195] a problem that can be addressed only by greater governmental intrusion and less individual freedom.

Thirdly, the Internet undermines democracy by encouraging cyber-balkanization. Not only do TV and the Internet depopulate "third places," where people can work towards social consensus, but the tailored news-feeds of the Internet's echo chamber allows a fuller immersion in a post-modern How-I-Feel ethic, as I tune out voices that I would rather ignore, and as I sidestep the exchange of reasons that defines democratic debate. Asked at the 2006 Online News Association convention whether RSS feeds prevented her from seeing the broader picture, a young panellist shot back, "I'm not trying to get a broader picture. I'm trying to get what I want."[196]

Slacktivism

The decentralized structure of the Internet is potentially a democratic feature. However, democracy also depends on people putting aside some of their individual desires in order to contribute to the common good, while the Internet's expressivist bias tilts instead towards How-I-Feel individualism. The emphasis on individual expression plus a democracy-fed sense of social justice yields slacktivism, a popular postmodern method of political engagement. We "Like," we "Share," we even sign Avaaz online petitions—whatever allows us to remain in front of our computers—but we avoid active political involvement. After 276 schoolgirls were kidnapped from Chibok, Nigeria, in 2014 to become the concubines of Boko Haram terrorists, the hashtag #BringBackOurGirls sped around the world, retweeted 6.1 million times by 2016.[197] Even Michelle Obama and British Prime Minister David Cameron held up #BringBackOurGirls signs for Webcams. At its worst, hashtag activism allows people to feel righteous just because they appear on the Internet for 30 seconds with a sign. Defenders of hashtag activism rightly counter that we don't want private citizens rushing off to battle Boko Haram, that hashtag activism spurs politicians to take action, and that consensus matters. But the problem is that we shake our fingers at complex problems requiring socio-economic development and anti-corruption measures.

---

[195] Sean Foley et al., 2–3, 22, 32.
[196] Bauerlein, 138.
[197] According to *Wikipedia*.

A case even more symptomatic of the pitfalls of slacktivism was the Kony 2012 campaign by Invisible Children. For many years in Uganda, the Joseph-Kony-led Lord's Resistance Army had massacred people, raped women, and enslaved child soldiers. The Kony 2012 viral campaign was supposed to make him famous, and thereby ensure his capture. As a quest for publicity, the campaign succeeded brilliantly, a signal example of the postmodern dominance of the image. As a quest to help Ugandans, not so much. A film on the issue received more than 100 million views in less than a week. People signed pledges, bought Kony 2012 T-shirts and bracelets, and donated money, lifting Invisible Children's revenue to almost $32 million, double that of the previous year. Of the $16 million in expenditures, almost two-thirds went to administration, mobilization, and media, leaving just over a third to be spent on actual programmes that might benefit former child soldiers.[198] Critics explained that the Ugandan rebels had real grievances, and that the conflict wouldn't be ended by neutralizing Kony.

One of the obvious effects of slacktivism is precisely to simplify problems so that they can be solved by keystrokes. Invisible Children has done important relief and development work in Africa and has helped convince some LRA soldiers to defect. Yet the lopsided distribution of the Kony funds diverts too much into spectacle. Cyber-culture, by itself, can't be blamed for slacktivism or for the decline of active commitments beyond the self. In Putnam's mid-1990s surveys, early Internet users were engaged with the community at the same level as non-users, and commitments had been declining since the 1960s, long before the Internet.[199] But cyber-culture intensifies the problem by leaving behind the intransigent real to settle in the malleable simulated world that Guy Debord prophesied, in which sharing Facebook videos is expected to end an insurgency.

MORE RESOLUTELY INTO SIMULATION

Already in 1998, when Disney's Animal Kingdom zoo opened in Orlando, visitors complained that the animals weren't realistic (i.e. Hollywood) enough—the crocodiles tended merely to lie in the sun. In contrast, the

[198] Tory Shepherd, "Remember Kony 2012? Well, it's 2013. What happened?" *Herald Sun* (Australia), 11 January 2013, accessed 5 April 2013, http://www.heraldsun.com.au/news/world/remember-kony-2012-well-its-2013-what-happened/story-fndl34gw-1226550575923. See also Invisible Children, "Highlights from FY2012," http://webinvisible.wpengine.netdna-cdn.com/wp-content/themes/invisiblechildren2.0/images/financials/forms/2012/highlights.pdf, accessed 27 April 2016.
[199] Putnam, 170.

animatronic crocodiles in other parts of Disneyworld slapped their tails and rolled their eyes—a far livelier spectacle.[200] For good reason, Jean Baudrillard pronounced simulation's coverage as the "death pangs of the real." His pre-Internet characterization of the media—"a marvelous instrument for destabilizing the real and the true"[201] could also gloss Facebook and the broad human migration online. On the one hand, our sophisticated technologies, such as CGI and motion-capture, couldn't exist without a profound knowledge of the physics of the real world. On the other hand, our simulations match neither the complexity nor the banality of the real. Kevin Kelly understandably loves how the Internet constantly gives the mind raw material for thought.[202] He enthuses, "Surrendering to the web is like going on an aboriginal walkabout. The comforting illogic of dreams reigns."[203] Only someone under the spell of simulation, ignorant of the wilderness, could equate clicking with walking.

More dangerous is the threat of the image to embodied community and political deliberation. Debord claimed that the spectacle affirms human life as mere appearance,[204] and Baudrillard, expanding, argues that we've entered a historical phase in which the image bears no relation to reality. In a society organized around the creation and consumption of images, the media anchors itself to spectacle, to both "the moral condemnation of terrorism" and "the brutal charm of the terrorist act." For Baudrillard, even the radio call-in show is nothing more than "a circular arrangement through which one stages the desire of the audience."[205] Although we could respond that call-in shows provide a public forum wherein political policy can at least be argued, Baudrillard could also point to the debasing of debate on TV (via talking points, via guests who take extreme positions) and on the Internet (via the echo chamber). The danger is that we may vacate the communicative reason that keeps alive a social contract and the notion of ethical commitments.

Baudrillard's position, sometimes equated with postmodernity, explicates the dangers of simulation. However, most communication, both online and off, does still present true information. Simulation long predates postmodernity, of course, although our vivid contemporary simula-

---

[200] Turkle, 4.
[201] Baudrillard, *Selected*, 220; *Simulacra*, 43.
[202] Kevin Kelly, "The Waking Dream," in Brockman, 21.
[203] Kevin Kelly, quoted in Turkle, 284.
[204] Debord, 9 (#10).
[205] Baudrillard, *Simulacra*, 6, 84, 80; *Selected*, 220.

tions make us less apt to notice how immersive books once were. Both the destruction and communication of the real, often in the same communicative act, have been with us probably since the invention of language and certainly since the beginnings of symbolic art, associated with the appearance of modern humans 100,000 years ago.[206] With the larger prefrontal cortex, came religious artworks such as the Löwenmensch sculpture (Lion-man, 35,000 ya),[207] and whether we call these works "counterfactual speculation," adaptive interventions in the environment, or simulations, the ability to imagine alternatives to the real gave us a key survival advantage.[208] It thus makes little sense to say, as Baudrillard does, that "the drive to spectacle is more powerful than the instinct of preservation."[209] By dropping the word "representation" in favour of "simulation," Baudrillard's argument circularly assumes the destabilization of reality, and ignores the way in which artistic and purported documentary representations belong to Habermas's order of communicative rationality.

Sixteen-year-old Rachel mistook simulation for reality when, on iwannabefamous.com, she wrote, "I want the thrill the happiness and the fun like I see in movies... I am sick of looking for a 'regular' job."[210] She takes the spectacle at face value, so that, as Debord predicted, her gestures are those of another, of the star.[211] Yet, without a robust conception of reality, we wouldn't even notice the irony of Rachel's comment. Contra Baudrillard, Torben Grodal argues that, until recently, it was easier to lie in print than with images, that there is no simple distinction between reality and communicative representations (including media), that communication always involves trusting certain communicators, and that what seems to be a crisis in representation is really a greater awareness of its problems.[212] Baudrillard's version of postmodernist thought ignores the more humanizing effects of new media in presenting unstereotyped foreigners,[213] for example, and, as Best and Kellner argue, his work ulti-

---

[206] Allen 49.

[207] Hoffecker, 101.

[208] Argyros 312. Dutton 5. Hoffecker, 101–2, 114–15.

[209] Baudrillard, *Selected*, 205.

[210] "Today's famous person is Rachel," 1999–2003, http://www.iwannabefamous.com/featured/rachel.shtml, accessed 2 June 2016. Niedzviecki, *Special*, 114.

[211] Debord 16 (#30). Best and Kellner, *Turn*, 90.

[212] Grodal, *Embodied*, 268–70; *Moving*, 36–7.

[213] Mark Poster in Baudrillard, *Selected*, 7–8.

mately invites political quietism.[214] Experienced media viewers can distinguish between the false and the true, fiction and non-, even when falsehood is presented in a documentary style (as I argued in the chapter on truth). To interpret *any* behaviour, not just media representations, requires cognitive analysis.[215] It quickly becomes apparent that the communications occurring in *King Lear* or in Amanda Todd's YouTube video are very different from Kate Winslet's photoshopped narrow waist on the cover of *GQ*, even though each of them involves simulation. Nevertheless, because images dominate online, and because, as David Williams says, in cyberspace "all realities are simulations,"[216] Baudrillard's fears can't be dismissed: "Communication" (with its rational strategies) "is too slow," he says, "The look is much faster."[217]

"Layered" Reality

In a cognitive analysis of cyber-culture's simulations, it may be too early to assess the layered effects of living simultaneously in real and virtual worlds. Between 2004 and 2014, Nicholas Felton digitally tracked his locations, the music he listened to, the videos he watched, his computing, driving, sleep, exercise, heart rate, weight, the beverages he consumed, and even his friends' moods and food consumption during their encounters with him. Overlaying Felton's body is his statistical summary of it. Unlike Benjamin Franklin, who kept track of his daily progress on his moral virtues, such as temperance and justice, Felton tracked mostly his physical body.[218] Franklin's project was not without simulation, since he did aim to superimpose a better self over his natural faults, but his goal of moral per-

---

[214] Best and Kellner, *Turn*, 96–100, 105. For Debord, in contrast, "no object is fully opaque or inscrutable" (Best and Kellner, *Turn*, 112). However, Debord also claims that, "The point is to actually participate in the community of dialogue and the game with time that up till now have merely been *represented* by poetic and artistic works" (Debord, 103 (#187). This suggests that he doesn't really trust art at all. Yet it is precisely the non-real, spectacle aspect of art that, since the Pleistocene, has been the greatest tool in human adaptation to the world. Although Debord makes a valid distinction between spectacle and existence, he seems to ask (impossibly, given human neural adaptations) for a world devoid of spectacle. This call for a revolution against human image-making is the opposite of Baudrillard's quietism.

[215] Grodal, *Moving*, 36–7.

[216] David Williams, *Imagined*, 250.

[217] Baudrillard, *Selected*, 189.

[218] Young, 8, 54, 33, 36. See also "Nicholas Felton," http://feltron.com/.

fection was profoundly social—such that even the virtue of frugality, which we might consider self-directed and almost an economic vice nowadays, Franklin approached in a socially productive way: "Make no Expense but to do good to others or yourself."[219] On the other hand, the data-map that Felton superimposed over the body is less social and far more self-involved.[220]

More intrusively, engineer and life-logger, C. Gordon Bell, wore a Microsoft SenseCam around his neck to automatically take photos of his surroundings and the people he interacted with.[221] Google Glass, the head-mounted computing device, goes beyond even SenseCam. Looking at a real restaurant, users simultaneously see restaurant reviews superimposed on the real building.[222] Eric Schmidt likes the idea of his devices searching without being asked to do so: "When I walk down the streets of Berlin... I want... my smartphone to be doing searches constantly 'Did you know? Did you know?.... This occurred here. This occurred there.' Because it knows who I am. It knows what I care about."[223] The layered real of Google Glass has some very beneficial applications. Surgeons performing cleft lip surgery in Lebanon were able to connect with doctors in New York who had more experience with the procedure. The doctors in New York used an iPad to mark where the incision on the two-year-old Lebanese patient should be made, and the surgeons in Lebanon, wearing Google Glass, could see on the patient's face precisely where to cut.[224] However, the first Google Glass addict has already been identified,[225] and Glass's critics worry about privacy for people within the range of the device's surreptitious recording. Andrejevic called it a materialization of Žižek's Big Other[226]—the social system watching us. In Jonathan Franzen's *Purity* (2015), even the founder of the "Sunlight Project," Andreas Wolf,

[219] Benjamin Franklin, *The Autobiography of Benjamin Franklin*, Electronic Text Center, University of Virginia Library, 83.

[220] Young, 36.

[221] Young, 100.

[222] Andrejevic, 148.

[223] Morozov, *Save*, 257–8.

[224] "AUBMC doctors conduct first virtually-augmented surgery in the region and third outside the US," American University of Beirut News, 22 April 2014, http://www.aub.edu.lb/news/2014/Pages/aubmc-gsf.aspx.

[225] Alter, 44–5.

[226] Andrejevic, 148.

who demands that everything become public and be placed on the Internet so as to disinfect it, also asks that a life-logger's camera be turned off.[227] Other layered realities abound. Fake celebrity photos have become commonplace; the music of Hatsune Miku is popular in Japan, even though she is a hologram[228]; and in 2010, the Gregory brothers created a viral sensation by "songifying" a news interview. After a home invasion and attempted rape of his sister in a Huntsville, Alabama housing project, Antoine Dodson gave a passionate WAFF-TV news interview that caught the attention of the Gregorys. Using an Auto-Tune program, they changed the pitches of Dodson's words to make him appear to sing, "He's climbin' in yuh window, snatchin' yuh people up… hide yuh kids, hide yuh wife." The remix became the "Bed Intruder Song" and (apart from major music studio releases) the most-watched YouTube video of 2010. In a different way from Google Glass, the "Bed Intruder Song" layers reality, superimposing a catchy tune on a disturbing crime. For Baratunde Thurston, the problem with the song is twofold: the song distorts the painful underlying events, and people laugh at Dodson's unintentional activation of African-American stereotypes. What heartened Thurston was that Dodson took control of his own meme.[229] The Gregory brothers shared half of the profits with Dodson and he parlayed his fame into other ventures, moving his family out of the Huntsville projects and to Los Angeles. Dodson felt ambivalent about the postmodern simulation, but decided that "it's taking a terrible situation and making at least something positive out of it."[230]

In a sense, every artist, from the political cartoonist to the historical novelist, overlays the real with irony and symbol. Other songified videos— such as Charlie Sheen's drug-braggadocio "Winning" or politicians'

[227] Franzen, *Purity*, 513.

[228] de Waal, *Bonobo*, 204.

[229] The Gregory brothers, "The Bed Intruder Song," https://www.youtube.com/watch?v=hMtZfW2z9dw, accessed 22 April 2016. See also "Antoine Dodson," *Wikipedia*. Andy Carvin, "'Bed Intruder' Meme: A Perfect Storm of Race, Music, Comedy And Celebrity," *NPR*, 5 August 2010. Thanks to Carissa Taylor for drawing this to my attention.

[230] Mitchell Peters, "Gregory Brothers Take Antoine Dodson to Hot 100," *Billboard*, 19 August 2010, http://www.billboard.com/articles/news/956772/gregory-brothers-take-antoine-dodson-to-the-hot-100. "Bed Intruder" Singer Moves Family into New Home," *US Weekly*, 16 September 2010, http://www.usmagazine.com/celebrity-news/news/bed-intruder-singer-moves-family-into-new-home-2010169.

speeches—created less controversy.[231] Will we acclimatize to technologies that make people appear to do things that they never did in real life, or will those who unwillingly had their images remixed and layered sue for control? As the Internet suffuses our world, we come closer to Baudrillard's description of postmodernity as a defeat of the real. In the Songify videos, the line between reality and simulation is still fairly clear, but with the photoshopping of models and with Adobe's Voco software, which allows one to manipulate audio recordings and *change* the speaker's words, the line becomes very blurry. The effects—politically potent untruths and sexual desire for falsified versions of women—are pernicious. Most troubling of all is the Deepfakes phenomenon, in which the FakeApp program is used to create very convincing simulations of people engaged in acts (mostly pornographic) that they never performed. Deepfakes have the potential to wipe out the line between simulation and reality, as Jordan Peele has warned in his fake video of Obama calling Donald Trump a "dipshit" and telling everybody to "Stay woke, bitches."[232] Some individuals will be harmed by falsified videos, while others may escape responsibility for misdeeds by blaming falsified videos.[233] If Baudrillard's understanding of simulation defines postmodernity, we have not yet succeeded in dispensing the real, with but cyber-simulations are threatening to do so.

Internet Addiction and Mediated Lives

Besides the public threat to our shared reality, there are also individual costs when our postmodern simulations get more and more sophisticated. Preferring TV and computer screens, many young people have stopped attending performing arts events. Between 1982 and 2002, the proportion of young adults in audiences dropped from 18.5% to 11.2%.[234] Even non-sedentary games such as Wii Sports do not fulfil the elusive promise of making the screen more real. Players assumed that Wii Sports would

[231] The Gregory brothers, "Songify This – Winning – a song by Charlie Sheen," 7 March 2011, http://www.youtube.com/watch?v=9QS0q3mGPGg, accessed 22 April 2016.

[232] James Vincent, "Watch Jordan Peele use AI to make Barack Obama deliver a PSA about fake news, *The Verge*, 17 April 2018, https://www.theverge.com/tldr/2018/4/17/17247334/ai-fake-news-video-barack-obama-jordan-peele-buzzfeed. See also Stephen Maher, "The Year of Fakes," *Maclean's*, January 2019, 12–13.

[233] See, for example, Franklin Foer, "Reality's End," *The Atlantic*, May 2018, 15–17.

[234] Bauerlein, 200.

help them lose weight, but most game-players simply ended up doing less exercise. More importantly, Internet and video-game addictions have been implicated in ADHD-like symptoms,[235] as people sacrifice reality for virtual lives. At the rehab centre reSTART, near Seattle, 29-year-old Brett Walker was among those who struggled to overcome technological addictions to the many little spikes of dopamine that make online life and gaming so exciting. For Walker, the detox was an attempt to escape *World of Warcraft*, which had dominated 4 years of his life. He says, "I could do whatever I wanted [online], go where I wanted... The world was my oyster." But the game destroyed his real life—weakening him physically, draining his bank account, and isolating him socially.[236] Danny Hartzell of Tampa Bay, who lost his job in the Recession of 2007–8, owned a huge video-game collection, and it made his wife miserable to see him playing *World of Warcraft* for 10 hours at a time.[237] Even those who can still function in real life realize that the long hours spent online have lowered their quality of life. Hank, a law professor in his late 30s, spends at least 12 hours a day on the Internet. He says, "[It] makes the flat time with my family harder. Like it's taking place in slow motion. I'm short with them." After dinner, he can't wait to get back online.[238] This makes sense: quick gratification online primes us to demand the same in the real world.[239] Former Microsoft VP Linda Stone admits, "The Internet stole my body, now a lifeless form hunched in front of a glowing screen."[240]

A dangerous social effect of the screen's postmodern simulations is that American soldiers who engage in drone warfare suffer *lower* rates of PTSD than do regular military personnel.[241] Good for the soldiers; not so good for civilians near the drone targets. At places such as Creech air force base near Las Vegas, invulnerable drone operators with video-game skills sit in front of screens and "pull the weeds." In other words, they pilot very real Hellfire missiles in Afghanistan and Pakistan to blow up terrorists and whoever else happens to be in the vicinity. Only infrared images of people appear on the screen—no faces—so the operators relate to "heat signs," not to people. Dehumanized images make the strikes feel simulated,

---

[235] Small, 66.
[236] Roberts, 1.
[237] Packer, 342.
[238] Turkle, 288.
[239] Roberts, 61.
[240] Linda Stone, "Navigating Physical and Virtual Lives," in Brockman, 219.
[241] Peron.

unreal, an effect that the operators' language confirms. Strikes are called "bug-splats," and the smaller black shadows (i.e. children) are called "fun-sized terrorists."[242] Some operators do worry about the many civilians they kill in drone strikes, and quit the job, but because the computer screen distances the operators from the targets, killing is not the main stressor. The main stressors are the 12-hour shifts in box-sized rooms, low meaning, low salary, shift work, and the difficulty of maintaining a relationship with one's family.[243] To the moral question raised by explicit video games—Is a vice I engage in while playing a game still a vice?[244]—we must say yes.

At the far end of this layered reality is full-scale immersion in virtual realities via headsets and gloves. Even with earlier immersive technologies, computer scientist Jaron Lanier explains, "your brain starts to believe in the virtual world instead of the physical one. There's an uncanny moment when the transition occurs." He programmed unusual limb placements and extra limbs, yet found that it wasn't difficult to control them as his brain began to accept them as parts of his own body. Theoretically, anything can become part of one's body, even clouds. For Lanier, this gives the virtual experience a "revelatory" character, the feeling of a boundless body. "I fully expect morphing to become as important a dating skill as kissing," he says.[245]

Next Step, Transhuman?

"I want to mutate… into whatever it is human beings are slated to turn into next," declares Julien in *Generation A*,[246] and, indeed, some of the advances in simulation during the postmodern era move us towards transhumanism. Sales of wearable technologies increased exponentially to about $2 billion by 2013, and were expected to reach $18 billion by 2018.[247] Drugs like Viagra and now Vyleesi are being marketed not to

[242] Ed Pilkington, "Life as a drone operator: 'Ever step on ants and never give it another thought?'" *Guardian*, 19 November 2015, http://www.theguardian.com/world/2015/nov/18/life-as-a-drone-pilot-creech-air-force-base-nevada.

[243] Peron.

[244] Achouche.

[245] Lanier, 185–7.

[246] Coupland, *Generation A*, 15.

[247] "Facts and Statistics on Wearable Technology," Statista: The Statistics Portal, accessed 19 May 2016, http://www.statista.com/topics/1556/wearable-technology/.

correct dysfunction, but to change the nature of the individual's desire. The latest i-limbs can convert muscle contractions into electronic impulses that control the simulated limb's movement. When asked whether he would wish for his legs back, Hugh Herr, who has two prosthetic legs, says, "Absolutely not.... I think normal bodies are boring."[248] Neuroscientists have converted brain activity (with the help of implanted electrodes) into digital signals. A Brown University team has developed systems allowing quadriplegics to use brain signals to control cursors and even prosthetic arms.[249] Implanted microchips have become widespread for livestock and pets, though, in the human world, devices such as the "VeriChip" have been slower to catch on. In the early 2000s, the Baja Beach Club in Barcelona encouraged patrons to get microchips implanted into their arms to store credit card information, yet concerns about cancer and security derailed marketing plans. More recently, however, employees at the Swedish startup hub Epicenter have had a small microchip injected into the fleshy area between the thumb and the index finger. Twenty-five-year-old Sandra Haglof, who had a chip implanted says, "I want to be part of the future."[250]

More vexed are attempts to simulate the social and emotional content of animal and human minds. In Japan, lack of companionship, especially for the elderly, has led to companionable robots. "Paro," marketed since 2004 and looking like a cuddly baby harp seal, makes eye contact, reacts to a number of words, and shows several emotions. It responds positively to petting, less positively to aggression. For some of the elderly who have to rely on sociable robots, the need for *any* relationship may understandably outweigh the fact that the "relationship" is simulated. But a 30-year-old man says, "I'd rather talk to a robot. Friends can be exhausting. The robot will always be there for me. And whenever I'm done, I can walk

[248] Lunau, "Building," 52.
[249] Alessondra Springmann, "Move a Mouse Cursor with Your Brain," *PCWorld*, 2 November 2010, http://www.pcworld.com/article/209553/Move_a_mouse_cursor_with_your_brain.html. Jason McBride. "Mind Games." *Maclean's*, 7 January 2013, 40. David Ewing Duncan, "The Brain-Computer Interface That Let a Quadriplegic Woman Move a Cup," *The Atlantic*, 16 May 2012, http://www.theatlantic.com/health/archive/2012/05/the-brain-computer-interface-that-let-a-quadriplegic-woman-move-a-cup/257275/.
[250] James Brooks, "Cyborgs at Work: Employees Getting Implanted with Microchips," NBC Miami, 3 April 2017, http://www.nbcmiami.com/news/tech/Cyborgs-at-Work-Employees-Getting-Implanted-With-Microchips-417962503.html?akmobile=o.

away."[251] The necessary comfort that these robots provide shades into convenience, since, unlike people, they make few demands for time and emotion. In our How-I-Feel universes, we needn't worry about this Other's emotional needs.

Worldwide, the most pervasive companionable robot is, of course, the smartphone. People speak of loving their cell phones, since they embody the presence of friends and family, yet even when friends and family are present, cell phones dominate. The times that she was without her cell phone, a television producer in her mid-40s admits, "I felt like I had lost my mind," and many people describe the loss of their cell phones as like a death.[252] In a 2006 survey, a third of young adults admitted that they couldn't live without their cell phones,[253] though perhaps they wouldn't go as far as the characters in *Super Sad True Love Story* who commit suicide rather than face a future without their äppäräti.[254] The flight from face to Facebook, from telephoning to texting has increased the sheer number of written messages that we exchange, but the human quality of those messages is another matter entirely.

Hunger for the Unreal

Trying to understand her teenage son Gabe's passion for the fictional online game Futopia, the psychologist Candace in Richard Powers's *Generosity* calls the passion "Infinite hunger for the unreal," and asks, "Why should that be useful in little boys?"[255] A haunting question, since it implicates reading and film no less than cyber-culture. We are postmodern to the extent that the Internet has become Futopia, a simulation beyond all our previous counterfactual speculations. The ensuing cyborg self—at the intersection between human and machine, between the given and the made—no longer remembers the cosmos reverently, and can, as Donna Haraway argues, liberate us from the domination of nature.[256] Shortenings of attention span, ever-greater simulation, and the distancing from one

[251] Turkle, 8–10.
[252] Turkle, 246, 16.
[253] The survey was by Pew (Bauerlein, 82).
[254] Shteyngart, *Super*, 270.
[255] Powers, *Generosity*, 95.
[256] See Donna Haraway, from *A Manifesto for Cyborgs* (1985), *The Norton Anthology of Theory and Criticism*, 3rd ed., Vincent Leitch, ed., New York, W.W. Norton, 2018, 2045–8. See also David Williams, *Imagined*, 238.

another are evidence of human freedom, but they also partake in the post-modern dilemma, since there's no objective measure to tell us how much of these are too much. If we can maintain the civilization that sustains it, the Internet's alternate world will accompany us, for better and for worse, an expression of infinite human variety. Yet these changes do represent a danger for the exchange of reasons that underlies democracy. A lot will depend on whether we can continue to tend our human connections in the real world. On the political level, a lot will depend on whether we can detect simulations and maintain some measure of online democracy, to limit political manipulation, corporate control, and individual lawlessness.[257] On the individual level, our enchanting cyber-culture, like drugs and alcohol, is already creating a postmodern underclass of those unable to balance their real lives with their alternate worlds. In the fictional *Generosity*, an ice storm causes an enchanted dark to fall and, as every screen blacks out, people begin talking to strangers, but Gabe's greatest anxiety is that the computer has shut down before he could save his game. In the real world, Mark, a 20-year-old college student, explains that the most *important* thing that older people need to understand is that young people can't just pause an online, multiplayer game "and hop to it."[258] How insulated Gabe and Mark are from humanity's earlier, more primal, dangers! Looking at the endlessness of Futopia's postmodern simulations, Russell (the boyfriend of Gabe's mother) thinks, "When we run out of resources, we can always move here."[259] He knows, of course, that if we run out of resources, the server farms will be the first to fall silent.

[257] In his novel *Neuromancer* (1984), William Gibson correctly predicted that cyberspace would increase corporate power and weaken the public sphere. See David Williams, *Imagined*, 245.

[258] Twenge, *iGen*, 59.

[259] Powers, *Generosity*, 168–170, 159.

CHAPTER 6

The Nation

As a borderless cyber-mediated postmodernity continues to erode tradition, community, and, at times, rationality and democracy, some observers
expect, even hope, that the nation-state will dissolve too. The nation-state
was the great success story of modern community, argues Bauman, though
in order to succeed it suppressed some communities, their local customs,
and their languages.[1] Taking measure of World War II and of his friend's
death, Michael Ondaatje's Count Almàsy comes to a postmodernist conclusion in *The English Patient*: "We are deformed by nation-states. Madox
died because of nations…. Erase the family name! Erase nations! I was
taught such things by the desert."[2] Almàsy's lesson is also Ondaatje's: he
has said that the novel is about "the dangers of love of country."[3] The
borderless world of the desert in the novel offers a pluralist hope, a hope
quickly dashed because neither national army understands the desert, and
Almàsy's beloved Katherine Clifton ultimately pays with her life when he
inaccurately calls her his wife, erasing her national identity.[4] *The English
Patient* is symptomatic of how, in the twentieth and twenty-first centuries,
the nation has increasingly come under pressure from within and without.
From within, the postmodern individual, aware of the nation's oppres-

---

[1] Bauman, *Liquid*, 173.
[2] Ondaatje, 138–9.
[3] "Michael Ondaatje and Anthony Minghella interview on *The English Patient*," Charlie
Rose, 1996, published 16 July 2016, https://www.youtube.com/watch?v=ScjsILH9Ud4.
[4] See David Williams, *Imagined*, 226–7, 240–4 on Almàsy's post-national identity.

© The Author(s) 2019
R. Kramer, *Are We Postmodern Yet?*,
https://doi.org/10.1007/978-3-030-30569-7_6

sions and less inclined to make sacrifices for the larger group, avoids political involvement, a process aided by the reconceptualization of the individual as consumer rather than citizen. And from without, wide-ranging trade deals and the moral authority of the pluralist UN have eaten into the sovereignty of the nation.

On and off, people continue to entertain the fantasy of a nation-race unity, most notoriously in the case of Nazi Germany, and most recently among the populist nationalists in Hungary, Poland, Austria, the US, and Brazil. However, it's not always easy to distinguish populism from a more rational unwillingness to jettison the goods of the nation for the fully deregulated world envisioned by a globalizing elite. State-building involved a rational calculus centred around a dominant group, but usually welcoming many groups in subordinate roles: witness the white Anglo-Saxon-dominated American "melting pot" and Canadian "mosaic." Barring a major disaster, a return to national identity on the visceral model of tribe or race is unlikely in the West. Despite the atavism of Brexit and Donald Trump's "Make America Great Again," most of the evidence suggests that the postmodern era is witnessing the slow, though uneven, divorce of nation from tribe. The late 1990s marked the point, worldwide, when the percentage of countries with policies *favouring* ethnic minorities rose above the percentage discriminating against them. High-profile police shootings notwithstanding, the US has seen a significant *decline* in racist violence, racist jokes, and racialized poverty in recent decades.[5] In a more individualist and human-rights-oriented culture, it has grown easier for subordinate groups within the nation to point out that they have not been treated equally—so we saw civil rights marches, assertions of aboriginal title, and, in reaction, defensive assertions of white tribal identity.

Politically we aren't fully postmodern yet. National sovereignty has not dissolved to the extent hoped for or feared. We are witnessing something like the selective religious adherence that is the subject of the next chapter: fewer and fewer people feel a duty-bound allegiance to the nation, but favour a rational patriotism that assigns a mostly protective role to the nation. Tighter immigration rules and protectionist measures to shelter my industry, yes; service in the military, no thanks.[6] So, for example,

---

[5] Pinker, *Better*, 384–92; *Enlightenment*, 218–20.

[6] Recently both the American and Canadian armies have had difficulty meeting recruitment goals. Jim Tice, "Army recruiting market tightens but service expects to make 2016 goal," *Army Times*, 23 February 2016, https://www.armytimes.com/story/military/

Trump's attempt to give Wisconsin dairy farmers access to Canada's closed, supply-managed dairy market received enthusiastic support from Democrats, while his Muslim travel ban had to be reframed, and, even then, required a Supreme Court decision.

The relative decline in patriotism is surprising, since political marketing consistently aims for the gut, where emotion defeats policies and rational discourse. Parties have sought to shape public opinion through spectacle, personality, emotion, and even the purchase of Twitter followers from companies such as TwitterWind.[7] In the summer before the 2016 US election, estimates suggested that up to 80% of Donald Trump's 10.3 million Twitter followers were either bots that he paid for or people who never actually logged onto Twitter.[8] Voters, far from declining the manipulation, have rewarded whoever promised the most. But it's precisely this intrusion of pop culture and memes into politics that, for two reasons, helps to create a more *calculating* patriotism. First, now that soundbite and image address the citizen as consumer, the political message becomes appealing mainly if it's good for me (not, as from time immemorial, if it's good for my group). Secondly, citizens are increasingly aware of the manipulation, and are less likely to give in unreservedly to manufactured patriotism. These developments are clearly postmodern in the role played by simulation and rising individualism, but such developments also work against postmodern simulation in that rationality—a self-interested rationality, to be sure—plays an important part.

INDIVIDUALISM: DISTRUST OF THE POLITICAL

It has become a postmodern truism that people don't trust establishment politicians. Four out of five Americans are dissatisfied with the government. Confidence in Congress fell from 40% in the 1970s to 7% in 2014.

careers/army/2016/02/23/army-recruiting-market-tightens-but-service-expects-make-2016-goal/80624982/. Lee Berthiaume, "Canadian military losing soldiers at increasing rate as headcount drops to level not seen in years," *National Post*, 27 January 2016, http://news.nationalpost.com/news/canada/canadian-military-losing-soldiers-at-increasing-rate-headcount-drops-to-level-not-seen-in-years.

[7] Rudder, 214.

[8] Nick Bilton, "Trump's Biggest Lie? The Size of His Twitter Following," *Vanity Fair*, 4 August 2016, http://www.vanityfair.com/news/2016/08/trumps-biggest-lie-the-size-of-his-twitter-following. Trump is not alone—the practice is common among politicians and retailers.

Even confidence in the Supreme Court declined to one-third by 2014.[9] We can't blame corrupt politicians for the change, for corruption is more difficult in the age of Internet surveillance. According to some scholars, politicians have been "desacralized" because of the growing exposure of their personal lives in the media,[10] but I would argue that there are more important causes. Firstly, income disparity is a factor, since countries with less disparity (the Nordic countries and Switzerland) show more trust.[11] Both Donald Trump and Bernie Sanders, so different politically, appealed to voters because they stood outside of party establishments and stressed the unfairness of the present globalized system. Secondly, scepticism in general is on the rise in the postmodern era. Thirdly, individualism means that I expect to have my wishes heeded, yet my opinions carry little weight in Ottawa or Washington. Objectively, that shouldn't be so disillusioning—why should a single voter step ahead of the other 36 or 324 million? Yet, if I've been told constantly how important I am as an individual, it *is* disillusioning. Young voters are targeted by advertisements using individualistic motivations such as "Express yourself."[12] It shouldn't shock us, then, that more than two-thirds of young people agree that "Our generation has an important voice, but no one seems to hear it."[13] Robert Lane has shown that much of our happiness is centred on self-determination, which, in the postmodern era, has come to mean maximizing "subjective well-being"—happiness. Unfortunately, democracy, with its complex checks and balances, doesn't make people happier in a direct way. Acts that benefit society or promote the economic equality of others don't necessarily *feel* rewarding to the individual voter,[14] so if How-I-Feel is a primary ethical marker, there will be collateral damage to democracy.

Possibly because subjective well-being isn't connected to democratic values, only half of young adults agreed that they should, in order to be good citizens, pay attention to government and politics.[15] This suggests a fourth reason for decreasing confidence in public officials: people,

[9] Mounk, 100.

[10] Stanyer, 162.

[11] Stephen D. King, 158.

[12] Twenge and Campbell, 290.

[13] Bauerlein, 185; Maich and George, 159.

[14] Lane, 334, 231, 272–3, 277.

[15] Bauerlein, 19. Among college freshmen, those who thought it essential to keep up with politics declined from 60% in 1966 to 34% in 2004. Young adults were much less likely to read the news than were older adults (Twenge, *Me*, 141–2).

especially young people, know less and less about politics. In a 2006 National Assessment of Educational Progress exam, a photo of the words "COLORED ENTRANCE" above a theatre door baffled two-thirds of American high school seniors. Only a third of 15- to 26-year-olds in 2003 knew which party held the majority in their state legislature, and a handful more knew which party controlled Congress. In contrast, nearly two-thirds could name the *American Idol* winner. Similarly, Grade 9ers did far better at naming the Three Stooges (from a *bygone* media era) than at naming the three branches of government. Mark Bauerlein blames this not on purposeful ignorance, but on the way that the immediate world of friends, sitcoms, pop music, and Facebook crowds out the rest of the world.[16] Keeping current with the news correlates with civic involvement,[17] but, generationally, Internet news-readers (and especially those with 10+ hours per week on social media) show less interest in actual social and political issues[18] and less civic involvement than those who read newspapers or watch TV news, the older media forms that historically undergirded the shared community of the nation.[19] On the positive side, young people's political values are more likely to *influence* other aspects of their lives.[20] On the negative side, the unwillingness to take an active part in shaping the polity may also explain why young people in the 2000s are more likely than those in the 1960s to think that they aren't in control of their lives.[21]

These factors have led to some distressing outcomes in the postmodern era. For one, younger generations are less politically involved, and vote less than their parents did. In the US, about three-quarters of young adults rarely vote.[22] Political freedom, Bauman suggests, has for many people come to mean freedom *from* politics.[23] Between 1972 and 2000, voter participation by Americans under age 35 dropped 16% or more, with the largest drop among the youngest voters. Because of massive efforts to get young voters out, federal participation numbers rose between 2004 and 2016, but it's too soon to tell whether the increase represents a change in

[16] Bauerlein, 17, 19, 13.
[17] Putnam, 218, 220.
[18] Twenge, *iGen*, 176–7.
[19] Putnam, 219–21, 250–1.
[20] Roberts, 222.
[21] Twenge, *Me*, 139.
[22] Twenge, *Me*, 138; Twenge, *iGen*, 282.
[23] Bauman, *Does*, 204–5.

attitude or just an effect of some highly polarized elections.[24] In support of the attitudinal hypothesis is the worrisome fact that 97 million people voted for their favourite *American Idol* in 2008, while only 70 million for Barack Obama.[25]

Realizing the power of social media, Labour supporters Yara Fowler and Charlotte Goodman realized that their best bet to get the youth vote out in the 2017 British national election was through Tinder. They convinced hundreds of their friends to turn over their Tinder profiles to a chatbot that nudged young people to vote Labour.[26] Millennials were just as likely as Generation Xers and Boomers to sign petitions online, but less likely to vote, and less likely to contact an elected official, whether online, by phone, or by letter.[27] iGeners seem to have a somewhat greater interest in social issues than Millennials do, but that hasn't yet translated into political interest or action, leaving the field open for populists and authoritarians.[28] The worry is that young people might withdraw from democratic institutions. The greatest predictor of voting, though, is not age but educational level: if education lags, so will political involvement.

A second outcome can be, as Kirby suggests, "a child's conception of politics." He argues that cinema's love affair with ancient, mythological, and apocalyptic scenarios reveals that we've lost patience with the complexities and horse-trading required by real politics. As evidence, he cites the popularity of *Lord of the Rings*, *The Matrix*, *Star Wars*, *Gladiator*, *Troy*, and *Alexander*.[29] Simplistic cures for complex problems have always been attractive, yet Kirby's point is valid: the recent glut of superhero movies and several populist successes is exactly what he would have predicted. The major weakness in his assessment is his failure to recognize that mythological works of art search for principles that *precede* political

---

[24] Twenge, *Me*, 143–4; Greenberg, 26; Pew, "Millennials," 63, 80. Estimates are that 50% of eligible Americans aged 18–30 voted in 2016. CIRCLE (The Center for Information and Research on Civic Learning and Engagement), "An Estimated 24 Million Young People Voted in 2016 Election," 9 November 2016, http://civicyouth.org/an-estimated-24-million-young-people-vote-in-2016-election/.

[25] D. Shields, 109.

[26] "The Current," CBC Radio One, 27 June 2017. Yara Rodrigues Fowler and Charlotte Goodman, "How Tinder Could Take Back the White House," *New York Times*, 22 June 2017, https://www.nytimes.com/2017/06/22/opinion/how-tinder-could-take-back-the-white-house.html.

[27] Pew, "Millennials," 83.

[28] Twenge, *iGen*, 281–2. See also Mounk.

[29] Kirby, *Digimodernism*, 152–3.

horse-trading, focus groups, and strategic voting. We may interpret *Lord of the Rings* as proto-fascist or *Batman* films as excusing vigilantism, but their search for moral principles is at least as important as the depiction of realistic political negotiations. Nevertheless, it's true that films containing more complex visions of the political process—*Good Night, and Good Luck* (2005), *Charlie Wilson's War* (2007), *Milk* (2008), *Mandela* (2013), *Selma* (2014), and *The Big Short* (2015)—have tended to be less popular.

In David Bergen's *The Matter with Morris* (2010), Morris arrives, after his son's war death in Afghanistan at a postmodern, individualist disillusionment with politics, losing patience with "the convoluted logic of politicians and generals."[30] He knows that the word "freedom" was a rhetorical device designed to convince people to fight. So, in a funny, yet heart-rending scene, Morris walks the Winnipeg streets, asking people "Are you free?" Bergen ultimately draws back from the public sphere, and it's unclear whether Morris's feeling that there is no direct connection between his son's death and the public good means that there *is* no connection (that the Afghan War wasn't a public good) or that Morris doesn't *recognize* the complex, if ambivalent, goods. Perhaps because appeals to the grand narratives of community have so often been manipulative, How-I-Feel ideology tends to deny that a public good such as the destruction of a terrorist base or the education of women might compensate for war.

Despite what their superhero tastes might imply, Millennials tend to be politically progressive. Even *conservative* Millennials are more open than their elders are to same-sex marriage and to governmental poverty reduction, and are more critical of big business.[31] These attitudes show increasing allegiance to individualism. However, advances in such areas as LGBTQ and minority rights, hailed by postmodernist scholars as a welcome change from "the former politics of repressive unity,"[32] mask a decline in civic participation. Recent generations learned from their Boomer parents who, enchanted by TV, participated less in civic life. By the turn of the millennium, American Generation Xers were already "less interested in politics, less informed about current events (except for scandal, personality, and sports), less likely to attend a public meeting, less likely to contact public officials… less likely to work with others on a community project, and less

---

[30] Bergen, *Morris*, 10.
[31] Roberts, 223.
[32] Bertens, 247.

likely to contribute financially to a church or charity or political cause."[33] As the grand narratives decline, so does participation. Attitudes may be progressive, but they are often, as Robert Samuels notes, shaped by an ironic mockery that is reflexively anti-government. Media humiliation of people in authority replaces constructive participation.[34] Among Millennials, interest in politics continued to decline, coupled with an even more disturbing trend: fewer people think that it's important to live in a democracy.[35]

Single political issues can still motivate people. Campaigners and fund-raisers in the US now use "micro-targeting," sending ads about hot-button issues tailored (by big data algorithms) to individual voters. Bush-strategist Karl Rove successfully used same-sex marriage and abortion in 2004 to rouse social conservatives and Christian evangelicals.[36] Trump did the same, capturing the endorsement of evangelical kingmaker James Dobson by promising to put evangelical-vetted justices on the Supreme Court to repeal *Roe v. Wade.* As a result, Trump, who has no interest in faith, drew a higher percentage of evangelical voters than did George W. Bush, an evangelical. The Obama administration also played to single issues with "We the People," billed as "Your *Voice* in Our Government," a website that invited citizens to create petitions. If a petition reached 100,000 signatories, the White House had to respond. Some petitions did seem significant, such as the bid to legally recognize non-binary genders, and another to stop the Department of Justice from obstructing India's attempt to hold Union Carbide legally responsible for the toxic Bhopal gas leak. Others were frivolous—such as the petition for the President of the United States to recognize Kazakhstan's contribution to a safer world—and the 3349-strong petition to give Alaska back to Russia because 16,000–10,000 years ago "Siberian Russians" first settled Alaska. In March 2014, the largest petition was a request to stop an impending trade deal between Taiwan and China, something entirely outside of American purview. Responses to successful petitions seemed merely to restate government policy, suggesting that the website functioned as a public opinion poll for the Democrats, rather than as a true venue for broader political participation. By 2017, the site was being used in coordi-

---

[33] Putnam, 261.
[34] Samuels, 6–7.
[35] Mounk, 100, 105, 107, 109–10.
[36] Roberts, 204.

nated lobbying campaigns by Democrats to push Trump to release his tax returns and by Republicans to repeal the National Firearms Act. The website could potentially be valuable, but participants' political contributions are limited to a click.[37] As well, when voters concentrate on individualized issues, they don't have to seek principled compromises.[38]

Consumer, Not Citizen

Tucked inside the postmodern Trojan horse of individual freedom is a danger: our increasing tendency to think of ourselves mainly as consumers with rights rather than citizens with rights and duties. Michael Schudsen justly balks at this distinction "between virtuous citizens… and venal consumers"—consumers have fought important battles against unscrupulous businesses and governments, and African-Americans had to fight to sit in white-only restaurants[39]—yet it's true that consumers do feel less and less obligated to pay for common goods.[40] During Canada's 2005 federal election, the Liberals promised a national public day care. Under the citizenship model, everyone contributes to roads, schools, and day care, because these are public goods. However, the Conservatives correctly predicted that a more individualistic, consumer-friendly strategy would beat out the notion of public goods. They countered with the slogan, "Fund the child (not the system)," and offered a "child-care" cheque of $100 per month for every child under five. Under the guise of consumer choice, it gave stay-at-home parents a windfall, and, to the real target audience (the majority of voters who didn't have young children) it gave a ready explanation as to why they, as consumers, had no responsibility in the matter. Why should taxpayers without small children foot the bill for day care? The Liberals then made the mistake of suggesting that the windfall would be spent on "beer and popcorn," not child-care. "It was political suicide," Maich and George report, "to tell a narcissistic electorate that government knows better."[41] Following this logic, Manitoba's NDP government promised senior citizens relief from school taxes. Seniors had no children in school, so why should they pay? No mention was made of seniors' dis-

---

[37] See "We the People: Your Voice in the White House," https://petitions.whitehouse.gov/, and Morozov, *Save*, 106.

[38] Roberts, 205.

[39] Maich and George, 177–80.

[40] Grossberg, 185.

[41] Maich and George, 183–4.

proportionate use of the public healthcare system, or, more to the point, that an educated populace was good for the country as a whole.

Using similar arguments that consumers are the best judges of where to spend their money, many US jurisdictions shackled governments by requiring referenda for any tax increases. Bauman would call such developments "opinion poll rule,"[42] and agree with Catherine Needham that, "the citizen, unlike the consumer, is not always right."[43] In "opinion poll rule," voting becomes a form of self-expression. Pinker astutely remarks that the benefits of democracy do not come mainly from elections, but from limits on government power and from the government's responsiveness to its citizens.[44] Are we postmodern yet? Yes, our gradual replacement of citizen with consumer, of public good with individual interest, is surely a postmodern change. As the fictional tax auditor DeWitt Glendenning Jr. laments in *The Pale King*, "We think of ourselves now as eaters of the pie instead of makers of the pie. So who makes the pie?"[45]

These developments extend earlier trends described by Putnam, who showed that between the 1970s and mid-1990s *expressive* forms of political action such as writing a letter to the newspaper hadn't declined nearly as much as *cooperative* forms, such as serving on a committee.[46] If, as Bill Bishop contends, we mainly engage in politics as a form of self-expression, then it's natural for us to protest and boycott more but to vote less.[47] The outrage in 2017 about United Airlines forcibly removing Dr David Dao from his seat at the start of an oversold flight arose, Cathy O'Neil suggested, because we identified with him as a *consumer*. None of us wishes to relinquish our gains as consumers, and Ian McEwan's character Dr Perowne in the novel *Saturday* (2005) goes even further, saying, "It isn't rationalism that will overcome the religious zealots, but ordinary shopping and all that it entails – jobs for a start, and peace, and some commitment to realizable pleasures, the promise of appetites sated in this world, not the next." Yet this cheerful wealth-of-nations kowtowing to selfishness reveals a less friendly face when Perowne gets annoyed that the public sphere (in the form of a possible terrorist attack) might interfere with his

---

[42] Bauman, *Discontents*, 63.
[43] Morozov, *Save*, 117.
[44] Pinker, *Enlightenment*, 381.
[45] Wallace, *Pale*, 138, 136.
[46] Putnam, 45.
[47] Monica Hess, "The G-r-r-r-eat Breakfast Boycott," *Washington Post*, rpt *Winnipeg Free Press*, 17 December 2016.

weekly squash game, and he begins to think it a fundamental liberty that his enjoyment shouldn't be interrupted.[48] As O'Neill says, to believe that human dignity is the entitlement of those who can afford a ticket price narrows dignity far too much.[49]

The postmodern consumer, in effect, depoliticizes politics. Pornographer Larry Flynt offered $1 million to anyone who would provide details of his or her sexual relationship with high-ranking American politicians, and James Stanyer documents a statistical rise in focus on politicians' private lives from the 1980s to the 2000s, particularly in the US, Britain, France, and Australia, a process he calls "a politicization of the personal lives of politicians." For voters to investigate politicians' attitudes towards race and gender, for certain gay activists to chase lawmakers out of the closet, and for the media to expose the extra-marital affairs of politicians who champion family values is, indeed, a politicization of the personal. Yet Stanyer's interpretation fails to explain why, when politicians appear on entertainment shows, they are explicitly asked to avoid politics, or why we have seen a huge increase in personal exposure, far beyond any personal stake in policy.[50] What's happening is less politicization than a form of celebrity entertainment.

Consumers in a celebrity culture learn to value politics for entertainment, not policy, and, if the citizen is a consumer, it makes sense for politicians to emphasize a personal brand, to rely on Twitter and soundbites, and to evade reporters' questions by sticking to a talking-point script.[51] The relentless coverage of Donald Trump on CNN, Fox, and MSNBC is a direct function of TV ratings. Political strategists also understand that personal display leads to electoral support, as happened with Trump and his populist baseball cap,[52] with Obama and his family, and, in Canada, with Justin Trudeau and Sophie Grégoire Trudeau, though nobody quite reached the revelatory standard set by Tony Blair during his 2005 campaign when he boasted that he was "up for it" five times a night. His wife Cherie confirmed this important political information. (At the same time, Blair complained that media coverage was too intrusive, especially with his

[48] McEwan, *Saturday*, 126, 108.

[49] Cathy O'Neil, "Why do we treat dignity as a commodity?" *Winnipeg Free Press*, 26 April 2017, A7.

[50] Stanyer, 107–8, 59–65, 153, 158, 163, 91, 96, 51, 53, 103.

[51] Heath, *Enlightenment*, 212.

[52] Kellner, *Nightmare*, 11, 18, 24, 26.

children.)[53] The marketing of the personal is both affective and yet incredibly calculating. Prior to the 1996 US election, the Clintons used focus groups to decide on a vacation spot, a process that sent them off to hunt in Arkansas.[54] It's not just the marketers but the voters too, who are to blame, when they vote according to irrelevant personal factors. Personalization can invest political issues (such as LGBTQ rights) with personal salience and interest, but Bauman warns that, "Public issues which resist such reduction become all but incomprehensible."[55] Vincent Harris, who worked for Rand Paul, Ted Cruz, Mike Huckabee, and Benjamin Netanyahu, explains, "If politicians want to get their news and information delivered to people, they have to be entertaining... and visual.... People are online to watch cat GIFs and to see pictures of Kim Kardashian."[56]

Political campaigns are increasingly treated like any other marketing campaign, becoming exercises in postmodern simulation. Campaign managers are careful to poll voters for issues that anger them, and to target especially the "low-information voters," those who will respond best to a simplistic pitch. During Republican primaries, Donald Trump was successful at welcoming on board that sizeable group of disengaged voters who rarely or never participated in community activities.[57] Canadian campaign manager Nick Kouvalis got the intemperate Rob Ford elected as Toronto's mayor, and, in 2016–17, threw his weight behind Conservative Party leadership contender Kellie Leitch, teaching her to become more aggressive and Trump-like in her use of Twitter. Instead of tweeting photos of visits to seniors' homes, she began attacking "Liberal and media elites," claiming that the Liberal government funded groups allegedly tied to Hamas, and demanding values tests for immigrants. She did this because polling data revealed that those Conservatives who decided the party's leader tended to be white males with an average age of 66.[58]

Leitch failed, but many Americans who voted for "Change We Can Believe In" during Obama's 2008 victory, were buying a brand, not policies. Political marketers try out arguments and slogans on focus groups, and later test voters' emotional engagement by measuring *autonomic*

[53] Stanyer, 2, 21.
[54] Stanyer, 37–8.
[55] Bauman, *Liquid*, 37.
[56] Murphy, 29.
[57] Yoni Appelbaum, "Losing the Democratic Habit," *The Atlantic*, October 2018, 76.
[58] Martin Patriquin and Charlie Gillis, "How to make a candidate," *Maclean's*, February 2017, 26–9.

responses. No need for voters to know exactly what is meant by "Change We Can Believe In," "Make America Great Again," or George Bush Sr.'s "A Thousand Points of Light." The marketing emphasis lies on how the political brand *feels*, what Lawrence Grossberg calls "affective politics."[59] Spouses matter too. Of Grégoire Trudeau, Clive Veroni says, a "political spousal brand… has to be both independent and subservient to the 'master brand.' A good piggyback brand increases the value of both brands."[60] And affective politics finds no shame in making its appeals via pop culture, as the late Sen. John McCain did in *Time Magazine*'s top tweet of 2010. When Snooki, from the reality show *Jersey Shore* complained that Obama was taxing tanning beds, McCain tweeted, "@Sn00ki u r right, I would never tax your tanning bed! Pres Obama's tax/spend policy is quite The Situation."[61] Politicians such as Newt Gingrich built careers on the knowledge that the postmodern simulations of TV ruled, that voters responded best to symbols, emotion, and partisan rhetoric rather than to reasoned policy.[62] Instead of seeking consensus, he made fiery televised speeches to an empty legislative chamber, and tried to weaponize legislation via names such as the American Dream Restoration Act and the Taking Back Our Streets Act.[63] This emotional marketing reached a zenith in the Trump presidency, yielding such gems as Trump's wish to grant a posthumous pardon to Muhammad Ali, even though Ali's conviction for refusing the American draft had long ago been overturned.

Entertainment-driven politics can bite not just the hapless voter but also the media-savvy politician. David Frum's words have proved prophetic: "Republicans originally thought that Fox worked for us and now we're discovering we work for Fox… The thing that sustains a strong Fox network is the thing that undermines a strong Republican party."[64] His prophecy came true in Fox-favourite Donald Trump's hostile takeover in 2016 of the Republican Party. Cyber-mediated technologies also lean towards simulations that modify reality. Lobbyists such as Quinn Gillespie have sought to influence American legislators by creating brief "grass*top*" coalitions—

[59] Grossberg, 180–1.
[60] Kingston, "Just Watch," 33.
[61] John McCain, @SenJohnMcCain, Twitter, 9 June 2010, https://twitter.com/senjohnmccain/status/15800359514.
[62] Packer, 23.
[63] McKay Coppins, "Newt Gingrich Says You're Welcome," *The Atlantic*, November 2018, 54–6.
[64] Roberts, 207–8.

simulations of grassroots movements—to give the false appearance that the grassroots had mobilized around an issue.[65] Which is more disturbing, the fictional parody in *Wag the Dog* (1997), where a president starts a war with Albania to distract voters from media reports of his attempt to seduce an under-age "Firefly Girl," or the actual invasion of Iraq in 2003 on the pretext of neutralizing Weapons of Mass Destruction that the Bush administration knew didn't exist? An anonymous Bush aide, arguing against the notion that reality determines political decisions, said, "That's not the way the world really works anymore. We're an empire now, and when we act, we create our own reality. And while you're studying that reality... we'll act again, creating other new realities, which you can study too."[66]

Some of these characteristics of postmodern-era politics aren't new. Natural selection within a social species rewards deception if it raises our status or our group's status, and natural selection also primes us to closely monitor powerful figures and potential cheaters on a personal level. New, in the postmodern era, is the way media and big data information allow political groups to use our harvested preferences against us in very sophisticated ways. The developments in entertainment and simulation are concerning, given the correlation between reason and democracy, but rational education can immunize us against the appeals of power and image. Education levels and intellectual ability (holding all else constant) predicted future rule of law, democracy, and prosperity. Without downplaying the evolutionary history of violent male competition or the fact that early nation-states were more or less protection rackets, Pinker lists a number of links between reasoning ability and peaceable values: people with higher IQs commit fewer violent crimes, cooperate more quickly, tend to value individual autonomy over authority and tradition," favour freer markets, and favour democracy. There is reason for hope. Combining freedom of political speech, civil rights, and restraints on the power of the executive into one score, the Polity IV Project found in 2015 that the world had slowly been getting more democratic.[67] Some aspects of postmodern individualism support this trend, though the rise of populism does not. Progress isn't guaranteed because federal and global institutions require that reason override both How-I-Feel and our evolved biases that favour kin and group-mates.[68]

---

[65] Packer, 165.
[66] Suskind.
[67] Pinker, *Better*, 40, 661–5; *Enlightenment*, 200–4.
[68] For the relationship between reason and federalism, see Heath, "Reason."

Decline of the Public Sphere

Strong party affiliation has taken on a postmodern hue, and has become, surprisingly, a bedfellow to diminishing political involvement. It might seem paradoxical that in the postmodern context individualism can often *increase* political tribalism. But it's less paradoxical when we consider that face-to-face encounters are needed to allow people to see the humanity of those with whom they disagree. Postmodern communications technology—TV, the Internet, and the smartphone—have depopulated those mediating "third places"—coffee houses, bars, restaurants, libraries, churches, and concert halls—where people meet and public opinions are exchanged.[69] Without unplanned public encounters, attitudes become more entrenched.[70] That depopulation, along with the decline of community groups, makes it more difficult to represent peoples' concerns to government bodies and to interpret government policies to the people.[71] At the same time, social balkanization—people moving to politically homogeneous neighbourhoods[72]—has increased alongside cyber-balkanization. In the US, partisanship has increased, including in academia, and, although many Americans consider themselves moderates, these moderates are less likely to vote.[73] Between 1972 and 2008, Republicans and Democrats came to disagree nearly twice as strongly on core issues.[74] Whereas in the 1960s, only 1 in 20 Americans would have been troubled by a child marrying someone from the other party, by 2012 the rate had dropped to 1 in 3 for Democrats and 1 in 2 for Republicans.[75] Ironically, much of the disagreement is not substantive. When Geoffrey Cohen gave American conservatives and liberals two different welfare policy options, liberals, as expected, were more likely than conservatives to favour the "generous" option. When he tried the same experiment but said that Republicans had authored the generous proposal, he found that liberals chose the *less* generous policies (which they believed had been authored by liberals) while conservatives chose the generous policies

---

[69] Quan-Haase, 158.
[70] Roberts, 127.
[71] Lane, 250.
[72] Roberts, 198.
[73] Pinker, *Enlightenment*, 371–2.
[74] Roberts, 200.
[75] Roberts, 201; Twenge, *iGen*, 267.

(which they believed had been authored by conservatives). And all participants unanimously denied that party endorsements affected their choices.[76]

Contrary to the twentieth-century fear of Big Brother intruding into our private spaces, Bauman argues that the *public* sphere is more endangered at present by the private. He adds that for this reason there are no more dystopias being written.[77] He's wrong about dystopias, but those very dystopias reinforce the wisdom of his political assessment. Many of the great contemporary dystopias—Atwood's *Maddaddam* trilogy, David Mitchell's *Cloud Atlas* (particularly Sonmi-451's story), Wallace's *Infinite Jest*—sense the greatest danger either from *private* corporations or from governments controlled by private corporations. Less sophisticated dystopias, such as *V for Vendetta* (2006), continue to fight yesterday's wars—the individual fighting the Big Brother nation—as if repressive governments were still the main danger in the West. Even the sophisticated *Super Sad True Love Story* worries that the nation knows too much about our private lives and that it will stifle dissent. Bauman, in contrast, fears a *weakened* nation-state, which would abandon global governance structures and encourage greater communal violence, preventing an ethical response to the Other.[78] The dystopias that Bauman doesn't know—Cormac McCarthy's *The Road* and Atwood's *Maddaddam*—fear exactly the deregulated Hobbesian state of nature that Bauman warns would accompany the dissolution of the nation-state. Only towards the end of Atwood's third novel do God's Gardeners grope their way towards a reinstated public sphere that isn't just a reflection of corporate or religious ideology. "Any true liberation," Bauman rightly insists, "calls today for more, not less, of the 'public sphere.'"[79]

MULTILATERALISM AND GLOBALIZATION

If the nation and its public sphere are under internal threat from rising individualism, is a similar level of threat discernible in the international sphere as a result of postmodern deregulation? Among the more curious attempts to dissolve the grand narrative of the nation is the "seasteading" movement, based on the notion that if homesteaders build an ocean platform outside of the 200-nautical-mile limit over which a state has jurisdic-

[76] Greene, 89.
[77] Bauman, *Liquid*, 61.
[78] Bauman, *Liquid*, 193; *Postmodern Ethics*, 131–2.
[79] Bauman, *Liquid*, 51.

tion, platform and homesteader would be free of the state's legal control, and would, in effect, create a micro-nation. Although seasteading exists mainly at the level of fantasy,[80] in 1967 one British citizen, Roy Bates, took over an old World War II gun platform, the Roughs Tower, 3 miles off the England's coast in the North Sea. Bates proclaimed himself Prince of Sealand. Because 3 miles was the limit of British jurisdiction at the time, Bates declared the platform *terra nullius*, and, as in the case of pirate radio stations, the British government didn't bother to interfere. After an attempted coup in 1978 by German lawyer Alexander Achenbach went awry, Bates held Achenbach prisoner, and German authorities sent a diplomat to secure his release. Bates interpreted this as the German government officially recognizing Sealand. Upon Bates's death, his son Michael inherited the realm. Of course, no nation, including Germany, recognizes Sealand, though for only £99.99, one can become a Knight in the Sovereign Military Order of Sealand.[81] The postmodernist hope is that the individual or small community might attain sovereignty. In a similar, but more important development, the Dutch organization Women on Waves has invoked the principle that outside of territorial waters, the laws that apply are those of the flag under which the ship sails. Women on Waves provides abortions near countries where abortions are illegal, thereby challenging one national sovereignty via another, more liberal, national sovereignty.

A more far-reaching instrument for potentially dissolving the modern state has been postmodern multilateralism. According to Robert Cooper, the world is moving away from modern imperialism, towards postmodern multilateralism. Indeed, as with contemporary ethics, in the international sphere there is no objective "foundation" from which we can easily judge the value and justice of a nation's policies and actions. Were nations to act like individuals, an attitude invited by scepticism about grand narratives, we'd soon arrive at a medieval patchwork of heterogeneous law.[82] Arrayed against this tendency are multilateral institutions such as the UN (called "the only truly global organization in the history of mankind"[83]) and the European Union (EU). The postmodern model gives priority to trade

[80] See http://www.seasteading.org/.

[81] Wikipedia, "Principality of Sealand," https://en.wikipedia.org/wiki/Principality_of_Sealand, accessed 4 August 2016. "The Principality of Sealand" [official website], http://www.sealandgov.org/, 2015.

[82] Cooper, 79.

[83] Hanhimäki, 5. As of 2015, the UN had 193 member states.

negotiations and soft economic power of the sort that created the EU as a buffer against the use of force,[84] and the lowering of trade barriers has interlocked us all in complex ways. American Supreme Court justice Stephen Breyer cites a number of cases in which he and his colleagues had to decide how far laws made in other countries—copyright laws, for example—should also apply inside the US. This is important, since the US belongs to over 800 organizations, from the International Olive Council to the World Trade Organization (WTO) that place binding rules on member businesses.[85] Globally, power is increasingly diffuse. The UN Security Council veto notwithstanding, no individual nation can control the processes of the UN or of agreements such as General Agreement on Tariffs and Trade (GATT) and the WTO. This is one reason why the US has complained bitterly about the UN: American interests are not treated as primary.[86]

Multilateral institutions, just like the nation, are creatures of modern reason and humanist ethics, attempting to coordinate competing tribes and traditions, yet multilateral institutions also challenge the grand narrative of the sovereign nation by broader appeals to human rights, based on the values of postmodern individualism. Assessing the shifts in peacekeeping since World War II, Alex Bellamy and Paul D. Williams argue that post-Westphalian conceptions of sovereignty are tilting away from the Westphalian stance that the nation is sovereign and towards the human-rights stance that when nations fail to protect their citizens from crimes against humanity, they surrender their moral right to sovereignty, thus inviting interference from other nations.[87] This notion was endorsed by all UN-member nations in 2005 as the Responsibility to Protect (R2P), shifting the ground from state security to human security,[88] often directly challenging national sovereignty. But this shift doesn't imply a libertarian conception of individualism. Pluralism is limited, since the *Universal Declaration of Human Rights* sets out a humanist ethical consensus,

[84] Cooper, 36–7; Ferguson, *Colossus*, 239.

[85] Stephen Breyer, "America's Courts Can't Ignore the World," *The Atlantic*, October 2018, 104–6.

[86] Ferguson, *Colossus*, 297–8; Gareis, 249.

[87] Bellamy and Williams, 4–5.

[88] Gareis, 57. UN Charter Articles 2(4) and 2(7), which prohibit the use of force against the territorial integrity or domestic jurisdiction of independent states, have been treated as subordinate to the Preamble and Article 1(3), which affirms fundamental human rights (Bellamy and Williams, 47–8).

rooted in the liberal democratic tradition that can clash with various nationalist, religious, and political agendas.

The movement from national public spheres to transnational deregulation raises Bauman's crucial question—"Can we have a global democracy?"[89] The decline in the use of vetoes by the five permanent members (P5) of the UN Security Council in the last 30 years suggests a shift towards democratic negotiation and contractarianism, even though the use of vetoes in relation to Syria and the Crimea/Ukraine reveals the continuing difficulties in multilateral negotiations.[90] Recent peacekeeping successes include Iran-Iraq (1988–91), Namibia (1989–90), Honduras-Nicaragua-Guatemala (1989–91), Iraq-Kuwait (1991–2003), El Salvador (1991–5), Cambodia (1991–3), Mozambique (1992–4), Haiti (1993–6), and Kosovo (1999–2012).[91] According to Virginia Fortna's analysis, international peacekeeping has been successful in about 80% of cases.[92] Despite evidence that some "peacekeeping" efforts consist of bids for geopolitical hegemony (Russia in Georgia, Nigeria in West Africa, and the US in Iraq), and despite tragic disasters in Somalia, Rwanda, and Bosnia, the UN has often successfully kept combatants apart and prevented much bloodshed. The catastrophic failure and genocide in Rwanda were due, in large part, to the Clinton administration's reversion to the Westphalian system of non-interference, keyed by the failed interference in Somalia. But even after the genocide in Rwanda, UNAMIR (United Nations Assistance Mission in Rwanda) persisted to rehabilitate the justice system, restore telecommunications, and rebuild infrastructure, while in Bosnia, peacekeepers from NATO and the EU prevented a return to war.[93] The relative weakness of international organizations is easily satirized, as in Mohsen Makhmalbaf's film *Kandahar* (2001), where Nafas believes that a little UNO flag will protect her car from robbers in Afghanistan. Yet Makhmalbaf also gives a dignity to the human troop, on foot after being robbed, silhouetted against a desert sky, led by Nafas's feigned husband holding up a little UN flag.[94]

[89] Bauman, *Does*, 28, 76, 244.

[90] Hanhimäki, 53, 137, 70.

[91] Freeman, 113; Hanhimäki, 80–5; Gareis, 108–10; Bellamy and Williams, 97–9, 246, 266–73, 276–7.

[92] Fortna, 173; Bellamy and Williams, 1, 232; Pinker, *Better*, 315. When belligerents gave consent to the peacekeeping forces, wars were prevented at the even higher rate of 95%.

[93] Bellamy and Williams, 44, 112–14, 284–8.

[94] *Kandahar*. Dir. Mohsen Makhmalbaf. Avatar Films, 2001, 17:00.

But if we think of the UN only in terms of wars prevented or not prevented, we fail to register other positive facets of postmodern multilateralism. The UN has taken on "second generation" tasks: disarmament, refugee repatriation, support for democratic processes and elections, civil policing, public administration, and justice.[95] Despite vast and continuing income inequities between nations, the UN has contributed hugely to the global South in terms of life expectancy, education, income levels, and child mortality rates.[96] It was also the UN, in the 1960s, which first called for international pressure against South Africa because of apartheid, though the movement didn't gain traction until African-Americans pushed for economic sanctions.[97] UN-Security-Council-driven economic sanctions eventually convinced Iran to sign a nuclear deal to significantly limit Iran's nuclear capabilities. On the other hand, American defiance of the UN's International Atomic Energy Agency (IAEA) findings in Iraq eventually led to the Iraq War.[98] This was particularly ironic and damaged American credibility, since the US insisted that Iraq must obey all UN legal requirements, yet when Iraq proved uncooperative, the US, like Iraq, ignored the UN, invoked the principle of national sovereignty to act in its own interest, and pursued a war that was illegal according to international law.[99] At the same time, the US is reluctant to abandon the UN's multilateral legitimacy. With North Korea testing ICBM missiles in 2017, the US ambassador to the UN, Nikki Haley, threatened trade action against China for ignoring Security Council sanctions against North Korea.[100]

Although many UN states have committed significant human rights violations, "talking the talk" of human rights often leads to "walking the walk," as rights become normalized and institutionalized, and as governments become more image-conscious.[101] In this era of postmodern multilateralism, UN norms have widely become reference points for state

---

[95] Gareis, 109.

[96] Hanhimäki, 92, 99, 101, 105.

[97] Freeman, 204.

[98] Hanhimäki, 68–9.

[99] According to the UN Chapter VII, Article 51, nations have the right to defend themselves in the face of an attack or an imminent attack. This was why the UN cleared the way legally for the US to invade Afghanistan. However, no imminent threat existed in the case of Iraq (Gareis, 92–4, 262–5. Bellamy and Williams, 138–9).

[100] Edith Lederer, "US warns China on trade with North Korea," *Winnipeg Free Press*, 6 July 2017.

[101] Freeman, 11, 104, 160.

behaviour.[102] According to Red Cross surveys, civilians in 12 war-torn societies wanted more, not less intervention. Only 10% disapproved of interventions, while almost 70% wanted more intervention.[103] A 2013 global survey suggests that around the world, three-quarters of people favour increasing the UN Security Council's military interventions.[104]

International criminal tribunals after the Yugoslavian and Rwandan genocides eventually led to the 1998 establishment of another global, multilateral governmental structure, the International Criminal Court (ICC), now supported by 123 nations (though not by the US, Russia, China, India, Saudi Arabia, and Israel, among others).[105] The US, despite its relatively good human rights record compared to the other resisting nations, cited its fear of politically motivated prosecutions, but American unwillingness to submit to international standards has also played a major role—as became clear in the continuing Guantanamo Bay detentions.[106] Although Amartya Sen thinks that it's unrealistic to bring the world under a common constitutional framework, Sen also praises institutions such as the UN, which represent precisely such a framework, and which treat democracy as "government by discussion," not just majority rule.[107] Since the UN consists of people with "divergent goals" striving for provisional agreements,[108] it exhibits the contractarian aspect of postmodern ethics, though negotiations often fail. Even the US and China supported the jurisdiction of the ICC for cases of war crimes in Darfur and Libya (by abstaining from the Darfur vote and by voting in the Libyan case), despite the fact that Sudan and Libya hadn't ratified the ICC statute.[109] Yet, in late 2018, National Security Advisor John Bolton vowed that the US would obstruct the ICC if it attempted to investigate possible American war crimes during the Afghan War. Evidently, the US and China agree with the normative moral principle that justice overrides national sovereignty, yet they balk at surrendering portions of their own sovereignty. As with Early Modern kings who considered themselves to represent the law and yet to

[102] Gareis, 284–5.
[103] Freeman, 113.
[104] Hanhimäki, 7.
[105] Freeman, 55, 94. Gareis, 197. Cohen, 209.
[106] Hanhimäki, 122, 124. Bellamy and Williams, 138.
[107] Sen, 140–1, 409, 324.
[108] Hanhimäki, 27.
[109] Gareis, 199–200.

stand above it, in time, the UN's P5 will more and more become subject to the multilateral laws they enforce.

Some plaintiffs have tried to nudge the justice system even closer to a global democracy than the ICC has. The son of Zahra Kazemi—a Canadian-Iranian photographer who was allegedly raped and murdered in an Iranian jail—challenged the State Immunity Act, which prevents Canadians from pursuing cases against foreign governments in Canadian courts. Stephan Kazemi argued that such laws run counter to Canada's Charter of Rights and Freedoms, but the Supreme Court found that only parliament, not the courts, could provide a remedy.[110] A similar result occurred after seven Guatemalan protesters were shot, allegedly by security personnel employed by Vancouver's Tahoe Resources, the owner of the Escobal Mine in Guatemala. A Canadian judge took the Westphalian route, ruling that the charges must be answered before Guatemalan, not Canadian, courts, and he stayed the charges.[111]

More successfully, Mayan women in Guatemala were able to pursue serial rape charges against the gangs who evicted them from disputed property of the Canadian company Hudbay Minerals. Charges were also brought forward in relation to nine shootings and a murder. Instead of addressing unsympathetic Guatemalan courts, the petitioners litigated in Ontario, and Superior Court Justice Carol Brown took the post-Westphalian, postmodern route, ruling that the women could proceed.[112] Seeded, here, is the notion that Western companies should be held to the standards of Western democracy no matter where in the world they operate. Companies can no longer count on laxer standards in foreign countries to shield themselves from prosecution. Even the Internet is not immune, given the recent Canadian Supreme Court's decision in 2017 to order a *worldwide* implementation of a Canadian court decision, requiring Google to stop indexing websites associated with Datalink Technologies

---

[110] Stephan Kazemi, "Harper's broken promise of justice for my mother," *Toronto Star*, 10 July 2015, https://www.thestar.com/opinion/commentary/2015/07/10/harpers-broken-promise-of-justice-for-my-mother.html.

[111] McMillan, "Lawsuit against Tahoe Resources Inc. stayed by Supreme Court of British Columbia," November 2015, http://www.mcmillan.ca/Lawsuit-against-Tahoe-Resources-Inc-stayed-by-Supreme-Court-of-British-Columbia.

[112] Roger LeMoyne, "Mining for the Truth," *Maclean's*, 14 July 2014, 43–4. Amelia Berot-Burns, "Hudbay Court Case," MICLA (McGill Research Group Investigating Canadian Mining in Latin America), 5 February 2015, http://micla.ca/blog/4181/hudbay-court-case/.

Gateways, a company that persistently sold industrial network interface hardware created by another company.[113]

Organizations such as Avaaz have also shown that domestic lobbies can mobilize global public pressure campaigns to convince nations not to enact repressive legislation—for example, in Uganda's attempt to make homosexuality punishable by death—and to call multinational giants such as Monsanto to account for harmful practices. Such trends undermine modernity's grand narrative of the sovereign nation. So do the various degrees of self-government that indigenous communities have gained in Canada, for example. Although Canada's treaties with indigenous peoples were multi-juridical at the time of their signing in the late nineteenth and early twentieth centuries, they were not treated as such until the postmodern era.[114] We see neither a full postmodernist pluralism, in which the state's minority members can freely remake the rules of association (creating their own separate small narratives), nor an absolute sovereignty in which the state is completely free to define morality and political rights within its own borders. In 2007, an overwhelming majority of countries adopted the UN's *Declaration on the Rights of Indigenous Peoples*, which limits national sovereignty with respect to indigenous minorities. Only four countries (including Canada and the US) voted against the adoption, with 11 abstentions; Canada eventually withdrew its objection in 2016.

What Robert Cooper calls the postmodern system of international relations emphasizes reasoned negotiation—contractarianism—rather than complete sovereignty or geopolitical balance. In a simplified but accurate description, he outlines a historical movement from hard to soft power: the premodern state's agricultural economy adds the modern state's industrial production, and then adds the postmodern state's information economy. Cooper, in 2003, considered European nations to be postmodern in relation to each other (though the Cold War had forced them to deal with Warsaw Pact countries according to older principles); Japan was a postmodern state surrounded by states existing in an earlier age; the US was still a modernist empire-building state; Russia was poised between modernist empire-building and postmodern-style multilateral treaties (though nowadays it has regressed significantly). When a nation uses force, postmodern openness and interrelatedness are waived, and the system

---

[113] Jim Bronskill, "Supreme Court rules Google order should be applied worldwide," *Winnipeg Free Press*, 29 June 2017.
[114] Borrows, 124–5.

reverts to modernist warfare, as happened in Kosovo. There, NATO's ideological premise—that severe human-rights abuses merit intrusion into national sovereignty—was post-Westphalian and postmodern, but Serbian "modern" nationalist force could only be met with modern force, not "postmodern" negotiation. Even the end of the Cold War in 1991 was marked not by territorial takeover but by domestic changes, such as new constitutions, privatization, and membership in capitalist bodies, such as the WTO, the IMF (International Monetary Fund), and the EU. The postmodern EU is "a highly developed system for mutual interference in each other's domestic affairs,"[115] with many EU laws overshadowing national law,[116] precisely what Brexiters criticized. Henry Kissinger, arguing in favour of geopolitical balance, warned that when nations repeatedly intrude upon the sovereignty of other nations in the name of goodness, they risk replaying the religious wars of the seventeenth century, but, given the Holocaust and the Rwandan genocide, it's difficult to prefer Kissinger's modernist-inflected, Westphalian notion that national sovereignty should always remain inviolable.[117]

According to Cooper, the US, despite inventing the postmodern system, remains outside of that system as its "guardian," still operating as a modern state. Yet even the US is not as imperial as earlier empires were—it doesn't want new territory[118]—and its military interventions before the Iraq War often sought UN or at least NATO blessing, revealing a genuine uneasiness with the national version of the How-I-Feel ethic. During the multilateral postmodern era, there have also been fewer wars. US modern force is one reason—the "Pax Americana"—but equally significant factors, as Steven Pinker shows, have been the Humanitarian revolution in the eighteenth century, the Human Rights revolution in the twentieth, the slow feminization of western culture, literacy, and the escalator-effect of reason. Colonial wars have all but disappeared. Civil wars, the mass killing of ethnic and political groups, and terrorism have all declined relative to the world population, though we often fail to notice the decline, because of innumeracy, and because of the media policy of "if it bleeds it leads."[119]

[115] Cooper, 51, 40, 43, 108, 27.
[116] Ferguson, *Colossus*, 234.
[117] Cooper, 59–60, 29.
[118] Cooper, 44–6, 173.
[119] Pinker, *Better*, xxvi, 302, 296. Pinker argues that changes in education and individual IQ (even presidential IQ!) since the nineteenth century have allowed us, through reason, to limit our emotional involvements in conflicts, by recognizing the futility of the cycle of vio-

Of course, there are serious problems in attempting to create a post-national world order, and the EU exemplifies some of them. John Gillingham calls the EU a "secular faith," whose myth falsely congratulates itself on giving Europe peace and prosperity. He criticizes the EU for the lack of democratic accountability, for corruption, for the unwillingness to use military force to protect Ukraine, for a multiplying bureaucracy, for confusion about where and why EU jurisdiction ought to override national sovereignty, for member non-compliance in decisions, and for the single currency that puts weaker nations at economic risk. The failure of the EU to deal successfully with the debt crisis in Greece and elsewhere helped, in Gillingham's opinion, to bring about a European Depression, deeper and more ominous politically than the Recession of 2007–8, given the current rekindling of nationalism.[120] While many of the critiques are valid—particularly Greece's inability to devalue its currency to stimulate growth—it's not at all clear that Gillingham's models for economic success—the US and Margaret Thatcher—have played benign economic and democratic roles. Since the European Commission, presently too secretive, does consist of elected heads of state, it's a mistake to call it autocratic, though greater democratic oversight would clean up a lot of corruption and legitimize the EU's multilateral project. Gillingham rightly chastises the European Parliament for refusing to tackle the Volkswagen emissions scandal, yet he wants looser environmental standards. He also wants a more "flexible" labour market,[121] but this is code for "lower wages," and he generally avoids mentioning social costs, particularly the cost to workers when capital does as it pleases. Most damningly, Gillingham doesn't say how a war with Russia would yield a better outcome, or how a Europe without the EU and its international negotiation structure would have resulted in greater peace and prosperity than is presently the case.

The liberalization of trade has indeed brought significant benefits, and though Gillingham complains about how the European Court of Justice encroaches on national (democratically elected) legislatures in areas such as product standards,[122] he forgets to mention that (to name just one set of examples) many of the rights and liberties that make up English

lence and limiting our tendency to privilege our own interests over those of others (Pinker, *Better*, 642–70).

[120] Gillingham, 1, 7, 121, 116, 172–3, 66, 110, 152.
[121] Gillingham, 169, 177, 179, 196, 247, 84, 169.
[122] Gillingham, 72, 67.

common law came not through elected legislatures but through judicial activism. The great irony of Gillingham's approach is that he repeatedly calls for greater national power, which is incompatible with the EU,[123] yet simultaneously urges economic deregulation, which eviscerates national power. He does admit, ultimately, that the development of European law has been important even without agreement on a European Constitution.

Economically, the world has benefitted tremendously from postmodern multilateralism under GATT and then the WTO,[124] since trade is the likeliest scene of international win-win scenarios. Although, by 2010, income equality in the US dropped to lows not seen since the crash of 1929, *global* equality, which had been getting worse for at least three centuries, has improved since 1990.[125] Pinker, nevertheless, argues that income inequality is not the best measure of the effects of globalization. Instead, we should focus on the decline of extreme poverty, on the increases in social welfare spending, and on consumption (people's ability to buy what they want), which has increased far more than income. Globally, great strides have been made for those with income between the 10th and the 70th percentiles, and, of course, for those near the 100th percentile. In contrast, those between the 80th and 90th percentiles—in other words, the lower middle classes in the rich world—only saw a small gain. Thus, the Recession of 2007–8 was a recession mainly for North Atlantic countries, while incomes soared worldwide in the postmodern era of globalization.[126]

And the benefits of multilateral trade treaties are not just economic. Pinker, his tongue only partially in his cheek, reports the "Golden Arches theory" of international relations: except for the 1999 NATO bombing of Yugoslavia, "no two countries with McDonald's have ever fought in a war." It's not Ronald McDonald's relentless smile that keeps combatants apart, but the very nature of economic exchange. Although many factors can lead to war, Pinker gives plenty of evidence that trade decreases war. Trading partners are worth more alive than dead, and economic exchange encourages social emotions—guilt and anger, but also empathy, sympathy, trust, and gratitude. This is a positive side of consumerism and of the How-I-Feel ethic. Once upon a time, plunder enriched some nations, but in our interconnected world, wealth is created by exchange, credit, and

[123] Gillingham, 191, 251–2.
[124] Rodrik, *One*, 210.
[125] Piketty, 24, 61.
[126] Pinker, *Enlightenment*, 104–17.

division of labour. In the 70 years since World War II, only Israel and
Russia, out of 44 major developed countries, have expanded their territo-
ries through military conquest. Some commercial interests, such as the
arms industry, still have a vested interest in war, but for the most part
"gentle commerce" undermines the aggressor's impulse to attack first,
since many of the benefits will be available without war. Though trade by
itself doesn't produce equality, commerce is even more pacifying than
democracy, Pinker argues, because of "an openness to foreign investment,
the freedom of citizens to enter into enforceable contracts, and their
dependence on voluntary financial exchanges as opposed to self-sufficiency,
barter, or extortion."[127] These practices promote postmodern multilateralism and contractarianism.

We tend to see farmers, manufacturers, and building contractors as
contributing to economic growth because they produce tangible goods.
Yet, despite the finance industry's responsibility for the Recession of
2007–8, the goods of commerce depend also on merchants and bankers,
who are crucial in facilitating transactions.[128] If properly regulated,
merchants connect producers more efficiently to markets, and bankers
allow money to flow where it can be most effective. Bretton Woods and
GATT, pushing towards globalization, while still allowing individual
nations to determine their level of engagement, ushered in one of the
greatest periods of growth for the world economy. Following Bretton
Woods and after the implementation of GATT, countries dropped their
tariffs on many products, though smaller nations still had a voice and
effectively retained sovereignty, so that they could act in protectionist ways
for industries deemed to be under threat—agricultural subsidies being a
notable example.[129] The WTO eviscerated some of these protections, but
greatly increased trade, and even the flawed structures of the WTO are
much preferable to closed, hostile economies.

Deregulation

Of course, there is a darker side of the postmodern freedoms that gave us
globalization. Because of the benefits of trade, multinational corporations
have been able to argue that national strategies such as tariffs should be

[127] Pinker, *Better*, 284, 76–7, 245, 251, 259, 682, 287.
[128] Pinker, *Better*, 329.
[129] Rodrik, *Globalization*, 91, 110, 70–2, 75.

abolished entirely. And because the limited company has been such a boon to entrepreneurship, the corporation (a fictive individual for legal purposes) has latched onto the analogy of "individual" freedom: the fewer the rules, the better the economic outcome. Deregulation proclaims a new grand narrative: the market is wise.

But the market isn't wise. Transactions in stocks, bonds, derivatives, and currencies overwhelm trade in actual goods by several orders of magnitude, suggesting that private finance is far too mobile in comparison to the real economy.[130] The most open, globalized countries thus took the worst hits in the Recession of 2007–8.[131] It's also not the market's wisdom but the West's economic power that lets it defend its agricultural products with subsidies (while demanding freer trade in other areas). And the all-knowing market is myopic, often unwilling to see beyond the next quarter, as shown when the Dow Jones average immediately rose 135 points the day that the US pulled out of the Paris climate agreement in 2017. Since commerce is the biggest reason why people risk stepping beyond their countries in the first place, it's natural that contemporary structures such as the WTO and IMF would express the developed world's and especially America's self-interest,[132] but Dani Rodrik argues compellingly that lack of capital controls—the financier's postmodern "individualism"—invites boom-and-bust cycles. Currency values often don't reflect economic fundamentals, but reflect "bubbles, irrationality, myopic expectations, or short-term trading strategies." With what George Soros calls the self-reflexive nature of speculation,[133] short-selling can turn a national currency's believed weakness into a self-fulfilling prophecy, as investors flee.

During the 1997 Asian financial crisis, the South Korean, Thai, Indonesian, and Malaysian economies were all sound. The crisis was caused not by cronyism or excessive borrowing but by an irrational run on the bank, as investors caught a chimerical panic from other investors and withdrew their capital: the "wise" market suddenly got stupid and created the disaster that the players feared. Once the panic was over, the stupid market got wise again, as people realized that the Asian economies had sound fundamentals. The market's sudden insight came too late for some people, because during the crisis the US and the IMF forced huge interest

---

[130] Rodrik, *Globalization*, 107.
[131] Stiglitz, 236.
[132] Barber, 332–3.
[133] Ferguson, *Ascent*, 317.

rates on the affected Asian countries—50% in the case of Indonesia. People starved. The wisdom of the market, after all, is the collective wisdom of the twenty- and thirty-something men who, as Rodrik puts it, sit in front of computer screens and "move hundreds of millions of dollars across the globe at a keystroke," magnifying "the ups and downs in the market by acting like a herd and chasing phantom profits."[134] Just as nature can't give us a reliable ethics, the deregulated market isn't even reliable in *economic* matters, never mind in ethical or social matters, as the Asian crisis of 1997 proved.

It might appear that multinational corporations are *not* postmodern if they treat "the market" as a reliable grand narrative. A decade after the Asian crisis, the wise market gave us the US housing crash, which was fueled by real weaknesses—a hugely over-valued real estate market, leveraged banks, and excessive debt, both individual and national. Finance ("obeying" the market, while simultaneously shaping it) had skewed the rules to its own special interests by demanding the repeal of the Glass-Steagal Act, the lifting of capital controls, and deregulation generally. If a derivative was overpriced, the market eventually corrected that. But as soon as the market revealed the worthlessness of certain derivatives, banks cried for a bailout—in effect denying the wisdom of the market. Unlike during the 1997 Asian crisis, no market discipline was even contemplated because the US was involved.[135] Instead, interest rates were *lowered* to stimulate economic growth (and more borrowing). This time, banks refused to let the wise market work its magic. Rather, they engaged in the economic equivalent of basing one's moral decisions on "How I feel at the time." This is postmodern, and certainly has attractions for the individual person, bank, corporation, or nation. But selfishness fails miserably as a principle for making economic rules. Invoking the grand narrative of the completely free market not only ignores the boom-and-bust cycles, but also cynically disguises the fact that those who call for market freedom do so only when it's to their advantage. In other words, the market isn't really a grand narrative, since believers quickly left the market behind for an ego-based narrative whenever the market proved inconvenient. Deregulated economic "freedom" actually undermines a measured version of postmodern multilateralism.

---

[134] Rodrik, *Globalization*, 92–3, 106–7, 109.
[135] Stiglitz, 221–2.

Indeed, the market fails whenever it's too free. Without global regulation, we get a "race to the bottom," in which companies ruthlessly seek out the most unprotected national markets[136] and the laxest safety standards, while parking their capital in tax-evasion havens such as the Cayman Islands and the City of London Corporation.[137] The race to the bottom occurs even within the same country. Although Boeing share prices reached record highs in 2013 and received billions of dollars in tax breaks, the company threatened to move work from Seattle to non-union South Carolina if machinists refused to accept cuts to pensions and medical benefits.[138] Before the Recession of 2007–8, when one rating agency gave a financial product a poor grade, investment banks simply took their business elsewhere to get a better rating. Rating agencies quickly learned to give high ratings to even the most toxic financial products. The *market* decided this.[139] On the individual level, too, free markets reward sellers who exploit human weakness,[140] such as the inability to do mortgage calculations. Finance, left to its own devices, prefers light regulation, and skews rules to its own "individual" corporate interests, which are often opposed to those of nations and individuals.[141]

In terms of a global economics, we are surely postmodern, since, as in ethics, there is no final arbiter in negotiations, and the market cannot replace the nation in this role. At the same time, the wisest nations understand that it's still best to avoid an unbounded free-for-all. China and India have succeeded in recent decades partly because they kept a GATT-era control over their economies, even during the WTO's push for "deep integration." China's case is both stunning and instructive. An unhealthy command economy without private property rights was transformed into a capitalist economy and swiftly moved half a billion people out of extreme poverty. Instead of heading directly towards extreme postmodern deregulation, Chinese officials created a mixed economy. The government still commanded quotas from farmers to feed city workers, but allowed farmers to sell on a free market whatever they produced above the quotas. Instead

[136] Barber, 327.
[137] The market's "optimal" choice of the laxest standards reveals, like the peacock's tail, that what seems good for the individual corporation and its shareholders can be very bad for the larger group. See Heath, *Economics*, 32.
[138] Roberts, 159.
[139] Stiglitz, 92, 216–17.
[140] Sunstein, 10.
[141] Rodrik, *Globalization*, 125.

of leaping immediately to private property rights (which were considered politically suspect and in practice might have stalled before weak or corrupt courts), the central government allowed local townships or villages to market products, thereby creating an alliance between local governments and entrepreneurs. Special Economic Zones for intensive capitalist production were created. These zones lowered tariffs on inputs and allowed foreign firms to gain a foothold as long as they partnered with Chinese firms. During all this, the currency was pegged at an artificially low rate so that exports would do well and China wouldn't be swamped with speculative capital flows.[142] Rodrik argues that we should view selective protectionism not as a failure of free trade, but as a necessary effect of achieving international cooperation.[143] The postmodern market freedoms on offer are only selectively chosen, and the grand narrative of the nation is retained on other selected fronts. As in the case of postmodern ethics, negotiation is paramount.

Because there is not yet democratic global governance, economic globalization has tilted the playing field, Benjamin Barber argues, sharply towards the West and, in particular, towards American corporations. To keep its market advantage, especially for Hollywood, the US opposed UNESCO's 2005 convention on the protection of cultural diversity, which allowed for some safeguarding of (i.e. protectionism for) cultural expressions.[144] Globalization in such instances becomes a synonym for American cultural domination, not for a postmodern world with many centres. Against the grand narrative of wise, deregulated markets, Rodrik argues that international economies, just like national economies, obviously need *non-market* structures in order to be effective and in order to provide public goods that the market doesn't provide. Trade that is supposedly "free" still requires "regulations, standards, supervision, enforcement, lenders-of-last-resort," and infrastructure.[145] In other words, although there may often be a good case for lowering tariffs and loosening capital controls, there is no such thing as completely "free" trade, just as there are no ethics based entirely on How-I-Feel.

Free trade benefits some (consumers and multinational corporations) while hurting others: manufacturers who lose preferential access to the

[142] Rodrik, *Globalization*, xvii–xviii, 110–11, 149–55.
[143] Rodrik, *One*, 210.
[144] Barber, 163, 211, 226.
[145] Rodrik, *Globalization*, 105.

home market, workers whose jobs flee overseas, and farmers who must compete with cheaper foreign produce. A drop from a protectionist 20% tariff to a 5% tariff brings far more benefits than a drop from 5% to 0%, but even the more beneficial 15% drop creates winners and losers. Whether we can accept the resulting income redistribution is always an important political question, and it becomes even more urgent when the gains to be had get smaller in our less protectionist postmodern era. The US numbers are rather shocking—a *redistribution* of $50 for every $1 net *gain*—and Rodrik puts the change in graphic terms: "It's as if we give $51 to Adam, only to leave David $50 poorer."[146] This is a bit misleading, since the $50 doesn't disappear, but goes somewhere—perhaps to Western shareholders or to non-Western workers, but we must at least consider in each case whether the redistributions invited by postmodern economic freedom are just.

Under the WTO, the increase of capital's freedom has been matched by a decrease of national sovereignty and the power of labour. Reforms typically demanded by the IMF when loaning money include deregulation, lowered trade barriers and capital controls, cuts to government social spending, lowered corporate taxation, weakening of unions, and elimination of local content rules.[147] The tax burden gets shifted from capital to labour. In order to defend market price, the WTO makes export subsidies illegal, but market price tends to exclude social and external costs, because we lack international political organizations that can regulate costs such as environmental degradation and the loss of union protections. Although a nation can regulate minimum wage and prohibit work under unsafe conditions within its borders, the ability of a corporation to easily cross borders can subvert those local standards. The appellate court of the WTO legislates on trade matters and has at times usurped national sovereignty by, for example, ruling against EU bans on genetically modified products and hormone-tested beef, even though health fears, not protectionism, led to the bans, and even though the same ban applied to domestic trade. As well, higher American fuel emissions standards were found to discriminate against trade partners. In such cases, national sovereignty and democracy are weakened in favour of trade. Under NAFTA, US firms were awarded millions in damages because a

[146] Rodrik, *Globalization*, 57–8.
[147] Rodrik, *Globalization*, 164, 76, 78. Unions had already declined between 40%–79% in the US early in the postmodern era. Putnam, 81–2.

Mexican municipality refused to allow a toxic waste facility and because Canada banned certain gasoline additives. Freer trade has also allowed $500–800 billion (according to the World Bank) to flow *out* of developing countries illegally in the 1990s and 2000s, while only about $50–80 billion made its way back to those developing countries from the West in the form of aid. Rodrik therefore argues that "deep" globalization is incompatible with national democracy.[148]

In other words, we can't equate economic freedom with postmodern individual freedom in any simple way. Companies such as Airbnb and Uber assert that the individual is being freed and empowered as an entrepreneur, but, in reality, the new deregulated business plan pushes workers' salaries down below minimum wage and eliminates protections for the consumer.[149] Even more exploitative are the Internet's "Mechanical Turk" set-ups, in which workers compete to do tiny Human Intelligence Tasks (HITS) that computers can't do, such as detecting bias, tagging photographs, and culling inappropriate content. In operations such as Amazon's MTurk, workers must compete for brief contracts, and the oversupply of workers drives down the wage. Some crowdworkers like the individual freedom of working whenever they want, but the cost of such freedom is that workers have no rights, no benefits, and low wages—between $1.00–2.00/hour according to some estimates.[150] One CEO, Lukas Biewald of CrowdFlower (now rebranded as Figure Eight), admitted, "Before the Internet, it would be really difficult to find someone, sit them down for ten minutes and get them to work for you, and then fire them after those ten minutes."[151] In a process (sometimes voluntary, sometimes forced) of extricating the individual from the union of workers and renaming the individual an "independent contractor" in the gig economy, the worker gains flexibility, but loses a minimum wage, a pension plan, unemployment insurance, maternity benefits, health insurance, and sick leave. Just as a deregulated How-I-Feel is unjust, so, too, is its economic equivalent.

[148] Rodrik, *Globalization*, 192, 198, 53, 190–1, 78–80, 195–6, 188. Baker and Joly. Freeman, 199.

[149] Rushkoff, 46–7.

[150] Marvit. See also Ellen Cushing, "Amazon Mechanical Turk: The Digital Sweatshop," *Utne Reader* (Jan/Fe 2013), rpt from *East Bay Express*, https://www.utne.com/science-and-technology/amazon-mechanical-turk-zm0z13jfzlin.

[151] Marvit.

olars have found a bitter irony in the fact that capital and multina-
ᴜᴏᴨᴀᴜ corporations freely cross national boundaries, while migrant workers and refugees face strict border controls. Theoretically, capital goes
where it's most effective, but labour can't go where it's most needed,
where incomes could move towards parity. All around the world, people
strongly favour increased international trade, while balking at increased
immigration.[152] Capital thus operates in a postmodern world in which it
can move freely between weakened nations. At the same time, workers are
forced to operate in a modern world where national boundaries form
impermeable walls and hide the social consequences of deregulation.[153]

The effects of postmodern deregulation—who gains and who loses—
can be seen in Packard Electric (a division of General Motors) and Packard
employee Tammy Thomas. In the 1990s, Packard cut jobs and sent a lot
of work to the maquiladoras in Juarez. From 13,000 workers in the 1970s,
the labour force declined to 3000 in 2005, and the union's power declined
accordingly. At the same time, Packard's foreign workforce rose to
100,000, many of them in Mexico. Thomas, who had grown up as the
daughter of a drug-addicted mother and had been raised by her grandmother in Youngstown, Ohio, became a single mother and got a job with
Packard, making wire harnesses for GM electrical components. Like many
other workers, she got carpal tunnel syndrome, but she did make a good
wage, close to $25 an hour. By working a lot of overtime, she hoped to
retire early. Packard, however, divided the company in 1999 in order to
shed American workers. Thomas survived the first series of cuts, but now
she worked for Delphi Automotive Systems, which went bankrupt six
years later, partly because of management fraud, and partly for tactical
reasons. Only the North American operations went bankrupt—elsewhere
the company was still making money—yet the bankruptcy allowed Delphi
to fire all its North American workers. The economic tsunami hit Thomas

---

[152] Pew, "World Publics," 1. A Pew poll in 2007, just before the Recession, found that
support around the world for international trade was quite high (above 70% in most countries) with support for free markets somewhat lower. Only 7 of 47 countries showed less than
50% support of free trade, with Bulgaria the lowest at 42% (Pew, "World Publics," 1). In
2014, after the Recession, about half of the people believed that trade lowers wages.
Nevertheless, people in 44 nations not only supported trade (81%) but also supported foreign companies building plants (74%). Support for trade was lower in the US (68%), higher
in the developing world (Pew, "Faith," 2–3, 5).

[153] Ferguson, *Colossus*, 177. Stiglitz, 221. Bauman, *Wasted*, 79, 132. Wacquant, cited in
Bauman, *Wasted*, 84.

and all of Youngstown, as the tax base collapsed. After bankruptcy proceedings, the same company—General Motors—that had owned Packard from 1932 to 1999 miraculously re-emerged, still possessing most of the Delphi operations, but having shed its workers. About 150,000 jobs had been shifted outside of the US, where workers didn't have to be paid so much, and "Delphi was hailed as a model of cost-cutting through bankruptcy."[154] The power of the nation declines; corporations and shareholders get more freedom. But Tammy Thomas, sharing none of that postmodern freedom, can't cheer.

Reassertions of the National Grand Narrative

Faced with the many deleterious effects of globalization, the limits of international regulatory regimes, and the inability of sovereign nations to exert control, some people have called for a renewal of grand narratives of the nation. On the right, the success of Donald Trump and nationalist parties in Poland, Hungary, Italy, and Brazil show evidence of this: a disillusionment with postmodern freedom and multilateralism. Despite Trump's demagoguery, his eagerness to blame every ill on foreigners, his neglect to mention that most jobs were lost to automation, and his possible unawareness that consumers (including workers) had made significant gains,[155] he was not wrong to tell his core constituency of disenfranchised workers that globalized competition has out-sourced American jobs and put downward pressure on American wages.[156] Similarly, Brexiter antipathy towards immigrants and resistance against the increasing legislation coming out of Brussels arose most strongly among people in low-growth areas, where globalization has been a net loss. On the left, protesters disrupted the 1999 WTO meetings in Seattle and, more recently, rallied against Trans-Pacific Partnership negotiations, calling for an end to trade deals and market liberalization. Even more popular trade deals have been attacked. Chris Hedges explains how NAFTA bankrupted Mexican farmers by wiping out government subsidies for corn and bean crops, driving 2 million Mexican farmers off the land, and how some NAFTA-enabled

---

[154] Packer, 91, 150, 52, 91, 151–2, 231, 331.
[155] Pinker, *Enlightenment*, 117.
[156] Rodrik, *Globalization*, 85.

Mexican maquiladoras eventually fled across the Pacific to make use of even cheaper labour in China.[157]

Given their similar protectionist sentiments, it's not always easy to distinguish on a practical level between progressive attempts to protect disempowered workers and regressive attempts to resurrect the former glory of the nation by scapegoating immigrants. The leftist Takis Fotopoulos argues that votes for Trump, France's Marine Le Pen, and Britain's UKIP are appropriate anti-globalist responses to the erosion of workers' rights.[158] Both far-right nationalists and progressives want to turn back the clock on the newly integrated postmodern globe. What Hedges and Fotopoulos ignore is that between 1984 and 2012, extreme poverty was reduced in Mexico from about 27% of the population to about 3%,[159] and that, worldwide, freer trade has brought many millions of people out of poverty, particularly in China and India.[160] Despite the massive growth of human population, the number of people living in poverty has declined since its peak in the 1960s. (This is all the more impressive because the peak was one of absolute, not just relative numbers. The percentage of people in poverty declined from 90% in 1820 to about 50% in 1960). There are many reasons for this, including freer trade, and Max Roser says that if news outlets reported accurately, "they could have run the headline NUMBER OF PEOPLE IN EXTREME POVERTY FELL BY 137,000 SINCE YESTERDAY every day for the last twenty-five years."[161]

Ironies abound. For all of his jeremiads against "very unfair" trade deals, outsourcing, and the loss of American jobs, Donald Trump was, of course, very happy to let factories in Bangladesh and China make Donald J. Trump Collection suits, shirts, cuff-links, eyeglasses, and perfume.[162] Lest we think that the ironies apply only to millionaire entrepreneurs, however, it must be added that workers in my city buy their shoes at Walmart because they're cheaper than at Brandon's Union Shoes, even

---

[157] Hedges, 158.

[158] Fotopoulos, 30, 34, 282, 284–7.

[159] "Share living in extreme poverty vs. GDP per capita over time," World Bank statistics, quoted in Roser, Global Extreme Poverty IV.i, https://ourworldindata.org/extreme-poverty.

[160] Stephen D. King, 180, 251.

[161] Pinker, *Enlightenment*, 87–9.

[162] Rosalind S. Helderman and Tom Hamburger, "Trump has profited from foreign labor he says is killing US jobs," *Washington Post*, 13 March 2016, https://www.washingtonpost.com/politics/trump-decries-outsourced-labor-yet-he-didnt-seek-made-in-america-in-2004-deal/2016/03/13/4d65a43c-e63a-11e5-b0fd-073d5930a7b7_story.html.

though Union Shoes supports local charities, while Walmart does very little.[163] Walmart's Buy American campaign won praise, and "Made in the USA" signs advertised clothing imported from Bangladesh.[164] It's a win-win scenario: the consumer feels virtuous in pledging allegiance to the grand narrative of the nation while still getting the cheapest (globalized) deal.

An alternative populism on behalf of the poor—the 2011 Occupy Wall Street protests, the 2018 yellow vest protests in France—is full of ironies too. In art, utopian morality tales such as *Children of Men* (2006), *V for Vendetta* (2005), and even *Avatar* (2009) were applauded for their revolutionary group action,[165] while on the street, the Occupy movement returned to simplistic utopian arguments about good and evil (the 99% and the 1%), an outlook that hinders negotiation, especially when trade is at stake. Rising income inequality is certainly a bad omen for social peace and an incitement to populism,[166] but everyone (not just the 1%) has gotten wealthier, especially if wealth is measured in consumption.[167] As well, since trade is a key arena for multilateralism, a simple protectionist rejection of postmodern freedoms would not only be economically devastating to foreign workers and to developing economies, but also to the West and the purchasing power of its poorest citizens, never mind to global interrelations and community-building.

GLOBAL RULE OF LAW

On the one hand, the success of Trump and nationalist politicians worldwide implies a revival of the grand narrative of the nation. On the other hand, the fact that conservative populism is strongest among the oldest cohorts of voters, and that voters don't usually become more conservative as they age,[168] the increasing reach of global organizations such as the UN and the EU, a growing consensus against racism, and the rise of human rights alongside citizenship rights could suggest a great deal of support for a moderate path between the extremes of complete postmodern deregulation and a return to strict national sovereignties. Against this positive out-

---

[163] Packer, 103. Roberts, 83.
[164] Packer, 104.
[165] Hill, 152.
[166] Mounk, 16–7, 218–9. Fotopoulos, 39.
[167] Pinker, *Enlightenment*, 98, 104–8, 111–12, 114, 117.
[168] Pinker, *Enlightenment*, 341–2.

look, Yascha Mounk makes a strong argument that populism's appeal may bring democracies to crisis. In his view, the massive increase in lobbying, the power of bureaucrats to decide the details of international treaties, economic stagnation for the middle class in the West, all suggest that populists are correct to complain that their voices aren't heard. Examining 1779 policy issues over 20 years, one study found that almost all policy decisions favoured economic elites and special interest groups, while mass-based interest groups had little influence. That problem, Mounk contends, is magnified in multilateral organizations such as the EU: the complexities of integration are such that bureaucrats hold most of the power, while elected officials have less and less say in decisions, in effect stifling the voters' influence.[169]

Along the more moderate path than populism are two main responses to the deleterious effects of globalization's postmodern individualism: global rule of law and selective national sovereignty. Global rule of law points towards international regulations, for which the EU provides a model, albeit a flawed one. Proposals also exist for such things as an international bankruptcy court and an international lender of last resort. Proving that an entirely self-regulating market and small government don't lead to prosperity, successful capitalist countries have created extensive supporting institutions: trading regulations, strong legal regimes to protect property, police to punish cheats, national banks to prevent panics, redistributive tax systems to pay for public goods, health and safety standards to protect workers, and social safety nets to support those who flounder in the capitalist economy. Rich countries have both better markets *and* larger governments. Between the end of the nineteenth century and the present, public spending increased from below 10% to 40%, revealing that a mixed economy is the most effective in bringing about wealth.[170] Given this, we might envision a similar global social contract: better global regulation will aid the market by caring for the market's casualties. The EU, with its strong unions and legislation, does so by retraining workers whose work has been offshored,[171] and by allowing labour to move more freely to wherever the jobs are. During the Recession of 2007–8, Latvian

---

[169] Mounk, 77–8, 197, 293.

[170] Rodrik, *Globalization*, 208–9, 15–18, 22, 237, 234. Heath, *Economics*, 58–60. Although the US lags behind other Western nations in its social safety net, leftists such as Fotopoulos are mistaken about "the effective dismantling of the welfare state" (Fotopoulos, 39).

[171] Roberts, 152.

workers moved freely to other EU countries, to find work and send home wages.[172] Even flawed international structures (such as the IMF, which requires questionable cuts to public services in countries asking for loans) do provide a global public sphere where inequalities can at least be debated, a process far preferable to a complete Hobbesian deregulation. Inequities created by international trade organizations such as the WTO won't be solved by destroying them, but only by making them more sensitive to democratic and developing-world concerns.

Unfortunately, the diversity of nations makes a global democracy unlikely. In an era of postmodern scepticism about grand narratives, supra-national organizations such as the EU have an even greater struggle than do nations to inspire emotional attachment.[173] That's beneficial up to a point, since it keeps a lid on the rabid patriotism that fuelled so many wars. But a certain amount of emotional investment may be necessary to iden-tify with a group. As well, EU nations in 2005 couldn't agree on a consti-tution, which would have taken primacy over national constitutions and forced nations to obey legal judgements made in other countries.[174] Under imperialism, international standards were possible, if unjust. In the time of postmodern multilateralism, it's more difficult to arrive at global stan-dards, and those standards may still be unfair. During the Recession of 2007–8, Latvia, Hungary, and Greece had to submit to IMF conditions before receiving EU loans. At the same time, Greece and other hard-hit countries in the Euro-zone (Spain, Portugal, and Italy) could no longer devalue their currency to make investment and exports more attractive. This gave these South-European nations, as Rodrik puts it, "the worst of both worlds:" little central support and not enough freedom to chart their own paths. Brexit, meanwhile, will cost Britons dearly, but the devaluation of the pound also encourages British manufacturing. If such profound dif-ficulties loom even for the EU, with its shared history and religion, how much more difficult would it be for a global democracy?[175] Nevertheless, Rodrik agrees that international regulation is essential. Even bank leader Stephen D. King, who recommends freer financial flows, and who fears national regulations, understands that cross-border political institutions

---

[172] Rodrik, *Globalization*, 219–20.

[173] Pew Research polls from the early 2000s show that 90% of Europeans still felt "fairly" or "very" attached to their individual countries, but only 45% felt the same attachment to the EU (Ferguson, *Colossus*, 251).

[174] Gillingham, 137–9.

[175] Rodrik, *Globalization*, 223, 218–19, 220, 238.

are necessary.[176] Without some surrender of national sovereignty, we fall into the tragedy of the commons. Environmental problems, for example, are notorious for the unwillingness of individual nations to agree on regulations.[177] Ozone depletion was successfully addressed by the global UN,[178] and, at present, the only hope to address global warming also lies with the UN.

SELECTIVE NATIONAL SOVEREIGNTY

Are we postmodern yet? The rise of global multilateralism, the decline of political participation, the replacement of the citizen by consumers and spectators suggests so. If the UN is postmodern in trying to balance a plurality of national agendas, it is still not radically postmodern*ist* or relativist, because it seeks to place nations under the rule of law. Our allegiance to human rights makes us suspicious of the nation, which often threatens minority rights and reverts to imperialism, as in the US's 2003 decision to go to war with Iraq despite the Security Council's opposition.[179] It's thus tempting at times to cheer for the decline of the nation. However, in an era of relative order, it's far too easy to overlook the protective role that national governments also play. At present, we lack a full international constitution, so the Security Council can still put individuals on terror lists without due process. Jean Cohen also argues that, because of the dangers of Security Council imperialism against weaker nations, and because nations should be free to develop culturally in a way not predetermined by Western liberal democracy, we ought to make explicit the legal limits on when and how the international community may interfere with sovereign nations. Making *any* human rights violations a legal cause for intervention opens up too much room for hegemonic intervention, Cohen says, so we should only allow interventions when human security rights (personal liberty and bodily integrity) are contravened in genocide, ethnic cleansing, crimes against humanity, or war crimes.[180] It still falls to national governments to protect our social and cultural standards, to negotiate international agreements, and to provide almost all public services. The continuing

---

[176] Stephen D. King, 251, 226.
[177] Rodrik, *Globalization*, 247–50.
[178] Gareis, 235, 243.
[179] Gareis, 143, 148.
[180] Cohen, 274, 188, 211–16.

importance of the nation means that we haven't fully converted to a post-modern politics. During the Recession of 2007–8, it was sovereign nations that bailed out the banks, provided the liquidity for the market, initiated an economic stimulus, and revised the rules in order to prevent a repeat market failure.[181]

Rodrik suggests that it's possible and even desirable to keep national sovereignty alive in the postmodern era of globalization by, for example, expanding opt-out provisions such as the WTO Agreement on Safeguards (which allows for tariffs and subsidies when domestic firms or industries come under heavy fire). South Korea and Taiwan are sometimes held out as models for successfully globalized nations, but, in fact, both countries had subsidized and protected their young industries into the 1980s. If globalization only lets nations leverage the industries and capabilities it already has, then developing nations will always lag behind. They need some protection for fledgling domestic industries before opening them to the competition and opportunities of globalization. With respect to the financial sector, Rodrik argues that countries should be able to enforce their own standards, as the US did under Obama with new rules on banks' capital requirements and limits on bank size. To avoid a financial services race to the bottom, Rodrik suggests a small tax (one-tenth of 1%) on international currency transactions. With this equivalent of a toll-road, the nation can limit the appeal of very short-term profits, and link finance more productively to the real economy.[182] This would create an ordered postmodern multilateralism, preserving pluralism and many financial free-doms, without falling into a How-I-Feel regulatory void. Multilateralism would also be expressed in greater freedom for workers to cross borders. Here Rodrik proposes a partial opening up of developed countries' labour markets—3% of a nation's labour force—to a rotating series of guest workers from developing countries.[183] He argues that the ensuing global wealth gains would outstrip all of the free-trade measures proposed under the flagging Doha Round of WTO negotiations.[184] Such reforms would balance the desired capitalist expansion of the economy with some degree of fairness—applying to workers and not just to multinational companies—

---

[181] Rodrik, *Globalization*, xix, 237–8, 207. Gillingham, 122.

[182] Rodrik, *Globalization*, 253–5, 147, 145, 182, 262, 264, 108, 121, 283–4.

[183] Rodrik, *Globalization*, 266–8. Others, less sympathetic to workers in developed countries, call for a completely free labour market (Stephen D. King, 252, 236).

[184] Rodrik, *Globalization*, 266.

so that globalization wouldn't be just a tool of the elites. After all the rhetoric of free trade, such reforms would begin to right the balance between radically free areas of the economy (finance) and unfree areas (the labour market). The reforms would preserve some national economic sovereignty even as globalization proceeds.

Cohen likewise argues for a dual international political-legal order, retaining national sovereignty in most areas, but allowing global governance institutions (GGIs) such as the UN, the ICC, and the International Court of Justice to override national sovereignty at defined times. This would avoid a false choice between a Westphalian system and a completely pluralist system. We already see dual orders in many areas, including peacekeeping operations, where a country's highest-ranking officer in a UN contingent is nominally under UN command, but ultimately takes orders from the officer's home government. Likewise, soldiers in a UN contingent are immune from criminal prosecution except by their own national governments. A dual legal order appears in hybrid missions when the UN explicitly cedes command to a troop-contributing nation, and in missions which have the UN's moral support but which, because of the threat of P5 veto, cannot be pursued under the UN banner—for example, the so-called "illegal but legitimate" NATO campaign in Kosovo.[185]

Whatever shape future reforms take, the fantasy of complete political and economic deregulation can't be taken seriously. On the broad historical scale, strong federal governments reduce violence, if only because there are fewer units to fight each other. Gary LaFree and Orlando Patterson identify an inverted "U" relationship between crime and democratization. Both established autocracies and established democracies show low crime rates, though emerging democracies—because of typically weak central governments—show high crime rates and descend more easily to civil war. When governments falter, as in Russia and South Africa during the 1990s, crime rises. When national governments are strong and have reduced the violence committed by citizens against each other, the best opportunity for further reducing violence becomes reducing *governmental* violence. But this isn't done by encouraging civil wars in autocracies, as the US discovered in Iraq. Nearly all genocides after 1956 have taken place after a state failure.[186] Even in the authority-mistrusting postmodern era, collapses of authoritarian regimes rarely lead to democracy.[187]

---

[185] Bellamy and Williams, 58, 374, 59, 121. Cohen, 174, 212.

[186] Pinker, *Better*, 89, 202, 159, 336–7, 341.

[187] Diamond and Plattner, 63–6.

There is a perception that nation-states are fuelling a decline in democracy, but Larry Diamond and Marc Plattner give evidence that although there have been setbacks after 2005 in important nations such as Russia, China, Brazil, and Turkey (we could now add Hungary and Poland), democracy in general has held its own worldwide. Between 1970 and 2014, the number of electoral democracies increased from 35 to 110. There are legitimate concerns about polarization in centrist parties (the Donald Trump/Bernie Saunders phenomenon), and growing fears that parliaments and unions are losing power to the executive branches of government and to multinational companies. Other developments such as freedom-of-information acts, delegation of powers, parties' affirmative action to encourage female and racialized candidates, and public funding for political parties suggest that voters, even in our postmodern era of deregulation on the one hand and populism on the other, recognize the importance of legal structures, and that democracy is progressing.[188] The nation, though less belligerent and no longer as dominant in the West as it was in the modern era, continues to play a decisive role, even in a necessarily multilateral era.

[188] Diamond and Plattner, 6, 41, 11–12, 73–4, 102, 107, 42, 49–52.

CHAPTER 7

Faith and Other Grand Narratives

"Evil Spirits"

In 1999, St. Matthew's Anglican Church of Abbotsford, British Columbia, invited Moses Tay, Anglican Archbishop of Southeast Asia, to a celebration planned for October 2000. But when Michael Ingham, Bishop of New Westminster, heard of the invitation, he, with the support of senior Vancouver Anglicans, refused to allow Archbishop Tay into the diocese. The problem was that on an earlier visit to Vancouver, Tay had noticed totem poles in Stanley Park, and had organized a prayer meeting to exorcise the "evil spirits" associated with the poles. To make matters worse, Tay had spoken aggressively against homosexuality. Trying to be tactful and expressing a religious form of multilateralism, Ingham explained, "Both our relationships with aboriginals and our discussions around gay and lesbian spirituality would make [Tay's] presence difficult."[1] Such a response is indicative of rising distrust, even among the faithful, for traditional grand narratives. Just as postmodernity has weakened the imagined national communities that pull people together, so too has postmodernity contested the communities built on religious faith. While Christianity still provides meaning to Ingham, the freezing out of one church leader by another for attitudes that a few decades ago would have been called sound biblical doctrine demonstrates the remarkable and necessary ways in which postmodernity challenges the stories whereby we live.

[1] Ferdy Baglo.

R. Kramer, *Are We Postmodern Yet?*,
https://doi.org/10.1007/978-3-030-30569-7_7

229

e longer historical arc that postmodernists see begins with traditional religious faiths. These faiths undergo modernity's attacks, such as the rational critique of the *Bible*, and then new grand narratives arise: socialism, capitalism, scientific progress, humanism, to name a few. Finally, postmodernists arrive on the scene, distrustful even of these new grand narratives. The natural outcome of such scepticism is for Lyotard the rise of the *petit récit*, the small narrative that gives a provisional meaning to me and to my group, but makes no larger claims about the human world or the cosmos. Actual contemporary history is, of course, much messier than this postmodernist history implies. In North America, the wish to retain the grand narrative of Christian faith has often issued in something like Bishop Ingham's tentative version of the old story. Ingham has been influenced enough by modernity not to trust Christian denunciations of homosexuality, and by postmodernity not to dismiss either aboriginal spirituality or Christianity as naïve pre-scientific mythologies that are best shed. In this chapter, we will examine, firstly, many signs that, in North America, the grand narrative of Christianity has been significantly diminished; secondly, ways in which it continues to exert societal and individual influence; and thirdly, five varieties of postmodern accommodation made by people who lack the former confidence in faith stories but who still seek meaning, whether in the self, in small narratives, in a more tentative version of the Christian grand narrative, in pluralism, or in humanism, a grand narrative that in the postmodern West seems to be surpassing Christianity. Grand narratives have not been abandoned, even among sceptics—one can hardly fail to notice that the very attempt to refuse grand narratives inevitably coalesces into a new grand narrative about openness, freedom, and rights.

TRADITIONAL BELIEFS DIMINISHING IN A POSTMODERN CONTEXT

The resistance to Archbishop Tay's Christian grand narrative is not an isolated flare-up. Sociologist Christian Smith's 2007–8 surveys of American religious attitudes and behaviours, particularly those of young adults, form an excellent window into the *Zeitgeist*, because Millennials' expressed attitudes often reflect their parents' unspoken assumptions. Young adults are less certain about God, feel less close to God, adhere less to traditional, "biblical" teachings, and tend to think that religion should be private, rather than a factor in political and social debates. Worship-service attendance and religious commitment have declined significantly, subjective beliefs not quite as much.[2] In Canada, 2008 trends mirror those in the US. Among the younger Millennials (aged 15–19), one-third attend church services at least monthly, almost unchanged from 1992 (though if Philip Brenner is correct that church attendance is consistently over-reported, then the rate might be closer to one-quarter). At the opposite end of the spectrum, one-third of Millennials are either convinced or suspect that God does not exist. Belief in God has declined among all age groups, and only 13% of teens were prepared to call religion *very* important to them.[3] Less than half of teens said that they wondered about the purpose of life "a great deal" or "quite a bit." They worried more about the pressure to do well at school (75%), plans for what to do after finishing school (60%), lack of money, lack of time, losing friends, boredom, looks, and the fact that so many things in the world are changing.[4] In some surveys, nearly half of Millennials placed themselves among the undecided, emphasizing an unstructured and individualized faith.[5] Only 18% were very worried about their relationship with God, though God did beat out deciding whom to vote for, contributing to the community, and finding a spouse.[6] The changes point to generational change, not to age effects, because Millennials and iGeners are less religious than previous generations were at the same age, and belief in God, prayer, and biblical inspiration have all declined.[7] If we look at changes over a much longer period, the changes are even starker. Back in 1924, 91% of students in an American high school agreed that "Christianity is the one true religion and all people should be converted to it."[8] By the mid-2000s, one-third of American Millennials declared that they had no religion, twice as many as called themselves evangelical (15%).[9]

[2] C. Smith, 125, 139, 141, 213.

[3] An additional 17% say that religion is *somewhat* important (Bibby, 168, 178–9, 185). In Canada, rates of teens with no religion were highest in the North (51%) and British Columbia (44%), lowest in Ontario (23%). According to 2001 Canadian Census data, 16% of adults said that they had no religion, up from a pre-1961 level of 11% (Bibby, 177). Brenner, cited in Bass, 53.

[4] Bibby, 66.

[5] Greenberg, 6. Other surveys give similar numbers. See Twenge, *iGen*, 120; Bass, 46.

[6] Greenberg, 16–17.

[7] Twenge, *iGen*, 124–8.

[8] Pinker, *Better*, 392.

[9] Bass, 81.

Surveys of the general population present a similar picture of declining grand narratives of faith. Between the 1960s and the 2000s, church attendance in the US dropped by nearly half; in Canada, only one-third of Canadians still attended weekly church services in 2008, down from two-thirds in the 1950s.[10] In a 2012 nationwide poll, two-thirds of Canadians professed belief in God's existence, but only less than half agreed that, "religion is an important part of my life." Agreement was higher among women (46%) than among men (37%) and far higher among seniors (56%) than among young adults under the age of 24 (30%).[11] Emblematic is Natalie's wariness about higher powers in Trevor Cole's *Practical Jean*. Natalie declares that the funeral of Jean's mother was lovely, but also complains that the minister was "a bit wordy… a bit God-ish."[12] Many people retain a residue of faith, but even if some of the words remain the same, the meanings have changed, become vaguer, lessening the demands on the individual, as appears in Andrew Binks's autobiographical novel *Strip* (2013). There, the stripper, John Rottam, goes to church, but sneaks out before the end. "My real church," he thinks, "was somewhere in the back pew of the city bus: that is where I had time to examine my reflection. I didn't lack faith. Faith was all around me now: I had a home, a job, and a neighbour." He even calls his co-worker Brittany a "*goddess*" and her performance "holy" because she doesn't poke herself or squeeze her breasts.[13] More conventionally than in the novel, a real-life former believer explains that on Sunday mornings he now prefers to sleep in, read the *New York Times*, and run in the woods: "I worship nature. I see myself in the trees and in the butterflies. I am one with the great outdoors. I find God there. And I realized that I am deeply spiritual but no longer religious."[14] It's not surprising that the Grammy for Best Country Solo Performance in 2016 went to Maren Morris's "My Church," in which driving alone down the highway with an FM station turned up high replaces communion with other believers.

The survey data cohere with broad signs of weakening trust in grand narratives, resulting in an increase in libertarian attitudes and less respect for authority, religion, and patriotism. One clear positive effect is a measurable increase in tolerance. On the negative side of the ledger, charitable

[10] Putnam, 67, 71. Bibby, 164.
[11] Jack Jedwab.
[12] Cole, *Practical*, 51.
[13] Binks, 136, 162.
[14] Daniel, 5.

donations and group involvement have steadily decreased. Charity fell in relative terms in the US after the 1960s (though total giving rose with population increase), and the decline has continued in recent years with iGen. In other words, explains Putnam, we spend far more on ourselves than we used to. Evangelicals give more to the church, percentage-wise, than do mainline Protestants, yet Evangelical contributions, because they started higher, fell at a greater rate.[15]

Group involvement has also diminished as religion becomes more privatized.[16] A troubling trend is that the "Nones" (those who profess no religion) tend not to vote.[17] Pinker justifiably fears evangelical voters, who proved instrumental in electing Donald Trump, but one must also ask why religious "Nones," who favoured Hilary Clinton, couldn't find the motivation to vote. Since about half of association membership, personal philanthropy, and volunteering arise out of a religious context, the weakening of grand religious narratives has negative consequences for social and political organizations generally, in terms of both money and volunteers. The picture can be complex. It's not that people who are involved only in secular organizations give little. In fact, non-believers who do volunteer, volunteer at *higher* rates and give *more*. It's just that there are fewer of such "involved" secular people. And the correlation between religious giving and broader charity isn't a simple correlation in the postmodern context, since among the devout a growing percentage is being given to the church and less to other charities.[18] To counteract the decline of involvement, consultants suggest that nonprofit groups must get better at harnessing "selfish" altruism: people want to feel generous, but they also want to have fun while they're being generous. Mimicking the transformation of citizens, volunteers must be treated as consumers too. Consultants say that charities should "start thinking of their volunteer positions as a 'product' to be sold by promising 'an opportunity, a privilege, and a stride toward greatness.'"[19]

This waning influence of faith grand narratives also appears in small ways, as in the proliferation of coffee cups and cell phone activity during church services. Some faith practices such as "mindfulness," meditation,

---

[15] Putnam, 254, 123, 126. Twenge, *iGen*, 174–5.
[16] Putnam, 74.
[17] Pinker, *Enlightenment*, 438.
[18] Putnam, 66, 119, 126.
[19] Maich and George, 230–1.

and yoga have become unmoored from the religious traditions that informed them and have entered the marketplace. Now, for a small fee, one can perform the 26 traditional yoga postures in a hot room—"hot yoga" (it's copyrighted).[20] Jesus's claim that faith as small as a mustard seed can move mountains has been repackaged as "The Secret," graciously made public (and verified by Oprah): health and wealth follow the universal "Law of Attraction," flowing to those who think positively. On the one hand, why one shouldn't take up the best aspects of a religious practice? But on the other hand, faith communities warn against wrenching religious practices and scriptures out of their spiritual depths to be reborn as slogans, pop psychology, and get-rich-quick schemes.

In larger social developments, too, grand narratives of faith are weakening. The past century has seen the state take over many health and welfare organizations that were founded along religious lines, divorce is no longer a sin, and a strong majority of Canadians (71%), alongside a smaller majority of Americans (56%), now feel that religion should be kept separate from government.[21] During their decade in power ending in 2015, Canada's Conservatives avoided the divisive issues of abortion and same-sex marriage, despite lobbying from the base. In the US, conservative churches have had greater effect, recently emboldened by limits on abortion in several states, and by Donald Trump's pro-life appointments to the Supreme Court. Yet American churches haven't been able to stop abortion, or the Supreme Court's 5–4 legalization of same-sex marriage in 2015, or even the legalization of marijuana in several states.

Faith has increasingly come under scientific scrutiny, and, with Internet dissemination, evidence against biblical literalism has become better known. For example, scientific studies of intercessory prayer show that prayer has little or no effect on medical outcomes. In one double-blind study, neither the heart-bypass patients nor their prayer intercessors knew which patients were being prayed for. The study found no statistically significant differences in post-operative complications.[22] Such studies

---

[20] Maich and George, 216.

[21] Pew, "World Publics," 37. Worldwide, there is a lot of variation on this issue, often linked to local conditions. European results are generally closer to Canada, though some countries scored closer to the American results (Spain 51%, Russia 55%, Bulgaria 57%, and Italy 59%).

[22] The patients who were prayed for and who had been *told* that they were being prayed for had the *most* complications. Chance likely explains the result: *one* of the three groups must have the most complications, not very long odds. Although the authors controlled for many

rule out a purely "magical" effect of prayer, though their very rigour may mask the potential human and socially supportive effects of prayer that earlier studies found.

Accounts of near-death experiences in the afterlife have also tended to wilt under scientific and media scrutiny. Belief in hell is down, with hardly anybody expecting that they or their friends will go there,[23] but upbeat visions of heaven are still popular. *The Boy Who Came Back From Heaven* (2010) told of Alex Malarkey's time in a Christian heaven after he was severely injured in a 2004 traffic accident. Both he and his father, Kevin Malarkey, were credited as authors, but in subsequent years Alex repudiated the book, revealing that his father had exaggerated the events. In *Heaven is for Real: A Little Boy's Astounding Story of His Trip to Heaven and Back* (2010), 3-year-old Baptist preacher's son Colton Burpo, after an emergency appendectomy in 2003, also reported that he had visited a Christian heaven where the angels sang "Jesus Loves Me" and "Joshua Fought the Battle of Jericho," and where Colton met King David, Samson, the Apostles Peter and John, Mary, a brown-haired blue-eyed Jesus, Colton's great-grandfather (appearing as a 30-year-old), and a baby girl that his mother had miscarried.[24] Colton insisted that everybody in heaven had wings. Ghostwriter Lynn Vincent tried to dissuade him and his father from including that detail, but she was overruled.[25] Many believers nevertheless welcomed Burpo's story as a confirmation of the Christian grand narrative, the book spent years on the *New York Times* bestseller list, and a 2014 movie based on the book grossed about $100 million in its first year.

variables (including medical conditions and even faith groupings), they acknowledged that in addition to the anonymous intercessors, patients were being prayed for by family and friends, an effect difficult to control for. Yet given the large sample size (600 for each group), differences in "extra-curricular" prayer should average out. Herbert Benson et al. "Study of the Therapeutic Effects of Intercessory Prayer (STEP) in cardiac bypass patients." *American Heart Journal* 151: 4 (April 2006): 934–42, http://www.sciencedirect.com/science/article/pii/S0002870305006496.

[23] Bass, 42, 51. Nevertheless, Bill Wiese's *23 Minutes in Hell* (2006), too, was received as a confirmation of the traditional Christian story and was popular enough to carve out a speaking career for Wiese.

[24] "Heaven is For Real" Revisited December 7, 2012 ~ Colton Burpo at 13," Christian Broadcasting Network, *700 Club*, http://www.youtube.com/watch?v=m%2D%2DM5itPoqA. John Blake, "Proof of heaven popular, except with the church," *Belief Blog*, CNN, 19 May 2013, http://religion.blogs.cnn.com/2013/05/19/proofs-of-heaven-popular-but-not-with-the-church/.

[25] Ariel Levy, "Lives of the Saints," 15 October 2012, https://www.newyorker.com/magazine/2012/10/15/lives-of-the-saints-3.

However, alongside orthodox reports from beyond the grave appeared other, just as upbeat, reports that ran towards postmodern pluralism. During a coma, Eben Alexander, an Episcopalian neurosurgeon who only attended church at Christmas and at Easter, heard the Hindu mantra "OM" and saw a faceless and genderless God in an orb of light. The angels made no mention of hell, and instead told Alexander, "You are loved and cherished, dearly, forever. You have nothing to fear. There is nothing you can do wrong."[26] By May 2013, Alexander's book, *Proof of Heaven* (2011) had sold 1.6 million copies. And in Canada, near Thompson, Manitoba, an Anishinabe woman whose heart had stopped as she lay in 34-below-zero temperatures was rescued by two firefighters who worked on her until she returned to life. She had no book or movie deal, but recounted, "It was amazing. I knew I was alive, even though I seemed to be dead. It was something strange, wonderful and so beautiful. I had a vision which was all part of my Indian culture; I will never forget it and I am sure it will change the way I live."[27] Because the various accounts are irreconcilable, because we now have greater access to these irreconcilable accounts, and because out-of-body experiences can be created by stimulating the temporoparietal junction in the brain,[28] orthodox heaven carries much less weight outside of the church than it once did.

Seminaries and post-secondary religious institutions have struggled to balance scientific knowledge with a respect for traditional narratives. This struggle can be seen when church leaders are asked to speak on controversial topics. Between Christmas and Easter 1998, the *Winnipeg Free Press* queried a number of Christian leaders on topics that included whether Jesus was born of a virgin and whether he rose from the dead. Not surprisingly, a Pentecostal minister and a Ukrainian Orthodox priest strongly affirmed the literal truth of the Christian grand narrative, while two professors from the University of Winnipeg's theology school (associated with the liberal United Church) countered that the stories must be metaphorical. More interesting were the responses of John Friesen, Dean of the Canadian Mennonite Bible College (now Canadian Mennonite University),

---

[26] Eben Alexander, "Dr. Eben Alexander Shares What God Looks Like," Interview. Oprah Winfrey Network, December 2012, http://www.oprah.com/own-super-soul-sunday/Dr-Eben-Alexander-Shares-What-God-Looks-Like-Video. John Blake, "Proof of Heaven..."

[27] *Winnipeg Free Press*, 17–24 February 1981.

[28] See Olaf Blanke et al., "Linking Out-of-Body Experience and Self Processing to Mental Own-Body Imagery at the Temporoparietal Junction," *The Journal of Neuroscience*, 19 January 2005, 25(3): 550–57.

and John English, provincial superior of Jesuit priests. They sought to affirm the truth of the stories while still questioning their historical accuracy, leaning towards metaphorical interpretations but unwilling to go all the way. As much as they might like to speak as scholars or individuals, their statements would be perceived as ex cathedra. The hedging of even denominational authorities—authorities whose equivocating would once have threatened their jobs—suggests that the grand narratives have weakened in the postmodern era.[29]

The general trend can also be seen in the disappearance of something that was a fact of life among evangelical churches as late as the 1960s and 1970s: church discipline committees. Codes of conduct for members were taken seriously, and deacons would regularly admonish offenders, particularly teens with a taste for sex or alcohol. Among the youth of the 200-member Pentecostal church in which I grew up, the committee was unofficially known as "the stoning committee." But church discipline largely disappeared by the 1990s under two main pressures. Firstly, as Baby Boomers began their demographic coup in the churches, individualism began to dominate there just like everywhere else, with a direct correlation between the decline of teens' church attendance and the increase of individualistic language in books.[30] Charles Taylor has well described denominations as "affinity groups;"[31] indeed, individualist Boomers switched churches or left if they found a church's worship style uncongenial or its conduct expectations too onerous. Contemporary faith includes a consumerist agenda—more parties, less fasting.[32] Many churches began to re-conceptualize themselves in ways that could both weaken and humanize them: no longer as exclusive groups of saints, but as sinners in need of grace.

Secondly, increasing market-consciousness emphasized church growth and member retention, which gave birth to a new inclusiveness. Demographic changes led to "seeker-friendly" churches, churches that turned down the house lights to let high-quality rock music and spectacle attract young people. These changes have been adopted by the largest evangelical churches, emphasis turning from membership and discipline to attendance and religious experiences. Now, coffee, sports, day care, and socializing figure heavily. As with "Oasis Church" or "The Meeting Place"

[29] Kandeith McArthur, "Divided in Faith." *Winnipeg Free Press*, 1 February 1998, B1, B4.
[30] Twenge, *iGen*, 138.
[31] Taylor, *Secular*, 449.
[32] Charles, 16–17.

in Winnipeg, denominational names disappear in favour of place names or names signifying "community." The Immanuel Pentecostal Church that I attended has been rebaptized for a more individualized era as "My Church." Bible school administrators, too, saw the consumer-choice writing on the wall and began rebranding Bible schools as colleges in order to increase enrolments: Ontario Bible College in Toronto became Tyndale College in 1998; Northwest Bible College in Edmonton became Vanguard College in 2004; and so on across Canada. The renaming also required that colleges submit themselves to secular standards and programme assessments.

The postmodern media have played a significant role in undermining the strength of traditional grand narratives. With TV, the "'holy" could be debunked quickly, widely, and then, with the Internet, perpetually. The fall of popular televangelist Robert Tilton spanned both the early postmodernity of TV and the more recent effect of the Internet. In his heyday, the handsome Tilton—folksy in image, but a sophisticated mass marketer—pulled in $80 million dollars a year through prosperity gospel shows on 200 American TV stations. Then, in 1991, the ABC-TV programme *Primetime Live* revealed that his employees threw prayer requests into the dumpster after the cheques had been harvested. Tilton responded that, to the contrary, he had laid his body on the prayer requests and wept on them to the point that the ink had caused an allergic reaction in his capillaries. Tilton had also secured millions of donations by using tactics such as photographs of starving Haitian orphans. *Primetime Live* found that all the orphanages but one were bogus; and that the real one received only minimal support in exchange for posing as the face of Tilton's charitable work.[33] The speed and reach of the TV exposé cut deeply into Tilton's empire and his show was cancelled a couple of years later.

The Christian grand narrative was also made risible by scandals involving Jimmy Swaggart, and PTL Club's Jimmy Bakker, by statements from televangelists such as Jack Van Impe, who predicted that the "millennium bug"' at the end of 1999 would set the apocalypse in motion,[34] and by viral videos of Tilton. Tilton, a bad actor when he tried to convey sincerity,

[33] ABC-TV's 1991 *Primetime Live* broadcast with Diane Sawyer can be seen on YouTube at "Robert Tilton: Televangelist Scandal," 29 May 2012, http://www.youtube.com/watch?v=7fXjZpPMmaQ.

[34] "2000 Time Bomb," [TV Programme from 1999]. Uploaded 29 Dec 2011, http://www.youtube.com/watch?v=uEUCjaOQs9U.

habitually scrunched his eyes shut every time that the Holy Spirit got hold of him. Someone spliced together a fart-track with VHS footage of Tilton scrunching, and the tape went viral on the Internet under such titles as "Pastor Gas" and "The Joyful Noise." A 2017 Google Video search for "Robert Tilton" yielded "The Farting Preacher" at positions #2, #3, and #4, with his healing claim, "we've seen midgets grow," at position #13. Exposés of and satire against evangelistic excesses are not new, but, whereas print, radio, and TV coverage was mostly limited to a day or two after the story broke and mostly to a secular audience, the Internet makes the stories and parodies widely and perpetually available, preventing the evangelists from keeping the information out of followers' hands. James Randi's popular YouTube videos exposing the techniques of faith healers such as Peter Popoff had similar meme-like effects. Randi caught Popoff's wife secretly radioing Popoff information from prayer request cards as he was speaking, so that he seemed to be receiving "a word of knowledge" from God about audience members. Popoff and Tilton still found a few buyers for their style of gospel by purchasing airtime on Black Entertainment Television, but for the most part evangelical culture moved on. Even in North American Pentecostal churches, faith healing has a far lower profile than it once had, as the Christian grand narrative softens its claims.

Of greater social importance was the 2006 case of Rev. Ted Haggard, deposed from his position as leader of the National Association of Evangelicals and from the pulpit of the 14,000-strong New Life Church in Colorado Springs for using crystal meth and for having a homosexual encounter with a masseur. Haggard had spoken against same-sex marriage, and, once the masseur outed him, many evangelicals were forced to become more receptive to what homosexuals had long argued, that homosexuality was an orientation. After 3 years of exile, enforced by his termination agreement with New Life Church, Haggard wanted to return to Colorado Springs to start a new church. It helped that, unlike Tilton or Popoff, Haggard wasn't a con artist, had the support of his wife and children, and seemed at least partly honest about his fall. As he prepared to restart his ministry, he commented on the reach of postmodern media: "What you put on the Internet, that's gonna stay there for somebody to find theoretically forever, along with everybody's comments. So, Number 1, there's no such thing as time. And Number 2, there's no such thing as distance. So it *used* to be that, back in the old days, when somebody would get in trouble, they'd just need to move 40 or 50 miles, or a hundred miles, and they could start again. Not anymore. Which is one of the reasons why we needed to come home."[35] Haggard restarted his ministry in 2010, beginning St. James Church in a barn, moving to larger premises when his congregation grew to beyond 300, and finding some acceptance by the larger Christian community.

Haggard's case in relation to the Christian grand narrative wasn't clear-cut. Although he still treated homosexuality as a sin, he insisted that because of his experience he became more accepting of homosexuals and drug addicts. He came out in favour of civil marriage for homosexuals, arguing that homosexuals should be treated equally and that the state is outside of biblical mandates. His minimal admission to bisexuality was congruent with the warming attitudes towards LGBTQ orientations among young Christians, and his case has become an object lesson, suggesting that if the leader of the National Association of Evangelicals couldn't suppress his homosexual orientation, then the grand narrative of Christianity had been, for two thousand years, mistaken on the issue.

In response to their respective scandals, Tilton took the modernist approach, Haggard the postmodern. Tilton continued to assume a strict division between those (himself, ABC-TV) who could control the medium and those who couldn't (his target demographic of middle-aged and older low-income women without much media literacy). He scaled back his expenses and TV shows, but continued to use the Internet in a way similar to his use of TV, presenting a controlled message with very little reference to his difficulties of the 1990s. In the 2010s, he ran a *Success-N-Life* website, hosted a meagrely attended monthly service at a Marriott Hotel in Culver City, California, and engaged in the multilevel marketing of Stella Vita nutritional supplements. Though his income was obviously far less, he continued to proclaim God's financial largesse by bringing in enough money to maintain a lavish lifestyle.

Haggard's response, in contrast, assumed a postmodern world, where media might still be controlled by the few, but where most people are online. In such a world, the most effective response is to take the Oprah guest approach: overwhelm the negative message by revealing not less but *more* than the media managed to uncover and by proclaiming an individualized "truth" in an emotional, How-I-Feel manner. Haggard recognized that the publicity value of a story of fall and redemption was huge. He

[35] Forman, Bill. "The resurrection of Pastor Ted." 1 October 2009, *Colorado Springs Independent*, 28 May 2013, http://www.csindy.com/colorado/the-resurrection-of-pastor-ted/Content?oid=1450688.

allowed an HBO version of his story to be filmed, his wife Gayle published a bestseller called *Why I Stayed*, and he had a sympathetic filmmaker do a scandal documentary featured on Tedhaggard.com. In the documentary, he calls himself a bisexual, and his children talk about their shock at hearing of their father's sexual indiscretion. Damage control and Christian prejudices made complete honesty unlikely: his target audience loved stories of sin and redemption, but because many evangelical Christians still considered homosexuality a sin, Haggard likely couldn't tell the whole truth about his sexual orientation.

As Pastor Gas shows, the Internet also undermines traditional grand narratives by extending parodies into public forums. In 2005, when fundamentalists wanted to mandate the Christian grand narrative by enshrining the teaching of intelligent design in Kansas schools, Bobby Henderson responded with one of the most popular parodies of religion in the postmodern era, Pastafarianism—the Church of the Flying Spaghetti Monster—and he requested that its tenets be taught in schools too. *The Gospel of the Flying Spaghetti Monster* describes the beginnings of the universe, "THEN THE FSM SAID, "Let there be light," and there was light.... He called the light Day, and the darkness He called Night or 'Prime Time.'" In answer to sceptics, who scoff at the *Bible*'s story that the cosmos was created in a day, the *Gospel* qualifies, "[The FSM] then spent the next ten to one hundred years painstakingly preparing the universe to appear older than it actually is. Photons were placed individually, en route to earth, ostensibly emitted millions of years ago from stars across the galaxy. In reality, we know that each photon was divinely placed and red-shifted appropriately to make the universe appear to be billions of years old."[36] One-upping a challenge issued by creationists, the website *Boing Boing* offered $1 million (in "Intelligently Designed currency") to anyone who could produce "empirical evidence which proves that Jesus is not the son of the Flying Spaghetti Monster."[37]

With its popular website, Pastafarianism quickly moved beyond a literary parody, claiming many "adherents" around the world. Nico Alm, on learning that he could only wear headgear for his Austrian drivers' license photo if the headgear formed part of his religious observance, petitioned for the right to wear a pasta strainer—the "official" headgear of Pastafarianism. It

---

[36] Henderson, 70, 51.

[37] Xeni Jardin, "Boing Boing's $250,000 Intelligent Design challenge (UPDATED: $1 million)," 19 Aug 2005. http://boingboing.net/2005/08/19/boing-boings-250000.html.

took 3 years and a psychological examination, but in 2011 Alm prevailed,[38] though Aaron Williams was unable to obtain the same right in New Jersey. Outside the 2012 Global Atheist Convention in Melbourne, a small group of Christians protested, led by a woman who used a microphone to keep up a loud hectoring of her atheist opposition. The next day, about 20 Muslim protesters also arrived during the lunch break, chanting responsive slogans such as "Ayaan Ali Hirsi Burn in Hell! Burn in Hell!" and waving signs that said, "Atheism is Hellfire; Islam is Paradise," while the atheists counter-chanted "Bullshit," "Where are the women? Where are the women?" and sang, "Always look on the bright side of life," the song that the crucified Brian sings on the cross in Monty Python's *Life of Brian* (1979). Amid this shouting match between tradition and modernity, postmodernity also showed up, less obtrusively. A couple of Pastafarians briefly stood beside the Muslims as if in support of their protest—the Pastafarians "agreed" with the Muslims that the universe had been created, though they had a different name for the creator—not Allah or God, but the Flying Spaghetti Monster. While the Muslims appeared in traditional Middle Eastern attire, the Pastafarians wore pasta strainers and one held high a pack of spaghetti.

As an attempt to break the hold of the Christian grand narrative on education and government, Pastafarianism is an outgrowth of modernity. However, unlike modernity's parodies of religion (*Candide* or *Waiting for Godot*, for example), Pastafarianism pushes its ironies into non-literary spheres. Bobby Henderson estimated in 2009 that about 80,000 people called themselves Pastafarians. He has fought to gain tax-exempt status for his parody faith, but he also fears the loss of credibility that might happen if Pastafarianism were to become an official religion burdened by money.[39] In order to rise above the publicly limited role of literary satire, Pastafarianism is presented as an actual religion, though anti-dogmatic. Of course, it doesn't have the institutional reach of a religion (houses of worship, regular rituals, and institutional discipline) and it isn't intended as a new grand narrative. The "boutique religion," as Henderson calls it,[40]

[38] "Austrian driver allowed 'pastafarian' headgear photo." *BBC News*, 14 July 2011, http://www.bbc.co.uk/news/world-europe-14135523. Retrieved 26 July 2011.
[39] Antonio Martinez Ron. "Bob Henderson: 'I get about 20 sightings of the flying spaghetti monster every week." *La Informacion*, 8 September 2009, accessed 6 June 2013, http://noticias.lainformacion.com/arte-cultura-y-espectaculos/Internet/bob-henderson-i-get-about-20-sightings-of-the-flying-spaghetti-monster-every-week_m9oE9hq4aGMh-VmlG70lkN/.
[40] Henderson, xiv.

isn't a threat to "Love your neighbour as yourself," but it is a drag on attempts by faith groups to make public institutions conform to the faith's grand narrative. Despite the weakness of Pastafarianism's ethical implications (as we saw in the ethics chapter), it plays an important role in limiting the public power of religious grand narratives.

While not framed as direct interventions into the public sphere, postmodern artistic parodies of faith such as *Pulp Fiction* are similarly nested inside a mischievous style. Unlike Voltaire and Beckett on the one hand, or Bobby Henderson on the other, however, Tarantino blurs the lines between parody and faith. One of *Pulp Fiction*'s two hit-men, Jules, bows before *some* moral limits, while the other, Vincent, treats the world as ethically nil. Ethics takes on a religious cast in the film, from avoidance of *haram* pork sausage—"I don't wanna eat nothin'," says Jules, "that ain't got enough sense to disregard its own feces"—to the possibility that a miracle saved the two hit-men when a "Fourth Man" sprays bullets at them from close range and yet misses. Vincent treats their survival as a vagary of chance, whereas Jules insists, "We just witnessed a miracle and I want you to fuckin' acknowledge it!"[41] Since it's the "miracle" that makes Jules decide to give up being a hitman, Tarantino tempts us to see Jules's decision as the postmodern equivalent of a conversion, and to sense holiness in the suitcase's grail-like glow. The film's time loop underlines the blessing and cleansing of Jules.[42] In the religious interpretation, the sceptical Vincent witnesses a second miracle the next day, when Mia comes back to life after an overdose, but he still fails to change his ways, and must therefore pay with his life.

Sceptics argue that *Pulp Fiction* demonstrates a purely nominal redemption in which Vincent, Jules, and the audience learn nothing.[43] In a pluralist world, where each ethos has its own small logic, for a hitman to renounce first-degree murder could be considered a victory of faith, but Tarantino is less interested in morality than in irony. Isn't it funny to watch two hit-men have a theological discussion? When, after Jules's conversion, Vincent blows the brains out of their captive in the back seat, Jules says, "I will never forgive your ass for this shit. This some fucked-up repugnant shit!"[44]

---

[41] Tarantino, *Pulp*, 171, 139.

[42] Gavin Smith, "When You Know You're in Good Hands," 1994, Tarantino, *Interviews*, 99.

[43] Jonathan Rosenbaum, *Movies as Politics*, Berkeley: University of California Press, 1997, 173, 178.

[44] Tarantino, *Pulp*, 158.

out that Jules is mostly repulsed by the mess made in the car. Both ᴜ.ʜᴇ miracles and the jokes appear to be self-serving. In the sceptical view, the suitcase's golden glow is just a metaphysical conceit, a postmodern nothing: whatever is in the suitcase doesn't exist because the writer never specified it. A film is a series of signs; and the *signs* of redemption are not redemption.

Works more complex than *The Gospel of the Flying Spaghetti Monster* or *Pulp Fiction* further undermine grand narratives of faith through the convolutions produced by simulation. In Jonathan Lethem's novel *Chronic City* (2009), New Yorkers find a seeming Holy Grail on the Internet, a "glowing peach-colored chaldron" that smashes every frame and context. Is the chaldron simply a well-staged consumer item or is it (as the characters Perkus and Chase think) fundamentally holy? It turns out not to be a thing at all, but a hologram, designed by Linus Carter, who also designed everything in the virtual reality *Yet Another World* (the novel's equivalent of *Second Life*). There, he deposited a few chaldrons, scarcity driving up their price. Even before the discovery of the hologram, the narrator, Chase Insteadman, hopes to make *himself* "into a kind chaldron, to generate a love field broad enough to enclose our fear." This is far too ambitious for the former child-star Chase, but it points the chaldron in a humanist direction, making it both less and more than an object of worship. There are reports that the designer Carter wanders his own invented landscape "hidden inside an anonymous and humble avatar, perversely dedicating himself to trying to persuade other players of the unimportance of chaldrons."[45] Despite these intimations, Lethem never really develops the humanist content. Like some postmodern works after the decline of grand narratives, *Chronic City* is quicker to notice simulation than to invite a humanist sense of wonder or of morality. In artists as diverse as Lethem and Tarantino, we see the postmodern dilemma: becoming sceptical about grand narratives that created community in the past, but finding nothing to replace them except simulations or the self-serving human heart.

TRADITIONAL BELIEFS CONTINUING

In general, postmodernity extends modernity's distrust of the grand narratives of faith. Yet it's worth remembering that we only began speaking of *post*modernity, after all, because science couldn't answer questions of

[45] Lethem, *Chronic*, 141, 151, 255, 332.

meaning, and because postmodernity cast a cold eye on even the modernist narrative of reason and scientific progress. Even in the postmodern era, the grand narratives of faith have retained some ontological power because it's beneficial in many ways for the individual to participate in a faith community. The correlation of religious practice with happier lives, healthier bodies, and lower rates of cognitive decline may arise from coordinated social rituals such as praying and singing.[46] Christian Smith notes that among young adults the religiously "devoted" generally had better life outcomes than the "disengaged." Depression was lower among those who regularly attended faith services than those who did not, even though the "Devoted" did not have fewer traumatic events in their lives or feel less guilty. The "Devoted" had better relationships with their parents, gave more to charity, volunteered more, engaged in fewer risky behaviours such as binge drinking, took part in more social activities *unconnected* with churches, were healthier, were more educated, and were less likely to be unemployed.[47]

Other studies have found similar practical benefits to religious attendance, though survey data hasn't been entirely consistent. Owens et al. found that women with high religiosity tended not to hook up sexually, but religiosity didn't seem to stop men from doing so.[48] A recent Canadian longitudinal study found that faith, paired with church attendance, inculcates healthy habits, reduces risky behaviour, and brings assistance from fellow believers.[49] The protective effect of faith against depression was strongest in highly stressed populations and quite as protective as a college education or perceived social support. Attendance—taking part in a caring community—mattered, whereas merely placing importance on spiritual values, identifying as a spiritual person, or occasionally attending services had no protective effect. In fact, a *higher* rate of depression appeared among those who characterized themselves as "spiritual" but *didn't* regularly attend religious services.[50]

---

[46] Susan Pinker, *Village*, 73, 75.
[47] C. Smith, 261–75.
[48] Jesse Owen et al., 658.
[49] Balbuena et al.
[50] Both monthly and occasional attenders felt that they had social supports, non-attenders less so. Balbuena et al. The study controlled for "income adequacy, age, family and personal depression history, marital status, sex, education, and perceived social support." See also Haidt, 267.

It is sometimes argued that the beneficial effects are a function of self-selection: the depressed and the unhealthy are less likely to attend faith services.[51] Such an explanation fails, because by far the strongest determinant of attendance is whether one's parents attended, indicating that socialization into the community plays a far stronger role than self-selection. More likely, those who attend are, merely by virtue of attendance, likely to make more community contacts and to be prodded, by those contacts and by sermons, into other communal activities. At the very least, as Putnam argues, the causal arrow goes both ways: people are more socially connected because they go to faith services, and because they are more socially connected, they're more likely to go to faith services. Regular worshippers talk with a surprising 40% more people daily,[52] and young people who grew up in religious homes are more likely to feel that they can speak to their parents about anything.[53] People won't suddenly adopt a dubious faith narrative just because it provides meaning and community, but if it *does* provide meaning and community, they won't be as quick to drop it, even if they have doubts.

Continuing attachment to a faith community is sometimes viewed as a form of nostalgia. One could cite a host of novels and films in which the loss of faith is a necessary prelude to adulthood. Michael Redhill, however, approaches the question with greater complexity through the character Lillian in his story "Mount Morris" (2003). Lillian's attachment to knick-knack angels strikes her ex-husband Tom as infantile. She has progressed from her native Christianity to meditation religions, to group therapy, and then to angels, which, in Tom's eyes, is "like praying to Jiminy Cricket." He thinks, "You had to be willing to look at the hardest things in life and admit they were beyond your understanding." But it's Tom who looks away from the hardest things. He'll sleep with Lillian on his yearly trip through town, yet because Lillian, nursing her aged mother, seems pathetic, he's careful not to renew their failed marriage. He senses that Lillian, wrestling with aging and death, has "moved on from the angels,"[54] but he doesn't know to what or where. Lillian's serial ties to faith narratives aren't delineated, but they do seem to have prepared her to care for

[51] See, for example, Colby Cosh, "Church: the Happiest Place on Earth." *Maclean's*, 29 April 2013, 13.

[52] Putnam, 67.

[53] Seventy-one percent of young people raised in religious homes feel this way, compared to 56% in homes "where religion was less important" (Greenberg, 14).

[54] Redhill, *Fidelity*, 7, 9.

another human being in a way that Tom's scepticism hasn't. Ha
been surrendered in a meaning-bereft postmodern society?

A second factor that has prevented the disappearance of the granu
ratives of faith is that they undergird certain resistance identities. For
Bauman, any strong racial or religious identification with a grand narrative
counts, by definition, as "fundamentalist," and always offers an easy, but
proto-totalitarian, solution to the potentially terrifying freedoms of postmodernity.[55] Manuel Castells also describes various fundamentalisms as
"resistance identities," calling them both dangerous and "the most daring,
uncompromising challenge to one-sided domination of informational,
global capitalism."[56] This strict dichotomy appears in novels such as Zadie
Smith's beautifully written *White Teeth* (2000), where the brothers Millat
(the radical Islamicist) and Magid Iqbal (the genetic engineer) represent,
respectively, an implacable tradition and a heedless modernity. In Smith's
satire, the Islamicist Millat can't shed the pleasures of modernity, while
Magid seems hollow and inattentive to the dangers of genetic engineering. In actuality, however, Bauman and Castells's hyperbolic notion of an
"uncompromising challenge" describes only a small, if forceful, minority
of Muslims and Christians. The popular notion that fundamentalist
terrorism is on the rise, a notion that underwrote the US Homeland
Security Act of 2002 and Richard Dawkins's and Chris Hedges's critiques
of religion, has no statistical basis.[57] Despite Bauman's analysis, neither
Christian evangelicalism nor strict Islamicism are identities to which people "flee" in response to the intolerable freedoms of postmodernity. Faith
identities are overwhelmingly received identities. In Canada, for example,
conservative churches grew in the 1970s and 1980s not because people
converted and fled to them, but because they were able to retain their
young and bring in members from mainline denominations that were
liberalizing.[58]

Nevertheless, it's fair to speak of conservative evangelicalism as a resistance to postmodernity's pluralism. From a more nuanced position, David
Lyon argues that fundamentalism is an intellectually significant response

---

[55] Bauman, *Discontents*, 184.
[56] Castells, quoted in Lyon, 47–8, 114.
[57] See, for example, Pinker, *Better*, 350–2.
[58] See Reginald Bibby and Merlin B. Brinkerhoff, "Circulation of the Saints Revisited: A
Longitudinal Look at Conservative Church Growth," *Journal for the Scientific Study of
Religion* 22: 3 (Sept. 1983): 253–262. Bibby, *Fragmented Gods*, Toronto: Stoddart, 1987,
28–9. Bibby, *Restless Gods*, Toronto: Stoddart, 2002, 72–3.

to pluralism, demanding "moral accountability and a sense of cultural direction."[59] The conservative Promise Keepers, founded in 1990 by University of Colorado football coach Bill McCartney, has harnessed post-modern spectacle to resist unwanted features of the contemporary world such as absentee fatherhood, female leadership, and homosexual rights. As an inter-denominational, "big-tent" organization, PK, on the one hand, encourages men to support their pastors, whatever the pastor's gender, and cites the biblical example of a female-led household. On the other hand, these paper claims don't always mesh with the agendas of PK speakers. The PK statement on equality—"Promise Keepers believes that men and women are completely equal at the foot of the cross"—neatly obscures the question of whether men and women should have equal social rights and equal representation in leadership roles.[60]

Yet to focus only on the politically regressive elements of the "resistance" identity is to miss other aspects of moral accountability. PK also resists the kinds of sexual freedoms that can encourage men to become absentee fathers. Throughout evolutionary history, men have had less at stake in reproduction than women have, and the availability of pornography, divorce, and abortion has increased masculine freedom to the point that absentee fatherhood has become a significant social problem. The most emphasized PK "promises" encourage sensitivity to the needs of women and children. The one PK event that I attended in the late 1990s took note of the biological, hormonal, and psychological differences between (heterosexual) men and women (at a time when conventional wisdom had it that gender was purely a construction) and emphasized communication across gender differences. Margaret Visser has suggested that, "the gentling of the male is always one of the most urgent aims of civilization,"[61] and PK makes "gentling" or "feminization" more palatable to men by upping the masculinity quotient in other ways. Men are encouraged to "lead" their families into godliness. Spiritual life is addressed through the equivalent of the motivational half-time football speech, as "Coach Mac," in a promotional video for the 2013 *Awakening the Warrior* conference, begins, "I'm talkin' to warriors. Oh, you might not know

---

[59] Lyon, 117.

[60] Promise Keepers website, "FAQs: Controversial Issues," http://www.promisekeepers.org/about/faqs/faqs-controversy. The female-led household is Lydia's in *Acts* 16:14–15. Promise Keepers website, "7 Promises," http://www.promisekeepers.org/about/7-promises.

[61] Margaret Visser, *The Geometry of Love*, Toronto: HarperCollins, 2000, 170.

you're a warrior…"[62] PK resistance has thus been psychologically savvy: securing men in a traditional gender identity by validating the "warrior" and regressively criticizing homosexuality, while inviting men to express Christianity's "feminine" sensibility without calling it that.

Resistance identities, as expressed by groups such as PK, are important signs that the grand narratives of faith aren't about to disappear—in 1995, 738,000 men attended 13 PK conferences, and, in 1997, between 800,000 and 1 million men walked in the 1997 *Stand in the Gap* rally in Washington—but it's also easy for conservatives and liberals alike to over-estimate the significance of such phenomena as a wholesale reassertion of the Christian grand narrative in North America. With the difficult task of continually upping the entertainment ante, PK, by 2008, could only muster 25,000 men in seven cities,[63] ultimately voted off the island by the same postmodern media culture that first brought it to prominence.

A third development working against the disappearance of grand narratives of faith, and sometimes touted as the saviour of the orthodox form of the Christian grand narrative, is the rise of "southern" Christianity. Whereas religion is declining in Europe and Canada, churchgoing rates are still fairly strong in the US, and positively booming in Latin America, Africa, and the Pacific Rim.[64] The more conservative south is gaining traction, via demographics, over the more liberal north, with the result that some denominational stances on family, LGBTQ rights, women's roles, abortion, and church/state ties are becoming more conservative.[65] Archbishop Tay's spiritual warfare against Vancouver totem poles is merely one expression of this. In Islamic circles, the southern push for *Sharia* law is a cognate phenomenon. Despite southern Christianity's obviously conservative and patriarchal doctrines, it still expresses some features of postmodernity: emphasizing individual biblical interpretation and American populism, encouraging lay-people to spearhead expansion, enlisting market forces, and allowing women to take important roles, especially in independent and Pentecostal congregations.[66]

[62] Bill McCartney, promotional video for Promise Keepers 2013 *Awakening the Warrior* conference, Promise Keepers website, main page, http://www.promisekeepers.org/, accessed 3 July 2013.
[63] Promise Keepers website, "PK History," http://www.promisekeepers.org/about/pk-history.
[64] Lyon, 23.
[65] Jenkins, 187, 240, 247–8.
[66] Jenkins, 77, 96.

As with resistance identities, one should neither underestimate how much southern Christian energies will reshape their host societies, nor fail to recognize the limits of this phenomenon. Western Christians sometimes entertain a fantasy of return to an originary Christian grand narrative through the combined energies of Africa, South America, and Asia.[67] Others fear this. British geneticist Steve Jones predicts that he and his fellow atheists will remain in the minority because religious people have more children, witness the differential birth rate between secular Europe and religious Africa.[68] However, the rise of southern Christianity is also linked to specific circumstances. Philip Jenkins notes that in Africa, social and political chaos helped lead to a great increase in Christian conversions, and that, in the south generally, weak economies have played a large role in church growth. Fundamentalist churches often form an alternative "health, welfare, and education" system, so that one can leave the "wide impersonal world" for a smaller, more caring community. The greatest increases in southern Christian numbers have been among Pentecostal and independent churches, where often a "prosperity gospel" combines with warm fellowship, greater emotionalism, and more spontaneity in worship, attracting people, particularly in areas of high poverty and low education.[69] We can expect that, wherever political turmoil, war, or economic failure persist (whether in the south *or* in the north), the grand narratives of faith will play a strong role.

However, if economic and social conditions continue to improve, existential reasons for staying in an intimate community may remain, but some of the social welfare draws of such communities disappear, especially if the community makes strong disciplinary demands on the individual. Not surprisingly, the 2007 Pew Global Attitudes survey, involving 47 countries, showed a broad inverse relationship between a country's religiosity and its GDP. As wealth rose, religiosity generally declined, and the only significant outliers from this broad band of decline were Kuwait (near the middle of the GDP scale, yet near the top of the religiosity scale) and the US (at the

---

[67] The subtitle of Jenkins's book—*The Next Christendom: The Coming of Global Christianity*—hints at this return. Andrew Wall claims that via the African Church, Westerners can witness first-century Christianity (Jenkins, 166).

[68] Jamie Merrill, "Steve Jones at the Hay Festival: Falling birth rates in Europe and rising ones in Africa could spell decline in atheism," *The Independent*, 10 June 2014, http://www.independent.co.uk/news/world/politics/steve-jones-at-the-hay-festival-falling-birth-rates-in-europe-and-rising-ones-in-africa-could-spell-decline-in-atheism-9436397.html.

[69] Jenkins, 74, 93, 97, 168.

top of the GDP scale and at the middle of the religiosity scale). The belief that only faith in God can guarantee morality declined the most in the Ukraine, India, Slovakia, and Kenya,[70] countries that all had significant increases in GDP (before 2008 for Ukraine). What some commentators call "compressed modernity"—a quick transition from a traditional society to a modern capitalist state—may still wreak havoc on Jenkins's projections of the growth of southern Christianity. With increases in wealth and higher education in the global south, one might expect that grand narratives (whether Christian or other faiths) will shift closer to the patterns in European humanism or North American selective adherence. Education makes certain beliefs—treating homosexuality as a sin, for example—less plausible, and the education of women decreases the birth rate.

A fourth factor that energizes grand narratives of faith is their beneficial effect on society as a whole, not just on the individual. Food banks, shelters for the homeless, and relief and development organizations still depend heavily on the Christian church for monetary support and for volunteers. Religion and education are the two greatest factors in civic engagement. Regular worshipers and those for whom religion is very important visit friends more often, entertain at home more often, attend club meetings more often, and belong to more non-religious organizations.[71] Regularly maintained social ties are a crucial part of the equation.[72] In this way, the benefits that grand narratives provide to the individual shade into the common good. A recent Canadian study calculated that for every dollar a congregation spends on its own programmes, the surrounding community gets $4.77 in services.[73] That's only the monetary contribution; the real point, of course, is the larger social good that flows from day cares, youth programmes, refugee assistance, divorce prevention, alcoholism programmes, incarceration prevention, suicide prevention, and space for social programmes. Like their secular counterparts, churchgoers in the postmodern era have become less involved in civic and community affairs than in the past, but the tie between regular worship and community involvement is still fairly strong.

[70] Pew, "World Publics," 41, 34.

[71] Putnam, 67.

[72] Balbuena et al. The Balbuena study, ending in 2008, showed that monthly church attenders also joined other organizations at a rate (50%) much higher than occasional attenders (about 25%) and non-attenders (about 20%) did.

[73] Mike Wood Daly, The Halo Project, Phase 1: Valuing Toronto's Faith Congregations, Cardus, June 2016, http://haloproject.ca/phase-1-toronto.

New Grand Narratives: Science, Environment

Since the colonization of North America, Christian faith communities have been the dominant, but not the only way through which North Americans made meaning and bound themselves to grand narratives. According to Christian Smith, committed traditionalists now comprise 15% of the American population. This is a significant, but relatively small portion, and the question arises of what other grand narratives motivate people in the postmodern era. At the very least, a grand narrative tells us what we ought to do and why. Nationalism (until the middle of the twentieth century) and socialism (until the 1990s) also gave meaning to many human lives and adjudicated between competing moral claims. Neither narrative, however, carries the same force in the early twenty-first century. Nationalistic rhetoric, which declined with the lowering of tariffs and the decrease of national wars, resurfaces whenever unemployment rates rise, but is nationalism still a central grand narrative in the West? In 1914, nearly an entire generation of young men were prepared to die for their countries; nowadays, nationalism restricts itself to anti-immigration policies and protectionism. Successful right-wing parties are more likely to make laws blocking property tax increases than they are to call for a draft. As we've already seen in the previous chapter, the nation now functions more as a tool for prosperity and protection than as a meaning-giving narrative. Socialism's decline can be seen in the virtual disappearance of socialist governments, in the weakening of unions, in the co-opting of socialized policies such as universal medical insurance by centrist parties, and in the market-friendly evolution of social democratic parties in Europe and Canada, especially whenever they form national or provincial governments. Socialism's victorious competitor, capitalism, has become a signature postmodern narrative, and is often used to adjudicate claims, but even as capitalism's story of progress and plenty explains economic exchange and political stability, it hasn't made much headway in the postmodern cathedral as a *meaning*-giving grand narrative. Almost nobody testifies that consumption provides a reason for living.

What about science? Is it replacing religious grand narratives? Science gives a grand and convincing story about the rise of *Homo sapiens* and the first 4 billion years of biological life, forces us to question the reality-status of the faith stories we live by, and has an institutional basis in the education system. Those who have sought to minimize the philosophical force of science's grand narrative by denying its material descriptions of the world (creationists), or else by treating it as just another social construction (post-structuralists), have looked foolish. Evolutionary psychology erodes the grand narratives of faith by insisting that natural, not mystical, accounts best explain the world. They explain not only biological life, but also religious hierarchies and the human attachment to faith groups, because "membership in dominance orders pays off in survival and lifetime reproductive success." Irreconcilable faiths can all have positive effects: "Anything will serve," says E.O. Wilson, "as long as it gives the individual meaning."[74] But there's a problem here, as we've seen in the chapter on ethics, in that evolutionary psychology can't say why, morally, we *should* act in one way and not in another. If *anything* will serve, why did the Roman gods fall out of favour, or the worship of Darwin not catch on?

Most influential grand narratives, including faiths, must nowadays accommodate themselves partly to reason and empiricism, yet science itself has generally failed to give higher meaning to people's lives, at least to people outside of the academy. Scientists occasionally test out gospel-like language. Richard Dawkins, after dismissing God, wants to offer "Inspiration," but is reluctant to engage in flights of rhetoric: it should be enough, he says, to recognize how "staggeringly lucky" we are to be alive under the sun, in comparison to the "unborn trillions."[75] If it is logically suspect to speak of the "unluckiness" of the non-existent (never mind to estimate their number!), others have likewise articulated the emotional resonances of a scientific mythos. Psychologist Bruce Hood says, "Holding another's brain in your [sic] hands for the first time is the closest to a spiritual experience I have ever had."[76] With greater eloquence, Ian McEwan's neurosurgeon Henry Perowne in *Saturday* gets at the majesty of the evolutionary grand narrative—"an unimaginable sweep of time, numberless generations spawning by infinitesimal steps complex living beauty out of inert matter"—and of the human brain—"the wonder will remain, that mere wet stuff can make this bright inward cinema of thought, of sight and sound and touch bound into a vivid illusion of an instantaneous present, with a self, another brightly wrought illusion, hovering like a ghost at its centre."[77] Nevertheless, in *Nutshell* (2016), McEwan's foetus-narrator

[74] E.O. Wilson, *Consilience*, 283–4, 281.
[75] Dawkins, 404.
[76] Hood, 5. Frans De Waal describes a workshop in which an astronomer was moved to tears as he discussed the place of humanity in the cosmos (De Waal, *Bonobo*, 106).
[77] McEwan, *Saturday*, 56, 254.

recognizes the moral pitfalls of extrapolating from biological fact to human meaning: "The biologists also suggest that my father's wisest move is to trick another man into raising his child while he—my father!—distributes his likeness among other women.... Too much to bear, too grim to be true." Still, at the narrator's moment of birth, McEwan makes the most mundane object, a blue towel, miraculous, as the narrator takes his "stately ship of genes" through the birth canal towards a blue sea: "The lambent towel beaming its colour summons the Goharshad mosque in Iran that made my father cry at dawn."[78]

George Levine's *Darwin Loves You* wittily promises to turn such emotions to account. Fearing, in the George W. Bush era, a "fundamentalist religiosity that has entered almost every phase of our public lives," Levine imagines a secular re-enchantment that would allow the world to "make sense entirely on its own terms," apart from human grand narratives. But as soon as he couples science with meaning, science begins to function as a grand narrative, nature quickly taking on the colours of the human spirit. Levine's failure is instructive. Wanting to avoid E.O. Wilson's reductionism, which claims that "there is no Eden," Levine can only disembark at Romanticism, with Darwin as the great soul.[79] Similar transformations occur when science points at other secular saints, martyrs, or icons. In the stirring, though idealized, film *Agora* (2009), the early fifth-century philosopher Hypatia becomes a martyr for scientific truth. Icons, such as the penguins in Luc Jacquet's equally moving documentary, *March of the Penguins* (2005), enchant us with the beauty and courage of biological life. Of course, the real cargo carried by the penguins, by the bright inward cinema of thought, and by the worshipping foetus, is not really science but humanism. To recognize that the penguins take on the colours of the human spirit, one need only compare our warm emotional response to baby penguins with our much cooler response to the equal biological wonder of baby snakes.

A playful, postmodern approach to science as a grand narrative appears in Charlie Kaufman's brilliant film, *Adaptation* (2002). The title refers both to the *character* Charlie's attempt to adapt Susan Orlean's book *The Orchid Thief* for the screen and to biological life's adaptation to various environments. When Charlie asks, "How did I get here?" the film responds immediately with a shot of a field of lava, subtitled "Hollywood, CA, Four

---

[78] McEwan, *Nutshell*, 33, 196.
[79] Levine xii, 25, 53.

Billion And Forty Years Earlier." The montage cuts from shots of a micro-scopic organism, to a fish climbing out of the water, to dinosaurs, to an asteroid hitting Earth, to the ice age, to a Cro-Magnon man seen from afar, and, finally, accounting for that extra 40 years, to the birth of baby Charlie.[80] As a *cinematic* sequence, this scientific "documentary" is no less artificial than Charlton Heston parting the Red Sea is. Later, the montage cuts from orchid-hunter John Laroche and his colleagues, waist-deep in a Florida swamp, to Laroche in his van listening to an audiobook, *The Writings of Charles Darwin*. In the dubbed sentence—"As natural selec-tion works solely by and for the good of each being, all corporeal and mental endowments will tend to progress towards perfection"[81]—Darwin isn't being teleological: while natural selection certainly doesn't work for the good of *each* being, it does favour adaptive attributes in species. However, Kaufman's irony drains out the grandeur that Darwin finds in the endless and beautiful forms of evolved life,[82] for immediately after the audiobook arrives at the word "perfection," the swamp montage cuts dia-lectically to looming alligators, whose "corporeal and mental endow-ments" are indeed a kind of "perfection"—if adaptation is the only measure. Shortly thereafter, we see a shot of the ghost orchid, perfect in a very different way. This time the beauty of the flower vouches for a more human-inflected grandeur in the evolutionary story.

At first excitedly, the character Charlie informs his Dictaphone, "To dramatize the flower, I have to show the flower's arc, and the flower's arc stretches back to the beginning of life.... It is the journey of evolution. Adaptation. The journey we all take." All he has to do in order to write about the ghost orchid, he realizes, now despairingly, is to tie all of history together.[83] Unfilmable. Yet we've already seen such a film in the Four-Billion-And-Forty-Years-Earlier sequence, if only as parody. The post-modern evolutionary narrative proposes desire as the motive force, the main reason why human beings do things. Yet, when we search for a moral order in *Adaptation*, we are thrown back not on reproduction only, but on an incipient humanism. This is hardly a surprise, since humanism, the only grand narrative that has grown stronger in the postmodern era, is also the grand narrative most closely identified with scientific progress. The

[80] *Adaptation*. Dir. Spike Jonze. Columbia Pictures, 2001, 3:08.
[81] *Adaptation*, 6:45–7:20.
[82] Charles Darwin, *The Origin of Species*, New York: New American Library, 1958, 450.
[83] *Adaptation*, 39:46.

most perceptive scientists would say, with Steven Pinker (as he, too, turns towards humanism), "We don't *believe in* reason; we *use* reason."[84]

In comparison to science, other contemporary attempts to propose new or reconditioned grand narratives have criticized not only traditional faiths, but also humanism, seen as lacking in mystery or in care for animals and the biosphere. Although various New Age philosophies, goddess worship, Wicca, and the Gaia Movement have sought new grand narratives, and although some sympathizing artistic expressions, such as *The Da Vinci Code* (2003) and *Avatar* (2009) proved immensely popular, organized groups and adherents remain few. In *Generation A* (2009), Douglas Coupland articulates the effect of the Baby Boomer loss of faith upon the Millennial generation. The extinction of bees in the novel is closely linked to the manufacture of Solon, a popular drug that seems both a response to, and a cause of, what looks like postmodernity: "[Users] felt like they needed no other people in their lives.... They stopped dating and voting and seeking religion." Despite this, the five young narrators are all stung by bees at moments when they are in some way involved with the Earth, and, on Haida Gwaii (site of the last beehive), their personalities begin to merge towards "one big superentity," a communal identity that the grand narratives of faith formerly produced.[85] However, such environmental grand narratives are more likely to appear in literature than in communal activities.

Margaret Atwood's Maddaddam trilogy similarly broaches a faith structured around the environment. The God's Gardeners sect that becomes central in the last two books constitutes Atwood's attempt to envision a post-Christian faith rooted in pantheism: Jesus, it turns out, chose fishermen as disciples in order to neutralize two fish-killers.[86] Atwood's imagined future falls into three stages. First comes Christian civilization, tied to global warming denial—"the Devil Wants You to Freeze in the Dark." The second stage produces the post-humanist scientist, Crake, who tries and fails to wipe away religion, mystery, and babies, with their "huge car-

---

[84] Pinker, *Enlightenment*, 424–5, 352.

[85] Coupland, *Generation A*, 256–7, 283, 295. A reconditioned grand narrative also appears briefly in Jonathan Franzen's *Freedom* (2010), where Walter, nearly fanatical in his atheism, puts faith in the pantheistic music of Conor Oberst: "Oberst works the word 'lift' into every song," Walter enthuses, "It's like religion without the bullshit of religious dogma" (Franzen, *Freedom*, 370). Franzen intends readers to take Walter seriously here, even though his expectations of rock music seem rather inflated.

[86] Atwood, *Flood*, 195–6.

bon footprint."[87] The third stage ushers in pantheism via God's Gardeners and via the genetically re-composed race of Crakers (who deify both their sky-god creator Crake, and the nature-goddess Oryx, from whom they learned recycling).

Recently, some Christian churches have attempted to incorporate environmentalism, in a style faintly reminiscent of God's Gardeners, but real, gut-level faith in the new grand narrative is lacking. For example, a 2014 Mennonite service in Hamilton, Ontario took place in a park, with the congregants arranged in a circle, singing U2's "I Still Haven't Found What I'm Looking For" and spiritual director Jeff Druery's environmentally themed songs that prophesy a future in which we talk with our sister- and brother-animals.[88] A 2015 liturgy at Knox United Church in Brandon, Manitoba, invoked the "Creator Spirit," and the Call to Worship began,

> We invite our fauna family to worship with us,
> All our kin living on this planet."

The trickster Raven also decorated the cover of the service order. Atwood herself visited A Rocha, a group that practises a Green branch of Christianity, and participated in a fundraiser.[89] There is even a Green Bible (2008), with an introduction by Archbishop Tutu and supporting essays by such figures as Brian McLaren, Pope John Paul II, and scholar N.T. Wright. Nevertheless, although one might want to interpret such glimmerings as a possible future for Christianity, the most sympathetic congregations can't retain their younger members, while growing evangelical congregations show little interest in environmental religion.

THE UNDECIDED MIDDLE

If grand narratives of faith are being eroded and new grand narratives aren't catching on, where are we headed? Amy Hungerford and John McClure prematurely celebrate what Hungerford calls a postmodern "belief without content." According to McClure, novelists who "live in oblique relation to the structures and discourses of institutional religion"

---

[87] Atwood, *Maddaddam*, 112, 117, 238.
[88] Jeff Douglas Druery, "Someday," *the Other Side of Night*, https://jeffd.bandcamp.com/track/someday, 2013. See also http://www.music.studentopencircles.com/.
[89] Atwood, "Planet," 38:30.

become the new priests, and "their literary practice is a species of religious practice."[90] Hungerford and McClure arrive at a mystical state where faith and doubt, religion and secularism are indistinguishable. McClure describes small, fragile, and transitory post-secular communities,[91] but his "new" category is no more than secularism with a few religious metaphors. Most of McClure's authors don't participate in any religious community and wouldn't call themselves "post-secular."

Others have argued that faith has been re-channelled into figures such as Princess Di or into phenomena such as Dungeons and Dragons.[92] "Know the sacred through pop," recommends Andrew Boyd, tongue-in-cheek.[93] Hungerford wants a piece of this action too, insisting that faith shows up in the restlessness of the Internet, in Las Vegas, and in quantum physics.[94] The Internet and Las Vegas may well give us insight about lived religion (quantum physics not so much), but pop phenomena manifest only very limited and reductive aspects of religious faith, are invariably evanescent, and fail to create real communities. A bit more discriminating than Hungerford is Margaret Miles, who says that contemporary culture is forged not in the church but in the movie theatre, where Americans ponder moral quandaries.[95] This is true. Film and literature reveal much about contemporary faith and ethics, and do help to make meaning, but—lacking bodily community, or shared beliefs and practices—art forms by themselves can't really function as new faiths.

For young people of declining faith, no other strong narrative has replaced religion: "less religious youth are less strongly identified with anything at all."[96] Yet something other than chance still guides people's moral choices, even if the guiding narratives aren't "grand." Looking at the two ends of Christian Smith's survey data, we see vigorous faith narratives at one end (15% of Millennials), complete secularism at the other

[90] Hungerford, xiv, xvi.

[91] McClure, 4.

[92] Lyon makes the claim about Princess Di (32), though he is otherwise an astute commentator. Role-playing games (maybe video games too) and imagination can give an experientially immersive *meaning* to one's life, but only temporarily. In Jennifer Egan's *The Keep*, Howard, seemingly on the model of Dungeons and Dragons, plans to counter postmodern aimlessness by refurbishing a rundown castle and turning it into a place where Christ, witches, and goblins can reappear.

[93] Andrew Boyd #325.

[94] Hungerford, 20.

[95] Quoted in Christopher Deacy, 4–5.

[96] Greenberg, 15.

(also 15%). But that leaves out 70% of the population. Hints of 1
tudes of this group appear in the following statistics. Although or
third of Millennials view religion as either *very* or *somewhat* important,
over 80% seek the comfort of a religious wedding and a religious funeral.
Two-thirds also want religious rites such as baptism or child dedication for
their children.[97] Greenberg calls the people who neither tie themselves
securely to tradition nor dismiss religion "the undecided middle." In
Christian Smith's schema, the first category ("selective adherents") is
helpful, while the other two categories ("the spiritually open" and "the
religiously indifferent") give no indication how members form their moral
choices. Instead, I would break the undecided middle into five categories:

1. *Ego-based personal narratives:* Since we can't know a transcendent
   truth, we base our ideals on what's best for us and on how we feel
   at the time.
2. *Small narratives:* Since we can't know a transcendent truth, we
   base our ideals on, and work for the good of, the smaller group to
   which we belong—our family, political party, church, nation, race,
   or gender.
3. *Selective adherence:* Since neither modernity nor postmodernity
   offer compelling *meanings* to replace the grand narratives of faith,
   we continue in the old stories, albeit much more provisionally.
4. *Pluralist adaptation:* Since neither modernity nor postmodernity
   offer compelling *meanings* to replace the grand narratives of faith,
   we discriminately or indiscriminately combine meanings from a variety of faith sources.
5. *Humanism:* Since the grand narratives of faith aren't true, we create a new narrative that emphasizes human flourishing and a communal human good instead of a numinous transcendence.

Ego-Based Personal Narratives

One popular response to the decline of grand narratives, a response that
appears both among those in the undecided middle and among those
whose faith has disappeared, has been a rise in ego-based personal narratives, narratives mainly concerned with the individual's material and psy-

[97] Bibby, 179.

chological well-being. The ego-based narrative is not just a matter of egocentrism. People adhering to *any* grand narrative can be egocentric, but they must mask and sublimate their egocentrism under broader group goals. The growth of individual freedom, however, has made it socially acceptable treat the self as a moral arbiter, occasionally with a religious aura. Most of the time, ego-based narratives aren't articulated as explicitly as other narratives, but we can see the ego-based narrative's spoor in quasi-religious self-help materials. Rhonda Byrne's *The Secret* became a bestseller by initiating readers into the gnosis that they are the source of the universe's magic, and that through understanding "The Law of Attraction" they can induce a financial windfall. "The Power – to have everything good in life – is inside you," proclaims Byrne.[98] A testimony offered by Lulu, a 50-year-old woman, is typical of the wonders wrought by self-generated magic. After her divorce, Lulu picked up *The Secret* at a yard sale, and she was inspired to move to Washington State. There, her finances declined to the point that she had to spend a month living out of her car, but she downloaded the movie *The Secret* onto her iPad, spending her nights watching it, imagining that she was walking with the man of her dreams in a foreign country. Down to her last $20, she bought two Powerball lottery tickets, and won $2 million dollars. She invested the money in a company, and she testifies, "Now I'm engaged to the owner of the company and I just completed my first novel which will be published in June."[99] Lulu's story is just one of the 2360 stories listed under "Finances" on *The Secret* website. The stories under "Faith" aren't much different.

Congregational minister Lillian Daniel interprets the "spiritual but not religious" (SBNR) phenomenon as similarly egocentric, because it denies the value of the religious community. When someone introduces herself as SNBR, Daniel wants to respond, "Thank you for sharing, spiritual-but-not-religious person. You are now comfortably in the norm for self-centred American culture, right smack in the bland majority of people who find ancient religions dull but find themselves uniquely fascinating." This uncharitable, never-uttered response balks at an individualized spirituality.

[98] Rhonda Byrne, "The Power," *The Secret Official Website*, 19 July 2013, http://thesecret.tv/thepower/.

[99] B. Lulu, "Never Lose Faith Especially in the Darkness," Stories about Finances, *The Secret Official Website*, 16 July 2013, accessed 19 July 2013, http://thesecret.tv/stories/stories-read.html?id=22655.

For Daniel, SBNR represents a laissez-faire attitude towards sin in that one is unwilling to have one's attitudes challenged by other believers.[100] SBNR belief seems to be a prelude for dropping faith altogether.

Less explicit signs of the ego-based narrative are the decline in charitable giving, the pressure on charities to call their volunteer positions steps towards greatness, the decline in political involvement and in group involvement, and the fast-growing "You Sell" advertising pitch.[101] The decline of grand narratives gives a tacit encouragement to free riders. When Bibby queried theist and atheist teens about their values, he noticed that the atheists placed significantly less emphasis on some traditional virtues. Theists placed greater value than atheists on trust (88% to 78%), honesty (86% to 75%), concern for others (72% to 54%), politeness (71% to 57%), forgiveness (72% to 44%), working hard (61% and 49%), and patience (55% to 35%). Bibby also asked teens to respond to scenarios. Atheists felt better than theists about crossing the street on a red light and making traffic wait (64% to 58%) and about giving someone "the finger" (53% to 34%). Atheists were also far less likely than theists to return $10 given to them by mistake (26% to 47%), and to plan involvement in their community in the future (53% to 76%).[102] To treat Bibby's results as an important gloss on the decline of religious grand narratives is not to say that atheists lack these virtues, or that they don't value other important virtues—freedom and rational thought, say—on which theists might score lower. Nor is it to claim that theists always act on the virtues that they espouse. But it is to recognize that when people claim not to value something, they're probably telling the truth; and that in the gap left by the departing grand narratives of faith, ethical ego-based narratives can come to dominate. Contra to Bauman's pluralist hope that we will allow *many* gods into our postmodern breasts, we may end up with only one god—the self. Lenny in *Super Sad True Love Story*, Vince and even Jules in *Pulp Fiction*, and the young people that Christian Smith interviewed all have difficulty reasoning about why they performed certain actions.

For David Bergen's Morris, grieving his son's death in Afghanistan, an ego-based narrative is a temptation throughout *The Matter with Morris* (2010), and the attraction is inversely proportional to the strength of his parents' Mennonite grand narrative. Morris remembers hearing a provi-

---

[100] Daniel, 7, 83.
[101] Maich and George, 21–2.
[102] Bibby, 171.

dential story in which his Grandfather Schutt avoided the Soviet draft because he had earlier given a free bag of wheat to a soldier. But the story's moral doesn't convince Morris: "If he, Morris Schutt, had lived the clean and generous life of his grandfather, would his son Martin be alive? Not so. Life was not theatre. Good deeds were not rewarded so easily. There was no grand arc of a story. Only novelists were inclined that way.... His existence here in 2007... was founded on commerce and vanity. 'Moral virtue' was dead."[103] Morris is right that hazard won't bend so obediently to the wishes of faith. But the "death" of moral virtue is a non sequitur here, an easy way for Morris to excuse himself for visiting prostitutes, and Bergen allows Morris slowly to realize the limits of an ego-based narrative.

Ultimately, Daniel is right to fear that ego-based narratives can offer little basis for community. Near the dawn of the postmodern era in the early 1960s, Emanuel Levinas argued that "sensation breaks up every system."[104] By the late 1990s, Bauman concluded that the contemporary equivalent to religious peak experience was postmodern sensation-gathering,[105] enfeebling religious commands such as "love your neighbour as yourself." An ego-based narrative allows me to become a free rider, but, paradoxically, the narrative is partly illusory, because my moral decisions are more communally determined than I think, and because I expect everyone else to operate according to an altruistic narrative. Any "altruistic" narrative is effectively a "grand" narrative: I want the other person's altruism to apply in a wide variety of situations, especially where it concerns me, rather than to apply based on how that person feels in the moment. In other words, while ego-based narratives can be important in challenging the claims of grand narratives (especially those that oppress the individual), ego-based grand narratives are not sustainable in a social species.

Small Narratives

A less ego-driven version of postmodern faith owes its articulation to Jean-Francois Lyotard's promotion of the *petit récit*, the "little" narrative, as a response to the perceived philosophical failures of grand narratives.[106] The small narrative draws a circle bigger than the self, but smaller than human-

---

[103] Bergen, *Morris*, 192.
[104] Levinas, 59.
[105] Bauman, *Discontents*, 180.
[106] Lyotard, 60.

ity, asking us to argue moral issues based on what's good for our particular community. "Il faut cultiver notre jardin," Voltaire famously wrote at the end of *Candide*—"we must cultivate our own gardens." Quite compellingly, in a film such as Alejandro Iñárritu and Guillermo Arriaga's *21 Grams*, the family replaces spiritual certainties for the individual. So as long as Cristina Peck's family lives, she can remain drug-free, but when an accident claims her husband and children, the world loses all its meaning. With grand narratives hollowed out at one extreme and ego-based narratives far too narrow at the other, why not marshal one's forces around family, friends, neighbourhood, gender, race, or nation? No need for outsiders to accept our terms of reference. Mini-van ads and political rhetoric are directed at Voltaire's small gardeners for whom the family is the supreme good, while calls for special status come from "identity politicians" who take their groups as the crucial frame of reference.

One of the difficulties with the "small narrative" is its slipperiness: one can adopt different, even contradictory narratives depending upon the circumstances. Canada's federal government congratulated itself on banning asbestos in Canada to keep Canadians safe, but, at the same time, justified continued sales of asbestos to Third world countries because those sales benefit the Canadian economy. Only those inside the small narrative circle really count, in this case citizens. In another example, Terry Nelson, former chief of the Roseau River Anishinabe First Nation in Manitoba supported the Idle No More protests in 2012 as protests designed to take the hand of colonialism off Canadian First Nations communities. But when he was ousted from his position as Roseau River chief by the reserve's custom council (a traditional, non-Western check on the democratic process to which each of the reserve's 20 families contribute a member), he invoked Western one-person-one-vote ideals.

Small narratives can remain stable and compelling as long as they don't have to deal with an Other outside the circle. When Western Muslims protested the treatment of Palestinian Muslims, but then gave credence to an Israeli conspiracy during 9–11 or ignored the Holocaust denial of Mahmoud Ahmadinejad and others, the situation was much the same as when North American Christians protested the persecution of Christian minorities in Sudan but mustered little indignation at attacks on aboriginal culture via residential schools or the persecution of Muslims in Bosnia. Narrow, group-centred arguments—under the rubric of "multiple knowledges"—are tempting when a dominant culture oppresses a subordinate group or bans that group's traditional practices, but as soon as the broader world enters, the narrow "we" is driven to generalize. Particular practices—the potlach, say—can be castigated as primitive (according to a Christian grand narrative) or defended simply because it belongs to a traditional Northwest Coast aboriginal spirituality that was once banned by Christian Canada. While the source and emotional resonance of any social practice may originate in a small narrative, a defence of the practice must eventually take the Other into account and answer to much broader conceptions of rights, freedoms, and moral goods. Christian arguments about who may be served communion and about what women may do in the church have with good reason been submitted to such scrutiny. Jewish leaders such as Jonathan Sacks, former Chief Rabbi of the United Hebrew Congregations of the Commonwealth, seek to limit the tribal aspects of their tradition and instead emphasize its universalist implications.[107] Neither arguments in favour of, nor those against a particular practice can convincingly resort to the escape clause of "local" knowledges.

Small narratives have clearly been important in the postmodern era in pointing out the oppressions of grand narratives. In David Bergen's *A Year of Lesser* (1996), Johnny Fehr struggles to attach himself to the grand narrative of Christianity, with funny and tragic results. Early on, he hopes, naïvely, that baptism will be the magic pill to make him love his difficult wife Charlene. But others sense differently. His son Chris's girlfriend Melody intuits that unredeemed, dark-hearted Johnny is the best bet to take her from Manitoba across the US border for an abortion that even Chris doesn't know about. A more philosophical challenge to Christianity comes from the physicist Michael, who doesn't believe in evil. Schooled in Nietzschean *ressentiment*, Michael repeats the simplistic blanket indictment that Christian conversion is only the rancour of the sick, and he expounds a theory, "based on good research," that "Jesus and Judas were lovers."[108] Apart from a minor (and debated) reference in Josephus, the only first-century sources for the life of Jesus are contained in the *New Testament*, which offers no evidence for such a theory. Michael is likely alluding to the "young man" mentioned in the *Secret Gospel of Mark*, a work optimistically dated by some scholars between the first and the middle of the second centuries, but also a work that its "discoverer," Morton Smith, conveniently managed to avoid producing. However much one might sympathize with Smith's subtle and ingenious recasting of Jesus as gay, the *Secret*

[107] See Sacks, *Not in God's Name*, especially 49, 152, 169, 195–6.
[108] Bergen, *Lesser*, 162–3.

Gospel of Mark is evidently a twentieth-century forgery.[109] Yet the repression of same-sex love *does* apply to the house-church's Pastor Phil, justifying an outburst from Johnny. Hoping to give "a faithful interpretation" of Melody's praying in tongues, Johnny hilariously transposes Michael's ideas into his own register: "Jesus Christ was a fag.... There is this theory which is quite possible.... Seriously, I mean, why didn't the man have any women?"[110] Up against biblical stories that are much larger and more powerful than he is in the small Mennonite community, Johnny can only offer a small counter-narrative cry of self-defence against Jesus: Jesus doesn't understand my sexual desire. Johnny throws his lot in with a family unit that gives meaning to his existence, centring his morality mainly on his new partner, Loraine. Even so, the content of Johnny's resistance leans away from the small narrative and towards a humanism that, unlike religious faith, doesn't rely on transcendental categories to make decisions about sexuality, homosexuality, and abortion. Author Bergen says, "Unlike my father, who believed in an angry but forgiving God, I wanted to hold to the mysterious and if that was my only form of faith, so be it."[111]

In Cormac McCarthy's post-apocalyptic *The Road*, the father draws a small moral circle that includes only himself and his young son. Killing an attacker, the father considers himself ethically justified (as do we) since he kills in order to protect his son, whom he considers his "warrant," the only possible manifestation of the word of God.[112] When Oprah asked McCarthy, "You haven't worked up to the God thing, have you?" he replied, "It depends what day you ask me."[113] The questions raised by *The Road* about small and grand narratives are both personal—with McCarthy's idealization of the fictional boy rooted in his idealization of his youngest son,[114] born when McCarthy was about 65[115]—and more general, with the origins

---

[109] See Bart Ehrman, *Lost Christianities*, Oxford: Oxford University Press, 2003, 67–89. Donald Akenson calls the debate "post-modern scholarly theatre." *Saint Saul*, Montreal & Kingston: McGill-Queen's University Press, 2000, 84–9.

[110] Bergen, *Lesser*, 199.

[111] Bergen, "And You Arrive on the Other Side with Nothing," *Writing Life*, Constance Rooke ed., Toronto: McClelland, 2006, 49, 45.

[112] C. McCarthy, 5.

[113] Kenneth Lincoln, *Cormac McCarthy: American Canticles*. New York: Macmillan, 2009, 14.

[114] John Cant, *Cormac McCarthy and the Myth of American Exceptionalism*, New York: Routledge, 2008, 272.

[115] David Kushner, "Cormac McCarthy's Apocalypse," *Rolling* Stone, 27 December 2007, 43–53, http://74.220.215.94/~davidkus/index.php?option=com_content&view=article&id=61:cormac-mccarthys-apocalypse-&catid=35:articles&Itemid=54.

of religion appearing late in the novel as the boy attempts to talk to his dead father. Here the boy follows the *Homo sapiens* of the Upper Paleolithic, who began to put grave goods in with dead family members, the warrants of the group's small narratives. But early in the novel, after the father designates the son as holy, the son pushes towards a grand narrative beyond the familial unit, urging his father to feed the tramp "Ely" and to return the clothes of the thief who stole their supplies. In Levinasian terms, the boy recognizes the Other as a face, breaking the boundary of the father's small narrative, and moving towards a humanist grand narrative.[116] Necessary as small narratives may initially be in countering the oppressive grand narratives of majority cultures, small narratives will only be taken seriously if they generalize their notions of responsibility and justice, thereby turning into selective adherence, pluralism, or humanism.

Selective Adherence

A third group in the "undecided middle" comprises people who still have strong ties to traditional faiths, but who no longer adhere to all of the faith's teachings. "Choose religion cafeteria-style," *Life's Little Deconstruction Book* wittily recommends, "Have beliefs, but don't believe."[117] From an outsider's point of view, the picking and choosing of doctrines, the waning of discipline, and the imitation of popular cultural forms may look self-deceiving or droll. Hal Niedzviecki criticizes the tendency to modify grand narratives, mocking Jewish congregations that don't keep all the Sabbath laws, Christians who don't attend services weekly, and Catholic Christians who disagree with papal views. "Tradition-lite," Niedzviecki names this, "Tradition without responsibility."[118] He demands that adherents perform their faith in orthodox ways, though *he himself*, of course, won't do so. He calls for a stark choice between either an irrational faith in a grand narrative or a complete refusal of faith.

Despite Niedzviecki's barbs, many "believers" haven't given up faith—there's still a discipline involved in committing oneself to a faith group—

---

[116] Tony Davies mistakenly treats *The Road* as if it were an anti-humanist work (T. Davies, 134), as if works that imagine an apocalypse must by definition be highly critical of humanism.

[117] Andrew Boyd #227, #326.

[118] Niedzviecki, *Special*, 36, 38–9, 57.

but are moving towards the less absolute versions that in our time ... also helped to reduce inter-communal violence. These "Selective Adherents" ignore certain doctrines of their faith, for example teachings on sex, alcohol, drugs, birth control, hell, or service attendance, and sometimes even central doctrines, such as the divinity of Christ.[119] Selective adherents to tradition express postmodernity by giving the *individual* a greater say in determining right and wrong, and express modernity in reasoning about which faith elements are true. As Diana Bass puts it, while some Christians built "museums to creationism" and "asked for more belief about increasingly unbelievable things," others were fleeing creeds and doctrines, though still believing in Christ's call to "love your neighbour as yourself." She avoids questions about the historicity of the resurrection, and instead asks, somewhat disingenuously, "Do you trust in the resurrection?"[120] For selective adherents, modernity's rationalism shakes the foundations of faith, but since neither reason nor postmodern individualism offers a compelling *meaning* to replace the grand narrative, selective adherents continue in the old stories, less stridently and less securely. Christian Smith treats selective adherence ironically, implying that it is absurd to allow the individual to decide the content of a faith, but, in fact, church councils have always decided which teachings to require, which to make optional, and which to ignore. Institutionalization allowed believers either to forget that cafeteria choices had been made or to interpret deviation from earlier teachings as God-led.

We can see selective adherence in Bass, who fell into a "belief gap," while hearing a sermon "likening Jesus to an imperialist warlord,"[121] as well as in Bishop Michael Ingham, whom we met at the outset of this chapter, as he upheld aboriginal traditions and homosexual spirituality in Vancouver. Catholic philosopher Charles Taylor, though he strongly defends transcendence, hints at his own selective adherence and admits that the historical "move to secular humanism... has been a great gain for human kind." He speaks of a "stabilized middle condition... where we have found a way to escape the forms of negation, exile, emptiness, without having reached fullness."[122] For Taylor, the purpose of religion isn't a response to meaninglessness, but the creation of community, and it must

[119] See C. Smith, 156–7, 167, and Bass, 112.
[120] Bass, 108–11, 129.
[121] Bass, 105.
[122] Taylor, *Secular*, 717–18, 637, 6.

include the promotion of human well-being. We can also see selective adherence in former Anglican Archbishop Rowan Williams, who tries to walk the line between humanism and Christianity. He refuses to dismiss others' non-Christian symbolic worlds, yet struggles to avoid relativism. Instead of seeing God as a "useful fiction" (one response to modernist critiques of biblical sexism, racism, and homophobia), Williams acts "as if" there is "a really existent God" who offers "a context of grace" for "any imaginable future." With the "as if" approach, the Christian assertion still comes from the *Bible*, but isn't absolute and refuses to prejudge other perspectives.[123]

In the evangelical context, selective adherence arises in theological debates between those such as Brian McLaren (*A New Kind of Christian*, 2001), who take seriously modernity's criticisms of Christianity, and those, such as Andrew Wilson (*Unbreakable*, 2014), who assert the primacy of the *Bible* no matter what it says. Mega-church pastor Rob Bell argued in *Love Wins* (2011) that, since God is love, traditional accounts of hell can't be literally true. *Love Wins* cost Bell his ministry position at Mars Hill Bible Church, but then became a bestseller and turned him into a Christian celebrity in the larger, more pluralist culture. What is new in the postmodern era is the ability of individual churches and individual believers to make selective choices with relative impunity.

From the perspective of traditional commentators, selective adherence is often seen as a road away from faith. One *Mennonite Brethren Herald* writer complains about a free-rider mentality: "I … see a generation asking the church to bend over backward for them while lightheartedly hinting they might still prefer to relax at home every Sunday even if the church does bend over backward."[124] From a secular perspective, selective adherence is a welcome development. Many Christians today, in their actions, hew more closely to the recent norms of "nonviolence and toleration" than to the beliefs of early Christendom, Steven Pinker observes, "a benevolent hypocrisy for which we should all be grateful."[125] The balancing act for churches has been difficult. How does one take the *Bible* seriously as a guide and yet resist biblical injunctions against tribal religions, homosexuality, and women's equality?

---

[123] R. Williams, 88–91, 115.

[124] Peter Epp, "Why don't young adults go to church?" *Mennonite Brethren Herald*, August 2013, 16.

[125] Pinker, *Better*, 17.

Some aspects of selective adherence have been unexpected. Given the modernist notion that education liberates one from the shackles of superstition, religious participation ought to be declining most among the college-educated. But the opposite is true. Those with higher education are *more*, not less, likely to be involved in faith groups.[126] This is less surprising when we consider that college-educated people are more involved in the community generally. Religious involvement generally reinforces other identities, encouraging civic connections, familial connections, and self-understanding.[127] We are not, despite Bass's hopes, on the cusp of a Fourth Awakening,[128] but given the better life outcomes for the "Devoted" cited earlier, it's understandable why the educated might want to participate in a faith community.

Attempts in North America to renew traditional beliefs in a selective way can be seen outside of the Christian tradition too. Eden Robinson, a part-Heiltsuk member of the Haisla First Nation in British Columbia, seeks to reincorporate aboriginal spirituality in works such as "Queen of the North" (1996), *Monkey Beach* (2000), and *Son of a Trickster* (2017). In *Monkey Beach*, Ma-ma-oo is the conduit for tradition, while the failure of indigenous cultural institutions, mainly seen as the effect of residential schools, is expressed through Karaoke and Lisa, Ma-ma-oo's granddaughter. Karaoke superficially allies herself with contemporary nihilism in "Queen of the North," but that seems to be a pose. A potentially helpful, potentially malevolent Tree Spirit, shows up surreptitiously as Arnold in "Queen" and more explicitly in *Monkey Beach*, where his manifestations to Lisa signal her shamanic abilities. After one of her supposed friends rapes her, she rejects the little man—"If you couldn't stop it, what good are

---

[126]Twenge, *iGen*, 134–5. C. Smith, 249.

[127]Greenberg, 15. Twenge, *iGen*, 134. Belief is lower among scientists. Only one-half of American scientists believe in God, while 83% of the public does. Forty-one percent of scientists don't believe in either God or a higher power, while only 4% of public doesn't believe. Belief is higher among younger scientists than among older. In the 18–34 age group, 66% of scientists believe in God or a higher power, while the number drops in each subsequent age group down to a low of 46% in those over age 65. Other aspects of the survey suggest that the believing scientists are selective adherents. Almost all American scientists (97%) believe that humans and other living things evolved over time, while only 61% of Americans believe this. A huge majority of scientists (87%) also think that evolution is due to natural processes, but only 32% of the Americans think so (Pew, "Scientific," 36–7). Evidently, the scientists who believe in God reconcile that belief with a non-providential view of human evolution.

[128]Bass, 222–3, 262–3.

you?"[129]—but she finds value in her tradition, and the repeated appearance of trickster-like crows and ravens in *Monkey Beach* and *Son of a Trickster* suggest that Robinson does too. The trickster Wee'git appears both as a man and as a raven in *Son of a Trickster*, and the title character Jared, who can see spirits, tries to free himself from the dysfunctions associated with being one of Wee'git's 532 children.[130] Some figures that Robinson's characters encounter—*b'gwus* and Wee'git, for example—are rooted in traditional stories, while gothic plot elements and other characters such as the Tree Spirit combine Haisla tradition with Robinson's own spiritual inventions.[131] She imagines a selective adherence, in that characters reorient themselves towards tradition rather than assuming a specific array of traditional practices. As her novels confirm, she's not interested in writing morality tales or in a full return to tradition,[132] yet she uses trickster tales to teach protocol and behaviour.[133]

Michael Chabon likewise gives voice to those who adhere selectively to Judaism. His novel *The Yiddish Policemen's Union* (2007), an alternate world in which the 6 million Holocaust victims didn't die but were shipped to a homeland in Sitka, Alaska, verges on the blasphemous at times. For example, a chicken, about to feel the *shochet*'s knife, reportedly announces, "in Aramaic, the imminent advent of the Messiah." Several characters—Rabbi Heskel Shpilman, Hertz Shemets (an agent for a Mossad-like group), and Alter Litvak—are involved in a conspiracy to drive the Arabs off the Dome on the Rock and to re-establish the Temple in Jerusalem. They give lip service to Judaism, but make their beds in *realpolitik*, preparing to utilize Heskel's kind-hearted, homosexual, drug-addicted son Mendel Shpilman as putative messiah (Chabon nodding both to John Barth's postmodern Max Spielman and to the traditionalist Chabad Rebbe Menachem Mendel Schneerson). Although Chabon's Mendel can neither overcome addiction nor fight the Orthodox prohibition against homosexuality, his blessings *work*, shaking at least one character's "faith in faithlessness." In

[129] Robinson, *Monkey*, 259.

[130] Robinson, *Son*, 307, 312.

[131] See Traci Vogel, "Bordering on the Dream World," (Interview with Eden Robinson), *The Stranger*, April 12–18, 2001, http://www.thestranger.com/seattle/bordering-on-the-dream-world/Content?oid=7062.

[132] Ariel Gordon, "In Conversation with Eden Robinson," *Winnipeg Free Press*, 4 February 2017.

[133] Canadian Press, "Unlikely teen hero key to coming of age tale," *Brandon Sun*, 15 March 2017.

addition, through Sitka detective Berko Shemets (son of the agent Hertz and a Tlingit mother, Laurie Jo Bear), Chabon imagines a selective adherence to Judaism as Berko calls his Zionist father to moral account. Berko has the same birthday as the putative messiah, but is a far less tortured figure than Mendel is.[134] Chabon, who with his wife, Ayelet Waldman, belongs to Oakland's Reform Temple Sinai, cannot remain fully inside Judaic law (which persecutes homosexuals and underwrites Zionist aggression), but fears that to drop the tradition entirely would be to become unmoored.

David Foster Wallace, who suffered all his adult life from serious depression and eventually took his own life, attempted selective adherence. Wallace long counted himself among a generation of ironists whose patron saint was David Letterman. According to Wallace, these "highly intelligent, motivated career-track people" don't believe in politics or religion and are quick to read cynical motives into civic and political activism. As his mental struggles intensified, Wallace sought communities tied to a higher power, communities such as Alcoholics Anonymous, where he had to drop his sense that he was the smartest person in the room and submit himself to clichés, such as "Your best thinking got you here." In the early 1990s, as he turned 30, his girlfriend, the poet Mary Karr, nudged him towards Christianity. Although Wallace began to pray and thought that he might even receive the sacraments, the priest judged that he wasn't ready to become a believer.[135] Like many of his increasingly individualist generation, Wallace chafed at most kinds of discipline, including a full commitment to Karr.

In the late 1990s, having returned to the Midwest and about to publish his masterwork, *Infinite Jest*, Wallace made several tentative visits to a Mennonite Church in Normal, Illinois, which his friends, Doug and Erin Poag, attended. Because Wallace spoke in interviews of meeting Doug "at a Mennonite house of worship," commentators were quick to anticipate a conversion. In fact, however, the "house of worship" was an AA meeting, Wallace having become Doug's sponsor.[136] Wallace posted St. Ignatius's Prayer in his bathroom, a prayer which, emphasizing generosity and labour,[137] expresses the selective face of a grand narrative emptied of metaphysical assertions.

[134] Chabon, *Yiddish*, 13, 125, 117.
[135] Max, 114, 139, 166.
[136] Max, 220; Beck.
[137] Lipsky, 302.

Although Wallace dropped his selective adherence and finally lost out to depression, *Infinite Jest* expresses his earlier hopes. Hal Incandenza, modelled partly on Wallace himself, spirals downward; Don Gately, modelled partly on an AA acquaintance called Big Craig,[138] heads upward. Gately recovers from addiction by laying scepticism aside. Hospitalized and medicated, Gately speaks with a wraith that can't be purely imaginary, since it mentions "pirouette," a word Gately doesn't know. Gately thinks that the wraith may be "like the legendary Pulsing Blue Light that AA founder Bill W. historically saw during his last detox, that turned out to be God telling him how to stay sober via starting AA and Carrying the Message."[139] Alternatively, the wraith might be The Disease, trying to get him to accept Demerol and thus fall off the wagon. Wallace explicitly alludes to Dostoevsky's *The Brothers Karamazov*, in which the devil appears to Ivan Karamazov. The rationalist Ivan considers the devil a hallucination, until the devil admits that he has rheumatism, a thought Ivan is certain didn't come from his own head. "Nothing human is beyond the possibility of Satan," Ivan's devil avers.[140] The reader of *Infinite Jest*, however, will quickly realize that Gately's wraith speaks in the idiom of the deceased filmmaker James O. Incandenza (Hal's father). Yet this doesn't derail the faith narrative, since Gately has never met Hal's father. In such a way, Wallace's novel, less sceptical than Wallace himself, keeps open a metaphorical, selective way of talking about God.

Pluralist Adaptation

Even more tentative towards faith traditions than selective adherents are, but not ready to dismiss religious metaphysics as humanists do, are the pluralist adapters. According to Lipovetsky, hypermodern atomization and "individualist disintegration of the social bond" creates a new need for religious faiths, so people turn to "*à la carte* religions." He's referring to people who combine Eastern and Western religious practices, but the description can be applied more broadly to those who combine various beliefs without necessarily seeking coherence.[141] Pluralist adapters run the

---

[138] Max 141.

[139] Wallace, *Infinite* 833.

[140] Dostoevsky, 579. See also Timothy Jacobs, "The Brothers Incandenza: Translating Ideology in Fyodor Dostoevsky's *The Brothers Karamazov* and David Foster Wallace's *Infinite Jest*," *Texas Studies in Literature and Language* 49:3 (Fall 2007): 265–92.

[141] Lipovetsky, 63–4.

gamut from New Age beliefs—more than a third of American Christians feel comfortable with astrology, reincarnation, and spiritual energy in mountains and trees[142]—to E.O. Wilson's materialist inversion of Pascal's wager: "Accept the faith… but treat this world as if there is none other." No pluralist adapter himself (Wilson left his Southern Baptist roots early),[143] his description captures a significant portion of the undecided middle— those people who still feel a tenuous connection with a faith but no longer take part in communal practices. By 2008 in the US, two-thirds of people believed that "many religions can lead to eternal life."[144] Talented Canadian poet and singer Leonard Cohen's popularity into his 80s was attributable, at least in part, to his role as a kind of secular priest, combining Jewish, Christian, Buddhist, and Scientology symbolism with sexual freedom.

One of the most prominent pluralist adapters has been Oprah Winfrey. When she left Jeremiah Wright's United Church of Christ, an upscale African-American church in Chicago, she spoke of a "fatigue with organized religion." Though she continued to classify herself as a Christian, she began to speak in a creedless way about self-transformation, insisting, "Ultimately I am Spirit come from the greatest Spirit." While interviewing Madonna, Winfrey discovers, "I'm a closet kabbalist;" with Deepak Chopra, she's more of a Hindu; and with health and wealth guru Rhonda Byrne (*The Secret*), Oprah reveals, "I've always lived by the secret."[145] At times, it's difficult to distinguish between Winfrey's pluralism and an ego-based narrative. A "Best Life Week" on *The Oprah Winfrey Show* in January 2009 ran thus: "Your Weight (Monday), Your Health (Tuesday), Your Spirit (Wednesday), Your Money (Thursday), and Your Sex Life (Friday)."[146] With "your" as the salient term, it's not unreasonable for "your wish to lose a few pounds" to receive equal billing with "your spirit." The ethical pitfalls of How-I-Feel are obvious when Winfrey says, "I don't just like me. I adore me. I adore that I feel a connection to other people that really makes me feel like a part of something that is bigger than myself…. And I adore that I have a great generous spirit…. Last week I found some slippers that felt wonderful, so I bought them for all the women in the control room at the studio."[147] Oprah is the great exemplar,

---

[142] Pew, "Many," 2.
[143] E.O. Wilson, *Consilience*, 269, 6.
[144] Bass, 51.
[145] Winfrey, quoted in Lofton, 68, 4, 70, 43.
[146] Lofton, 53.
[147] Winfrey, quoted in Lofton, 34.

the one who has learned to love her fallible self, thus liberating the divine spark and taking away guilt when she buys things for herself.

Kathryn Lofton finds parallels between Oprah and some of the most successful contemporary Christian churches, such as Joel Osteen's Lakewood Church in Houston. Although broadly popular evangelical churches retain a backroom scaffolding of dogma, public worship leans towards uplifting songs and positive-thinking sermons. What clearly engages people is the "life application" method of *Bible* study, a method that Oprah borrowed for her Book Club by repeatedly asking her participants, "What in the book most related to you?" The guests, not the book, became the subject of discussion.[148] Oprah's danger of falling back into an ego-based narrative is a problem for pluralist adaptation generally: if I never defer to moral authorities, if I alone decide the value of each piece in the pluralist puzzle, and if my welfare is paramount, then what differentiates pluralism from my will?

Still, the outward focus in Winfrey's gospel makes it pluralist, not merely ego-based. Although Lofton satirizes Winfrey as offering religion "safely couched within a girl-power democracy and capitalist pleasure,"[149] one cannot ignore the ways in which her show and her Book Club created post-religious communities that brought women together in supportive ways. If it seems silly to believe that one can prime the money pump by attuning oneself to one's divine self, Oprah's refusal to believe in random suffering[150] nudged many audience members into taking responsibility for their lives. It's also noteworthy that after the horrific events of 9/11, organizers of a five-hour inter-faith service at Yankee Stadium—"A Prayer for America"—looked to Winfrey as the person who could pull Christians, Muslims, Jews, Hindus, and Sikhs together. It wasn't just "celebrity recognition" and "consumer popularity;"[151] Winfrey's pluralism also meant that she could bring together people of various colours and various faiths. For many who cross cultures, as does surgeon and writer Atul Gawande, pluralism has a kind of inevitability. Although sceptical about rituals, Gawande agreed to spread his father's ashes on the Ganges River, with the proper priestly rituals to facilitate *moksha*, the escape from the cycle of birth and death. Gawande even sipped from the Ganges and contracted a

---

[148] Lofton, 73, 178–80.
[149] Lofton, 49.
[150] Packer, 61.
[151] Lofton, 118–9.

Giardia infection, but felt that he had connected his father "to something far bigger than ourselves."[152]

Spiritual pluralism undergirds the moral conscience of much contemporary fiction. Earnestly and without nuance, Dan Brown's *The Da Vinci Code* (2003) and Umberto Eco's *The Prague Cemetery* (2010) pronounce pluralism good, religion bad. With less dogmatism, Abraham Verghese's *Cutting for Stone* (2009), Salman Rushdie's and Rohinton Mistry's novels, Neil Gaiman's *The Ocean at the End of the Lane* (2013), and Yann Martel's *Life of Pi* (2001) undermine the belief that any singular grand narrative can give us the truth about the world. Verghese's Hema, an unambiguously good character, keeps a Shiva lingam and a ceramic crucified Christ side-by-side in her closet shrine.[153] Beneficent divine figures of all sorts aid the living. Death isn't an end, and the transmigration of souls (from the dead Shiva into his twin Marion) is intended to be more than just metaphorical. Mistry's "Pavement Artist" in *Such a Long Journey* (1991) does sacred wall paintings of Zarathustra, the *Trimurti*, Baby Jesus, and many others, even of Dustoorji Baria, a possible con-man, leaving open the possibility that whatever good comes out of the grand narratives of faith could well arrive through an imposter. In Mistry's later novel, *Family Matters* (2002), pluralism—as symbolized by the cricket-playing mechanical Santa in a Parsi shop-window on a Hindu street—is a less viable option, but both Mistry and Verghese vouch for pluralism as a way of promoting coexistence in a multicultural world.

Life of Pi (2001)—which won the Booker Prize, and then, in its 2012 film adaptation, a Best Director Oscar for Ang Lee—imagines a nearly Unitarian faith. Stranded on a boat with animal predators and prey, Pi practises all faiths inexpertly, and even deifies himself, declaring, of his turban, "THIS IS GOD'S HAT!"[154] If Pi mythologizes what in fact was really a slaughter, the truth may corrode Pi's religious syncretism, but even if Pi's version of events is fabular, Martel implies that his pluralist faith is an appropriate imaginative response to the cruelties of the natural world. This verges on humanism, as does George Saunders's *Lincoln in the Bardo* (2017), where the characters experience a pluralist afterlife that doesn't fit into Buddhist or Christian conceptions. Saunders has said that he doesn't know what will happen after death, so he wanted to destabilize traditional

[152] Gawande, 260–3.
[153] Verghese, 208.
[154] Martel, 231.

notions. "The world itself has no meaning, no beauty, no ugliness,"[155] he insists, and yet the characters, especially Hans Vollman and Roger Bevins III, see inside each other's and inside Lincoln's spirit, creating a profound humanist empathy.[156]

* * *

Writing of communal identities, Bauman identifies a problem that also afflicts both selective adherence and pluralist adaptation: we want the freedom from grand narratives that postmodernity had promised, yet, at the same time, we want tradition to guarantee a "happy end." In the traditional scenario, God and community *precede* all choice and enforce loyalty, potentially a totalitarian scenario. In postmodernity, our individual choices are supposed to determine the community's grand narrative, its rules, its ethics. In the latter scenario, we are thrown back on our individual resources.[157] But after lucidly explicating the problem, Bauman can only offer pluralism—having *many* gods in one's breast—as a response. Of course, pluralism simply restates the postmodern dilemma without solving it. We can tolerate a wide variety of lifestyles, but when it comes time to act and legislate, we are forced to choose. Will we choose the foetus's health or the mother's autonomy? Will we affirm pluralist openness to all cultural practices or legislate against female circumcision? Selective adherence and pluralism have helped to reduce violence, but they have difficulty telling us *which* beliefs to act on.

Christian Smith mocks selective adherents and pluralist adapters alike, calling the American de facto religion "moralistic therapeutic deism." God is distant from human affairs, but He does want people to be happy and nice to each other. Pragmatism reigns: "religious faith becomes good *if* and *because* it makes people do better, if it helps them live more moral lives." Smith implies that the undecided haven't thought matters through. Sometimes, he calls them "moral intuitionists," who see morality as self-evident and consider their subjective feelings to be reliable moral guides, since those feelings are based on whatever morality the intuitionists learned

---

[155] Sam Pricket, "Consciousness Is Not Correct: A Conversation with George Saunders," *Weld*, 14 February 2017, https://weldbham.com/blog/2017/02/14/consciousness-not-correct-conversation-george-saunders/.

[156] Saunders, *Lincoln*, 171–5.

[157] Bauman, *Discontents*, 193, 195.

as children. Sometimes, he calls them "ethical consequentialists" who believe that if an act doesn't hurt others and isn't illegal, it's probably okay. This, he states, also makes most young people "soft ontological anti-realists" or "epistemological skeptics" or "perspectivalists" doubtful about a shared objective reality that could provide a stable basis for moral arguments between individuals.[158]

One senses some justification for Smith's frustration when one hears less reflective voices struggle to articulate a moral code. Asked about the discrepancy between his church's position on sexuality and his own decision to live with his girlfriend, one young man, "Brad," says, "I think it's all based on your situation, if that's what you want to believe at that kind of church, sure, that's great, if that's what they want to do. It's all relative." Brad believes in Jesus and sometimes goes to church, but on larger questions of morality, all he can do is appeal to majority opinion and to feeling. In a morally ambiguous situation, he would "take care of number one" and do the things that make him "happy." Relativism and the priority of personal feelings are common themes among many of the young adults that Smith interviewed. "June," who identified herself as a Satanist and who lost her child because of her drug habit, suggests that "everything, every situation has its right or wrong, really every situation is different." She believes in karma and thinks that there might be a God, but also thinks of life as a game and admits that she often manipulates others to get what she wants. If someone thought it fine to hurt another that would be wrong, but she probably wouldn't voice her opinion: who is she to judge? Pressed to explain how she makes decisions about right and wrong, she admits that the main determinant is what makes her happy.[159] Part of Smith's agenda is to drive people such as Brad and June off untenable relativist faiths, revealing them as a cover for ego-based narratives.

But if young "perspectivalists" are so foolish, why are there so many of them? The reason, I would argue, is that those people in the undecided middle have (sometimes unconsciously) apprehended the postmodern dilemma. It's always easier to describe the difficulties created by the ero-

---

[158] C. Smith, 166–8, 154, 292, 46, 82, 47, 163, 45. For the triumph of individualism, Smith, a Catholic, partly blames American evangelicalism with its emphasis on personal experience (C. Smith, 290–1). Individualism has indeed had a profound leaching impact on faith in grand narratives, but as Smith's own data show, conservative Protestants and Mormons have been affected *less* by the movement away from doctrinal claims than have Catholics and other mainline Christian groups.

[159] C. Smith, 11–25.

sion of grand narratives than to offer a solution. "Moralistic therapeutic deism," according to Smith, holds "that each individual is uniquely distinct from others and deserves a faith that fits his or her singular self; that individuals must freely choose their own religion; that the individual is the authority over religion and not vice versa; that religion need not be practised in and by a community; that no person may exercise judgments about or attempt to change the faith of other people; and that religious beliefs are interchangeable" because individual comfort matters more than "the integrity of the belief system."[160] Agreeing with Smith, Brad Gregory, tongue-in-cheek, chimes in, "How could a sincerely felt feeling be false?" Gregory complains that as a postmodern culture we have increasingly favoured emotion and morally conformist civility, resulting in a highly sentimentalized faith and in secular analogues such as self-realization programmes. He says, "The freedom of each American citizen to make doctrinal claims has always greatly exceeded that of any pope."[161] That's a bit of a red herring, but it does get at an important feature of selective adherence and pluralist adaptation: why *should* the pope or a church have the final word over my sexuality or my beliefs?

In the past, of course, doctrinal disagreements were mostly resolved not by reasoned faith or by community consensus, but by authority, exerting the powers of excommunication and coercive physical force. In criticizing "anti-realists," Smith implies that an objective reality—including moral matters!—would be easy to assent to, and sidesteps modernity's historical *reasons* for perspectivalism: "higher" biblical criticism that pointed to many contradictions in the *Bible*, so that it couldn't be taken in any direct way as God's voice; scientific education that questioned irrational beliefs; democratization that revealed abuses in hierarchical churches; the growing sense of a buffered self that was immune to attacks from demons or ministrations by angels; cosmopolitan cities that revealed Hindus, Muslims, Buddhists, and atheists to be good people; and the increasing social dignity given to the pursuit of individual human flourishing. Not all young people can articulate the philosophical or historical sources for their perspectivalism, but that doesn't disqualify their intuitions. It is particularly interesting that Smith should call his young subjects "anti-realists."[162] True, they would be less likely than he is to insist that our representations

[160] C. Smith, quoted in Gregory, 171.
[161] Gregory, 170, 65, 101–2, 98–9, 176.
[162] C. Smith, 290–1.

can convey objective truths about the world, so that technically they might not qualify as philosophical realists. Yet for him, a Catholic scholar, the "truths" about the world include the Virgin Birth, the deity of Christ, and resurrection from the dead—doctrines that require a great deal of massaging to fit them into the category of objective reality. Smith and Gregory too, as much as any "moralistic therapeutic deist," must assume that their sincerely held feelings can't be false.

Humanism

Going further than selective adherence or pluralist adaptation is perhaps the most widespread contemporary grand narrative in the West—the secular faith of humanism. Pinker describes the humanist grand narrative thus: "We are born into a pitiless universe…. We were shaped by a force that is ruthlessly competitive. We are made from crooked timber, vulnerable to illusions, self-centeredness, and at times astounding stupidity." However, human nature has also evolved the self-awareness of recursive thought, an instinct for language, and a capacity for sympathy, so that meaning arises because we care about ourselves and our kin, and reason allows us to widen the circle of our sympathy: "If I object to being raped, maimed, starved or killed, I can't very well rape, maim, starve, or kill you."[163] Like selective adherence and pluralist adaptation, humanism has a perspectivalist core and refuses to let traditional authorities determine our choices. Like those who rely on ego-based narratives, humanists believe that the power to reach fullness is within,[164] yet in contrast to ego-based narratives, humanism also calls for selfless adherence to certain ethical principles, and, in contrast to small narratives, it tries not to favour any particular group. Humanists preach the intrinsic value of human *individuals* above theories, systems, and institutions, with the goal either of freeing people from oppressive institutions or of shaping institutions (reforming prisons, demanding wheelchair access in public buildings) so that institutions serve individual needs. Despite its central significance in most contemporary ways of thinking, including faith-based ones, humanism often appears as unarticulated "common knowledge" rather than as an explicit grand narrative. A focus on rationality and equality is intended to rescue the grand narrative from unfounded beliefs on one side and from egoism on the other.

[163] Pinker, *Enlightenment*, 412, 410, 415, 434–5, 453.
[164] Taylor, *Secular*, 8.

Humanism is compatible with religious faith wherever faith places human flourishing and impartiality above supernatural beliefs and parochial ecclesiastical authority.[165] Smith argues that the membership decline of mainline Christian denominations is an expression of the cultural triumph of liberal Protestantism's core values: "individualism, pluralism, emancipation, tolerance, free critical inquiry, and the authority of human experience." If Christian denominations mimic humanist culture by valuing inclusiveness and diversity, Smith implies, members will bleed away[166]—denominations will pay for their larger cultural victory by losing their distinctive role. Yet if, counter to Smith's assumption, denominational allegiance isn't the only measure, the cultural gains wrought by the humanist grand narrative become apparent. Like other faiths, Christianity had, and has, strong currents favouring individual rights: Jesus's choice of simple fishermen as his disciples; the early church's continuing focus on individuals of negligible social status; social justice movements such as the one instituted by St. Francis; Quaker appeals to "the light within"; antislavery movements; and temperance campaigns that demanded the vote for women. Yet institutional Christianity also subordinated the individual via asceticism, church discipline, loyalty requirements in the post-Constantinian state church, heresy hunting by various Inquisitions, and control of the state in recent eras. Against such forms of control, humanism asserts itself.

The increase of humanist commitments may be seen in myriad ways: in the consistent broadening of human rights, in the growing mandate of the UN, in the relative decrease of violence, and in casualty dread. Under the rubric of "human rights," humanism underwrites the mission of state welfare agencies and international NGOs, and champions the Human Development Index as a better measure of progress than GDP.[167] The great increase in money and research devoted to health care is arguably an expression of humanism. School programmes—from Gay-Straight Alliances to programmes designed to foster self-reflection and moral growth—depend on humanism. For example, in Ralph Brown School and Champlain School, both in Winnipeg's poorer north end, teachers use meditation to attempt to combat self-harm and suicide ideation. Each student gets a Thrival Kit, which includes not only breathing exercise cards,

[165] Pinker, *Enlightenment*, 412.
[166] C. Smith, 288, 81.
[167] Wight, 202–3.

but also a copy of the Charter of Rights and Freedoms.[168] While humanism has come under fire from all sides—from the right for banishing God and mystery, from the left for drowning racial, class, and gender differences in a specious "universal" humanity, critics of humanism nevertheless rely on typically humanist assumptions, since both traditionalists and postmodernist sceptics demand rights and freedoms. Foucault thought of himself as an anti-humanist cheering the end of "man," and Derrida mistrusted humanism as another transcendental signified. Yet Derrida's anti-apartheid stance made "human" rights a transcendental signified, while Foucault's attempt to undermine the "normal," had the salutary effect of normalizing homosexuality in Western legal regimes, and amalgamating homosexual rights with human rights. The widespread acceptance of humanist values reveals that no matter our rhetoric, we haven't gotten rid of grand narratives, nor do we want to. Tony Davies astutely observes, "Some version of liberal humanism underpins almost all modern societies and political parties, left or right, except those organized around religious doctrines."[169]

Davies follows Levinas, declaring, "Humanity is neither a given essence nor an achievable end, but a continuous and precarious process of becoming human, a process that entails the inescapable recognition that our humanity is on loan from others, to precisely the extent that we acknowledge it in them."[170] Since individuals vary greatly and since many crimes against individual humans have been committed in the name of "humanity," one wouldn't want to require some essential feature before recognizing the humanity of another. Still, evolution has primed our species' psychology and behavioural repertoire, so that, despite our cultural variety, we react in predictable ways. Davies's description of "a humanity on loan from others if we acknowledge it in them," in fact, usefully presupposes that our humanity appears in our sociality. Like others who deny essences, Davies presupposes essential psychological features of *Homo sapiens*: he hopes that human adaptations such as social cooperation, empathy, and reciprocal altruism can combat other, darker adaptations, such as dominance hierarchies, vengeance, sexual jealousy, and predation, at least in regards to other humans.

[168] Jessica Botelho-Urbanski, "Combatting suicide risk by teaching meditation," *Winnipeg Free Press*, 1 March 2018, A04.
[169] T. Davies, 140, 151.
[170] T. Davies, 142.

In the past, social cooperation often depended on a shared religious faith, but now a central strain of the humanist faith—the attempt to renew ethical values on a non-religious basis—is deepening in the West. The 2007 Pew survey of Global Attitudes showed stark differences between Europe and the rest of the world on the question of whether one must believe in God to be moral. Majorities, sometimes overwhelming majorities, in most of the surveyed countries of Africa, South America, the Middle East, and Asia thought that one needed to believe in God to be moral.[171] In Europe, however, national majorities believed that one *does not* need to believe in God to be moral. The responses ranged from Sweden, where only 10% of people found belief in God necessary, to Germany and Ukraine at 39% and 42% respectively. Canada (30%) fit the European model, while the US (57%) remained anomalous, neither as low as Europe nor as high as the rest of the world.[172] A few years later, the numbers had dropped further, with only 18% of Canadians, 33% of Germans, and 53% of Americans continuing to say that one must believe in God to be moral.[173]

The renewal of ethical values on a non-religious basis can be seen in a practical way via the treatment of LGBTQ people. Contemporary humanism arose not just from Enlightenment philosophy but from practical attempts by the English Levellers, then Rousseau and Paine, to assert political rights,[174] and it's in the pragmatic battle for "human rights" that we see the profundities of the humanist faith most clearly. Although Christianity treated homosexuality as a sin, by 2007, large majorities of Western Europeans said that homosexuality should be accepted. Even in South American countries, those who accepted homosexuality rose to the majority or close to the majority. Canada, with a two-thirds acceptance rate, followed the European trend. The US, where half accepted homosexuality and 41% that it should be rejected, showed numbers comparable

---

[171] The most notable exceptions were China (with two generations of communism under its belt) and westernized Japan, where, respectively, only 17%, and 33% believed this (Pew, "World Publics," 33–4).

[172] In Germany, the numbers were up 6% from 2002, while, less surprisingly, Ukraine was down 19% from 2002. The US numbers were comparable only to South Korea, Mexico, and Chile (Pew, "World Publics," 33–4).

[173] Pew, "American-Western," 8–9, 2011. The Canadian numbers are more recent, from 2015 (Angus Reid, 21).

[174] T. Davies, 25. See also David Williams, *Milton's Leveller God*, and Christopher Hill, *The World Turned Upside Down*.

to less developed South American countries such as Peru and Venezuela.[175] Nevertheless, in 2011, American acceptance moved up to 60% despite high religiosity, [176] suggesting that Americans, including many American believers, are shifting towards a non-religious basis for values. The shift can be seen in Gus Van Sant's *Milk* (which recounted the shooting of gay activist and San Francisco city supervisor Harvey Milk), both in the way that the film presents a human rights narrative and in the film's reception: nominated for eight Academy Awards, it won two, and it received a positive review in the evangelical magazine *Christianity Today*. In every country, people under 40 are more accepting of homosexuality and more ready to believe that morality can be had without God.[177]

Inevitably, humanism has taken on the confessional features of a religious faith, as any grand narrative does. Supporters of the UN's *Universal Declaration of Human Rights* treat it as "a quasi-sacred text."[178] At the opening of the Canadian Museum for Human Rights, which was designed to be and is fast becoming a humanist cathedral, the cover of a special edition of the *Winnipeg Free Press* declared, "A BEACON OF LIGHT SHINES ON WINNIPEG."[179] Similarly, highly popular children's movies such as *Monsters University* (2013) and *Zootopia* (2016) translate the core beliefs of a humanist faith into the realm of individual diversity and equal opportunity. Taking on a dogmatic quality isn't necessarily a bad thing, insofar as racism, for example, is anathematized, rather than being a subject for consequentialist reasoning. Among the humanist sins in Robert McGill's novel *Once We Had a Country* (2013), one in particular stands out. A 16-year-old jilted girl, Lydia, is discovered to be the author of the graffiti, "Nigger Lover" (pointing at the protagonist Maggie's relationship with George Ray), and, subsequently, Lydia becomes symbolically outcast. Maggie refuses to feel sorry for her, despite her youth and romantic agony. Author McGill shares Maggie's horror to such an extent that he only hints at the N-word in the graffiti, but will not quote it directly in the novel.[180]

---

[175] Pew, "World Publics," 35.

[176] Between 2007 and 2011, the acceptance rates for homosexuality rose from 82% to 91% in Spain, from 81% to 87% in Germany, from 83% to 86% in France; and from 71% to 81% in Britain (Pew, "World Publics," 35; Pew, "American-Western," 11).

[177] Pew, "World Publics," 36. By 2011, two-thirds of Americans under age 30 said that homosexuality should be accepted (Pew, "American-Western," 11).

[178] Freeman, 40.

[179] Supplement to the *Winnipeg Free Press*, 20 September 2014, 1, 2, 6.

[180] McGill, 351, 299.

Sins against human rights do feel unforgivable, and certain humanist words function as argument-stoppers: "freedom," "rights," "respect," "non-discrimination," and "choice." Even those who *don't* treat the *Universal Declaration of Human Rights* as a sacred text almost always consider their own human rights as non-negotiable and fundamental to their human flourishing. Still, the emotional, blanket attachment to these argument-stoppers troubles people who don't fully share the humanist faith. Charles Taylor rightly cautions that it's important to argue about *which* choices, freedoms, and rights, and at what *cost*.[181] Nevertheless, the brain cannot reason fully without emotion,[182] and one wouldn't want to deny humanism its transcendence—Luc Ferry, to differentiate humanism from traditional faiths, speaks of "horizontal transcendence"[183]—as long as the wished-for transcendence is recognized as such and not smuggled in as common knowledge to silence dissenting voices.

Despite the importance of humanism as a compelling postmodern faith, when one looks for a conscious framing of the humanist grand narrative and its ethical foundations, the results sometimes feel disappointingly thin. The 1933 *Humanist Manifesto I* declared that the universe is self-existing, not created, and recommended that we quickly reconstitute "religious institutions, their ritualistic forms, ecclesiastical methods, and communal activities" along humanist lines.[184] The 2003 *Humanist Manifesto III*, however, drops such language—perhaps remembering Auguste Comte's abortive nineteenth-century humanist church with its worship of Humanity.[185] Paul Kurtz, a father of American humanism, struggled to articulate the reasons behind a humanist moral code. He understood that the universe described by science is indifferent to humans, but also felt that people would only be attracted to the "New Atheism" and "a self-reliant humanism" if humanism contained genuine ethical alternatives to religion. He knew which ideals he wanted to push—"a positive attitude towards

---

[181] Taylor, *Secular*, 478–9.

[182] In Antonio Damasio's patients who had severe damage to the ventromedial prefrontal cortex, their emotionality dropped down to nothing. They could still reason and even scored well on moral reasoning tests. However, they couldn't make appropriate decisions in everyday life and tended to alienate everyone around themselves (Haidt 25, 33–4).

[183] Taylor, *Secular*, 677.

[184] American Humanist Association, "Manifesto I."

[185] As long as Comte insisted that the world was progressing from fetishism to monotheism to positive science, he drew the interest of John Stuart Mill and George Eliot. But as soon as Comte tried to imagine a new church, his followers balked at the new and elaborate rituals. T. Davies, 28–9, Manuel and Manuel, 725–30. Taylor, *Secular*, 390.

life," "a safer, more productive, peaceful, and harmonious society," "a meaningful life of satisfaction, exuberance, and creative joy," "a kind of *natural cosmic piety*, stimulated by awe at the magnificence of nature," enlightened self-interest combined with a compassionate empathetic altruism and love. What he *didn't* know was how to get from the indifferent universe to humanist moral values. We should, he says, do good deeds not for God's sake but for their own sake.[186] But what could it possibly mean to do good deeds for the deeds' sake? In effect, this avoids the question of what we should do and why. He refers often to choice and free will, but rarely says why we should make one ethical choice and not another.

To explicate the humanist response, Kurtz sets up six ethical quandaries. Here are some of them: "A married woman with two children falls passionately in love with a married man with children. Should they get divorced and remarry?" Harry Truman orders the nuclear bombing of Hiroshima—should the pilot obey? Dick Cheney approves of torture in order to prevent future terrorist attacks—should we permit this? Human rights or human flourishing can't help us here, and in each case, Kurtz fails to give guidelines for resolving the ethical dilemma: the love-struck mother will have to "weigh alternatives carefully;" meanings "vary from person to person;" certain rights are "widely accepted." Even after invoking the Geneva Convention, he can come to no conclusion about Truman's bomb and Cheney's "enhanced" interrogations. Rather, he says, "We need to take into account the values that we cherish and the moral (and/or legal) principles that we believe we are constrained to follow." If we start creating designer babies, we should "only develop those talents that we consider morally worthwhile." Such banal replies teeter on the shifting moral perspectivalism that Smith criticized in Millennial adults. This isn't surprising, in light of Kurtz's statement, "I can find no ontological foundation for ethics." In only one of the six quandaries—"a suffering relative pleads with you to assist him in committing suicide"—does Kurtz take a position that is defensible on humanist grounds. Given the humanist goods of bodily integrity and individual freedom, it follows that physician-assisted death ought to be permitted. But in his response, Kurtz begs the question, saying, "Humane societies will permit active euthanasia."[187] The logical circularity of "humane" is not surprising if humanism is an emotional, faith-like, grand narrative, not just a reasoned response to ethical quandaries.

[186] Kurtz, 20, 15, 227, 248, 228, 249, 192, 232. Kurtz's emphasis.
[187] Kurtz, 208, 247, 216–7, 209–10, 245, 240, 209.

Case Study: Humanist Chaplain Bart Campolo

The shift towards a humanist faith is exemplified in popular Christian minister and social activist Tony Campolo's humanist son, Bart Campolo. As a young man, Bart Campolo followed his father into the Christian ministry, and when, after 15 years, Campolo's small inner-city ministry in Philadelphia expanded into other cities, he left it to start over in Cincinnati—he wanted to serve individual poor people in a relational ministry rather than to head the organization. His de-conversion happened slowly, over 30 years, on a variety of fronts: the hard rational questions that modernity asks religion were amplified by disillusioning personal experiences. Early on, a young mother, Shonda, rebuffed Campolo's attempts to convert her, revealing to him that she had been gang-raped at age 9. Since God was both all-powerful and all-good, her Sunday School teacher informed her, He must have allowed the attack in order to bring about some future good. Although Campolo didn't recognize the modernist philosophical problem of evil, he understood, in his gut, the profound threat that her case posed to God's sovereignty. His sense that poverty and other ravaging social circumstances prevented people from being good made him doubt the free will that seemed necessary for conversion to a Christian lifestyle. He increasingly doubted the authority of the scriptures when he realized that his homosexual friends were simply oriented differently, not more sinful than he was. He didn't understand why God could only save humans by slaughtering Jesus on the cross, and he became enchanted with the process of evolution, attitudes that were supported by his reading of the new atheists, especially Sam Harris. Other pressures on his faith, also arising from modernity, took most of their force, however, from postmodern individualism: his impulse to affirm the goodness in people made him distrust the notion that humans are inherently depraved by original sin. But the final straw that converted Campolo to humanism came in 2011, when he lost control of his bicycle and crashed headlong into a tree. For a month, he wasn't himself—suffering headaches, unable to concentrate, crying often, and becoming angry over small things. Although his recovery made him love life intensely, he recognized that he was mortal without reprieve, that his *soul* was mortal, and that when his brain died, he would disappear forever.[188]

---

[188] Campolo and Campolo, 18, 14–5, 17, 93–5, 24, 94, 19–22.

Since Campolo's Christian parents had always disciplined him not in terms of absolute rules but in terms of the *harm* his wrongdoing did to others, taking God out of the equation was a logical next step. Like Steven Pinker, Campolo argues that the universe is indifferent to us, and that morality arises in the relationship of one human being to another, while God and Jesus are projections of our own, human ideals. When Campolo finally acknowledged his humanism, he thought, "Holy mackerel! Evangelizing people to love, justice, and community is going to be a whole lot easier now that I don't have to convince them to buy a whole set of unbelievable Iron Age myths at the same time!" He eventually became the first Humanist Chaplain at the University of Southern California, where he now attempts to foster community and bring pastoral care to people interested in a secular spirituality.[189] Unlike the individualists who call themselves "spiritual but not religious," Campolo works through a community.

Campolo's journey reveals the strengths and also the limits of humanism as a grand narrative. In his "Humanize Me" podcast, he says that his moral basis ultimately boils down to a gut-level love of sentient life and human flourishing, but he recognizes that the notion of human flourishing is too broad and is interpreted too variously to be a reliable moral guide.[190] More debilitating, the free-rider problem that appears in all faiths is amplified in humanism. Like Dawkins, Campolo thinks that good deeds done without a sense that God is watching are somehow purer and more praiseworthy,[191] yet, as we've seen, atheists feel less tied to traditional virtues, while religious people tend to have better life outcomes in terms of risk behaviours, depression, health, work, relationships, and education. It may be that fearing God's displeasure makes self-control easier, while fuller social relationships, which are built by church attendance, contribute both to the knowledge that others are watching and to a sense of communal happiness. Talking to other post-Christians, Campolo finds that they don't miss the Ten Commandments, the Great Commission, or Jesus's substitutionary death; what they miss is the singing, the potluck dinners, and the meetings with their friends every week to inspire each other. It may be easy for Campolo to gather together college-aged people who, away from home and losing their faith, seek a like-minded commu-

---

[189] Campolo and Campolo, 106, 132, 112, 93, 24, 65–6.

[190] Bart Campolo, Humanize Me Podcast, Humanize Me 320, "Where do You Get Your Morality? https://bartcampolo.org/humanizeme.

[191] Campolo and Campolo, 109.

nity, but, in the teeth of an indifferent universe, it has proven far more difficult to establish such communities on a wider basis. Campolo seems to recognize the limits of his new faith when he says that humanism has the most majestic and truest narrative, but that, "we haven't yet learned how to make it sing."[192]

* * *

It's the indifferent universe that haunts the most persuasive expressions of the humanist grand narrative. In Ian McEwan's *The Children Act* (2014), a 17-year-old Jehovah's Witness, Adam Henry, invites a martyr's death rather than accept a blood transfusion (which would mediate the drugs necessary to counteract his leukaemia), but Judge Fiona Maye grants the hospital the right to transfuse, against Adam's and his parents' wishes. What blindsides Adam is his parents' subsequent tears of joy. They had obeyed God's hard command, and yet they received their son back alive. Adam interprets their thoughts: "Blame the judge, blame the godless system, blame what we sometimes call 'the world.' What a relief."[193] There is initially something self-congratulatory here on the part of the humanist author McEwan in that Adam's martyrdom becomes a drama of self-exaltation rather than a yearning for transcendent values, and in that Adam quickly repudiates *Bible*, God, and Kingdom Hall, nominates Fiona as the adult in the room because of her rational humanism, and begs to live with her. Of course, reason and humanism have no better answers than do Jehovah's Witnesses to the impossible question, "Why is there something instead of nothing?" Nevertheless, as a metaphor for the many secular conversions in our day, Adam's trajectory from the Witnesses to Yeats, Berryman, and Mahler makes sense.

To McEwan's credit, he is honest enough not to turn Fiona into a humanist saint. She refuses to let Adam live with her. Moreover, the indifferent universe had terrorized her humanism during an earlier court case, when, also against the parents' religious principles, she allowed a viable Siamese twin, Mark, to be separated from his unviable twin Matthew, in effect saving Mark by condemning Matthew to death. Sex with her husband Jack became difficult after that. So did sleep: "While Jack at her side quietly snored, she seemed to peer over a cliff edge. She saw in the remem-

---

[192] Campolo and Campolo, 62–3, 70.
[193] McEwan, *Children*, 144.

bered pictures of Matthew and Mark a blind and purposeless nullity."
Later, she finds Jack's summary of a geology lecture equally oppressive—
"the weight of meaningless time"—as she imagines a future geologist
scraping through the six inches into which our civilization, cities, roads,
and maybe a few bones have been compressed. Even Mahler proves inadequate. McEwan's reply, after Adam's renewed and wasteful martyrdom,
is Fiona's and Jack's muted but tender reconciliation, and Fiona's acknowledgement that, against all professional judgement, she should have let
Adam live with them: "Adam came looking for her and she offered nothing in religion's place, no protection, even though the Act was clear, her
paramount consideration was his welfare."[194] Here, McEwan defends The
Children Act as a secular, individualist, and loving piece of humanist legislation, but he coordinates this public and morally *inexpensive* expression of
humanism with the private and *costly* deontological demand made on
Fiona, a demand that in the past was the province of religiously motivated
self-sacrifice. McEwan clearly desires it as an expression of humanist faith,
but he seems to recognize that, without a transcendent reward, such sacrifices become less likely, pitting, as they do, the happiness of one individual merely against the happiness of another. This certainly doesn't
negate the value of humanism in public institutions but it suggests the
limits of humanism as a meaning-giving ethic.

Attempts to articulate the assumptions behind the humanist grand narrative stress the value of the individual by invoking one of Kant's categorical imperatives. Kurtz says, "We should always consider persons as ends in
themselves and never as merely a means to an end."[195] The *Humanist
Manifesto III*, signed in 2003 by E.O. Wilson, Richard Dawkins, and 22
Nobel laureates among others, sounds a similar Kantian note: "Ethical
values are derived from human need and interest as tested by experience.
Humanists ground values in human welfare shaped by human circumstances, interests, and concerns and extended to the global ecosystem and
beyond. We are committed to treating each person as having inherent
worth and dignity, and to making informed choices in a context of freedom consonant with responsibility."[196] The humanist grand narrative and
its empathic identifications are evoked whenever an audience is made to

---

[194] McEwan, *Children*, 26, 31, 184, 220.

[195] Kurtz, 229.

[196] American Humanist Association, "Humanist Manifesto III," 2003, http://american-
humanist.org/Humanism/Humanist_Manifesto_III.

live for a while inside the skin of someone of little or no caste, from the gauche outsiders of *Napoleon Dynamite* (2004), to the overweight African-American teen in *Precious* (2009), to the transsexual woman Bree in *Transamerica* (2005). The fundamental dignity of every human being guides the audience's emotional reaction.

Humanism's strong individualist basis often prevents it from being seen as a grand narrative—it often looks like a small narrative, centred on one group of victims or another—but in the humanist grand narrative, these victims stand in for all of us. We see this in genocide films such as *Schindler's List* (1993), *The Pianist* (2002), *Ararat* (2002), *Hotel Rwanda* (2004), and *Fugitive Pieces* (2007), and in films showing systematic human rights abuse, such as *El secreto de sus ojos* (2009; *The Secret in Their Eyes*), which depicts Argentina's Dirty War. The humanist faith requires right action, not purity or ritual, so that someone as conflicted as Oskar Schindler may indeed become a humanist saint.

Steven Spielberg's more ambivalent *Munich* (2005) shows Mossad agents assigned to murder the Palestinian murderers of 11 Israeli Olympic athletes. The agents struggle between a small narrative (oriented only towards Jews) and a humanist narrative (oriented broadly towards human rights). Tony Kushner and Eric Roth's screenplay questions not so much the lack of due legal process for the Palestinian terrorists, as the collateral civilian casualties. Predictably, the Zionist Organization of America, with its small-narrative focus on what is good for Israel, called for a boycott of *Munich* because it humanized the Palestinian terrorists and supposedly dehumanized Israelis.[197] Actually, the terrorists were depicted much more critically than the Israelis were. The ZOA wanted what Spielberg had offered in *Saving Private Ryan* (1998), where the small narrative triumphs: whatever is good for America is morally good. In *Schindler's List*, because of the unambiguous nature of the Nazi evil and its huge scope, it was reasonable to equate human lives with Jewish lives. However, given the more difficult ethical problem of Palestine, Kushner and Roth sought a larger humanist frame of reference, refusing to favour small-narrative moral self-congratulation.

---

[197] Morton Klein, "ZOA: Don't See Spielberg's 'Munich' Unless You Like Humanizing Terrorists and Dehumanizing Israelis," Zionist Organization of America, 27 December 2005, http://zoa.org/2005/12/102082-zoa-dont-see-spielbergs-munich-unless-you-like-human-izing-terrorists-dehumanizing-israelis/.

In non-Western worldviews, too, humanism seems to have made significant gains. A major factor in the huge popularity of the novels *The Kite Runner* (2003) and *A Thousand Splendid Suns* (2007) was Khaled Hosseini's personalization of the human rights narrative. The protagonists witness a textbook list of human rights abuses—racial prejudice, religious totalitarianism, sexual oppression, gender inequality, illegal confinement, lack of due process—but can do little about them. In a more complex way, the characters in Mo Yan's *Frog* (2009) respond to an official Chinese ideology that uses humanism to buttress the ethical value of the Chinese Revolution. When the hospital administration wants to expel the severely injured Chen Bi, one of his friends demands of the nurse, "Is a humanistic spirit alien to you people?" The nurse responds, "I only work here. If you people are flush with humanistic spirit, then pay his medical bills. I think our director would reward each of you with a plaque that says: Model Humanist." If at such a moment it's difficult to tell whether Yan is advocating or satirizing humanism, later on, the case is simpler when the narrator Tadpole finally has a surrogate child, and experiences "the most solemn feeling a human can know – the love of life." This is underscored thematically by the clay dolls, by the photos of babies at the surrogacy clinic, and by all of the tragedies that China's one-child policy causes throughout the novel, as necessary as that policy seems to Tadpole and possibly even to Yan. The one thing that Tadpole can't forgive himself for is the death of his first wife Renmei and her child because of his willingness to go along with the government's policy. He tries to console himself with the notion that the surrogate child is a reincarnation of that earlier foetus, but fails: "I understand... that I was not just the chief culprit, but the only one.... Every child is unique, irreplaceable."[198]

Whether fully expressed in contemporary political arrangements or not, humanism rests on an ideology of equality and on a valuing of individual humans as ends. Humanism turns claims about human rights into an emotional declaration of a creed that sometimes supersedes and sometimes reorients previous faiths. If the new faith isn't always held consciously, the evidence in film and literature suggests that it is growing, and that in the postmodern era, it is now a faith, alongside tradition, selective adherence, and pluralist adaptation, that gives meaning and motivates people to act charitably outside of their individual or group interests.

[198] Yan, 281, 303, 321.

CHAPTER 8

Conclusion

Are we postmodern yet? As both the structure and the content of this book have argued, the question cannot be answered on the general level. In terms of factual truth, the answer is unequivocal: we are not postmodern and never were. Strong forms of postmodernist relativism have proven to be self-contradictory and unworkable. Despite fake news, our propensity to skew the truth on behalf of our group, and the popularity of "multiple knowledges" (the unconsidered version of pluralism), we still, as always, place a premium on factual truth. Yet, in many areas of ethics, the issues are far more vexed. Since we neither agree on values nor rely on power to enforce an agreement, and since we have collectively begun to treat this disagreement not as a tragedy but as an irreducible fact of the human condition, we are indeed postmodern. We have rightly granted greater freedom to the individual to the point that pluralism has become a cardinal value. This is a postmodern condition, and we haven't left it behind, even though the most fashionable commentators are less apt to use the term "postmodern" anymore.

According to Charles Taylor, we try to authorize our own values, and this raises a difficult question: "Can the values we take as binding really be invented?"[1] One answer would be to say that we've always invented values. But an important thread of this book has been to insist that our values are rarely *self*-authorized, since many of them arise out of our primate evolution and many we hammer out together in political, juridical, and faith

---

[1] Taylor, *Secular*, 588–9.

© The Author(s) 2019
R. Kramer, *Are We Postmodern Yet?*,
https://doi.org/10.1007/978-3-030-30569-7_8

groups. Our evolved human psychology operates in particular ways that have never been postmodern: certain ethical principles (such as reciprocal altruism or preferential treatment of kin) apply so strictly that, even across very diverse cultures, we must speak of human universals. The most we can do, in this regard, is to structure our societies—by means of faith, government, law, and social practices—to make room for the benefits of our evolved psychology and to rationally limit it in areas where it does real harm. On a practical level, our wide agreement on basic elements of human rights across diverse constituencies makes us both postmodern and, at the same time, very un-postmodern. The human rights attack on earlier grand narratives is a pluralist, individualist, and therefore a *postmodern* attack, yet the resulting agreement about human rights arrives at a new and mutually comprehensible grand narrative—not so postmodern—on which basis ethical negotiations can occur and contracts be imagined.

The difficulty of finding a single coherent answer to the title's question is repeated in other contexts. Ethical uncertainty has opened the way to a desirable postmodern individualism, as we find less and less reason to think that the individual should be sacrificed to the dictates of the group. Although I've detailed some of the shortcomings of individualist How-I-Feel ethics throughout the book, it's important to remember that the widening circle of sympathy began with feelings, not just reason, and would eventually issue in children's rights and animal rights. With the exaltation of the individual's freedom and personal feelings to a central ethical good, even traditionalists have become more self-indulgent, as I've argued. Yet individualism will also bite us if we don't recover or invent structural—un-postmodern—ways to limit self-indulgence and to ensure that we don't drop our familial and human responsibilities. As nations, we are only beginning to build a multilateral global culture in which the international rule of law (and other sovereignty-limiting structures) are absolutely essential for human flourishing and social justice. As with the individual, so, too, with the nation: the person-to-person postmodern ethical dilemma is magnified exponentially when whole societies assert their sovereignty at others' expense, and can't negotiate a fair relationship.

As well, despite how much some of our traditional social structures are replicated online, our cyber-culture is highly postmodern in facilitating pluralism and in favouring simulation, isolation, and emotion over bodily presence, community, and reason. Cyber-culture forces us to recognize that our simulations always were postmodern—that film, fiction, writing, even speech already had a postmodern quality in that they replace things and deeds with mere signs. The first-century writer of the apocryphal *1 Enoch* said, "Men were not created for such a purpose, to give confirmation to their good faith with pen and ink."[2] On the contrary, we *were* made for this—this neocortical hunger for the unreal—but not *only* for this.

In the late twentieth century, when postmodernism was academic high fashion, it seemed to some of its defenders, and to many of its traditionalist and modernist detractors, to be a synonym for relativism. But relativism was never a good description for how most people, including postmodernists, actually operated. To equate postmodernity with relativism is very quickly to reach the *cul de sac* of ego-based narratives or small narratives. Particularly when we ask *others* to do things, we attach ourselves to some larger narrative, whether that narrative looks back to a traditional faith or ahead to a new home in humanism or both at once. Taylor delineates how the modern shift towards secularity has involved the validation of human desire against ascetic or "higher" goals, but he also identifies an important caveat that is confirmed by our human quest for meaning: without "higher" goals, we feel "the emptiness of the repeated, accelerating cycle of desire and fulfillment," to the point at which everyday desire comes to seem terribly flat.[3] This is indeed a postmodern problem. Even humanists seek a larger, universal meaning that they frame in a "horizontal transcendence." The more complex inheritors of modernity, such as Steven Pinker, have recognized that, as important as reason is, we are only able to make the kinds of moral determinations that are necessary to make if we do so through what Taylor calls a "constitutive good,"[4] what others have called a grand narrative. Against the trumpeting of the early prophets of postmodernism, we do, indeed, continue to agree on truth and human rights. So does the contemporary era really inject enough ontological uncertainties, conceptual simulations, technological advances, and changed practices to call postmodernity a new historical period? My answer has been a qualified yes. At the moment that we demand a place at the table where social contracts are negotiated, postmodernity rightly asks us to put our larger meanings and grand narratives in brackets as we take the interests and the good of others into consideration. Cultural conditions have changed on too many fronts—ethics, understandings of the individual,

[2] *1 Enoch* 69:10. R.H. Charles, ed., *The Apocrypha and Pseudepigrapha of the Old Testament*, Vol. 2 (1913), Berkeley, CA: Apocryphile Press, 2004.

[3] Taylor, *Secular*, 253, 406, 309.

[4] Taylor, *Sources*, 92–5.

cyber-simulations, national sovereignty, and faith—to speak of a straight-forward and unbroken continuation of modernity.

If postmodernity referred mainly to theorists such as Foucault and Rorty who in various ways declared that relativism reigned over morality and even knowledge, then it would be necessary, as some scholars have done, to speak about "post-postmodernism."[5] Yes, there is a "Post-postmodernism" *Wikipedia* page, but if, as I have argued, postmodernity consists of the various cultural expressions that arise when grand narratives decline and when we agree to disagree about ethical foundations, it becomes much more difficult to speak of "post-postmodernity," because no culture or group or philosophy has surmounted or solved this disagreement. We are clearly beyond "postmodern*ism*," the relativist philosophy that we never really adhered to, but not beyond "postmodernity," the historical era of which postmodernism is a symptom. We can speak of *returns* to tradition or to modernity, and we can speak of ways in which we've attempted to *address* the postmodern condition—procedurally through contractarianism, ethically and existentially through humanism, selective adherence, and pluralist adaptation—but there is no evidence of a "post-postmodern" consensus.

$$*\quad*\quad*$$

Where this line of history will take us, no one knows. In one of his most evocative phrases, Nietzsche said, "Since Copernicus, we have been drifting towards X."[6] Scott Durham celebrates a kind of soft apocalypse, what he sees as a postmodern dissolution of the world into appearances—the Nietzschean moment that the artist finds himself free of "the vengeful and moralizing judgments of the 'truthful man.'" The truthful man, also known as the philosopher, tries to pass judgement on the image "as a truthful or deceptive representation, which either reaffirms or subverts the

---

[5] Jeffrey Nealon, with some wit, defends his indefensible title, *Post-Postmodernism* (2012). Jeremy Green speaks of *Late Postmodernism* (2005), and many scholars have named their books "After Postmodernism." Already in 1990, scholars who wanted to be part of the next new thing were asking the question-begging question, "What was postmodernism?" (McHale, *Cambridge*, 3; McHale, "What Was"). Apparently, Alan Wilde used the word "post-postmodern" as early as 1976 (Burn, *Franzen*, 17).

[6] "Ever since Copernicus man has been rolling down an incline, faster and faster, away from the center—whither?" Nietzsche, *Genealogy*, 291. It's unclear who had the brilliant idea of loosely translating the unknown destination as "X."

founding truths of the prevailing order of things."[7] What Durham fails to consider is that merely in *living*, we (and artists no less than philosophers) make moralizing judgements all the time. My car is for sale. As the seller, I must decide whether to reveal the truth about its engine difficulties or not. The Canadian federal government institutes a carbon tax; several provinces challenge the tax. As voters, we cannot help but judge whether the tax represents an unnecessary intrusion into our economic lives or a true accounting of what must be done to avert global warming. It's not only Durham's "truthful" straw man who makes the moralizing judgement, but everyone who chooses to buy a particular product or not, to surrender to the aura of particular movie or not, to laugh at a particular joke or not, to let one's feelings decide a particular moral question or not.

Thinking about the many benefits given and many wounds inflicted by postmodern changes, it would be highly reductive to speak of postmodernity as simply a good or bad development. I've argued that our lives are several layers deep, in that we haven't abandoned our evolutionary past, our faith traditions, or the lessons of scientific modernity. We've accumulated worldviews, a sort of cultural neocortex. It's impossible to limit our evolutionary biases and to maintain individual virtues without some form of tradition—How-I-Feel is unreliable. Yet it's impossible to maintain human rights without some form of modernist reason that strictly limits tradition. In other words, we still rely on tradition and modernity, but in a more sceptical, postmodern way.

As a species, we are doing something complicated and historically new, and we all have a stake in how the experiment turns out. We could try to abandon the older layers and keep only the most recent layer of individualism, but what if we're living off the moral equity of previous generations? We have no way of knowing if that's so until we arrive in the future. If, as Norbert Elias, Steven Pinker, and Charles Taylor in various ways have argued, "civilized government and rule of law" are "external expressions of a certain mode of self-discipline,"[8] then a too-indulgent form of individual freedom could threaten the very institutions and human rights codes that allow *individualism* to flourish. Speaking about perception, film theorists Barbara and Joseph Anderson say that information about changes to our environment allows us to assess which changes are in our

---

[7] Durham, 11, 19.
[8] Taylor, *Secular*, 394.

best interests.[9] This is the approach I've tried to take, a corrective, I hope, both to traditionalist accounts (that tend to complain about the direction of cultural change) and to postmodernist accounts (that tend to celebrate every change). Postmodernity involves a series of related, yet discrete changes and reactions to changes in the environment—often, though not exclusively the technological environment. We have been drifting towards X: there is no pre-given diagnostic tool that will tell us whether a particular change—screen immersion or the WTO—will ultimately be for good or for ill, but by understanding the dangers and successes of our recent practices, we may be able to keep civility alive. We must evaluate each change by itself, and our best approaches to the changes will be at least four layers deep—involving our evolutionary psychology, tradition, modernity, and postmodernity.[10] And that's a good thing.

[9] Anderson and Anderson, 351.
[10] McHale, "What Was."

WORKS CITED

Achouche, Mehdi. 2014. The Technological Utopia in Hollywood: The Surrogate as Contemporary Paradigm for Post-Humanity in Surrogates (2009) and Gamer (2009). *Visions of Humanity in Cyberculture, Cyberspace and Science Fiction.* Ninth Global Conference, Mansfield College, Oxford, July 15.

Ackerman, Rakefet, and Morris Goldsmith. 2011. Metacognitive Regulation of Text Learning: On Screen Versus on Paper. *Journal of Experimental Psychology: Applied* 17 (1): 18–32.

Ahmed, Akbar S. Postmodernism and Islam: Where to After September 11? In Goulimari, 140–5.

Allen, John S. 2009. *The Lives of the Brain.* Cambridge, MA: Belknap Press.

Alter, Adam. 2017. *Irresistible: The Rise of Addictive Technology and the Business of Keeping Us Hooked.* New York: Penguin.

American Humanist Association. 1933. Humanist Manifesto I. *The New Humanist.* http://americanhumanist.org/Humanism/Humanist_Manifesto_I

———. 2003. Humanism and Its Aspirations: Humanist Manifesto III. http://www.americanhumanist.org/Humanism/Humanist_Manifesto_III

Anderson, Benedict. 1983, 1991. *Imagined Communities.* London: Verso.

Anderson, Perry. 1998. *The Origins of Postmodernity.* London: Verso.

Anderson, Joseph, and Barbara Anderson. 1996. The Case for an Ecological Metatheory. In *Post-Theory,* ed. David Bordwell and Noël Carroll, 347–367. Madison: University of Wisconsin Press.

Andrejevic, Mark. 2013. *Infoglut.* New York: Routledge.

Angus Reid Institute (with contributions from Reginald Bibby). 2015. Religion and Faith in Canada Today: Strong Belief, Ambivalence and Rejection Define Our Views. www.angusreid.org/faith-in-canada/

© The Author(s) 2019
R. Kramer, *Are We Postmodern Yet?*,
https://doi.org/10.1007/978-3-030-30569-7

Ansari, Aziz, and Eric Klinenberg. 2015. *Modern Romance*. New York: Penguin.

Argyros, Alexander. 1991. *A Blessed Rage for Order: Deconstruction, Evolution, and Chaos*. Ann Arbor: University of Michigan Press.

Atwood, Margaret. 2003. *Oryx and Crake*. Toronto: Random House.

———. 2009. *The Year of the Flood*. Toronto: McClelland & Stewart.

———. 2013. *Maddaddam*. Toronto: McClelland & Stewart.

———. 2015. *On the Planet of Speculative Fiction*. Interviewed by Synne Rifbjerg, Louisiana Literature Festival, Louisiana Museum of Modern Art, Denmark, August 2014, published on March 3. https://www.youtube.com/watch?v=aOWYdX50qQc

Badiou, Alain. 2013. *Philosophy and the Event*. With Fabien Tarby. 2010. Trans. Louise Burchill. Malden: Polity.

Baglo, Ferdy. 1999. Canadian Bishop Blocks Asian Church Leader from Visiting His Diocese. *Christianity Today*, November 1. http://www.christianitytoday.com/ct/1999/novemberweb-only/41.0d.html

Baker, Raymond, and Eva Joly. 2009. Illicit Money: Can It Be Stopped? *New York Review of Books*, December 3. http://www.nybooks.com/articles/2009/12/03/illicit-money-can-it-be-stopped/

Balbuena, L., M. Baetz, and R. Bowen. 2013. Religious Attendance, Spirituality, and Major Depression in Canada: A 14-Year Follow-Up Study. *Canadian Journal of Psychiatry* 58 (4): 225–232.

Ball, James. 2017. *Post-Truth: How Bullshit Conquered the World*. London: Biteback.

Barber, Benjamin. 2007. *Consumed*. New York: W.W. Norton.

Barbetta, Gian Paolo, Paolo Canino, and Stefano Cima. 2019. *Let's Tweet Again? The Impact of Social Networks on Literature Achievement in High School Students: Evidence from a Randomized Controlled Trial*. Dipartimento di Economia e Finanza, Università Cattolica del Sacro Cuore, Working Paper Series, n. 81, May.

Bass, Diana Butler. 2012. *Christianity After Religion*. New York: HarperCollins.

Baudrillard, Jean. 1994. *Simulacra and Simulations* (1981). Trans. Sheila Glaser. Ann Arbor: University of Michigan Press.

———. 2001. *Selected Writings*. 2nd ed. Edited by Mark Poster. Stanford: Stanford University Press.

Bauerlein, Mark. 2008. *The Dumbest Generation*. New York: Penguin.

Bauman, Zygmunt. 1993. *Postmodern Ethics*. Oxford: Blackwell.

———. 1997. *Postmodernity and Its Discontents*. Cambridge: Polity.

———. 2000. *Liquid Modernities*. Cambridge: Polity.

———. 2004. *Wasted Lives: Modernity and Its Outcasts*. Cambridge: Polity.

———. 2008. *Does Ethics Have a Chance in a World of Consumers?* Cambridge, MA: Harvard University Press.

Bauman, Zygmunt, and Keith Tester. On the Postmodernism Debate. In Goulimari, 22–31.

Beatty, Paul. 2015. *The Sellout*. New York: Farrar, Straus and Giroux.

Beck, Ervin. 2012. David Foster Wallace Among the Mennonites. *CMW Journal* (Center for Mennonite Writing) 4: 6. http://www.mennonitewriting.org/journal/4/6/david-foster-wallace-among-mennonites/#page1

Bellamy, Alex J., and Paul D. Williams. 2010. *Understanding Peacekeeping*. 2nd ed. Malden: Polity Press.

Beller, Mara. 1998. The Sokal Hoax: At Whom Are We Laughing? *Physics Today* 51: 9. (Ebscohost, 25 May 1999, 10p).

Bergen, David. 1996. *A Year of Lesser*. Toronto: HarperCollins.

———. 2006. And You Arrive on the Other Side with Nothing. In *Writing Life*, ed. Constance Rooke. Toronto: McClelland & Stewart.

———. 2010. *The Matter with Morris*. Toronto: HarperCollins.

Bertens, Hans. 1995. *The Idea of the Postmodern: A History*. New York: Routledge.

Bérubé, Michael. 2006a. *Rhetorical Occasions*. Chapel Hill: University of North Carolina Press.

———. 2006b. *What's Liberal about the Liberal Arts? Classroom Politics and "Bias" in Higher Education*. New York: W.W. Norton.

Best, Steven, and Douglas Kellner. 1997. *The Postmodern Turn*. New York: Guilford Press.

———. 2001. *The Postmodern Adventure: Science, Technology, and Cultural Studies at the Third Millennium*. London: Routledge.

Bethune, Brian. 2014. The End of Neighbors. *Maclean's*, 40–43, August 18.

Bibby, Reginald. 2009. *The Emerging Millennials*. Lethbridge: Project Canada.

Binks, Andrew. 2013. *Strip*. Gibsons: Nightwood.

Borges, Jorge Luis. 1964. *Labyrinths*. New York: New Directions.

Borrows, John. 2010. *Canada's Indigenous Constitution*. Toronto: University of Toronto Press.

Boyd, Andrew. 1999. *Life's Little Deconstruction Book*. New York: Norton.

Boyd, Brian. 2009. *On the Origin of Stories: Evolution, Cognition, and Fiction*. Cambridge, MA: Belknap Press.

Brockman, John, ed. 2011. *Is the Internet Changing the Way You Think?* New York: HarperCollins.

Browne, Rachel. 2015. Welcome to the Future of Reading. *Maclean's*, 86–88, January 5.

Burn, Stephen. 2008. *Jonathan Franzen at the End of Postmodernism*. New York: Continuum.

Campolo, Tony, and Bart Campolo. 2017. *Why I Left, Why I Stayed*. New York: HarperCollins.

Carr, Nicholas. 2010. *The Shallows: What the Internet Is Doing to Our Brains*. New York: Norton.

Carroll, John. Zygmunt Bauman – Mortality and Culture. In Jacobsen et al., 143–147.

Centers for Disease Control and Prevention (CDC). 2013. Youth Risk Behavior Surveillance – United States, 2013, 13 June 2014. *Surveillance Summaries* 63: 4. http://www.cdc.gov/healthyyouth/data/yrbs/results.htm

Chabon, Michael. 2007. *The Yiddish Policeman's Union*. New York: HarperCollins.

———. 2009. *Manhood for Amateurs*. New York: HarperCollins.

Charles, Sébastien. Paradoxical Individualism: An Introduction to the Thought of Gilles Lipovetsky. In Gilles Lipovetsky, *Hypermodern Times*.

Coen, Ethan, and Joel Coen. 1996. *Fargo* (screenplay). London: Faber & Faber.

Coggins, Jim. 2009. Review: Teenagers More Moral, Less Religious…, April 16. http://www.canadianchristianity.com/nationalupdates/090416survey.html

Cohen, Jean L. 2012. *Globalization and Sovereignty*. New York: Cambridge University Press.

Cole, Trevor. 2006. *The Fearsome Particles*. Toronto: McClelland & Stewart.

———. 2010. *Practical Jean*. Toronto: McClelland & Stewart.

Cole, Julie. 2012. Harder Named as Briercrest's 'Young Alumnus of the Year.' *Bcast*, April 3. http://briercrest.ca/bcast/news/article.aspx?id=1408&type=5

Cooper, Robert. 2003. *The Breaking of Nations*. Toronto: McClelland & Stewart.

Coupland, Douglas. 2009. *Generation A*. Toronto: Random House.

———. 2010. *Player One*, CBC Massey Lectures. Toronto: Anansi.

Davies, Tony. 2008. *Humanism*. 2nd ed. London: Routledge.

Davis, Phil. 2008. Is Google Making Us Stupid? Nope! *The Scholarly Kitchen*, June 16. http://scholarlykitchen.sspnet.org/2008/06/16/is-google-making-us-stupid-nope/, 9 June 2011.

Dawkins, Richard. 2006. *The God Delusion*. Boston: Houghton Mifflin.

de Waal, Frans. 1996. *Good-Natured: The Origins of Right and Wrong in Humans and Other Animals*. Cambridge, MA: Harvard University Press.

———. 2013. *The Bonobo and the Atheist: In Search of Humanism Among the Primates*. New York: Norton.

Deacy, Christopher. 2001. *Screen Christologies*. Cardiff: University of Wales Press.

Debord, Guy. 2005. *Society of the Spectacle* (1967). Trans. Ken Knabb. London: Rebel Press.

DeLillo, Don. 1997. *Underworld*. New York: Scribner.

DePaulo, Bella. 2015. *How We Live Now*. New York: Simon & Schuster.

Deresiewicz William. 2011. The Children's Hospital: On David Foster Wallace. *The Nation*, July 4–11. http://www.thenation.com/article/161456/childrens-hospital-david-foster-wallace, 15 June 2011.

Derrida, Jacques. 1970. Structure, Sign and Play in the Discourse of the Human Sciences (1967). In *The Structuralist Controversy*, ed. Richard Macksey and Eugenio Donato. Baltimore: Johns Hopkins University Press.

———. 1978. Structure, Sign and Play in the Discourse of the Human Sciences (1967). In *Writing and Difference*. Trans. Alan Bass. Chicago: University of Chicago Press.

———. 1974, 1997. *Of Grammatology* (1967). Trans. Gayatri Spivak. Baltimore: Johns Hopkins University Press.

Diamond, Larry, and Marc Plattner. 2015. *Democracy in Decline?* Baltimore: Johns Hopkins University Press.

Dosse, François. 1997. *History of Structuralism, Vol. 2, The Sign Sets, 1967-Present.* Trans. Deborah Glassman. Minneapolis: University of Minnesota Press.

Dostoyevsky, Fyodor. 1957. *The Brothers Karamazov* (1880). Trans. Constance Garnett. New York: Signet.

Douzinas, Costas. Human Rights in Postmodernity. In Goulimari, 50–73.

Durham, Scott. 1998. *Phantom Communities: The Simulacrum and the Limits of Postmodernism.* Stanford: Stanford University Press.

Dutton, Dennis. 2004. The Pleasures of Fiction. *Philosophy & Literature* 28: 453–466.

Egan, Jennifer. 2006. *The Keep.* New York: Random House.

———. 2010. *A Visit from the Goon Squad.* New York: Random House.

Eribon, Didier. 1991. *Michel Foucault* (1989). Trans. Betsy Wing. Cambridge, MA: Harvard University Press.

Esmaeili, Peyman. 2004. Interview w Stanislaw Lem. *Shargh*, July. http://www.lem.pl/cyberiadinfo/english/interview2/interview.htm. Accessed 7 Jan 2008.

Ferguson, Niall. 2004. *Colossus: The Rise and Fall of the American Empire.* New York: Penguin.

———. 2008. *The Ascent of Money.* New York: Penguin.

Fischer, Claude. 2011. *Still Connected: Family and Friends in America Since 1970.* New York: Russell Sage Foundation.

Flesch, William. 2007. *Comeuppance: Costly Signaling, Altruistic Punishment, and Other Biological Components of Fiction.* Cambridge, MA: Harvard University Press.

Foley, Sean, Jonathan Karlsen, and Tālis Putniņš. 2018. Sex, Drugs, and Bitcoin: How Much Illegal Activity Is Financed Through Cryptocurrencies? *Social Science Research Network* (SSRN), January. https://papers.ssrn.com/sol3/papers.cfm?abstract_id=3102645

Fortna, Virginia. 2008. *Does Peacekeeping Work? Shaping Belligerents' Choices After Civil War.* Princeton: Princeton University Press.

Fotion, Nick. 2000. *John Searle.* Princeton: Princeton University Press.

———. 2003. From Speech Acts to Speech Activity. In *John Searle*, ed. Barry Smith. Cambridge: Cambridge University Press.

Fotopoulos, Takis. 2016. *The New World Order in Action.* Vol. 1. San Diego: Progressive Press.

Foucault, Michel. 1965. *Madness and Civilization* (*Folie et déraison*, 1961). Trans. Richard Howard. New York: Random House.

———. 1970. *The Order of Things* (*Les mots et les choses*, 1966). New York: Random House.

———. 1984. *Discipline and Punish* (*Surveiller et Punir*, 1977). Trans. Alan Sheridan. *The Foucault Reader*. Edited by Paul Rabinow. New York: Pantheon.

Foy, Jeffrey E., and Richard J. 2008. Gerrig, "How Might Literature Do Harm?" *Style* (Summer–Fall): 175–178 (Academic OneFile, Web, 5 May 2010).

Franzen, Jonathan. 2010. *Freedom*. New York: Farrar, Straus, Giroux.

———. 2015. *Purity*. Toronto: Penguin Random House.

Freeman, Michael. 2011. *Human Rights*. 2nd ed. Cambridge: Polity.

Freitas, Donna. 2013. *The End of Sex*. New York: Basic Books.

Gaiman, Neil. 2013. *The Ocean at the End of the Lane*. New York: HarperCollins.

Gareis, Sven. 2012. *The United Nations: An Introduction*. 2nd ed. New York: Palgrave Macmillan.

Gartner, Zsuzsi, ed. 2010. *Darwin's Bastards*. Vancouver: Douglas & McIntyre.

———. 2011. *Better Living Through Plastic Explosives*. Toronto: Penguin.

Gatehouse, Jonathan. 2014. Over Our Heads. *Maclean's*, 46–48, September 15.

Gawande, Atul. 2014. *Being Mortal*. Toronto: Random House.

George, Lianne, and Steve Maich. 2009. It's All About You. *Maclean's*, 38–40, January 26.

Gillingham, John. 2016. *The EU: An Obituary*. London: Verso.

Gladwell, Malcolm. 2013. *David and Goliath*. New York: Little, Brown.

Gottschall, Jonathan, and David Sloan Wilson, eds. 2005. *The Literary Animal: Evolution and the Nature of Narrative*. Evanston: Northwestern University Press.

Goulimari, Pelagia, ed. 2007. Introduction. In *Postmodernism. What Moment?* Manchester: Manchester University Press.

Grant, Iain Hamilton. Postmodernism and Politics. In Sim, 25–36.

Greenberg, Anna. 2004. OMG! How Generation Y is Redefining Faith in the iPod Era. (Reboot, www.rebooters.net). http://www.civicyouth.org/PopUps/OMG.pdf

Greene, Joshua. 2013. *Moral Tribes: Emotion, Reason, and the Gap between Us and Them*. New York: Penguin.

Gregory, Brad. 2012. *The Unintended Reformation*. Cambridge, MA: Harvard University Press.

Grodal, Torben. 1997. *Moving Pictures: A New Theory of Film Genres, Feelings, and Cognition*. Oxford: Clarendon Press.

———. 2009. *Embodied Visions: Evolution, Emotion, Culture, and Film*. Oxford: Oxford University Press.

Grossberg, Lawrence. Affect and Postmodernity in the Struggle Over 'American Modernity.' In Goulimari, 176–201.

Haidt, Jonathan. 2012. *The Righteous Mind*. New York: Random House.

Hanhimäki, Jussi. 2015. *The United Nations: A Very Short Introduction*. New York: Oxford University Press.

Harris, Sam. 2010a. *The Moral Landscape*. New York: Simon & Schuster.

———. 2010b. Science Can Answer Moral Questions. *TedTalks*, February. https://www.ted.com/talks/sam_harris_science_can_show_what_s_right?language=en

Hart, David Bentley. 2003. *The Beauty of the Infinite: The Aesthetics of Christian Truth*. Grand Rapids: William B. Eerdmans.

Harvey, David. 1990. *The Condition of Postmodernity*. Cambridge, MA: Blackwell.

Hauser, Marc. 2006. *Moral Minds: How Nature Designed Our Universal Sense of Right and Wrong*. New York: HarperCollins.

Heath, Joseph. 2010. *Economics Without Illusions* (2009). New York: HarperCollins.

———. 2014a. *Enlightenment 2.0*. Toronto: HarperCollins.

———. 2014b. Reason Versus Passion in Politics. Big Thinking lecture, February 20. *Federation for the Humanities and Social Sciences*. http://www.youtube.com/watch?v=nWdbVB-sDpg&feature=share&list=UUirwy%2D%2DDhRDqgLIujCUY4VA

Heath, Joseph, and Andrew Potter. 2004. *The Rebel Sell*. Toronto: HarperCollins.

Hedges, Chris. 2009. *Empire of Illusion: The End of Literacy and the Triumph of Spectacle*. Toronto: Random House.

Hein, Grit, Giorgia Silani, Kerstin Preuschoff, C. Daniel Batson, and Tania Singer. 2010. Neural Responses to Ingroup and Outgroup Members' Suffering Predict Individual Differences in Costly Helping. *Neuron* 68: 149–160, http://www.sciencedirect.com/science/article/pii/S0896627310007208

Henderson, Bobby. 2006. *The Gospel of the Flying Spaghetti Monster*. New York: Random House. http://rpcmp.ru/canon/GOSPEL.pdf

Henrich, Joseph, Robert Boyd, Samuel Bowles, Colin Camerer, Ernst Fehr, Herbert Gintis, and Richard McElreath. 2001. In Search of Homo Economicus: Behavioral Experiments in 15 Small-Scale Societies. *American Economic Review* 91 (2): 73–78. Business Source Premier, EBSCOhost. Accessed 22 June 2017.

Hertz, Barry. 2014. The One Story That Could Save Your Life. *Maclean's*, 64, September 1.

Hill, Val. Postmodernism and Cinema. In Sim, 143–155.

Hobbes, Thomas. 1968. *Leviathan* (1651). Harmondsworth/Middlesex: Penguin.

Hoffecker, John F. 2011. *Landscape of the Mind: Human Evolution and the Archaeology of Thought*. New York: Columbia University Press.

Homer-Dixon, Thomas. 2001. *The Ingenuity Gap*. Toronto: Random House.

Hood, Bruce. 2012. *The Self Illusion*. Toronto: HarperCollins.

Hosseini, Khaled. 2007. *A Thousand Splendid Suns*. Toronto: Penguin.

Hungerford, Amy. 2010. *Postmodern Belief: American Literature and Religion Since 1960*. Princeton: Princeton University Press.

Hunt, Lynn. 2007. *Inventing Human Rights: A History*. New York: W.W. Norton.

Jacobsen, Michael, Sophia Marshman, and Keith Tester. 2007. *Bauman Beyond Postmodernity*. Aalborg: Aalborg University Press.

James, Carrie. 2014. *Disconnected: Youth, New Media, and the Ethics Gap.* Cambridge, MA: MIT Press.

Jameson, Fredric. 1991. *Postmodernism, or, the Cultural Logic of Late Capitalism.* Durham: Duke University Press.

———. 2001. Postmodernism and Consumer Society (1988). In *The Norton Anthology of Theory and Criticism,* ed. Vincent Leach, 1960–1974. New York: W.W. Norton.

Jedwab, Jack. 2012. In God We Canadians Trust? *Association for Canadian Studies and Leger Marketing,* April 11. http://www.acsaec.ca/pdf/polls/In%20 God%20Canadians%20Trust%20II.pdf

Jenkins, Philip. 2011. *The Next Christendom: The Coming of Global Christianity.* 3rd ed. New York: Oxford University Press.

Johnson, Denis. 2009. *Nobody Move.* Toronto: HarperCollins.

Joyce, Richard. 2006. *The Evolution of Morality.* Cambridge, MA: MIT Press.

Keen, Suzanne. 2007. *Empathy and the Novel.* New York: Oxford University Press.

Kellner, Douglas. 2016. *American Nightmare: Donald Trump, Media Spectacle, and Authoritarian Populism.* Rotterdam: Sense.

———. Reappraising the Postmodern: Novelties, Mapping and Historical Narratives. In Goulimari, 102–126.

King, Stephen D. 2013. *When the Money Runs Out: The End of Western Affluence.* New Haven: Yale University Press.

Kingston, Anne. 2014. Get Ready for Generation Z. *Maclean's,* 42–45, July 21.

———. 2016. Just Watch Me. *Maclean's,* 30–34, June 13.

Kirby, Alan. 2006. The Death of Postmodernism and Beyond. *Philosophy Now* 58 (November–December), 34–37. http://www.philosophynow.org/issues/58/ The_Death_of_Postmodernism_And_Beyond

———. 2009. *Digimodernism.* New York: Continuum.

Klinenberg, Eric. 2012. *Going Solo: The Extraordinary Rise and Surprising Appeal of Living Alone.* New York: Penguin.

Konrath, S., E. O'Brien, and C. Hsing. 2011. Changes in Dispositional Empathy in American College Students Over Time: A Meta-Analysis. *Personality and Social Psychology Review* 15 (2): 180–198.

Kross, Ethan, Philippe Verduyn, et al. 2013. Facebook Use Predicts Declines in Subjective Well-Being in Young Adults. *Plos One,* August 14. http://www. plosone.org/article/info%3Adoi%2F10.1371%2Fjournal.pone.0069841

Kurtz, Paul. 2013. *The Turbulent Universe.* New York: Prometheus.

Laland, Kevin, and Gillian Brown. 2002. *Sense and Nonsense: Evolutionary Perspectives on Human Behaviour.* Oxford: Oxford University Press.

Lane, Robert E. 2000. *The Loss of Happiness in Market Democracies.* New Haven: Yale University Press.

Lanier, Jaron. 2010. *You Are Not a Gadget.* New York: Random House.

Lehman, David. 1998. The Questions of Postmodernism. *Jacket*, 4, July. http://jacketmagazine.com/04/lehman-postmod.html

Lemert, Charles. 2005. *Postmodernism Is Not What You Think: Why Globalization Threatens Modernity*. Rev. ed. Boulder: Paradigm.

Lethem, Jonathan. 2009. *Chronic City*. New York: Random House.

Levinas, Emmanuel. 1969. *Totality and Infinity* (1961). Trans. Alphonso Lingis. Pittsburgh: Duquesne University Press.

Levine, George. 2006. *Darwin Loves You*. Princeton: Princeton University Press.

Lipovetsky, Gilles. 2005. *Hypermodern Times*. Trans. Andrew Brown Malden. Massachusetts: Polity.

Lipsky, David. 2010. *Although, of Course, You End Up Becoming yourself: A Road Trip with David Foster Wallace*. New York: Broadway.

Lofton, Kathryn. 2011. *Oprah: The Gospel of an Icon*. Berkeley: University of California Press.

Lunau, Kate. 2010. The Touch-Screen School. *MacLean's*, 59–61, January 30.

———. 2013. Building a Better Human. *Maclean's*, 46–52, October 21.

Lyotard, Jean François. 1984. *La Condition Postmoderne*. Paris: Les Editions de Minuit, 1979, *The Postmodern Condition*. Trans. Geoff Bennington and Brian Massumi. Minneapolis: University of Minnesota Press.

Maich, Steve, and Lianne George. 2009. *The Ego Boom*. Toronto: Key Porter.

Mangen, Anne, and Don Kuiken. 2014. Lost in an iPad: Narrative Engagement on Paper and Tablet. *Scientific Study of Literature* 4 (2): 150–177.

Mangen, Anne, Bente R. Walgermo, and Kolbjørn Brønnick. 2013. Reading Linear Texts on Paper Versus Computer Screen: Effects on Reading Comprehension. *International Journal of Educational Research* 58: 61–68, http://www.sciencedirect.com/science/article/pii/S0883035512001127.

Manuel, Frank, and Fritzie Manuel. 1979. *Utopian Thought in the Western World*. Cambridge, MA: Harvard University Press.

Martel, Yann. 2001. *The Life of Pi*. Toronto: Random House.

Marvit, Moshe Z. 2014. How Crowdworkers Became the Ghosts in the Digital Machine. *The Nation*, February 5 (24 Feb 2014 issue). https://www.the-nation.com/article/how-crowdworkers-became-ghosts-digital-machine/

Max, D.T. 2012. *Every Love Story Is a Ghost Story: A Life of David Foster Wallace*. New York: Viking.

McCarthy, Cormac. 2006. *The Road*. New York: Random House.

McCarthy, Tom. 2010. *C*. Toronto: Random House.

McClure, John A. 2007. *Partial Faiths: Post-Secular Fiction in the Age of Pynchon and Morrison*. Athens: University of Georgia Press.

McEwan, Ian. 2005. *Saturday*. Toronto: Random House.

———. 2007. *On Chesil Beach*. London: Random House.

———. 2014. *The Children Act*. Toronto: Penguin Random House.

———. 2016. *Nutshell*. Toronto: Alfred A. Knopf.

McGill, Robert. 2013. *Once We Had a Country*. Toronto: Knopf.

McGonigal, Kelly. 2012. *The Willpower Instinct*. New York: Penguin.

McGowan, John. They Might Have Been Giants. In Goulimari, 92–101.

McHale, Brian. 1987. *Pöstmodernist Fiction*. New York: Routledge.

———. 2007. What Was Postmodernism? *Electronic Book Review*, December 20. http://www.electronicbookreview.com/thread/fictionspresent/tense

———. 2015. *The Cambridge Introduction to Postmodernism*. New York: Cambridge University Press.

McKnight, Zoe. 2015. The Real Reason Crime Is Falling So Fast. *Maclean's*, 38–42, July 31.

McLaren, Brian. 2001. *A New Kind of Christian*. San Francisco: Jossey-Bass.

Meeker, Mary. 2014. *Internet Trends, 2014*. Code Conference, Kleiner Perkins, Caufield Byers. *Quartz*, May 28. https://qz.com/214307/mary-meeker-2014-internet-trends-report-all-the-slides/

———. 2018. *Internet Trends, 2018*. Kleiner Perkins, @ Code. *Quartz*, May 30. https://qz.com/1292515/mary-meekers-2018-kpcb-internet-trends-report-all-the-slides-plus-highlights/

Meredith, Martin. 2005. *The Fate of Africa*. New York: Perseus.

Miller, James. 1993. *The Passion of Michel Foucault*. New York: Doubleday.

Mistry, Rohinton. 1991. *Such a Long Journey*. Toronto: McClelland.

———. 2002. *Family Matters*. Toronto: McClelland.

Mitchell, David. 2004. *Cloud Atlas*. Toronto: Random House.

———. 2014. *The Bone Clocks*. Toronto: Random House.

Moody, Rick. 2010. *The Four Fingers of Death*. New York: Little, Brown.

Morozov, Evgeny. 2013. *To Save Everything, Click Here*. New York: PublicAffairs.

Morton, Timothy. 2013. *Hyperobjects: Philosophy and Ecology After the End of the World*. Minneapolis: University of Minnesota Press.

Moulthrop, Stuart. 1991. Essays in Postmodern Culture. In *You Say You Want a Revolution: Hypertext and the Laws of Media*, ed. Eyal Amiran and John Unsworth, 1993. Oxford: Oxford University Press.

Mounk, Yascha. 2018. *The People vs. Democracy*. Cambridge, MA: Harvard University Press.

Murphy, Jessica. 2015. Dirty, Viral Tricks. *Maclean's*, 28–29, April 27.

Myers, Tony. 2003. *Slavoj Žižek*. New York: Routledge.

NAEP (National Assessment of Educational Progress). 2013. Mathematics and Reading: Grade 12 Assessments. *Nation's Report Card*. http://nationsreport-card.gov/reading_math_g12_2013/#/. Accessed 2 July 2014.

NASE (National Association for Self-Esteem). 2010. *Self-Esteem*. http://www.self-esteem-nase.org/booster.php#. Accessed 5 June 2012.

Newton, K.M. Performing Literary Interpretation. In Waugh 475–485.

Niedzviecki, Hal. 2004. *Hello, I'm Special: How Individuality Became the New Conformity*. Toronto: Penguin.

Nietzsche, Friedrich. 1956. *The Birth of Tragedy* and *The Genealogy of Morals* (1870–1, 1887). Trans. Francis Golffing. Garden City/New York: Doubleday.

Nussbaum, Martha. 2004. Beyond 'Compassion and Humanity. In *Animal Rights: Current Debates and New Directions*, ed. Cass R. Sunstein and Martha Craven Nussbaum, 299–320. New York: Oxford University Press.

Ondaatje, Michael. 1992. *The English Patient*. Toronto: Random House.

Owen, Jesse J., Galena K. Rhoades, Scott M. Stanley, and Frank D. Fincham. 2010. 'Hooking Up' Among College Students: Demographic and Psychosocial Correlates. *Archives of Sexual Behavior* 39 (3): 653–663.

Packer, George. 2013. *The Unwinding: An Inner History of the New America*. New York: Farrar, Straus & Giroux.

Pamuk, Orhan. 2001. *My Name is Red* (1998). Trans. Erdağ Göknar. Knopf: New York.

Peron, Alcides. 2014. Virtuous War and UAVs: The Inhibition of the Friction and Trivialisation of Violence. *Visions of Humanity in Cyberculture, Cyberspace and Science Fiction*. Ninth Global Conference, Mansfield College, Oxford, July 14.

Pessl, Marisha. 2006. *Special Topics in Calamity Physics*. New York: Penguin.

———. 2013. *Night Film*. Toronto: Random House.

Pew Research Center. 2007a. How Young People View Their Lives, Futures and Politics: A Portrait of "Generation Next", January 9. http://www.people-press.org/files/legacy-pdf/300.pdf

———. 2007b. World Publics Welcome Global Trade – But Not Immigration. The Pew Global Attitudes Project, October 4. http://www.pewglobal.org/files/pdf/258.pdf

———. 2009a. Many Americans Mix Multiple Faiths (Pew Forum on Religion and Public Life), December 9. http://www.pewforum.org/2009/12/09/many-americans-mix-multiple-faiths/

———. 2009b. Scientific Achievements Less Prominent Than a Decade Ago. The Pew Research Center for the People and the Press, July 9. http://www.people-press.org/files/legacy-pdf/528.pdf

———. 2010a. The Decline of Marriage and the Rise of New Families. Pew Research Social and Demographic Trends, November 8. http://www.pewsocialtrends.org/files/2010/11/pew-social-trends-2010-families.pdf

———. 2010b. Millennials: A Portrait of Generation Next. Pew Research Social and Demographic Trends, February 24. http://www.pewsocialtrends.org/files/2010/10/millennials-confident-connected-open-to-change.pdf

———. 2011. The American-Western European Values Gap. Global Attitudes Project, November 17. http://www.pewglobal.org/files/2011/11/Pew-Global-Attitudes-Values-Report-FINAL-November-17-2011-10AM-EST1.pdf

———. 2014. Faith and Skepticism About Trade, Foreign Investment, September 16. http://www.pewglobal.org/files/2014/09/Pew-Research-Center-Trade-Report-FINAL-September-16-2014.pdf

———. 2018. Social Media Fact Sheet. Internet and Technology, February 5. https://www.pewinternet.org/fact-sheet/social-media/

Pew Research Center and Andrew Perrin. 2015. One-Fifth of Americans Report Going Online 'Almost Constantly', December 8. http://www.pewresearch.org/fact-tank/2015/12/08/one-fifth-of-americans-report-going-online-almost-constantly/#comments. Accessed 25 Apr 2016.

Piketty, Thomas. 2014. *Capital in the Twenty-First Century*. Trans. Arthur Goldhammer. Cambridge, MA: Harvard University Press.

Pinker, Steven. 1994. *The Language Instinct*. New York: HarperCollins.

———. 2011. *The Better Angels of Our Nature: Why Violence Has Declined*. New York: Penguin.

———. 2018. *Enlightenment Now: The Case for Reason, Science, Humanism, and Progress*. New York: Penguin Random House.

Pinker, Susan. 2014. *The Village Effect*. Toronto: Random House.

Powers, Richard. 2009. *Generosity: An Enhancement*. New York: Farrar, Straus, & Giroux.

Pozner, Jennifer. 2010. *Reality Bites Back: The Troubling Truth About Guilty Pleasure TV*. Berkeley: Seal.

Putnam, Robert D. 2000. *Bowling Alone: The Collapse and Revival of American Community*. New York: Simon & Schuster.

Quan-Haase, Anabel. 2013. *Technology and Society: Social Networks, Power and Inequality*. Don Mills: Oxford University Press.

Rachman, Tom. 2014. *The Rise and Fall of Great Powers*. New York: Penguin Random House.

Radesky, Jenny S., et al. 2014. Patterns of Mobile Device Use by Caregivers and Children During Meals in Fast Food Restaurants. *Pediatrics* 133 (4): 843–849; online 10 March 2014, http://pediatrics.aappublications.org/content/133/4/e843.full?sid=bd4d9e74-dfa8-4894-b2e4-4ea47d1650b6.

Rawls, John. 1999. *A Theory of Justice*. Rev ed. Cambridge, MA: Harvard University Press.

Redhill, Michael. 2003. *Fidelity*. Toronto: Random House.

Regnerus, Mark. 2000. On Hooking Up, Marrying Down, and How Women's Success Lowers the 'Price of Sex'. Interview with Kate Lunau. *Maclean's*, 16–17, February 14.

Richerson, Peter J., and Robert Boyd. 2006. *Not by Genes Alone: How Culture Transformed Human Evolution*. Chicago: University of Chicago Press.

Roberts, Paul. 2014. *The Impulse Society*. New York: Bloomsbury.

Robinson, Eden. 2000. *Monkey Beach*. Toronto: Random House.

———. 2010. Queen of the North. In *An Anthology of Canadian Literature in English*, ed. Donna Bennett and Russell Brown, 3rd ed. Don Mills: Oxford University Press.

———. 2017. *Son of a Trickster*. Toronto: Knopf.

Rodrik, Dani. 2007. *One Economics, Many Recipes: Globalization, Institutions, and Economic Growth*. Princeton: Princeton University Press.

———. 2011. *The Globalization Paradox: Democracy and the Future of the World Economy*. New York: Norton.

Rorty, Richard. 1982. *Consequences of Pragmatism*. Minneapolis: University of Minnesota Press.

Rosen, Larry D., Mark Carrier, and Nancy A. Cheever. 2013. Facebook and Texting Made Me Do It: Media-Induced Task-Switching While Studying. *Computers in Human Behavior* 29: 948–958, http://www.csudh.edu/psych/Facebook_and_Texting_Made_Me_Do_It-Media-Induced_Task-Switching_While_Studying-Compuers_in_Human_Behavior-2013-Rosen_Carrier_Cheever.pdf.

Roser, Max. *Our World in Data*. Oxford Martin Programme on Global Development, University of Oxford. https://ourworldindata.org/

Rudder, Christian. 2014. *Dataclysm*. Toronto: Random House.

Rushkoff, Douglas. 2016. *Throwing Rocks at the Google Bus*. New York: Penguin Random House.

Sacks, Jonathan. 2015. *Not in God's Name*. London: Hodder & Stoughton.

Samuels, Robert. 2009. *New Media, Cultural Studies, and Critical Theory after Postmodernism*. New York: Macmillan.

Saunders, George. 2000. *Pastoralia*. New York: Penguin.

———. 2016. Who Are All These Trump Supporters? *New Yorker*, July 11, 18. http://www.newyorker.com/magazine/2016/07/11/george-saunders-goes-to-trump-rallies

———. 2017. *Lincoln in the Bardo*. New York: Random House.

Sen, Amartya. 2009. *The Idea of Justice*. Cambridge, MA: Harvard University Press.

Shafer-Landau, Russ. 2012. *The Fundamentals of Ethics*. 2nd ed. New York: Oxford University Press.

Shea, Theresa. 2013. *The Unfinished Child*. Victoria: Brindle & Glass.

Shields, David. 2010. *Reality Hunger: A Manifesto*. New York: Knopf.

Shteyngart, Gary. 2009. *Super Sad True Love Story*. New York: Random House.

———. 2014. *Little Failure*. New York: Penguin.

Sim, Stuart, ed. 2011. *The Routledge Companion to Postmodernism*. 3rd ed. New York: Routledge.

Small, Gary. 2008. *iBrain: Surviving the Technological Alteration of the Modern Mind*. New York: HarperCollins.

Smith, Zadie. 2001. *White Teeth*. London: Penguin.

Smith, Christian (with Patricia Snell). 2009. *Souls in Transition: The Religious and Spiritual Lives of Emerging Adults*. Oxford: Oxford University Press.

Sniderman, Andrew Stobo. 2012. Harper v. the Judges. *Maclean's*, 18–19, September 3.

Snipp-Walmsley, Chris. Postmodernism. In Waugh, 405–26.

Sokal, Alan. 1996a. Transgressing the Boundaries: Toward a Transformative Hermeneutics of Quantum Gravity. *Social Text* 46/47 (Spring/Summer): 217–252 (JSTOR, http://www.jstor.org/stable/466856).

———. 1996b. A Physicist Experiments with Cultural Studies. *Lingua Franca*, May/June. http://www.linguafranca.com/9605/sokal.html. Accessed 15 Feb 2002.

Stanyer, James. 2013. *Intimate Politics.* Cambridge: Polity.

Stephens-Davidowitz, Seth. 2017. *Everybody Lies: Big Data, New Data, and What the Internet Can Tell Us About Who We Really Are.* New York: HarperCollins.

Stiglitz, Joseph E. 2010. *Freefall: America, Free Markets, and the Sinking of the World Economy.* New York: Norton.

Storey, Robert. 1996. *Mimesis and the Human Animal.* Evanston: Northwestern University Press.

Strange, Jeffrey. 2002. How Fictional Tales Wag Real-World Beliefs. In *Narrative Impact: Social & Cognitive Foundations*, ed. Melanie Green, Jeffrey Strange, and Timothy Brock, 263–286. New York: Psychology Press.

Su, John. 2005. *Ethics and Nostalgia in the Contemporary Novel.* Cambridge: Cambridge University Press.

Sue, Derald Wing (adapted from). University of California, Santa Cruz, Academic Affairs. Tool: Recognizing Microaggressions and the Messages They Send. https://academicaffairs.ucsc.edu/events/documents/Microaggressions_Examples_Arial_2014_11_12.pdf

Sugiyama, Michelle. Reverse-Engineering Narrative: Evidence of Special Design. In Gottschall and Wilson, 177–196.

Sunstein, Cass. 2014. *Why Nudge? The Politics of Libertarian Paternalism.* New Haven: Yale University Press.

Suskind, Ron. 2004. Faith, Certainty and the Presidency of George W. Bush. *New York Times Magazine*, October 17. http://www.nytimes.com/2004/10/17/magazine/faith-certainty-and-the-presidency-of-george-w-bush.html

Tancer, Bill. 2008. *Click.* New York: Hyperion.

Tarantino, Quentin. 1994. *Pulp Fiction* (screenplay). New York: Hyperion.

———. 1998. *Quentin Tarantino: Interviews.* Edited by Gerald Peary. Jackson: University of Mississippi Press.

Taylor, Charles. 1989. *Sources of the Self.* Cambridge, MA: Harvard University Press.

———. 2004. *Modern Social Imaginaries.* Durham: Duke University Press.

———. 2007. *A Secular Age.* Cambridge, MA: Harvard University Press.

Timmer, Nicoline. 2010. *Do You Feel It Too? The Post-Postmodern Syndrome in American Fiction.* Amsterdam: Rodopi.

Tomasello, Michael. 2014. *A Natural History of Human Thinking.* Cambridge, MA: Harvard University Press.

Turkle, Sherry. 2011. *Alone Together.* New York: Basic Books.

Twenge, Jean. 2006. *Generation Me.* New York: Simon & Schuster.

———. 2017. *iGen*. New York: Simon & Schuster.

Twenge, Jean, and Keith Campbell. 2009. *The Narcissism Epidemic*. New York: Simon & Schuster.

Unwin, Peter. 2013. *Life Without Death*. Markham: Cormorant.

———. 2017. *Searching for Petronius Totem*. Calgary: Freehand.

Urban, Thomas. 2007. Blind Exorcism in Poland. *Süddeutsche Zeitung*. Trans. Lucy Powell, May 24. http://www.signandsight.com/features/1364.html, 30 May 2007. Accessed 4 May 2010.

Vattimo, Gianni. Postmodernity and (the End of) Metaphysics. Trans. David Rose. In Goulimari, 32–38.

Verghese, Abraham. 2009. *Cutting for Stone*. Toronto: Random House.

Vetlesen, Arne Johan. Bauman's Troublesome Moral Party of Two. In Jacobsen et al., 251–258.

Vollmann, William. 2003, 2004. *Rising Up and Rising Down: Some Thoughts on Violence, Freedom and Urgent Means*. New York: HarperCollins.

———. 2005. *Europe Central*. New York: Penguin.

Vosoughi, Soroush, Deb Roy, and Sinan Aral. 2018. The Spread of True and False News Online. *Science* 359 (6380): 1146–1151, http://science.sciencemag.org/content/359/6380/1146.full.

Wallace, David Foster. 1996. *Infinite Jest*. New York: Little, Brown.

———. 2011. *The Pale King*. New York: Little, Brown.

Watson, Nigel. Postmodernism and Lifestyles. In Sim, 62–72.

Waugh, Patricia, ed. 2006. *Literary Theory and Criticism: an Oxford Guide*. Oxford: Oxford University Press.

Weinman, Jaime J. 2012. Reality TV Is Caught Faking It. *Maclean's*, 63, February 13.

Wight, Jonathan. 2015. *Ethics in Economics*. Stanford: Stanford University Press.

Wiley, David. 1997. Transcript of the David Foster Wallace Interview. *Minnesota Daily*, February 27. http://www.badgerinternet.com/~bobkat/jestwiley2.html

Williams, David. 1986. After Post-Modernism. In *Trace: Prairie Writers on Writing*, ed. Birk Sproxton. Winnipeg: Turnstone.

———. 2003. *Imagined Nations: Reflections on Media in Canadian Fiction*. Montreal & Kingston: McGill-Queen's University Press.

———. 2009. *Media, Memory and the First World War*. Montreal & Kingston: McGill-Queen's University Press.

———. 2015. Film and the Mechanization of Time in the Myth of the Great War Canon. *English Studies in Canada* 41 (2–3): 165–190.

———. 2017. *Milton's Leveller God*. Montreal/Kingston: McGill-Queen's University Press.

Williams, Rowan. 2014. *The Edge of Words: God and the Habits of Language*. London: Bloomsbury.

Williams, Peter, and Ian Rowlands. 2007. *Information Behaviour of the Researcher of the Future*. A British Library/JISC Study, Work Package II, October 18. http://www.jisc.ac.uk/media/documents/programmes/reppres/ggwork-packageii.pdf, 9 June 2011.

Wilson, E.O. 1998. *Consilience: The Unity of Knowledge*. New York: Random House.

Wilson, David Sloan. 2002. *Darwin's Cathedral*. Chicago: University of Chicago Press.

World Health Organization (WHO). 2011. *Global Status Report on Alcohol and Health*. Geneva: WHO Press, http://www.who.int/substance_abuse/publications/global_alcohol_report/msbgsruprofiles.pdf.

Yan, Mo. 2014. *Frog* (2009). Trans. Howard Goldblatt. New York: Penguin.

Young, Nora. 2012. *The Virtual Self*. Toronto: McClelland & Stewart.

Žižek, Slavoj. 2001. *Enjoy Your Symptom! Jacques Lacan in Hollywood and Out*. Rev ed. New York: Routledge.

Zunshine, Lisa. 2006. *Why We Read Fiction*. Columbus: Ohio State University Press.

Index[1]

---

[1] Note: Page numbers followed by 'n' refer to notes.

© The Author(s) 2019
R. Kramer, *Are We Postmodern Yet?*,
https://doi.org/10.1007/978-3-030-30569-7

R

Rachman, Tom, 143, 164
Racism, 18, 63, 78, 104, 126–127, 283
Randi, James, 239
Rationality, *see* Modernity
Rawls, John, 97–99
Recession of 2007–8, 113, 120, 167,
    209–214, 218n152, 222, 223, 225
Redhill, Michael, 246
Reformation, 4, 61, 126, 163
Religion, 12, 71, 229–291
    atheism, 241–242, 256n85, 261,
        269n127, 284–285, 287–288
    creationism, 241–242
    decline of, 230–244
    environmental, 256–257
    and fiction, 257–258
    heaven, 235–236
    and individualism, 230–232,
        259–262, 273–274, 277n158,
        278–280
    moralistic therapeutic deism, 276–279
    New Age, 246–247, 256, 272–273
    parody of, 241–244
    pluralist adaptation, 272–279
    religiosity *vs.* GDP, 250–251
    resistance identities, 247–249
    selective adherence, 266–272
    service attendance, 245–246,
        245n50, 251n72
    and simulation, 244
    skepticism, 246–247
    'spiritual but not religious,'
        232, 260–261
    undecided middle, 257–259
    See also Ethics, traditionalist;
        Tradition
Republican Party (US), 30, 197, 199
Rise and Fall of Great Powers, The
    (Rachman), 143, 164
Rising Up and Rising Down
    (Vollmann), 51

Road, The (C. McCarthy), 200,
    265–266
Robinson, Eden, 269
Rodrik, Dani, 212, 213, 215–217,
    223, 225–226
Romanticism, 3, 79, 126
Rorty, Richard, 18, 77, 96, 296
Roseau River Anishinabe
    First Nation, 263
Rosen, Larry, 147
Roser, Max, 220
Ross, Andrew, 14, 20
Roth, Eric, 290
Rousseau, Jean-Jacques, 3, 50, 282
Rove, Karl, 192
Rudder, Christian, 169
Rushdie, Salman, 44, 275
Russia, 87n155, 168, 203, 205, 207,
    209, 211, 226, 227
Rwanda, 47, 48, 55, 203

S

Sacco, Justine, 169
Same-sex marriage, 66, 78, 170, 191,
    192, 234, 239
Samuels, Robert, 3, 192
Sanders, Bernie, 188
Saturday (McEwan), 194, 253
Saunders, George, 33, 41, 275
Saving Private Ryan (film), 290
Schindler, Oscar, 290
Schindler's List (film), 290
Schmidt, Eric, 163–164, 176
Schudsen, Michael, 193
Science, 13–14, 19–22, 45–46
    as grand narrative, 252–256
    and religion, 234–237
Screen time, 119, 135–137, 135n14,
    139–141, 144, 156n128,
    160–161
Sealand, 201

Printed by Printforce, the Netherlands